剑桥语言测试研究丛书

Assessing Language Teachers' Professional Skills and Knowledge

语言教师专业技能与知识测评

[英] Rosemary Wilson
[英] Monica Poulter
编著

林敦来 导读

外语教学与研究出版社
FOREIGN LANGUAGE TEACHING AND RESEARCH PRESS
北京 BEIJING

剑桥大学出版社
CAMBRIDGE UNIVERSITY PRESS

京权图字：01-2019-1950

图书在版编目 (CIP) 数据

语言教师专业技能与知识测评：英、汉／（英）罗斯玛丽·威尔逊（Rosemary Wilson），（英）莫妮卡·波尔特（Monica Poulter）编著；林敦来导读. —— 北京：外语教学与研究出版社，2019.11
（剑桥语言测试研究丛书）
ISBN 978-7-5213-1377-2

Ⅰ. ①语… Ⅱ. ①罗… ②莫… ③林… Ⅲ. ①英语－教师－教学能力－资格考试－研究 Ⅳ. ①G451.1

中国版本图书馆 CIP 数据核字 (2019) 第 273217 号

出 版 人　徐建忠
项目负责　李海萍
责任编辑　段长城
责任校对　解碧琰
封面设计　郭　莹
出版发行　外语教学与研究出版社
社　　址　北京市西三环北路 19 号（100089）
网　　址　http://www.fltrp.com
印　　刷　北京虎彩文化传播有限公司
开　　本　650×980　1/16
印　　张　30.5
版　　次　2019 年 12 月第 1 版 2019 年 12 月第 1 次印刷
书　　号　ISBN 978-7-5213-1377-2
定　　价　112.90 元

购书咨询：（010）88819926　电子邮箱：club@fltrp.com
外研书店：https://waiyants.tmall.com
凡印刷、装订质量问题，请联系我社印制部
联系电话：（010）61207896　电子邮箱：zhijian@fltrp.com
凡侵权、盗版书籍线索，请联系我社法律事务部
举报电话：（010）88817519　电子邮箱：banquan@fltrp.com
物料号：313770001

记载人类文明
沟通世界文化
www.fltrp.com

Contents

导　　读

一、简介

《语言教师专业技能与知识测评》(*Assessing Language Teachers' Professional Skills and Knowledge*) 是剑桥大学出版社"语言测试研究"（Studies in Language Testing，简称 SiLT) 系列丛书的第 42 册。丛书的总主编为 Nick Saville 和 Cyril J. Weir，本书由剑桥大学英语考评部（Cambridge Assessment English，简称"考评部"）的 Rosemary Wilson 和 Monica Poulter 主编。

根据剑桥大学英语考评部的官方网站[1]，教学资格证书根据服务对象分为两大类：个人认证和学校与政府认证。本书涉及的主要是个人认证，因此本部分先简单介绍英语语言教师证书（简称 CELTA）、英语语言教师文凭（简称 Delta）、英语教学能力证书（简称 TKT）[2]，以便读者理解本书中关于这些认证考试的研究。《剑桥英语教学框架》（*Cambridge English Teaching Framework*）（Cambridge English 2016）将教师资格分为基础、发展、熟练、专业四个等级，详细描述了对应级别语言教师应具备的的专业技能与知识。剑桥大学英语考评部将教学资格认证考试与此框架进行了关联（如图 1）。

---

[1] https://www.cambridgeenglish.org/teaching-english/

[2] ICELT（在职英语教学证书）也是个人认证，但因其将于 2020 年 7 月取消，且本书对此测试的讨论相对较少，在此不作介绍。

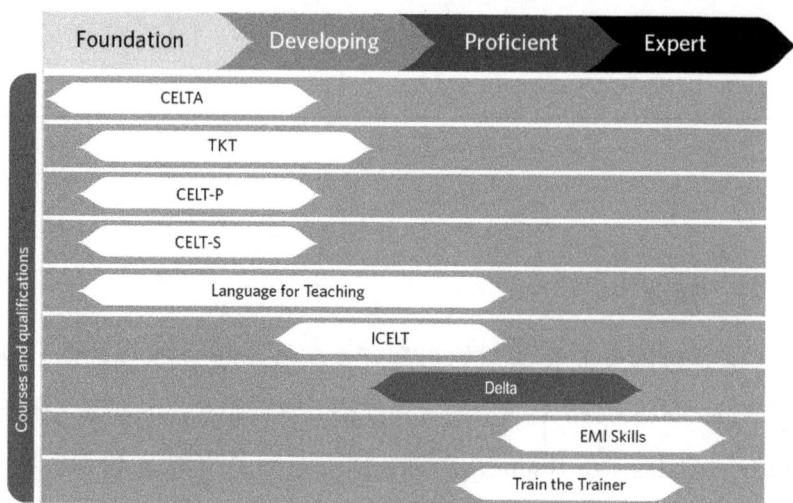

图 1　教师资格认证考试与《剑桥英语教学框架》的关联（Cambridge English 2016）

从图 1 和表 1 可以直观地看出，CELTA 和 TKT 属于入门级教师资格认证，而 Delta 则属于较高级的教师资格认证，它要求学员有一定的教学经验。表 1 列出了三种教师资格认证对学员的要求和认证特征。

表 1　CELTA、TKT 和 Delta 认证要求概览（改编自 Cambridge English 2014）

	对学员的要求		认证特征					
	教学经验	准入资格	教学对象年龄	能否职前参加	是否必须参与课程	是否评价教学实践	持续评价/课程作业	纸笔测试
CELTA	不要求	高等教育证书	成年人	能	面授或网络学习或混合	是	是	否
TKT 三个模块	不必要	不要求	小学、初中或成年人	能	不要求	否	否	是
Delta 模块一	最好有	初级教师认证	小学、初中或成年人	不能	不要求	否	否	是
Delta 模块二	必须有	初级教师认证	小学、初中或成年人	不能	要求	是	是	否
Delta 模块三	最好有	初级教师认证	小学、初中或成年人	不能	不要求	否	长篇作业	否

二、主要内容

本书分为四大部分：第一部分包含 2 章（第 1—2 章），为本书的绪论和剑桥英语语言教学资格认证考试简史；第二部分包含 5 章（第 3—7 章），主要汇报了剑桥英语语言教学资格认证考试中采用的测评方法是如何与教师发展乃至教师培训者发展紧密结合起来的；第三部分包含 4 章（第 8—11 章），从横向考察了剑桥英语语言教学资格认证考试中最具挑战性的几项标准；第四部分包含 5 章（第 12—16 章），讨论了剑桥英语语言教学资格认证考试与不同情境之间的交互，如考试后效、文化因素等。

第一部分　历史与背景

第 1 章　绪论　本章由本书主编 Rosemary Wilson 和 Monica Poulter 撰写。作者从 Hattie（2003）[3] 关于专家教师特征的深入研究为出发点，认为评价教学是非常复杂的活动，需要从多种渠道收集证据才能更加全面地反映教师的技能和知识。因此，要提供官方的，通常情况下也是高利害的教师认证，就需要采用标准化的方法来收集和印证证据。Ingvarson & Hattie（2008）主编的《教师专业认证评价》(*Assessing Teachers for Professional Certification*) 汇报了美国国家专业教学标准委员会（National Board for Professional Teaching Standards）关于在教师评价中收集和评价多渠道证据的复杂性，本书则从英语语言教学角度汇报语言教师认证评价。剑桥英语教学资格认证反映了当前国际上语言教师背景多样化的实际，开发了《剑桥英语教学框架》，设计了一系列针对不同对象的语言教师资格认证考试，采用多渠道收集证据的方式力求达到可靠的评价结果。本书主要采用质性研究的方法，从理论

3　本文献已在本书的参考文献中引出，故不再在本导读的参考文献中体现，其他类似情况同此处处理。

和实践角度汇报了剑桥英语教学资格认证中的测评问题和策略。

第 2 章　剑桥英语教学资格认证简史　本章由 Alan Pulverness 撰写，以叙事的方式记述了剑桥英语教学资格认证考试不断专业化的发展历程。第一阶段可以追溯到伦敦国际公司（International House，简称 IH）的职前语言教师培训课程。其中，提升意识的外语课、语法语音、教学法、课堂管理、实时课堂观察、教学实践以及培训者和同伴学员反馈等至今仍是剑桥英语教学资格考试中的重要因素，对学员的四个等级的评判（卓越、良好、中等、较差）也富有启发。第二阶段为英国皇家艺术协会（Royal Society of Arts，简称 RSA）的在职英语教师资格证书，面向两类教师群体：教授来自英国的成人英语学习者的教师和教授进入英国的移民英语学习者的教师。1977 年前该认证考试包含初试和复试，初试为语言能力测试，复试后来演变成成人英语教学文凭（DTEFLA）考试，由两场笔试和一场教学实操构成。笔试部分在主考的组织下先由助理考官完成评分，最终由主考官形成完整的报告。1977 年以来，该认证最大的变化是逐步建构起标准参照评价，对评价目标的描述更加细化和清晰，考官的数量不断增加，高级考官团成立并定期开展简报会。认证评价的标准化进程大力推进，并充分融合了当时流行的语言教学方法。从 1984 年到 1990 年，该认证逐步走向连续性评价，将课程内部的评价与外来考官的评价结合起来。该认证还根据形势推出了海外英语教师认证和海外英语教师文凭。第三阶段是从 IH 到 RSA 的发展。在 IH 的推动下，RSA 开始了职前教师培训和认证。由于 IH 采用四周强化训练模式，笔试不可行，同时外来考官也难以同时观察 12—18 名学员，因此 RSA 采用了考试中心之间的培训者互访制。培训者观察培训课程，调阅学员书面作业，观察学员教学实践，与受访中心的培训者和学员面谈，通过这种方式使得课程内容和评价标准一致化。培训者作为考官须接受每年一度的标准化会议。RSA 还改进了 IH 的四级评判标准，构建了 Pass I、Pass II 和 Pass 三级量表。随着海外课程和认证的进一步拓展，RSA 一年召开一次开放会议，课程培训师、主考官和顾问委员齐聚一堂讨论课程和认证项目的进展，构建了语言教师专业共同体。第四阶段为剑桥时代。1988 年 RSA 将教师培训课程和认证移交给剑桥大学考试委员会。20 世纪 90 年代中叶，CELTA 和 Delta 取代了原来的成人英语教学资格认证和文凭，形成新的教学大纲，教学框架更加清晰，具体目标描述更加详细。CELTA 中心要求以档案袋的方式详细记录学员的进步情况，从 46 个具体的目标来对学员进行最终评价。近年来，由于很多学员是非英语母语人士，CELTA 的受众更广，授课的形式和方式也因势而变。针对儿童英语教学，剑桥大学考试委员会开发了 CELTYL 和 CELTA 儿童模块。比起成人英语教学文凭，Delta 的导向更加实用，例如笔试部分要求分析、点评和评估学生的书面产出等内容。为了防止学员减少，Delta 构建了三个独立的模块，学员可以根据自己的时间和经费来完成。本章最后，作者简要介绍了教师评价的两项拓展考试，即入门级的 TKT 和介于 CELTA 和 Delta 之间的 ICELT（在职英语语言教学资格证书）。最后，作者指出，虽然课程结构调整了，评价工具更加得当了，考试方式也转变了，但是语言教师认证的基本原则和要素自 IH 以来始终未变。

第二部分　教学能力培养和测评

第 3 章　在职教师教育的良好实践：基于 Delta 的分析　本章由 Simon Borg 和 David Albery 撰写。本章中的在职教师教育（in-service teacher education，简称 INSET）指的是在职教师教育课程以及其他形式的培训。作者在国际教师教育文献综述基础上确定和讨论了教师教育，特别是语言教师教育中高效的 INSET 基于的一系列原则。这些原则为：1）认识到并利用好教师的先前经验、信念和知识；2）不应该定位为弥补教师能力的不足，而应该以发展的眼光，让教师基于丰富的先前经验得到提升；3）应该以综合的方式提高理论知识和实践知识；4）兼顾学者提出的理论和教师自身总结出的理论；5）应为教师合作学习提供机会；6）要避免教学法规约主义；7）要促进教学反思行为；8）应为教师提供积极的体验式学习；9）教师培训者要示范"良好的教学实践"；10）受训者要提供形成性和终结性的反馈，并以此调整课程实施和设计；11）应为教师提供持续的情境化的学习机会。作者运用上述 11 条原则来考察 Delta 第二模块。Delta 认证共有三个模块，模块一为理解语言、教学法和教学资源，模块二为教学实践能力培养，模块三为实践拓展和外语教学专业化。只有第二模块要求受训者参与配套课程，因为它包含持续的课程作业，包括教学观察以及纳入评价档案袋的一系列书面作业。Delta 是高利害认证，既要避免 INSET 只教授 Delta 所考查的内容，也要避免凸显教师的能力不足（原则 2），因此在 Delta 考试说明中既要关注教师个体的成长活动，也需要讨论外部考试可能带来的影响，并提供解决方案。Delta 通过以下两个密切相关的评价内容解决了这个矛盾：第一个是专业发展作业（Professional Development Assignment，简称 PDA），第二个是贯穿课程四个等级的语言系统和技能作业（Language Skills Assignments，简称 LSAs）。PDA 是形成性评价，是诊断性的课堂观察，学员基于此与导师制订课程计划。这个计划为学员教师的专业发展和正式的语言系统和技能作业测评提供参考。PDA 也让学员教师表达先前经验和信念，并通过问卷调查等形式帮助学员教师增强意识，将先前经验和信念与新的想法联系起来。PDA 采用的实验实践作业让学员教师尝试新的教学法，鼓励学员教师自己建构认识。PDA 还让学员教师学会反思。作者也分析了 LSAs 如何体现 INSET 原则，并列举了导师在课堂上对学员进行形成性反馈的样例及其如何体现 INSET 原则。总的来看，Delta 在教师发展和评价中取得了良好的平衡，促进了教师的反思实践。

第4章　语言教师评价中档案袋的角色　本章由 Neil Anderson 撰写。作者首先指出学科教学知识受到关注，对教师进行有效的评价不仅要反映教学实践，还要反映其背后的理念和对教学实践的调整，因此档案袋评价是最佳选择。首先，作者讨论了教学档案袋的定义和分类，以及教学档案袋应该包含的内容。接着，作者讨论教学档案袋作为教师发展和评价工具的主要优势，如它是行动研究驱动型，鼓励教师尝试新实践和想法，为教师提供反思的机会，历时性地评价教师能力更能反映教学过程的复杂性。然而，教学档案袋也有局限性，如可操作性不够强、评分信度低等。因此，作者认为要用好教学档案袋，首先要回答四个问题：1）学习档案袋和评价档案袋之间如何权衡？2）该采用什么评价标准？3）应该由谁来评价档案袋？4）要评价档案袋的哪些元素，如何分配权重？作者以 Delta 模块二的档案袋评价为例介绍了语言教师评价中的档案袋。作者详细介绍了 Delta 模块二档案袋的两个主线，即 PDA 和 LSAs，并阐述了 Delta 档案袋如何满足有效档案袋的四个特征，即行动研究驱动型、强调反思、历时评价和可靠的评价。

第5章　反思性实践：评价 CELTA 课程中的自我评估和同伴评估　本章由 Jo-Ann Delaney 撰写。本章的"评估"（evaluation）专指突显教师优缺点的教师反思，而"评价"（assessment）则专指教师培训者对学员评估质量的评价。本章主要考察的是评估的影响因素，对一些广为接受的反思过程提出了挑战。教师培训课程通常主张要培养反思性的实践者，认为通过反思教师能够将"所为"转化成"所想"；要更好地理解反思性实践，需要将理论和实践进行关联。作者简要回顾了 Schön（1992）、Kolb（1983）和 Brookfield（1995，2011）关于反思性实践的模型，以及 Lave & Wenger（1991）的合法边缘参与理论，指出反思性实践在教师学员自我评估和同伴评估中的两个问题：其一，它强化了理论与实践之间的距离必须缩小的观念；其二，学员没有足够的能力对自己的实践进行评估。评价反思性实践的问题在于学员会为了迎合培训员只表达可接受的内容，而非他们对教学的真实想法；学员产出的反思未能充分反映他们反思的全部内容。作者接着对 CELTA 中的反思性实践及测评进行了描述。为了探究学员对教学实践的价值和影响以及反思性实践的看法，作者汇报了一项涉及 6 名 CELTA 学员的长线质性研究。该研究印证了以下观点：学员认为自己没有足够的能力对实践进行评估，学员之间构建了统一战线，导致他们对同伴的评估缺乏批判性，学员之间的反馈更多地考虑组内的和谐气氛。因此，同伴评估存在诸多局限性。作者还汇报了一项研究结果，即培训者对学员自我评估和同伴评估的看法。作者通过网络问卷调查了 14 名经验丰富的教师培训者。研究显示，培训者认同学员自我评估和同伴评估的重要性。培训者虽然意识到学员给予同伴的评估批判性不足，但是他们很重视学员积极参与反馈；延迟反馈虽然会降低学员的反馈焦虑，但是也会导致学员遗忘很多细节。对此，一种办法是让学员撰写书面自我评估，但是这种办法也存在问题，因为从默会知识到陈述知识之间存在距离。即便如此，培训者还是认为，学员自我评估和同伴评估的质量并不构成问题，只是方法多样，总体上学员自我评估和同伴评估对学员的综合评定不会产生太大影响。作者最后总结了研究结果对实践的启示，如：适度调整学员与培训者的角色和责任，在教学实践反馈中更好地利用好培训者的专长，聚焦自我评估和同伴评估对实践的影响而非反思质量本身。

　　第 6 章　教学实践测评的标准化过程　本章由 Evelina D. Galaczi 和 Marie Therese Swabey 撰写。作为一种表现性评价，教学实践测评的信度问题备受关注。作者采用 Weir 效度框架中的评分效度，主要以

CELTA 为例，从评价标准、评估过程和条件、评价者特征、评分员培训和标准化、等级评定等五个方面探究了剑桥英语教学资格认证中测评的标准化过程。CELTA 的评价标准基于扎实的教师教育理论，详细清晰地描述了学员的学习目标。作为评估工具，它既以评价者为导向，又以学员为导向，大大降低了评分的主观性。在 CELTA 的评价模型中，培训者、外来考官、主考官、联合主考之间形成一套严密的评分系统，为学员提供了历时评估和共时评估。在测评条件方面，CELTA 管理手册详细规定了外来考官在评估前、中、后应该遵循的程序。CELTA 考官的选拔不仅重视考官知识基础，而且必须为现任培训者，并积极参与在职培训。作者还介绍了 CELTA 考官和培训者的培训和标准化程序。考官和培训者均需参加一年一度的网上评分考核，熟悉评价标准及其运用以保证评分信度。但是作者也认为，表现性评价中的评分差异是确实存在的，我们能做的就是尽量降低其影响。关于评分标准化程序，作者也根据研究提出了一些建议，如：考虑采用混合式的标准化程序，既能利用网络便利又有面对面讨论；节选多个教学实践课，提高基准课的代表性。最后作者介绍了 CELTA 等级评定，包含培训者、考官、等级审察（或授予委员会）三个层面的决策，最终将学员评定为 Fail、Pass、Pass B、Pass A 四个等级。

第 7 章　培养和评价英语语言教师培训者　本章由 Marie Morgan 撰写。作者首先回顾了语言教师常常被看作是非专业人士而被边缘化的背景，因而教师以及教师培训者的培训质量成为重中之重，一些培训标准，如《剑桥英语教学框架》，正是为提高培训质量而出台的。作者回顾了教师培训和教师培训者培训的模式。第一种模式是学徒模式。该模式下的教师培训者培训缺乏标准化程序，可能导致"外语教学实践者克隆"或"专业僵化"，无法保证对教师教学实践的标准化评价。第二种模式是基于能力的方法。它建构了具体的、可观察的良好教学的标准，用于培养和评价教师。这就涉及专业特长的问题，作者区分了两类专家："常规专家"和"顺应专家"。常规专家越来越高效地发展他们的运用能力，而顺应专家则能说明教学技能背后的原理，判断常规和非常规的技能是否合适，根据情境调整技能或使用新技能。顺应专家成为行业中的金标准。教学反思对教师发展的重要性已得到普遍认可，在职业生涯的不同阶段反思的内容深度会很不同，教师培训者同样体现出不同的反思深度和焦点。教师培训者同时还经历从一线教师到教师培训者的角色转换焦虑。作者接着对 CELTA 作了简单的介绍，并重点介绍了 CELTA 培训者培训项目。该项目分三个阶段培养教师培训者，旨在提供标准化的路径和方法，将语言教师提升为教师培训者。它支持个性化的内容订制，包含一些经验丰富的培训者的影子练习，融合了不同教学培训模型中的原理。作者在结论中指出，CELTA 培训者培训项目应该被看作是教师培训者的入门项目，教师培训者还应该参加一些合作项目，不断提升自己的辅导能力。CELTA 培训者培训项目使得很多教师成为教师培训者，但作为教师培训者，专业认同和个人认同则需要长期发展。

第三部分　具体标准的测评问题

本部分主要讨论的是剑桥英语教学资格认证中具体标准的解读和使用。挑选标准是学员感到最难的部分，如语言本身、学习者需求、基于教学知识构念的评价标准。

第 8 章　教师的语言能力：挪用和适切的问题　本章由 Jenny Johnson 和 Monica Poulter 撰写。作者首先指出，世界上 80% 以上的英语教师为非英语母语使用者，他们英语水平参差不齐，是否能胜任英语教学也饱受争议。同时，语言被看作是社会和文化行为，英语作为母语这个话题也是研究的焦点。语言教师的语言能力涉及社会和文化认同问题，教师测评框架必须提供标准来确保潜在的语言教师具有适当的语言能力。作者对英语的"母语"争议进行了综述，讨论了标准语的困境，并从实用角度分析了"中立准则"及其对教师培训的启示。CELTA 对教师的语言能力规定为 CEFR 的 C2 或者 C1 高水平。接着，作者通过一项 CELTA 语言能力调查，考察了 CELTA 培训者如何筛选具备合适语言能力的学员，以及他们面对不同语言水平的潜在学员时作筛选的过程。数据显示，学员的语言水平主要还是以得到普遍认同的受教育人士使用的英语为衡量标准，判断学员进入教师培训前的语言水平主要是看学员是否有"足够好的语言"可以作为学生的语言学习榜样，满足学生的期望。研究还显示，在挑选学员时，培训者采用的是实用主义和现实主义路径，不同环境中英语教师语言水平要求可以有所不同。"英语要好"和"能教英语"之间有紧密的关系，作者认为在保持准入语言水平标准的同时，要明确语言水平和教学技能以及教学对象语言水平之间的契合点，同时也要尊重世界上不同的英语变体及其对语言教学的影响。

第 9 章　语言意识：研究、规划、教学及其他　本章由 Martin Parrott 撰写，聚焦剑桥英语教学资格认证中反映的语言知识构成、语言观和语言评价方式，以及语言意识的不同方面和评价方法。作者首先从两个角度对剑桥英语教学资格认证中的语言意识进行考察并展开论述。这两个角度为：语言意识是关于语言的知识和实际运用；语言意识是批判性意识、反思和"语感"。作者认为，对教师在语言系统的陈述性知识方面，剑桥英语教学资格认证缺乏具体完整的描述语。TKT 采用客观题来测试学员的语言意识，作者认为这样的测试不能考查深层的语言意识。TKT 的 KAL 虽然对语言能力要求更高，但是对语言意识的测试类似于 TKT。Delta 模块一要求学员对语言现象发表评论，Delta 模块二有两个作业是关于语言系统的，学员需要撰写文章，探究语言意识，特别是语篇和语音意识。CELTA 及其少儿教师版教学大纲也包含了语言意识任务。ICELT 在课程的各个部分提供详细的标准来测试学员的语言能力，让学员在课堂中发现、分析和评估语言使用，以此提高语言意识。接着，作者从备课和教学实践角度讨论语言意识在语言分析、学习材料和寻找例证方面的体现。本章最后，作者简要地讨论了批判性意识在 Delta 模块二中的体现、反思在 ICELT 中的体现、语感在 Delta 中的体现与验证。

第 10 章 评价教师的灵活度和应对力 本章由 Rosemary Wilson 撰写。语言教学实践可以看作是富有变化的动态的过程，需要教师的临场表现。本章讨论的就是剑桥英语教学资格认证如何评判教师在课堂计划中的灵活度和教师应对学习者临场反应的能力。本章特别参考了评价报告中关于教师评判是否有效的例子。文献综述显示，教学是充满反思的互动的过程，是动态的，包含了师生的情感参与，在教学中很难将教师作为一个人和教学技艺分开。在评判教师表现时，要区别对待新手教师和有经验的教师在灵活度和应对力方面的表现，这点应该在教师评价标准中体现出来。作者接着介绍了 CELTA、TKT、ICELT 中的评价标准对教师灵活度和应对力的考查，并从评价标准和考官评论两个角度详细论述了 Delta 对教师灵活度和应对力的考查。最后，作者讨论了在评价教师的灵活度和应对力时遇到的评价方法论方面的挑战，即培训者作为培训者或导师和培训者作为考官之间的矛盾、考官本身的灵活度和应对力、考官作为个人和教学技艺难以区分。

第 11 章 TKT：教学知识的测试 本章由 Mary Spratt 撰写，探讨了 TKT 的构念，并介绍了其任务类型。TKT 检测的是教师学员的陈述性知识。作者在本章首先详述了 TKT 的构念界定，指出 TKT 以纸笔方式分三个模块测试教学知识：第一模块测试学员对语言和语言知识的认识、对语言学习背景和语言教学背景的了解；第二模块测试学员课程设计和备课的能力、选择和使用资源的能力；第三模块测试学员对课堂中教师语言和学生语言的认识以及课堂管理能力。作者将这些构念与 Grossman（1990）及其他学者对语言教师知识成分的论述作了对比分析，认为 TKT 虽然完整地测试了语言教师的教学知识，但是作为一项仅测试陈述性知识的测试，仍需谨慎对待从教学知识到教学实践能力的推断。作者认为，区分 TKT 测试和 TKT 培训课程是一种有益的思路。TKT 的培训课程大量采用了教学实践、微格教学、课堂观察、反馈、教学反思等实践性很强的活动，促使陈述性知识可转化成程序性知识，采用客观测试的 TKT 测试和注重认知过程的 TKT 培训课程应当相辅相成，以实现 Wallace（1991）的"反思圈"。

第四部分　测评的情境

第 12 章　TKT 在乌拉圭的影响（2005–2012）　本章由 Gerardo Valazza 撰写。作者首先介绍了剑桥英语考试委员会的"通过考试设计改进考试后效"（impact by design）理念，讨论了它的四个准则：规划、支撑、传达、监控与评估，提出了三个问题：1）TKT 对乌拉圭英语教师和学校产生的影响如何；2）这些影响如何反映教师的发展阶段；3）可以采用哪些策略提高乌拉圭教师在 TKT 中的表现。在对乌拉圭教育改革进行简要说明后，作者指出该研究是解释性的，目的是了解教师个人对现实的看法。研究采用的方法有问卷调查（通过电子邮件）和访谈。数据收集的来源有 TKT 学员、TKT 培训者和 TKT 项目主要决策者。研究结果显示，学员认为 TKT 从理论上和实践上对他们均产生了积极的影响，特别是教龄在 6—15 年的学员非常认可 TKT 的影响。从培训者的角度来说，TKT 为他们成为教师培训者提供了机会，促进了他们的专业发展，使得他们不仅成为教师培训者，而且作为语言教师的专业能力也得到了提升。从决策者角度来说，TKT 为一线教师提供了专业发展的机会，特别是 TKT 允许英语语言水平相对较低的教师参与国际认可的教师认证，成为专业的实践者。研究也汇报了学员和培训者对 TKT 培训材料的偏好。作者指出，总体上私立教育机构比公立学校从 TKT 受益更多，公立学校如果能更好地采用 TKT，将有助于乌拉圭实现其宏大的外语教学蓝图。

第 13 章　英语内容教学知识测试　本章由 Kay Bentley 撰写，讨论的是 2008 年启动的 TKT 模块，专注于内容与语言融合式教学 (Content and Language Integrated Learning, 简称 CLIL)。作者首先介绍了测试 CLIL 知识的理据，认为它为欧洲学生的生活和社会流动做了更好的准备。TKT 的 CLIL 基于 4Cs 框架，包括内容、交际、认知和文化，主要采用了选择题的形式来测试教师的 CLIL 知识。该模块分为两个部分，共 80 道题，测试四个方面的内容：CLIL 知识和原则、CLIL 课程设计知识、CLIL 课堂组织知识和 CLIL 评价知识。作者接着讨论了客观评价国际教师 CLIL 面临的四个方面挑战：1）如何让一项测试适用于学科教师和在不同的 CLIL 情境中的语言教师；2）如何界定 CLIL；3）如何看待 CLIL 情境中教师的语言水平和课堂中母语的使用；4）如何让 TKT 的 CLIL 有别于测试普通的语言教学知识的考试。最后，作者结合 TKT 的 CLIL 第二部分测试内容，比较了测试 CLIL 知识和测试普通的英语语言教学知识之间的异同，并从知识测试、语言测试、教学方法知识测试和资源知识测试四个方面介绍了 TKT 的 CLIL 测试的具体内容。

第 14 章　在局地情境中运用国际教师教育项目　本章由 Peter Watkins、Bill Harris 和 Alan Pulverness 撰写，主要运用不同地区（苏丹、俄罗斯、彼尔姆和巴基斯坦）情境中的三个案例来讨论学员在教师教育项目中的多样经历，以及这些项目如何被调整并运用于局地情境。语言教学必然要与当地的情境产生互动，国际化的教师教育课程不能直接强加于特定的情境，而要根据当地的文化逐步推进，培养学员的跨文化能力，让学员体会到新方法可以在真实的课堂情境中使用。

三个案例显示，在注重传授知识的文化中可以推行以学习者为中心的建构主义学习理论；CELTA 等教师培训项目有利于构建教师共同体；教师培训项目中习得的教学方法可以通过适当的调整来适应当地情境的需求。通过这些案例分析，作者认为国际化的教师认证不仅要设计契合当地情境的评价标准，还应该积极鼓励各培训中心讨论这些标准，增强当地"所有权"，提高国际化教师资格认证的灵活性。

　　第 15 章　理论与实践的整合：以毕尔肯大学的 Delta 为例　本章由 Simon Phipps 撰写。教师教育领域一直关注有效教学所需要的知识和技能，以及如何在教师培训项目中很好地传授这些知识和技能。本章汇报的是毕尔肯大学将 Delta 整合到硕士项目的案例。作者首先综述了教师教育的四种模式。第一种为学术模式，要求专家知识，聚焦理论，采用硕士课程实现；第二种为运用科学模式，要求专家知识，聚焦基于理论的实践，采用硕士课程实现；第三种为技艺模式，要求熟练工知识，聚焦基于实践的理论，采用硕士教学实习、导师制以及教师培训课程实现；第四种为反思性模式，要求广为接受的体验性知识，聚焦理论与实践的互动，采用教师培训课程实现。作者还对教师的学习进行了综述，认为有效的教师需要发展语言知识（语言使用和语言意识）、教学法知识（如何教语言）、教学技能和教学的批判性反思能力。教师教育的测评要回答评什么和怎么评的问题。在测评内容方面，难点在于很难区分内容和教学法，也就是需要考虑语言知识、关于语言的知识和如何教语言的知识，对于在职教师还得考虑教师的专长（丰富的知识基础、熟练的行为、高超的解决问题能力）以及教师的信念和反思，因此不仅要关注评价结果，还要关注评价过程。评价的方式则不仅要考虑效度和信度问题，也需要考虑可操作性。基于此，作者详细介绍了毕尔肯大学的一个三年在职硕士项目，特别是该项目在内容和结构方面如何整合 Delta 大纲及评价方式。最后，作者根据他完成的两项研究讨论了该项目对教师学习的影响，主要体现在反思性方法的积极影响，整合的评价手段对教师学习起到了积极的作用。此外，该项目的整合对教师信念和实践也起到了积极作用，一证两用也节省了学员教师的时间。

第 16 章　教学外部测评中的文化和情境　本章由 David M. Palfreyman 撰写，主要探讨 Delta 外来考官在教学测评过程中涉及的文化问题和文化意识。作者首先介绍了文化和情境、文化和教学、文化和教师教育、文化和测评等主要概念。在测评方面，剑桥大学考试委员会曾发起过"拓宽文化情境"的运动，来确保测评材料可理解、有意义且公平。作者认为，对于文化，较好的处理方法是首先确定适用范围较广的整体目标，然后再结合当地情境中的资源细化目标。Delta 中侧重"情境中立"的教学，让学员选择恰当的教学方法来应对具体情境的教学。作者在综述部分还援引了活动理论（Activity Theory）来考察外部测评中培训员、学员和考官的合作。本章采用的数据来自外来考官（英国本族语者）在英国和阿拉伯联合酋长国 Delta 教师培训项目中撰写的测评报告，也包括部分被标记为文化因素突显的报告。作者通过量化和质性研究，从课堂设计和备课、课堂气氛、语言使用和意识三个方面考察了报告中的文化因素。研究发现，文化意识是教师技能的重要成分；考官应该记住评价他人也是自己学习的机会；语言与文化紧密关联，教语言就要在学习者主体文化和目标语文化之间搭起桥梁；考官应该认识到教学的发展意味着教学方式发生变化，或者教学方式不变但意识发生转变。

三、本书特色与启示

本书是第一本关于语言教师专业技能和知识测评的著作。第一部分的简史为理解本书内容提供了重要的背景知识。第二部分从理论架构、评价方式和评分程序等方面综合讨论了剑桥英语教学资格认证的优秀实践，证明了能力培养与测评之间的和谐关系。第三部分则从教师语言能力、语言意识、灵活性和应对力、教学知识四个重点问题出发讨论剑桥英语教学资格认证所采取的策略。第四部分从教学情境出发，探讨剑桥英语教学资格认证所带来的影响及其与内容和文化之间的互动。归结起来，本书全面、系统地介绍了剑桥英语教学资格认证基于研究的教师能力测评实践。

本书论述的 CELTA、TKT 和 Delta 对我国中小学和幼儿园英语教师资格认证考试有重要的启示。我国于 2011 年由教育部师范教育司和教育部考试中心联合颁布《中小学和幼儿园教师资格考试标准及大纲（试行）》，2015 年开始实行教师资格证书全国统考，申请中小学和幼儿园英语教师资格者必须参加相应的笔试和面试，成绩合格后方可取得教师资格。与剑桥英语教学资格认证考试相比，笔者认为我国中小学和幼儿园英语教师资格考试可以在以下几方面深入探究。第一，构建中国英语教学框架，分等级对中国英语教师的专业技能和知识进行详细的描述；开发相应级别的英语教师资格认证，与该框架关联，增强中国英语教师培训的科学性和系统性。第二，对英语教师的语言能力作明确的要求。现有的资格考试只规定了申请者的学历要求，据此推断英语水平介于 CEFR 的 B1 至 B2 之间或更高（韩宝成、曲鑫 2016）。本书中关于教师语言能力和语言意识的讨论能够启发我们明晰本土化的英语教师语言能力要求，研制中国英语教师语言能力标准。第三，进一步明确中国英语教师资格证书的考试目标、考试内容，更加科学地设计考试任务。本书中的 CELTA 侧重考察课堂教学实践，TKT 侧重考察英语教师知识，Delta 则分模块关注了教学知识和教学实践。对实践性极强的教学能力进行测评，一次考试不能充分考查，本书中论述的档案袋评价和教学实践测评方法对我国中小学和幼儿园英语教师资格认证具有重要的启示。第四，表现性评价的评分信度是极具挑战性的，本书中讨论的多层考官培训模式和考官互访抽查的做法对我国中小学和幼儿园英语教师资格认证开发表现性评价任务也有重要的启示。第五，目前我国的中小学和幼儿园英语教师资格考试与培训是分离的，可以借鉴本书中讨论的做法，由专业机构开发英语教师专业能力培训课程，通过集中培训、网络课程、混合式教学的方式为职前和在职教师提供专业发展。对教学实践的评价则更适合在培训课程中由专业的教师培训者实施。另一种思路是像本书第 15 章那样，将引进国际英语教师资格认证课程与学位课程进行整合。

林敦来

北京师范大学

2019 年 2 月 14 日

参考文献

Cambridge English. (2014) *Delta Module One, Module Two, Module Three: Handbook for Tutors and Candidates*. Cambridge: Cambridge English Language Assessment.

Cambridge English. (2016) *Handbook for Teachers*. https://www.cambridgeenglish.org/Images/22191-tkt-clil-handbook.pdf

韩宝成、曲鑫.（2016）中外英语教师资格证书比较研究.《外语教学》（6），42–47。

Acknowledgements

The editors are grateful to all the authors not only for the time they have given to researching and writing their contributions but also for the spirit of openness with which they received suggestions from the editors, the Series Editors and the external reviewers. The editors would also like to thank the two external reviewers, Scott Thornbury and Richard Rossner, for their insightful and valuable feedback on an earlier draft of the manuscript.

Finally, the publishers are grateful to Oxford University Press and Alan Waters for their permission to use Figure 2 on page 281, which first appeared in *ELT Journal* issue 54 (2000).

Series Editors' note

Examinations specifically aimed at language teachers go back a long way in the history of Cambridge English language examinations. The University of Cambridge Local Examinations Syndicate (UCLES) instituted a Certificate of Proficiency in English (CPE) in 1913 alongside Certificates in Proficiency for teachers in other languages, viz., French and German. The 1913 Regulations for the Examinations for Certificates of Proficiency in Modern Languages and Religious Knowledge noted:

> The Certificate of Proficiency in English is designed for Foreign Students who desire a satisfactory proof of their knowledge of the language with a view to teaching it in foreign schools. The Certificate is not, however, limited to Foreign Students (1913: 5).

The emphasis in the early CPE was on the language proficiency of the candidates rather than their pedagogical expertise, though their knowledge of pedagogy was directly assessed, for example, in the writing paper. Proof of the suitability of the examination for practising or prospective teachers of English can be found in some of the CPE essay titles:

- 1920 The 'direct method' in the teaching of languages
- 1921 The value and importance of dialect
- 1922 The art of reading
- 1923 Intonation in speech as a mark of nationality

In addition papers in phonetics and grammar, as well as reading aloud, were particularly apposite components of CPE in terms of their relevance for the teacher in the English language teaching (ELT) classroom. A close relationship between assessment and the content of learning was an important consideration in this English language examination for actual or intending teachers of English in 1913.

This narrowly defined target audience would disappear from the regulations by 1933 and we find that by 1947 CPE was:

> ... open to all candidates whose mother tongue is not English and it is designed not only for prospective teachers but also for other students with a wide range of interest within the field of English studies (Regulations 1947).

The Diploma of English Studies was another Cambridge English language examination with potential for use as a teaching qualification. The Diploma of English Studies (DES) was an advanced, specialist examination in English Literature and background studies at post-Proficiency level. It was first offered in December 1945 to 16 candidates, eight in Egypt, at the British Institutes in Cairo and Alexandria, two at the Cultural Institute in Montevideo, Uruguay, and six at the Polytechnic in Regent Street, London.

The British Council was keen for the exam 'to be regarded abroad as a valuable qualification for foreign teachers of English' (letter to UCLES from the Council Secretary-General, dated 23 March 1945). In the January 1945 British Council UCLES Joint Committee minutes, it is clear that the Council (in the chair at this meeting) was pushing for the inclusion of a paper on the teaching of English in the Diploma examination but the Syndicate were unwilling to countenance such a move:

> **British Council request for a paper on the teaching of English.**
> It was understood that the Syndicate's representatives felt unable to commit the Syndicate at this stage; the proposal might involve the Syndicate in a far-reaching, long-term responsibility, and one aspect of this, which the Syndicate's representatives would first wish to discuss with the British Council, would be the necessary financial provision. The Chairman pressed the need, not only for a practical test, but also for an adequate record of a candidate's teaching practice over a period. It was agreed to refer the matter to an expert Committee to be called together for the purpose.

The issue of a paper on teaching methods was raised again at the July 1948 meeting following the 1947 UCLES/British Council conference for teachers from centres overseas:

> **Min.5(d) Proposal for a Diploma paper on Teaching Method.**
> There was further discussion on the proposal for the inclusion in the Diploma examination of an optional additional paper on the teaching of English as a foreign language. It was pointed out that, irrespective of the desirability of such a paper from the candidates' point of view, it was doubtful whether, in view of

the present lack of a recognised body of doctrine, it was a suitable subject for examination. The subject would be taken up again at a future conference.

Although there was a reluctance to embark on a test specifically for English language teaching at this stage, this was an area of Cambridge's work, which would eventually increase dramatically, in spite of this early reticence.

After the Second World War external circumstances played their part and there was a marked increase in the spread of English around the world as English became an international language. Crystal (1997) expands in detail on a variety of factors which led to the increasing dominance of English as a world language: access to knowledge, use in: international relations, the press, advertising, broadcasting, motion pictures, popular music, international travel, international safety, education, and communications (see also Graddol 1997, 2006). English was the lingua franca needed 'to meet the needs of international communication' (Howatt 1997: 263). This growth in the importance of English had a significant impact on educational systems worldwide and concomitantly on the numbers of English language teachers required. The increased demand for teachers led to a related increase in teacher training programmes of all kinds. With this demand for trained teachers came a demand for evidence of their ability. There was thus a pressing need for qualified teachers.

By the 1960s, the climate with regard to ELT qualifications had clearly changed and International House and the Royal Society of Arts (RSA) began offering English language teaching qualifications driven in the main by practical considerations rather than theoretical. In 1988 the well-established and respected RSA qualifications moved to Cambridge under the guidance of Lynette Murphy O'Dwyer who transferred from the RSA to UCLES at the same time. The training of English language teachers and the assessment of their competence was increasingly seen as an important part of ELT in general and the Cambridge landscape in particular (see Chapter 2 in this volume for details). The 1990s saw further changes to the former RSA examinations leading to the new Certificate in Teaching English to Speakers of Other Languages (CELTA) and Diploma in Teaching English to Speakers of Other Languages (Delta) and the addition of a separate Teaching Knowledge Test (TKT) in 2005.

Much has been written about the training of English language teachers over the last few decades, but unfortunately relatively little that relates to the assessment of knowledge, skills and ability in this area. This volume is one of the few to address this deficit and it is the first in the Studies in Language Testing (SiLT) series to consider assessment with regard to Cambridge English Teaching Qualifications (full details of the content of each of the qualifications discussed in this volume can be found on the website www.cambridgeenglish.org).

The editors of this volume explain in their introduction (Chapter 1) how the format in each of the chapters involves a discussion of key issues involved in a particular aspect of language teacher assessment together with an account of how those issues are addressed in the various Cambridge English qualifications. They have organised sections around themes that link the various chapters: history and background; development and assessment; the assessment of specific criteria; and assessment in context. Each section starts with an overview of the chapters within it.

The origins of the different qualifications can then be found in an account of their history by Alan Pulverness in Chapter 2, which makes clear that at first qualifications were aimed at prospective teachers whose first language was English and therefore competence in the language was assumed. The editors note how the changing nature of applicants for the qualifications can be found in the case studies in this volume by Peter Watkins, Bill Harris and Alan Pulverness (Chapter 14). The chapter shows the changing nature of English language users worldwide and raises the question of the level of linguistic competence required to teach a language effectively, which Jenny Johnson and Monica Poulter address in Chapter 8. Martin Parrott (Chapter 9) underlines the importance of language awareness, which underpins most of the decisions teachers have to make. Teachers' language competence and language awareness are particularly tested in spontaneous interactions with students, as discussed by Rosemary Wilson (Chapter 10).

When the source of evidence is short-lived, as in the case of a language lessson, the risk of unreliable judgement on the part of the observer is clearly a factor to be accounted for. The approach to ensuring reliability through standardisation of assessment is addressed by Evelina D. Galaczi and Marie Therese Swabey (Chapter 6).

The inherent tensions between training, development and assessment are explored from different perspectives with reference to the Delta by Simon

Borg and David Albery (Chapter 3), and by Simon Phipps (Chapter 15) in the case of an in-service teacher education programme at Bilkent University, Turkey. The reader is made aware that despite the perhaps inevitable tensions in a standards-based era, the need for formal summative assessment has taken on greater importance in training programmes and requires procedures, which may well conflict with the teacher development process.

The editors indicate in their introduction that a number of chapters in the volume refer to the complexity of the assessment process and draw attention to 'the unequal relationship between the parties involved in the assessment as well as the inter-personal factors which may impact on the behaviour of the students, the teacher being assessed and the observer making an assessment of the lesson'. The complicated interpersonal dynamics of the teaching/training situation are emphasised and examined by Jo-Ann Delaney (Chapter 5), David M. Palfreyman (Chapter 16), and Marie Morgan (Chapter 7).

The editors point to the need for multiple sources of evidence in order to gain a comprehensive picture of teachers' knowledge and skills. One effective way of collecting such evidence is through portfolios. Their use for different purposes and their specific content and role in the Cambridge English Teaching Qualifications assessment procedures are discussed by Neil Anderson (Chapter 4).

In some contexts a comprehensive teacher training qualification with a practical element is not possible. The discussion of the development of the Teaching Knowledge Test (TKT) by Mary Spratt (Chapter 11) and the test of Content and Language Integrated Learning (CLIL) by Kay Bentley (Chapter 13) offers an approach to assessing teachers' personal practical knowledge through paper-based tests in those situations where resources are limited. The impact of TKT in one particular country, Uruguay, is discussed in Chapter 12, which shows the role that formal assessment can play in promoting professional development.

Several chapters suggest areas for further investigation and it is hoped that this volume will encourage others to carry out and publish additional research in this important area. Cambridge English Language Assessment's quarterly *Research Notes* provides an ideal forum for this. For example, it would seem worthwhile investigating the potential for the use of technology in the assessment of teachers and how this may have positive or negative impact on issues of reliability.

In sum this volume presents an important set of papers with a wide coverage of critical issues in the neglected area of English language teaching qualifications and as such fills a serious gap in the literature on assessment. It represents a major contribution to our knowledge of this critical area and is a valuable addition to the SiLT series.

References

Crystal, D. (1997) *English as a Global Language*. Cambridge: Cambridge University Press.
Graddol, D. (1997) *The Future of English?* London: The British Council.
Graddol, D. (2006) *English Next: Why Global English May Mean the End of English as a Foreign Language*. London: The British Council.
Howatt, A. P. R. (1997) Talking shop: Transformation and change in ELT. *English Language Teaching Journal* 51 (3), 263–268.

Cyril J. Weir and Nick Saville
November 2014

Notes on contributors

Rosemary Wilson has had a long career as a language teacher, teacher educator, staff developer and academic manager in both the state and private sectors in the UK, Europe, the Far East, the USA and Australasia. She was a tutor and assessor for both CELTA and Delta as well as TEFL Subject Officer at UCLES (now Cambridge English Language Assessment). Her most recent post was at Birkbeck, University of London, where she set up and taught the new MA in TESOL/Language Teaching and led the college-wide Academic English programme, gaining a Birkbeck Excellence in Teaching Award for her work with students on planning and writing dissertations. She has now retired in order to live in the south of France.

Monica Poulter is currently Teacher Development Manager at Cambridge English Language Assessment. After teaching and training for a number of years in a variety of educational institutions in Germany, Czechoslovakia, Cameroon and the UK, Monica joined Cambridge English (then UCLES EFL) and for over 20 years has been involved in the area of teacher assessment. She has worked with teachers, trainers and external consultants in creating, revising and gaining recognition for the Cambridge English Teaching Qualifications and developing material to support assessors and trainers. A key focus has been to raise the status of ELT teacher training qualifications through establishing links with mainstream education programmes.

Alan Pulverness is Assistant Academic Director with Norwich Institute for Language Education (NILE) and a co-author of a number of ELT textbooks, including the award-winning *Macmillan Short Course Programme* (1993; 1995). He has been a CELTA and Delta trainer since the mid-1980s, and is an ICELT Chief Moderator and a Delta Assessor. He was Joint Chief Examiner for CEELT, the Cambridge Examination in English for Language Teachers. His most recent publications are (with Mary Spratt and Melanie Williams) *The TKT Course* (2005; 2011) and (with Brian Tomlinson) 'Materials for cultural awareness' in *Developing Materials for Language Teaching* (Tomlinson 2013). From 2000 to 2004 he edited IATEFL Conference Selections and he co-chaired the British Council Oxford Conference on the Teaching of Literature from 2002 to 2006.

Simon Borg has been involved in ELT for over 25 years, working as a teacher, teacher educator, lecturer, examiner, researcher and consultant in a range of international contexts. After 15 years in the School of Education at the University of Leeds, where he was a Professor of TESOL, Simon now works full-time as an ELT consultant. He specialises in teacher education and development (including monitoring and evaluation), teacher research, and research methods training, and is regularly invited to speak about these issues at international conferences. He is recognised as a leading scholar in the study of language teachers and has published extensively. He is also an editorial board member for leading language education journals.

David Albery has been working in ELT for nearly 25 years both in the UK and overseas. He has taught English language in a wide range of contexts, both private and public sector, and trained teachers and trainers in many different parts of the world. He has also held various ELT management posts and been responsible for highly regarded teacher training programmes. He currently divides his time between teacher training and teaching English for Academic Purposes at the University College London, Centre for Languages and International Education. He has written various books for teachers and has worked for Cambridge English in positions of responsibility for Delta assessment. His most recent publication is *The TKT Course KAL Module* (2012).

Neil Anderson has taught and trained in Hungary, Switzerland and England. He is currently a senior trainer at International House Budapest, where he is involved in CELTA, Delta and in-service training of teachers. He also works for the Distance Delta online training programme, as a CELTA, Delta Module Two assessor and a Team Leader for Delta Module Three. His particular areas of interest include classroom discourse analysis and fluency-to-accuracy approaches to language instruction such as task-based teaching and unplugged teaching. As part of his in-service training role, he is involved in teacher education through structured mentoring and the promotion of action research among more and less experienced teachers;

he is particularly interested in the benefits of reflective practice as part of situated learning.

Jo-Ann Delaney works as a senior lecturer in the Education Faculty at Canterbury Christ Church University. She taught ELT abroad and in the UK for over 15 years. She started working on CELTA courses in 1997 and has run full-time and part-time courses mainly in the UK Further Education sector. She is an experienced CELTA assessor and Joint Chief Assessor. Her research interests are in the area of teacher knowledge and teacher learning and she is currently working on a PhD on teacher learning on the CELTA course.

Evelina D. Galaczi is Principal Research and Validation Manager at Cambridge English Language Assessment. She has extensive experience as a researcher in language assessment and as an English language teacher, teacher trainer and programme administrator. Within Cambridge English Language Assessment, Evelina contributes to research on speaking assessment and on the Cambridge English Teaching Qualifications; she is also involved with a range of government projects and with training events on assessment literacy. Her current research interests include issues in performance assessment, the role of technology in speaking assessment, scale development and mixed-method approaches to research in language teaching, learning and assessment.

Marie Therese Swabey has been involved in English language teaching for more than 30 years as a teacher and a teacher trainer. She has taught in the UK in both the private and state sector and has worked overseas in Italy, West Africa, the United States and Canada. She has developed materials for teachers and trainers for Cambridge English and Cambridge University Press and has written for Delta and TKT exams. She is a CELTA and Delta Assessor and is Principal Assessor for TKT: Practical.

Marie Morgan is a freelance consultant, pre- and in-service ELT teacher trainer, trainer of trainers, materials writer, and English language teacher. She is a Senior Assessor, Inspector and Examiner with two examining bodies. She has worked with Cambridge English for over 20 years on a range of projects related to teaching qualifications. She holds an MA in TESOL (Distinction) from the Institute of Education, University of London.

Jenny Johnson is Academic Manager at Eastbourne School of English, UK. Previously, she was Director of Studies, then Head of Teacher Training, at International House, Barcelona, where she trained on CELTA courses. Jenny has been a coordinator of both the Teacher Trainers and Educators and Leadership and Management Special Interest Groups for IATEFL. She has presented at ELT conferences on various topics including 'non-native' trainees' experiences on CELTA courses, and has written several articles, including '"Non-native" English teachers on 4-week initial training courses: A study' (2012). She is a co-author with Susan Barduhn of the chapter 'Certification and professional qualifications', in the *Cambridge Guide to Second Language Teacher Education* (2009).

Martin Parrott is a teacher, teacher trainer, ELT management consultant and writer. He worked for many years for International House and in the British and French state secondary education sectors. He has designed and taught modules on Master's and Diploma courses at several British universities. He was Joint Chief Assessor for DTEFLA and contributed to the design of Delta. His most recent publication is the second edition of *Grammar for English Language Teachers* (2010).

Mary Spratt is an ELT consultant, trainer and writer. She works in teaching, teacher development, ELT research, and on several Cambridge Assessment qualifications. She is also the author and co-author of various ELT coursebooks and supplementary materials, such as *English for the Teacher* (1994), *Mission IELTS 1* and *2* (2010) and *The TKT Course Modules 1, 2 and 3* (2005, 2011). Mary has lived and worked in Italy, Portugal, China, Cyprus and Algeria. Her particular interest is the language of teachers of English.

Gerardo Valazza is currently the Director General and Cambridge English Centre Exams Manager at Instituto Cultural Anglo-Uruguayo (Anglo). He has been a teacher since 1989 and a teacher trainer since 1996 at Ahglo, where he also held other management positions: Head of Teacher Training (1999–2002) and Head of the Academic Department (2003–06). He has had articles and research papers published in *English Teaching Professional*, *IATEFL Voices*, OnestopEnglish.com and *Research Notes*. His main area of interest is teacher training and development. He holds an MEd in ELT from the University of Manchester and an RSA Diploma in TEFLA.

Kay Bentley started working in bilingual education in the Netherlands in 1997. There she taught students, and trained teachers to deliver subjects through a Content and Language Integrated Learning (CLIL) approach. In 2005, she returned to Britain and taught English as an Additional Language to non-British secondary students and also started training teachers new to teaching CLIL in primary and secondary schools in Spain. Kay became Chair of TKT: CLIL in 2007 then wrote *Primary Curriculum Box* (2009), and *The TKT Course CLIL Module* (2010), both published by Cambridge University Press. For Cambridge English Language Assessment, she was part of a team writing maths and science materials for new Egyptian bilingual schools then cross-curricular materials for trilingual schools in Kazakhstan. For Cambridge English Teacher, she authored an online CLIL course and moderated the content for a pilot course. She regularly trains European CLIL teachers, writes articles on CLIL and delivers CLIL workshops and presentations abroad.

Peter Watkins is currently a Principal Lecturer at the University of Portsmouth, UK, where he leads the MA in Applied Linguistics and TESOL programmes. He has been involved in both pre- and in-service teacher education for many years and has worked with teachers from all over the world. His research interests include the material used on teacher education programmes and the experiences of novice teachers. He has published widely and his books include *The CELTA Course Trainee Book* and *The CELTA Course Trainer's Manual*, both co-authored with Scott Thornbury (2007).

Bill Harris originally trained as a primary school teacher specialising in teaching French, but after seven years working in state schools, he decided to switch to TESOL. He taught and trained at International House for many years. Now freelance, he has worked on CELTA programmes all over the world in contexts as diverse as Vietnam and the USA, Morocco and New Zealand. His special interests include working with elementary learners and incorporating phonology into the classroom. Bill is a regular at the annual IATEFL conference and has given talks on a variety of training-related topics, including working with lexis in texts and how to promote quality teacher talk.

Simon Phipps is a freelance teacher training and educational consultant. He worked at Bilkent University School of English Language in Ankara for 20 years, where he was responsible for in-service teacher training and development. He designed and directed an in-house MA programme (Management in Education in ELT), and taught MA courses on linguistics, lexis and educational management. He has worked in ELT in the UK, Germany and Turkey since 1985, and has been involved in teacher education and teacher assessment since 1989. He has worked on Cambridge English courses since 1993, and has been an External Assessor for the Delta course since 1997. He has a PhD in Education, from the University of Leeds, UK, with a focus on teacher beliefs. His current professional interests include teacher cognition, teacher learning, teacher education research and educational management.

David M. Palfreyman is an Associate Professor at Zayed University, Dubai. Before moving to Dubai he worked in teacher training and development in Turkey and in the UK, and also taught in Italy and Spain. His current research interests include learner autonomy, the development of biliteracy and the contributions of sociocultural context (particularly the family and peer groups) to learning. He is the editor of *Learner Autonomy Across Cultures* (with Richard C. Smith) and of *Learning and Teaching Across Cultures in Higher Education* (with Dawn L. McBride).

Section 1
History and background

1 Introduction

Rosemary Wilson
Consultant, Cambridge English Language Assessment
Monica Poulter
Cambridge English Language Assessment

The current emphasis internationally on the importance of English language skills has had a significant impact on educational systems worldwide and, by extension, on the numbers of English language teachers required. This increased demand for teachers has in turn led to a related increase in teacher training programmes of all kinds linked to internationally recognised specifications of English language teacher competencies (Burns and Richards 2009). From the broader educational perspective, large-scale meta-analyses of studies of student achievement in all subject areas (Hattie 2003) highlight the key role that teachers play in student achievement and in particular the part that instructional quality plays in student success. A useful starting point for a discussion of teacher assessment is a related study that aimed to identify the qualities of expert teachers (Hattie 2003). The study drew on evidence from a series of activities designed to quantify the influence of specific attributes on student achievement. The detailed battery of tests included interviews with the teachers before and after each of a series of observed lessons, lesson transcripts, coded lesson observations by pairs of observers providing evidence such as student engagement as measured by time on task, interviews and surveys with students, artefacts such as teaching materials and responses to a number of scenarios about teaching and learning. Each of the pieces of evidence was then coded independently by a team of researchers, who were themselves assessed for inter-rater reliability.

The aim of the study was to identify specific characteristics of excellent teachers rather than to assess their performance but closer examination of the procedures used suggests the scope of evidence that is ideally needed in order to reach a judgement about teacher performance. Lesson observations may seem the most straightforward way to assess teacher performance but judgements will tend to be influenced by the subjective view of the observer. The use of a coding system or protocol promotes objectivity and encourages more standardised responses to teaching events. The presence of two observers also provides a balanced view; where this is not possible for logistical reasons, a comparison of assessments by different observers of a number of lessons taught by a particular teacher can provide a fuller picture of the teacher's performance. Teaching events are shaped by teachers' beliefs about teaching and learning as well as their thoughts about a particular lesson (Borg 2009), and their teaching will reflect these beliefs to a greater or lesser extent (Basturkmen 2012). The research study described above carried out interviews before and after lessons in order to capture teachers' planning processes before the lesson as well as their reactions to its effectiveness afterwards, while the use of scenarios elicited more evidence about their beliefs. In-class performances were further supported by artefacts in terms of teaching materials illustrating teachers' pedagogical knowledge through the way that information was selected, presented and tested. A more unusual aspect of the study was the inclusion of feedback from students both about particular lessons and teachers' general qualities.

This brief account of an in-depth research study demonstrates the challenges of assessing an activity as complex as teaching but also highlights the need for integrating *multiple sources of evidence* in order to provide a more rounded view of teachers' knowledge and skills. What can be observed is compared to 'the tip of an iceberg' by Turner-Bisset (2001: xii) in her study of the knowledge bases underpinning expert teaching: 'Under the surface of a seemingly effortless act of teaching is the other nine-tenths of the iceberg: a wealth of different kinds of knowledge on which the teacher has drawn for that particular teaching performance.' In the context of any programmes which provide formal, often high-stakes certification, a valid and reliable teacher assessment procedure needs standardised methods of collecting and collating evidence. A volume of essays documenting the development of an assessment framework for the National Board for Professional Teaching Standards for the US educational system describes the complexities of collecting and assessing multiple sources of evidence (Ingvarson and Hattie 2008). The assessment was complex as it needed to demonstrate achievement of national standards; it soon became clear that rigorous training was needed for assessors tasked with reviewing the evidence and assigning scores to define what constituted 'accomplished teaching'. In her contribution to the Ingvarson and Hattie volume, Pearlman (2008: 181) notes that 'no-one had thought about what might be the differences between training (of assessors) for the purposes of learning and development, and training for the purposes of legally defensible, operationally feasible scoring'; she describes the considerable challenges that were encountered in developing a reliable scoring system, with the need to develop manageable analytical criteria and holistic rubrics, and the difficulties of training a sufficient number of assessors to review the multiple sources of evidence without assessor bias or preference based on their own experience of teaching and teaching methods. While the collection of multiple sources of evidence may be seen as a solution to 'the tip of the iceberg' issue, the lengthy and detailed processes and procedures described in the volume illustrate that the multiple sources of evidence approach complexifies the assessment process and, without intensive training and monitoring, may increase rather than solve problems of ensuring reliability. The sources of evidence selected are perhaps best described as 'a union of insufficiencies' (Schulman 1988) designed to compensate for the inherent shortcomings in each of them. In this context of both theoretical complexity and practical limitations, this volume aims to illustrate one approach to teacher assessment in English language teaching. In doing so, we hope to contribute to the field of language teacher development and assessment by initiating a discussion on a topic of fundamental importance, but limited academic discussion.

The Cambridge English Teaching Qualifications encompass a series of certificates and diplomas designed for English language teachers at different stages of their professional careers. The development of the different qualifications is described in an account of their history in this volume by Alan Pulverness (Chapter 2), who makes clear that they had their origins in two specific teaching contexts in which the medium of instruction was of necessity English: multilingual classes in the UK and monolingual classes in other countries where the English-speaking teacher did not speak the students' language. It would be naive to ignore the fact that the majority of English language teaching worldwide is carried out by teachers who share their students' language and who may use that language almost exclusively as a medium of instruction. The renewed interest in bilingual teaching (Cook 2010) as well as in the use of specific translation activities in English-language classes (Kerr 2014) should also be considered. However, the historical context of the development of the qualifications is undoubtedly a key factor in their continued emphasis on using the language, in this case English, to teach the language.

Linked to the role of English as the medium of instruction, the account of the history of the qualifications makes clear that the first qualifications were aimed at prospective teachers whose first language was English and therefore competence in the language was assumed. The changing nature of applicants for the qualifications is demonstrated by the case studies in this volume by Peter Watkins, Bill Harris and Alan Pulverness (Chapter 14). It reflects the changing nature of English language users worldwide and raises the question of the level of linguistic competence required to teach a language effectively, as discussed by Jenny Johnson and Monica Poulter (Chapter 8). Assessment frameworks that are used internationally such as those in the Cambridge English Teaching Qualifications need to apply the same criteria to teachers and teachers-in-training from a wide range of language backgrounds while acknowledging the different strengths that individuals bring to their teaching. The interplay of the influence of linguistic competence, awareness of the target language and teaching knowledge and skills, as well as interpersonal qualities, reflects the holistic nature of language teacher assessment central to the discussion throughout this volume. Although all the assessment protocols in the Cambridge English Teaching Qualifications provide a list of analytical criteria, usually grouped together in domains or categories, the interrelationship between criteria and categories is apparent. The discussion of language awareness by Martin Parrott (Chapter 9) illustrates how the teacher's language awareness underpins most decisions that a teacher makes from planning through to teaching to reflecting on the lesson.

The study of expert teachers described previously highlighted the need not only for multiple sources of evidence but also for procedures for reliability of assessment. When the source of evidence is ephemeral, as in the case of a teaching event, the risk of subjectivity on the part of the observer is clearly a factor. The approach to standardisation of assessment in the Cambridge English Teaching Qualifications is addressed in detail by Evelina D. Galaczi and Marie Therese Swabey (Chapter 6). When observations are scheduled as part of a training programme, an observer familiar with the teacher-in-training may tend to base the assessment as much on their progress as on their achievement as well as other interpersonal factors. The inherent tensions between training, development and assessment are explored from different perspectives by Simon Borg and David Albery (Chapter 3) and by Simon Phipps (Chapter 15). Despite these tensions, in a standards-based era, the need for formal summative assessment has taken on greater importance in training programmes and requires procedures which do not always sit easily with the development process, for example the need to advise a teacher-in-training that a lesson is below the required standard. Indeed, anecdotal evidence suggests that such statements often begin 'With my assessor hat on', thus making a clear distinction between the roles of trainer and assessor. Transparency of assessment procedures is also increasingly demanded by the teachers themselves, in many cases in the interest of achieving their full potential but in others in order to play 'the rules of the game'; for example, choosing to teach more straightforward content for assessment purposes rather than more challenging topics. The decisions that teachers make at the preparation and planning stages of lessons can also make them more or less equipped to address any unanticipated interventions in a lesson, as discussed by Rosemary Wilson (Chapter 10).

A number of chapters in this volume refer to the complexity of the assessment process and draw attention to the unequal relationship between the parties involved in the assessment as well as the inter-personal factors which may have an impact on the behaviour of the students, the teacher being assessed and the observer making an assessment of the lesson. To ascertain teachers' impact on student achievement, evidence is needed of learning or progression in relation to the stated goals. Disengaged learners working through under-challenging tasks are evidence of ineffective teaching performance. However, it may be the case that students behave in supportive ways and co-operate with the teacher, while the teacher's behaviour may be influenced by what they think the observer expects. Observers may also be influenced by their own beliefs about teaching, which may conflict with the teacher's beliefs and learner expectations about what constitutes good teaching. The complicated interpersonal dynamics of the teaching/ training room are highlighted by Jo-Ann Delaney (Chapter 5) and David M. Palfreyman (Chapter 16), while Marie Morgan (Chapter 7) discusses an approach to training and standardisation procedures for English language teacher trainers.

The point has been previously made of the need for multiple sources of evidence in order to provide a rounded picture of teachers' knowledge and skills. One way of collecting and collating evidence is through the use of portfolios, in which teachers can include narrative accounts of their planning process, examples of artefacts such as teaching materials or samples of student work and comments on the effectiveness of lessons taught. Their use for different purposes and their specific content and role in the Cambridge English Teaching Qualifications assessment procedures are discussed by Neil Anderson (Chapter 4). The portfolios in question are highly detailed documents that are part of a resource-intensive teacher development programme. For other contexts with limited resources, the design of methods of assessment needs to be fit for purpose. The discussion of the development of the Teaching Knowledge Test (TKT) by Mary Spratt (Chapter 11) and the related test of Content and Language Integrated Learning (CLIL) described by Kay Bentley (Chapter 13) illustrate an approach to assessing teachers' personal practical knowledge through paper-based tests when resources are limited. The impact of the test in one particular country, as described by Gerardo Valazza (Chapter 12) indicates the role that formal assessment can play in promoting professional development.

This volume was proposed by the Series Editors of Studies in Language Testing and is the first to address assessment in the Cambridge English Teaching Qualifications. Indeed, it is one of the few volumes with a focus on English language teacher *assessment* as opposed to education or development; assessment seems to be the elephant in the room in language teacher education. Rather than issuing a general call for papers, the editors approached potential authors with substantial experience of the different qualifications and who were preferably actively involved as trainers and/ or assessors. This decision reflects the complex nature of the qualifications in terms of approach, procedures and terminology. Readers unfamiliar with the Cambridge English Teaching Qualifications will find full details of each qualification on the website (www.cambridgeenglish.org) but may find it more relevant to consider the principles of assessment involved than the precise details of the procedures. The format proposed for each of the chapters is a discussion of key issues involved in a particular aspect of language teacher assessment supported by an account of how those issues are addressed in one or more of the qualifications. Most of the chapters include small-scale qualitative investigations that draw on assessment reports, evidence from assessed portfolios, examination papers or a combination of these. One aim was to draw authors from different countries in order to reflect the international nature of the qualifications. That was partially successful in that a range of different contexts are described in several chapters but one regret shared by the editors is that most of the authors are first language speakers of English, a fact that does not reflect the composition of many course teams working with the Cambridge English Teaching Qualifications as well as the cohort of assessors. The organising principle for the volume developed along with the chapters themselves. The final decision was to organise the sections around the themes that linked the various chapters: development and assessment; the assessment of specific criteria; assessment in context. To foreground these themes, each section is introduced with an overview of the chapters within it. Organising the chapters into themes served to highlight the inter-related nature of the subject matter: is a chapter that discusses self- and peer-assessment linked to specific criteria more about development or more about specific criteria? In almost every case, each chapter could fit into more than one section and indeed the sections themselves could be reconfigured and renamed. It was assumed that most readers will select chapters at random and so key factual material about the relevant qualifications is included in each chapter as appropriate, despite the resulting repetition.

This volume has explored and discussed a limited number of themes drawing on descriptions and data from the Cambridge English Teaching Qualifications. The editors are aware of gaps both in the range of topics explored and the contexts discussed. We hope that these chapters will prompt others to identify additional areas for research or to undertake further research into some of the areas explored in this volume in relation to their own teaching context and assessment frameworks.

References

Basturkmen, H. (2012) Review of research into the correspondence between language teachers' stated beliefs and practices, *System* 40 (2), 282–295.

Borg, S. (2009) Language teacher cognition, in Burns, A. and Richards, J. C. (Eds) *The*

Cambridge Guide to Second Language Teacher Education. New York: Cambridge University Press, 153–171.

Burns, A. and Richards, J. C. (2009) Introduction: Second language teacher education, in Burns, A. and Richards, J. C. (Eds) *The Cambridge Guide to Second Language Teacher Education*. New York: Cambridge University Press, 1–8.

Cook, G. (2010) *Translation in Language Teaching*. Oxford: Oxford University Press.

Hattie, J. (2003) Teachers make a difference: What is the research evidence? Paper presented at the Australian Council for Educational Research, October 2003, available online: cdn.auckland.ac.nz/assets/education/hattie/docs/teachers-make-a-difference-ACER-(2003).pdf

Ingvarson, L. and Hattie, J. (Eds) (2008) *Assessing Teachers for Professional Certification: The First Decade of the National Board for Professional Teaching Standards, Advances in Program Evaluation*. Amsterdam: Elsevier Press.

Kerr, P. (2014) *Translation and Own-language Activities*. Cambridge: Cambridge University Press.

Pearlman, M. (2008) The evolution of the scoring system for NBPTS assessments, in Ingvarson, L. and Hattie, J. (Eds) *Assessing Teachers for Professional Certification: The First Decade of the National Board for Professional Teaching Standards, Advances in Program Evaluation*. Amsterdam: Elsevier Press, 177–209.

Schulman, L. S. (1988) A union of insufficiencies: Strategies for teacher assessment in a period of educational reform, *Educational Leadership* 46 (3), 36–41.

Turner-Bisset, R. (2001) *Expert Teaching, Knowledge and Pedagogy to Lead the Profession*. London: David Fulton Publishers.

Preface to Chapter 2

This volume presented an ideal opportunity to present a detailed account of the development of the Cambridge English Teaching Qualifications. The account of the history of the Cambridge English Teaching Qualifications by Alan Pulverness (Chapter 2) owes much to the paper by Hazel Orchard, former Deputy Director at the Royal Society of Arts (RSA), whose powers of recall of the minutiae of the decision-making process are legendary. Pulverness accessed the archives at Cambridge Assessment to trawl through documentation as well as interviewing key stakeholders and has pulled the somewhat motley sources together into a coherent story. The word 'story' is used advisedly because the theme that emerges strongly from the chapter is of the vision and energy of committed individuals. Pulverness begins the chapter with a quote from the late John Haycraft, the founder of International House and the originator of the intensive, classroom-based training courses from which the Cambridge English Teaching Qualifications have developed. Assessment was not formalised in those early days but Haycraft's 'frank grades' of 'Outstanding, Good, Moderate and Below Average' gave clear feedback to trainees as well as guidance to prospective employers. The foundations for more formal assessment were laid with the introduction of the RSA Certificate in Teaching English as a Second or Foreign Language, a notoriously difficult test that created the myth in English language teaching circles that it was impossible to pass 'The RSA' but just as impossible to fail a Post-Graduate Certificate in Education (PGCE). Pulverness refers to the Chief Examiner's report on the first examination for the RSA Certificate in 1967, with one of the main reasons for failure being 'Clarity and Limitation of Aims' and notes that achievement of aims remains a key issue. Assessment procedures needed to change as the number of candidates, courses and institutions offering the courses continued to grow. Pulverness also notes the more recent changes that technology has made to the process of standardisation throughout the Cambridge English Teaching Qualifications, enabling tutors and assessors anywhere in the world to take part in online training and updating.

2 A brief history of Cambridge English Language Assessment Teaching Qualifications

Alan Pulverness
Norwich Institute for Language Education (NILE)

Introduction

The history of Cambridge English Teaching Qualifications is a narrative of the ever-increasing professionalisation of English language teaching (ELT). From the first pre-service teacher training course at International House (IH) school in London in June 1962 to today's Certificate in Teaching English to Speakers of Other Languages (CELTA), from the Royal Society of Arts (RSA) in-service Certificate in the Teaching of English as a Second or Foreign Language to the current Diploma in Teaching English to Speakers of Other Languages (Delta) Modules, qualifications have been a major factor in raising the status of ELT within the Cambridge English network and gaining greater credibility for ELT as a profession, since many of those who started with an RSA or Cambridge English qualification have gone on to work in a range of different contexts worldwide.

Origins 1: International House

The IH training course was born out of practical necessity. As John Haycraft, co-founder of IH, writes in his autobiography:

> How could we get hold of reliable teachers more quickly? There was no agency supplying teachers, and university departments had no such service. Was there such a thing as a qualified teacher of English for foreigners? Did any real training exist? The answer was no … All I could do was observe new teachers, give them advice, and hope they would turn into reasonable teachers after three

months. What was required was a short practical course (1998: 193).

The first IH course was launched with a single advertisement which ran for three weeks in the *New Statesman* magazine and in *The Times* personal column. As Haycraft and his colleagues were unsure how many would-be teachers would enrol, this precursor of what became widely known as 'the 4-week course' lasted for just two weeks, with 12 trainees each paying a course fee of 8 guineas (£8.40).

Back in 1962 'the major textbooks available were Eckersley's *Essential English* and an Australian book called *Situational English*. There was also Bill Allen's *Living English Structure*, which gave straightforward analysis of English grammar from the learner's point of view. Also his *Living English Speech* which dealt with basic English pronunciation. These last two books were god-sends, not only for teaching foreign students, but also for teacher training' (Haycraft 1987: 2–3). In the absence of a body of research and professional knowledge to appeal to, and with barely any professional literature to refer to, for their 'short practical course' Haycraft and his wife Brita intuitively identified principles and developed procedures that can still be detected in today's Cambridge English teacher training qualifications: an awareness-raising foreign language lesson, sessions on grammar and phonology, sessions on methodology and what in a curiously deprecating phrase Haycraft called 'the platitudes of clear teaching techniques' (i.e. classroom management), observation of live classes and 'the core of the course' — teaching practice and feedback from tutors and fellow-trainees.

Haycraft describes the approach to language teaching methodology in beginners' classes as 'free of traditional academic fat':

> Without translating, new words had to be taught with pictures, mime, or blackboard drawing, or real objects brought into the class. Practice was done through repetition drills and acting out little situations. Writing came last ... We produced pithy teaching formulas that teachers could use to tackle the foreign students' common problems with English grammar, introduced stage by stage (1998: 194).

Haycraft's 'pithy formulas' have diversified and become immensely more sophisticated over the last 50 years, but all the principal elements of this early approach to the mechanics of effective language teaching are still evident on most CELTA courses. Indeed, in a paper written to celebrate the 25th anniversary of that first course, Haycraft characterises the design of the course in a series of rhetorical questions which (despite the advent of Task-Based Learning) have lost none of their relevance:

> The root of it was teaching Communication in an unfamiliar situation. How could one ensure this with a minimum of wasted time? How to make the language learnt memorable? Revision? How to involve all the students in classroom activities? How to ensure variety which kept the students alert? How to present, consolidate and freely practise new language? How to make students feel at ease and interested so that they wanted to learn? (1987: 4).

At IH, classes for teaching practice (TP) were initially offered to students as free lessons, but before long it was decided to charge a small amount so as to ensure greater commitment and more regular attendance. Whether or not to charge for these lessons is a question that is still debated in many CELTA centres. TP itself was delivered in 10-minute chunks, followed by a further 10 minutes of feedback from tutor, fellow-trainees ... and students! (In effect, this approach to TP could be seen as a prototype for micro-teaching, generally believed to have originated several years later at Stanford University, USA.) Observation quickly became part of the prevailing ethos at 40 Shaftesbury Avenue and later at 106 Piccadilly, to the extent that teachers would complain 'if they were not observed regularly, or they would request observation when they had difficulties, or wanted to try something new' (Haycraft 1987: 6). The course also developed a justified reputation for being extremely intensive and at the same time highly engaging, a description that would resonate with most of today's CELTA trainees. There was no certification: trainees received a report and were awarded one of four 'frank grades' — Outstanding, Good, Moderate and Below Average.

The course quickly became a key element of the IH operation, and of the symbiotic relationship between the course and their worldwide franchise network, as the overseas schools sought qualified teachers and IH London produced growing numbers of trainees in search of teaching posts. Although the original concept has been refined and formalised through successive incarnations, it has proved to be a remarkably robust model, whose essential components have remained constant, though scepticism from the world at large and in some sections of the language teaching community about the value of such a short initiation into language teaching has remained equally constant. The IH trainers, like the vast majority of their successors in centres around the world, continued to teach and so were not at risk of becoming detached from the reality of the classroom. Many of the early IH trainees became trainers themselves and what had been regarded, in Haycraft's words, as 'something of a ragbag profession' gradually formed itself into a professional community, whose influence eventually spread beyond the walls of IH: 'In the end our teachers' course graduates peopled BBC English, the British Council and the EFL [English as a Foreign Language] departments of innumerable universities' (Haycraft 1998: 244).

Origins 2: The Royal Society of Arts

The Royal Society of Arts (RSA) was founded in 1856 by the Royal Society for the Encouragement of Arts, Manufactures and Commerce. Education had been one of its chief concerns throughout the 19th century, and through its links with the Working Men's Institutes, the RSA had introduced a range of vocational and other practical examinations. By the early 1960s the RSA had a well-established reputation and already administered a qualification for teaching typing, shorthand and office skills.

The impetus for the RSA to develop an in-service teacher training scheme came through a formal approach from the Department of Education and Science (DES) three years after IH had set up its pre-service courses. The RSA was an obvious choice at the time, as it had already been identified by the Inner London Education Authority (ILEA) as a suitable provider of EFL examinations for large numbers of students working in London, and its examinations had gained currency in the Further Education (FE) and Adult Education sectors.

The consultative committee whose work led to the first RSA in-service scheme consisted of representatives from the DES, ILEA, FE colleges, the British Council and the Association of Recognised English Language Schools (ARELS). The RSA at the time had a dynamic culture where projects could be developed quickly and efficiently, without excessive bureaucracy, and the Certificate in Teaching English as a Second or Foreign Language was launched with the first Preliminary Examination in November

1966, just 12 months after the committee's inaugural meeting, with the first administration of the Final Examination following in June 1967.

The RSA Certificate (an in-service qualification not to be confused with the later Preparatory Certificate which evolved into CTEFLA and then today's CELTA) was directed at two groups of teachers: those teaching adult learners visiting Britain to learn English and those teaching adult immigrants, domains that have become known in the UK as EFL and English as a Second Language (ESL). It was assumed — notably by the British Council representative on the committee — that the scheme would be designed to address the needs only of teachers working in Britain. The distinctive needs of teachers working with the children of immigrants were also considered, though it was to be many years before there was a separate qualification for teachers of English to young learners. A sub-committee was set up to conduct research into the qualifications of the existing community of EFL and ESL teachers, and experience in Australia and the USA of teaching English to immigrants.

The Preliminary Examination in English, to give it its full title, was precisely that, a gatekeeping language test for teachers of English, which tested candidates' reading, writing, listening and speaking skills. A 2-hour written paper included a 700-word essay and a comprehension test. One standard rubric on this paper ran as follows: 'In the essay the majority of marks will be given for language rather than for content and form; the comprehension test will also test current usage.' The oral test required candidates to answer comprehension questions on a text read aloud, to give a 5-minute description of material (textual or pictorial) which they had been given 5 minutes to study, to discuss a given topic for 5 minutes with an examiner and to read aloud a given text. To be eligible to go on to take the Final Examination, candidates had to pass both the written and oral components. Exemption from the Preliminary Examination was granted to graduates from British universities and to trained teachers, on the assumption (which might no longer necessarily be the case today) that they would already have adequate language skills. The Preliminary Examination was discontinued in 1977.

Significantly for a scheme aiming to establish professional standards, centres were required to apply to the RSA for approval of courses, an unprecedented extension to the responsibility of an examination board.

Although it was to be a further 12 years before the introduction of a parallel scheme for overseas teachers of English, the RSA also made provision for candidates worldwide to enter externally for the Certificate, an option which was also withdrawn in 1977.

The Final Examination for the qualification, which was later to evolve into the Diploma in Teaching English as a Foreign Language to Adults (DTEFLA), comprised two written papers and a Practical Teaching Examination. The written papers tested procedural as well as declarative knowledge about teaching, with Paper I (2 hours) focusing on Principles and Practice of Teaching English as a Second or Foreign Language and Paper II (1 hour and 30 minutes) on Uses of Language Teaching Materials and Aids. Each paper was divided into two sections: Principles and Methods for Paper I; Materials and Aids for Paper II. Candidates were required to write essay responses to four questions on Paper I and three questions on Paper II, and in each paper they were obliged to answer questions from both sections. The Practical Teaching Examination (which soon became universally known as 'the RSA practical') consisted of two lessons with classes at distinct levels (one of which had to be elementary) which were both observed by an external assessor. Assessment visits included opportunities for the candidate to talk to the assessor before the lesson, to provide a brief overview of the class and the lesson to be taught, and after the lesson, to comment on aspects of the lesson that they wanted the assessor to take into consideration. (In today's Delta Module Two, in the interests of standardisation, this kind of exchange between candidate and assessor no longer takes place.) From 1973, centres were required to submit assessments of their candidates' performance in teaching practice on the course and of candidates' written work (based on a minimum of 10 written assignments), for consideration in borderline cases.

Each of the written examination papers had its own Chief Examiner, and papers were marked by a team of Assistant Examiners, initially under supervision, with Papers I and II each being marked by a different examiner, and borderline scripts double-marked. The Chief Examiners produced joint reports, which became increasingly detailed and informative over the years. This practice has continued, and current Cambridge English Principal Examiners' reports are freely available online, providing valuable guidance to prospective candidates as well as to centres and course tutors.

In the examiners' reports on the first round of practical tests held in

1967, one of the categories singled out for criticism in pass lessons and fail lessons alike was 'Clarity and Limitation of Aim'. The Chief Examiner's summary also noted the variable quality, apparent from the lessons seen, of the preparation given to candidates by different centres, and — evident in a significant number of cases — lack of awareness of underlying theories of language and learning and of available materials. Forty-five years on, today's candidates are generally well-read and appropriately prepared, and tend to exhibit far greater familiarity with theoretical principles, as well as with a wide range of materials, though 'Clarity and Limitation of Aims' remains a perennially key issue. Interestingly, one of the examiners' recommendations after the first round of practical assessments was that centres should consider the possibility of exchanging tutors, so as to avoid the 'very real danger [...] of institutions propagating a limited area of techniques which work with their own particular students, but not presenting to their teachers-in-training a broad picture of methods and approaches'. This proposal, for practical reasons, was rarely if ever followed up, although the desired exchange and dissemination of ideas and approaches has probably been achieved in recent years by tutors moving on to new posts and by a growing population of peripatetic freelance tutors.

The Certificate was subject to frequent reviews, partly because it was a new departure for the RSA, but also because the late 1970s and early 1980s was a fertile period of development in theories of language and learning, and consequently of innovative practice. Perhaps the most significant area of refinement to the scheme was in the basis for assessment. From 1977 onwards, in response to the need for rigorous assessment and taking a view of teaching as a set of observable skills, the RSA revised the scheme on a similar basis to the National Vocational Qualifications (NVQs), which also formed part of their qualifications portfolio. The Certificate became more explicitly competence based, with criterion-referenced assessment. In other words, Pass, Credit and Distinction grades were awarded on the basis of specific objectives achieved, and not simply on an aggregate mark. This implied the need to articulate objectives with ever-increasing specification and clarity. From the outset, these specifications were made fully transparent to centres and candidates, with the assessment form printed in the scheme booklet and criteria made even more explicit in the Assessors' Handbook. As we shall see, this tendency towards more rigorous specification of objectives and consequently, a more robust assessment framework, continued when the scheme was taken over by the University of Cambridge Local Examinations Syndicate in 1988. As the scheme grew, the pool of assessors expanded, and in 1977 the RSA set up a panel of senior assessors and introduced regular briefing meetings, where assessors viewed a videoed lesson as a vehicle for standardisation.

Standardisation, however, did not imply adherence to a standard lesson, though the belief persisted amongst candidates, if not amongst tutors, that there was indeed a standard 'RSA lesson'. At a time when there was considerable interest in so-called 'humanistic' approaches (a loose collection of unconventional and widely diverse methods such as Suggestopedia, the Silent Way and Community Language Learning) the senior assessors were at pains to assure centres that 'non-standard' lessons would be acceptable within limits, and one briefing meeting even included a session on alternative lesson types. One outstanding example of the limits being successfully tested was a candidate whose lesson consisted of an elaborate role play and featured minimal intervention from the teacher. The candidate received a Distinction on the basis of the quality of her planning and preparation and the rationale that accompanied her lesson plan, as well as the evident success of the students' performance. But this was exceptional, and one Chief Assessor's report sounded a warning note:

> It is clear that there are a number of quite strongly flowing streams in TEFL methodology and that there are those who have allowed themselves to be carried away by these to the point where candidates have offered lessons which might only marginally be considered to come within the regulations. Assessors have been very accommodating [...] However, it is, I believe, of some importance to note that the RSA scheme is concerned with what might be termed mainstream EFL teaching.

By 1980 the Certificate had gained sufficiently broad recognition to have become a prerequisite for employment in many institutions, in both the public and private sectors. The RSA was faced with an increasing demand from centres for the scripts of failed candidates to be re-marked. The numbers involved would have made this impractical and in any case the board felt that their marking system was already quite reliable. It was eventually decided to offer re-marking of examination scripts, and/or to provide detailed reports for failed candidates on payment of a reasonable fee, a provision that still exists as part of the current Delta Modules Two and Three. Re-marking remains available for Module One candidates.

From 1984 to 1990 there was a tentative move towards continuous assessment, with a pilot scheme for internal assessment, where coursework carried 40% of the overall mark. Despite fears that the international currency of the certificate might be devalued, a limited number of pilot centres administered this scheme, which involved four written assignments, an extended written project, a written examination and a practical test, all set and assessed by the centre, and sampled for final assessment by an RSA moderator. Response to the internal scheme was very positive, but administration costs, as well as the considerable workload involved, made it impractical to develop it on a larger scale. However, this experiment eventually led to an internally assessed option for the DTEFLA practical, whereby the course tutors would assess a number of lessons, with a final lesson being observed and judged by an external assessor. (A pilot scheme made it possible for this version of the DTEFLA to be run on a wholly internal basis — apart from the externally marked written examination.) Having seen the lesson, the external assessor would have a detailed discussion with the Course Tutor to agree the final grade. In cases where a candidate had performed very well throughout the course, including the internally assessed lessons, but had under-performed on the day of the external assessment, the assessor would often cede to the views of the course tutor(s), and it was the general feeling amongst tutors, assessors and candidates that this was a very fair approach. This option was taken up by a number of experienced centres and is preserved in today's Delta Module Two, whereby a series of lessons is assessed internally, with one final lesson externally assessed, though the final result is determined by the course moderators.

Another variant mode of delivery was an early example of distance learning, the IH 'correspondence course', designed for teachers in IH affiliate schools overseas, with locally supervised teaching practice. This was initially (in 1978) limited to IH candidates, though later extended to some British Council candidates. The course was carefully moderated and produced above average results. IH built on this experience in 2001, when they launched the Distance DELTA, and distance delivery has become increasingly common for the current Cambridge English Delta Modules One and Three, facilitated by the development of virtual learning environments such as Moodle.

When it was realised that the demand for in-service training was coming not only from expatriate and bilingual teachers, the RSA was also responsible for the introduction of another in-service scheme, the Certificate for Overseas Teachers of English (COTE), launched in 1975, and the Diploma for Overseas Teachers of English (DOTE). Nomenclature was problematic, and although 'Overseas' hinted at an ethnocentric perspective, it was rightly felt that 'Non-native' would be even more problematic. Cambridge ESOL resolved the problem by developing a single Diploma-level qualification (DELTA) in the late 1990s and by replacing COTE with the In-Service Certificate in English Language Teaching (ICELT) (2004). It is worth noting that a weighting similar to that in the RSA Preliminary Examination noted above ('the majority of marks will be given for language rather than for content and form') is now applied to the assessment of the Language for Teachers module of the ICELT, taken almost exclusively by teachers whose first language is not English.

Origins 3: From IH to the RSA

IH took a first step in 'exporting' its preparatory course in 1976, when they seconded one of their trainers to run a course for Bell Cambridge. Then, at the IATEFL conference in 1978, in response to a question from Steve Walters from Bell Norwich, John Haycraft agreed that RSA certification for the IH preparatory courses would be a welcome development. In 1977 the RSA Advisory Committee had considered but not pursued the idea of extending its provision of teacher qualifications to meet the growing demand for pre-service training. Despite some misgivings about the credibility and potential currency of such certification, when approached the following year by IH with a proposal for the Society to take over the administration and ratification of the Preparatory Certificate, the Advisory Committee approved the proposal, and a pilot scheme was run in 1979–80, and made available to a limited number of centres in 1980–81. When the pre-service and in-service schemes were renamed in 1983, the Certificate was re-designated as a Diploma (DTEFLA), while the label 'Preparatory' was dropped from the pre-service course and became known as CTEFLA, though the course and the qualification continued to be widely referred to as the 'Prep. Cert.'.

Rapid growth in demand for pre-service training and certification presented a particular challenge in terms of assessment. As the majority of courses were run along the lines of the IH intensive 4-week model, a written examination would clearly have been inappropriate as well as impractical. Equally, it was not possible for an external assessor to observe every single candidate in a cohort of 12 or 18 trainees. The creative solution to this challenge was to set up a scheme of inter-centre moderation, whereby every course would be sampled on two occasions by an assessor, who would not be an official from the RSA, but a practising tutor on Certificate courses at another centre. The assessor would observe input sessions, sample trainees' written assignments and observe the teaching practice of the trainees who happened to be teaching on the day of the visit. The assessor's visits included a formal meeting with the course tutors at which trainees' performance and their predicted grades were discussed, as well as a meeting between the assessor and the trainees, where any concerns could be aired. As well as providing a necessary means of moderating internal assessment practices, the assessor's visits helped to ensure a proper level of consistency across the CTEFLA community, giving trainees the important guarantee that wherever they did the course, they could rest assured that the same criteria and similar judgements would be applied. The visits also gave tutors the opportunity to exchange materials and ideas, and to benefit from the opportunity to observe colleagues' practical approaches, both to delivering training sessions and to the often delicate process of giving constructive, developmental feedback to inexperienced trainees. This mode of assessment still continues, in a more economical, though in terms of standardisation, equally effective, 1-day assessor's visit. (See Galaczi and Swabey, Chapter 6.)

Another way in which assessors were able to feel part of a professional community with shared understandings of assessment criteria was the requirement for attendance at annual standardisation meetings, at which they would discuss video recordings of sample lessons taught by trainees and discuss their views on the grades that should have been awarded. Often the most productive discussions were those which prompted the strongest divisions of opinion. The Chief Examiner would eventually divulge the 'recommended' grade, but the real value of the meetings lay as much in the process of discussion and debate as in the final judgement. Assessors who failed to attend two consecutive meetings were suspended from the list until such time as they attended another meeting. Twenty-first century technology has enabled the process of standardisation to be conducted more efficiently and economically, with video recordings of sample lessons circulated to assessors, who can upload their grades and comments to a dedicated Cambridge English website. At first, many assessors missed the opportunity to engage face-to-face in debates over borderline examples, but most have come to accept and appreciate the economic and more tightly controlled system of standardisation ushered in by Cambridge English in recent years, and the inclusive opportunities provided for all tutors and assessors to participate in and benefit from standardisation rather than the limited number who had access to meetings.

In its pilot year, the RSA Certificate was graded on a simple Pass/Fail basis, but in December 1980 this was replaced by a more nuanced division into three pass grades. Initially A, B and C, these were subsequently changed to Pass I, Pass II and Pass, as it was felt that 'C' carried connotations of failure. Although Cambridge English subsequently reverted to Pass 'A' and Pass 'B', they did not return to 'C', which remains a Pass.

As the number of centres expanded and the Certificate gained wider currency, it became increasingly important to articulate degrees of achievement and to ensure that their significance would be fully appreciated by stakeholders. Subsequently re-stated and elaborated, the descriptors for the original three pass grades are of particular interest, as they represented the first attempt to articulate levels of achievement on a pre-service training course, and marked a significant refinement of the original IH 'four frank grades'. It is worth quoting the descriptors, made public so as to provide potential employers, as well as trainees themselves, with a clear indication of the levels of competence achieved by the end of a course — and the scope for future development:

Pass I: A candidate receiving this grade will not only have improved considerably as a result of the course, but will also have shown some skill in the area of classroom technique and language awareness, as defined above. Someone with a Pass I would need considerably less guidance from an employer on taking up a first post.

Pass II: A teacher receiving a Pass II certificate will be someone who fulfils the requirements for a Pass grade and has exceeded the level of achievement for a Pass grade either in the area of classroom technique or language awareness. The latter will have been demonstrated through the analysis of language into appropriate teaching units or the preparation of effective teaching materials rather than through simple linguistic awareness. Experience suggests that a Pass II trainee will have excelled in one of two areas but it is possible that it could be awarded to those who have shown potential and have improved in both areas. Although they will continue to need guidance, they are likely to be more independent in the area(s) in which they have performed well on the course.

Pass: Pass grade certificates are awarded to candidates who have satisfactorily fulfilled all the requirements of the scheme. They will have shown potential for further development after the course, awareness of language learning problems and of classroom techniques. A successful candidate at this level should be able to produce lessons relevant to students' needs, giving adequate practice in all aspects of the language. Candidates achieving this grade will continue to need guidance from their employers to help them develop their potential and broaden their range of skills as teachers.

In 2013 more transparent descriptors were developed to bring the certificate in line with the more recently developed qualifications. (These can be found in Appendix A of the volume.)

With the increasing demand for courses overseas as well as in the UK, the RSA, traditionally a body whose functions had been limited to setting examinations and granting certification, soon recognised the wider implications of the innovative nature of the Certificate scheme, and 1986 saw the appointment of an Educational Adviser to monitor the scheme. As well as supervision of the running of the scheme, the Adviser was responsible for the monitoring of centres and reviewing the syllabus. This led to a more rigorous system of centre approval and to the establishment of criterion-referenced assessment profiling. However, the growing body of tutors delivering courses, often in geographically remote locations, inevitably felt somewhat detached from the thinking behind syllabus changes, and the RSA responded by introducing annual Open Meetings, where Course Tutors had the opportunity to comment on the running of the scheme, and the Chief Examiners and the Chair of the Advisory Committee could explain new developments. These meetings, like the standardisation meetings for assessors, also included standardisation exercises based on videoed practice lessons.

The sense of belonging to a professional community engendered by the Assessors Meetings and Open Meetings was enhanced by a seminar for tutors (March 1977) and a notable series of weekend conferences (Broadstairs 1977; Saffron Walden 1978; Exeter 1981, 1983) which were not limited to scheme-specific issues, but addressed wider themes in language teacher education and provided the foundations for developing ideas about Teaching English as a Second or Foreign Language (TESFL) across the profession, making a key contribution to the perception of English language teaching, at its best, as a profession.

By 1987, over 25,000 UK trainees had taken the preparatory course and gone on to teach all over the world, with the British Council and in private and state schools, as well as taking up posts with BBC English by Radio and Television and the ODA (Overseas Development Administration, predecessor to DFID — the Department for International Development).

The Cambridge era

By the end of the 1980s, the Certificate and Diploma schemes were well established and widely recognised in terms of both their validity and reliability, and 'the RSA' was firmly established in teachers' lexicons as a synonym for the Diploma. But the schemes, which were complex — and expensive — to administer, represented a relatively small proportion of the Society's work. It was felt by the RSA that a natural home for the teachers' schemes would be under the aegis of the University of Cambridge Local Examinations Syndicate (UCLES) — later known as Cambridge ESOL and now Cambridge English Language Assessment — with its comprehensive suite of examinations for language learners. An approach by the RSA was well received, and after lengthy negotiations, the hand-over eventually took place in September 1988, though as an interim measure in recognition of the strength of the RSA brand, the schemes were known for several years as the RSA/Cambridge Teaching English as a Foreign Language (TEFL) schemes.

Any initial scepticism across the profession about the move to Cambridge was soon dispelled by a combination of continuity, consultation and a carefully managed process of review and revision. A major aspect of continuity was the move to Cambridge from the RSA of Lynette Murphy O'Dwyer, a key figure in overseeing the schemes, who continued and consolidated this role in the new administration. Both pre-service and in-service schemes benefited from the marketing and administrative strengths of a larger organisation with a global reach. The essential course models and modes of assessment were preserved and changes introduced only gradually and after extensive consultation, energetically driven by Lynette Murphy O'Dwyer, who painstakingly sought the views of the entire constituency of course tutors and assessors.

As the schemes grew, it became increasingly important to demonstrate equivalence of practice and for candidates to know that the standards of judgement applied in one centre would be the same as those in any other centre. In a revision in the mid-1990s, the CTEFLA, always a rather unwieldy acronym, became the more user-friendly CELTA, with the DTEFLA and DOTE following suit as a joint qualification and becoming the DELTA. The revision that produced CELTA and DELTA brought EFL and ESL together in a single, unified syllabus, thus returning the qualification full circle to the scope of the original Certificate.

The reviews and revisions resulted in new syllabus documents with clearer frameworks and more detailed articulation of specific objectives, so that at Certificate level, candidates and potential employers alike would have a more precise idea of strengths and areas for improvement where continuing support would be needed. At Diploma level, too, the published syllabus would indicate the depth and breadth of professional knowledge attained, as well as the degree of practical skill required to emerge from a course with the qualification.

CELTA

The massive increase in the number of CELTA courses, and their expansion overseas, as well as the wish by Cambridge English for its ELT training qualifications to gain recognition within the UK National Qualifications Framework, has inevitably produced a need for Cambridge English to exercise greater control over every facet of the qualification.

Centres are now required to keep detailed records of trainees' progress through a course in the form of portfolios, which have to be maintained throughout the four weeks, containing trainees' written assignments (with evidence of double marking), their lesson plans (together with tutors' feedback and their own post-lesson reflections), and their signed agreement to notes arising from their tutorial meeting(s). Much of the assessor's visit is now spent meticulously checking and sampling these portfolios and standardisation is precisely that, a process of checking to ensure that tutors and assessors alike concur with the judgements of Chief Assessors on video recordings of sample lessons. Whereas becoming a trainer had traditionally involved a process of 'sitting next to Nellie', i.e. informally shadowing a course, there is now a highly formalised Trainer-in-Training scheme, whereby the aspiring trainer has to keep a portfolio recording the outcomes of double marking and shadow assessments, and which has to be approved before they can work independently on future courses. (See Morgan, Chapter 7.)

Many trainers lament what they see as the bureaucratisation of the qualification, not simply out of professional nostalgia, but because they feel it detracts from what had been the spirit of the scheme in the past:

> Personally, I am concerned that the course has lost some of its definition, that there isn't time for three whole sessions on the reading skill, those in-depth sessions on concept questions! [...] I miss those quirky bits of written work, way beyond the word limit! Now we are too busy ticking boxes, tweaking our portfolios. For the timetable has had to cede to a great deal of housekeeping and administration. (Blakeston 2003: 16)

Some of this 'housekeeping and administration' has been prompted by a demand for accountability in the occasional case of a complaint from a trainee, unhappy at having failed a course. On a course based entirely on continuous assessment of performance, there is a clear obligation for unimpeachable record-keeping, and tutors can no longer hedge their bets about eventual outcomes: each TP lesson has to be graded on its own merits (according to criteria applied cumulatively through the course) and the grades made known to the trainees, so that at any point during the course they know exactly where they stand. Final assessment is no longer summarised after the style of the three RSA grades of Pass cited above, but represents performance demonstrated by successful candidates in 46 specified objectives across the following five topic areas:

- learners and teachers, and the teaching and learning context
- language analysis and awareness
- language skills: reading, listening, speaking and writing
- planning and resources for different teaching contexts
- developing teaching skills and professionalism.

However, in the same period when there has been such tightening up of regulations and course specifications, there has also been a tendency for Cambridge to acknowledge some of the realities faced by many centres. For example, 3 out of the required 6 hours of observation may now be covered by observing videoed lessons and the minimum number of students in a TP class may now be as few as five for some lessons, as long as an average of eight students is maintained over the duration of the course; centres may now use their discretion in accepting 18- and 19-year-olds on a course; and discretion may also be exercised in cases where applicants do not have the normally expected educational level of university entrance. But perhaps the greatest shift has been in terms of trainees for whom English is not their first language. In keeping with a general preference for referring to 'expert users of English', an equal opportunity policy that dispenses with the invidious distinction between native and non-native speakers of English has made CELTA courses explicitly accessible to any applicant with a sufficient command of the language. (See Johnson and Poulter, Chapter 8.)

CELTA now has a justified reputation worldwide as the benchmark qualification for new entrants to the profession and as a glance at the job announcements in *The Guardian* education pages or *The Times Educational Supplement* will confirm, it is the basic requirement sought by employers in most reputable language schools and 'almost a pre-requisite for the DELTA' (Blakeston 2003: 16). In his view of the original IH 2-week course back in the early 1960s, John Haycraft was quite realistic about what such a course could hope to achieve: 'Our approach was based on giving trainees the enthusiasm and *savoir faire* to explore further once they had started teaching' (1987: 5) and in the late 1980s he was still warning trainees that the 4-week course would only get them as far as Paddington Station although their destination was Plymouth! Through the Cambridge English years, CELTA has benefited from the rigour of its external consultants and Assessment staff, from the investigations of researchers (Edwards 1997; Thaine 2004), and from writers and publishers who have, directly or indirectly, provided its manuals (Gower and Walters 1983; Gower, Phillips and Walters 1995; Harmer 1984; Scrivener 1994; Thornbury and Watkins 2007). But a 4-week course is still a 4-week course, and today's trainees, like that first cohort at IH, are still acquiring Haycraft's *savoir faire*, or resourcefulness, 'to explore further' when they walk into their first classroom.

Finally, it should be noted that although CELTA is very largely equated with the IH intensive 4-week course model, there have been centres that have offered it on a part-time basis over periods of up to nine months, with the same syllabus but allowing trainees more scope for development, and latterly an online CELTA, developed by Cambridge English together with IH, which delivers the course, apart of course from Teaching Practice, in a distance mode.

CELTYL and the Young Learners extension

Many teachers, having successfully completed their CELTA courses, find themselves in posts in private language schools where they are expected, at least for part of the time, to teach young learners. Recognising this, Cambridge English also developed an alternative version of CELTA, focusing on young learners — the CELTYL. But as relatively few trainees can determine at an initial stage of their training what age group they are going to teach, a more popular way of catering for the potential need for training teachers to work with young learners has been the YL extension to CELTA, usually delivered in two extra weeks (50 hours) and covering the following six units:

- language awareness
- the learner, the teacher and the teaching/learning context
- planning for effective teaching of young learners of English
- classroom management and teaching skills for teaching English to young learners
- resources and materials for teaching English to young learners
- professional development for teachers of English to young learners.

DELTA/Delta

Following the move to UCLES and an extensive consultation process across the profession, the DTEFLA, re-styled as DELTA, assumed a significantly more practical orientation. The written examinations that had previously consisted of a number of essay questions were now based on pieces of 'data' (samples of students' written text, samples of authentic texts and extracts from published ELT materials) for analysis, comment and evaluation. While continuous prose was generally still expected, the guidelines advised: 'Candidates are not required to write traditional academic essays' (Pilot Assessment Guidelines for Course Tutors and Assessors, October 1998). Assessed lessons were now to be complemented by written assignments of 1,750–2,000 words, as well as fully articulated lesson plans, complete with rationale for choices of methods and materials.

But enrolments for DELTA began to level off, despite the qualification being the most widely recognised professional qualification for those teachers who after two or three years' post-CELTA experience were seeking validation of their growing classroom competence and entry into a serious career in ELT. Courses over twice as long and twice as costly as the CELTA became increasingly inaccessible to potential DELTA candidates. By the first decade of the new millennium it was clear that this process of attrition was irreversible, and in 2008 Cambridge ESOL responded with a radical make-over that has transformed the qualification.

The Delta Modules are three free-standing elements which now combine to constitute the Diploma qualification:

Module	Title	Assessment format
One	Understanding Language, Methodology and Resources for Teaching	A written examination consisting of two parts, each 1 hour 30 minutes (externally marked)
Two	Developing Professional Practice	Assessed assignments incorporating background essays and observed teaching, including an externally assessed teaching assignment

Module	Title	Assessment format
Three	Extending Practice and ELT Young Learners, English for Special Purposes, Specialism (e.g. Teaching one-to-one); Management Option	An extended assignment of 4,000–4,500 words (externally marked)

Module One focuses on language awareness and on the theoretical principles underpinning effective language teaching, on practical applications and how these are informed by theory. Module Two aims to develop candidates' professional practice. It focuses on their teaching and is assessed through a portfolio of observed lessons, background written assignments and an externally assessed lesson.

Whereas Modules One and Two represent refinements of the core elements of the unitary DELTA, Module Three broadens the scope of the qualification in its requirement for an extended assignment in which candidates, choosing from a set of specialist teaching contexts, have to design a course for a specified group of learners, including needs analysis, diagnostic test(s), assessment instrument(s) and methods of evaluation. The syllabus provides tight specifications in terms of content and extent for five assessment categories, each of which is divided into three sub-categories. This highly prescriptive framework ensures that the assignment is marked with the same degree of objectives-driven rigour as the other two modules. As an alternative to the standard Module Three, Cambridge English has also introduced an ELT Management option, with the same 5-part structure, but based on situational analysis and proposals for implementing appropriate change.

For those who are moving into management roles and are looking for a more comprehensive qualification, Cambridge English also offers the International Diploma in Language Teaching Management (IDLTM). The IDLTM covers the following areas: Organisational Management, Managing Financial Resources, Human Resource Management and Communication, Marketing, Client and Customer Service, and Academic Management.

DELTA had been an acronym (Diploma in English Language Teaching to Adults), and although the revised qualification extended its ambit to include teaching young learners, the DELTA brand was so widely known and valued that it was decided to drop the title into sentence case and to make the acronym a word (Delta) so as to preserve the brand. The extremely flexible qualification framework, which does not impose any time limits between modules, recognises the professional circumstances in which candidates need to fit the courses into their working lives, and by splitting up the work involved, as well as the cost, has succeeded in reviving what was in danger of becoming a qualification that fewer and fewer teachers were in a position to undertake.

Expansion of assessments for teachers

TKT

The TKT (Teaching Knowledge Test) is a relatively recent (2005) addition to the Cambridge English suite of qualifications for teachers. Initially viewed by many only as an entry-level test that would simply precede the CELTA, it has now been adopted in over 60 countries, gaining Ministry recognition in many of them, as a test that may be appropriate for teachers in different circumstances at different stages of their careers. In some contexts it is being used as an initial step in a professional progression that continues through CELTA to the Delta Modules; in others it serves as a formal validation for teachers who may have a university degree in English and many years of practical experience, but lack any kind of qualification as teachers. The basic three TKT modules form a test of declarative knowledge *about* teaching, though latterly an additional module — the TKT Practical — has been introduced, which offers teachers at various stages in their careers the opportunity to gain a certificated practical qualification. This is assessed on the basis of one 40-minute lesson or two 20-minute lessons. TKT does not test language, and indeed the language of the questions in the test (apart from domain-specific terminology which is listed in a glossary published online) is deliberately restricted to B1 level, so as to make it fully accessible to candidates who may be working as teachers, yet whose own command of the language is limited. The three core modules test the following areas of teaching knowledge:

Module 1: Language and background to language learning and teaching
Module 2: Lesson planning and use of resources for language teaching
Module 3: Managing the teaching and learning process

Each of the three module tests lasts for 80 minutes and consists of 80 items.

The TKT also differs from other Cambridge English assessments for teachers in two important ways: it is not a Pass/Fail exam — results are categorised in four bands indicating degrees of competence demonstrated in test scores; and task types are restricted to formats such as multiple choice and sequencing that can be objectively marked and do not require specialist examiners. These factors make the test both appealing and affordable. The objectively scored formats have also made it possible to offer computer-based versions of the tests.

In addition to the three core TKT modules, there are also three 'specialist modules': TKT: KAL (Knowledge About Language), which tests knowledge of language systems more extensively than in TKT Module 1; TKT: CLIL (Content and Language Integrated Learning); and TKT: YL (Young Learners). (For further discussion of TKT see: Spratt, Chapter 11; Valazza, Chapter 12; Bentley, Chapter 13)

ICELT

A relatively little-known qualification for teachers, but one which continues to enjoy considerable support in a number of countries, ICELT (In-service Certificate in English Language Teaching), in terms of its recommended entry level and the demands it makes on candidates, lies somewhere between CELTA and the Delta Modules.

ICELT replaced the former COTE scheme for 'overseas teachers' and its Language for Teachers module also took the place of CEELT, the Cambridge English Examination in English for Language Teachers, a kind of English for Specific Purposes (ESP) test for language teachers. Although it does not specify a target teacher profile or teaching context, ICELT courses are almost exclusively organised outside the UK for teachers whose first language is not English. Like CELTA, ICELT involves a course, including sessions on methodology and language awareness, classroom observation and assessed teaching, but ICELT courses run over many months, often as long as a full school year, and assessment is continuous, with each course moderated by a local moderator and candidate portfolios sampled for second moderation by a team of UK-based Chief Moderators. And like Delta Module Two, its assessed teaching events are generally with the teacher's own classes and spread out over a period which allows for development.

The ICELT syllabus covers the following seven areas:

- language knowledge and awareness
- the background to teaching and learning English
- resources and materials
- planning and management of teaching and learning
- evaluation, monitoring and assessment
- professional development
- language for teachers.

These syllabus objectives are assessed across three components: Language for Teachers (four assignments), Teaching (four assessed lessons) and Methodology (four assignments), with Language for Teachers also available as a stand-alone module with two additional assignments. Following the same tendency noted above for an increasingly practical orientation in written assignments at Diploma level, ICELT assignments require teachers to consider areas such as teachers' and learners' language, planning beyond the single lesson and evaluating teaching materials. Assessment is informed by detailed sets of assignment-specific criteria, with differentiated bands of descriptors for different kinds of tasks in the Language for Teachers module.

In those countries where ICELT is well established (e.g. Turkey, Brazil, Mexico) it continues to fulfil a valuable function in providing a principled foundation for professional development for experienced teachers who are beyond the level of CELTA, but whose language competence and/or their level of methodological awareness would not qualify them to succeed at Delta level. (See Watkins, Harris and Pulverness, Chapter 14.)

In conclusion

Looking back over the 50-year history of ELT qualifications from the first 2-week course at IH to online delivery of the Delta Modules, it is interesting to note how fundamental principles and priorities have remained constant, even as course structures have been re-designed, assessment instruments have become more delicate and modes of delivery have been transformed.

Since the move to Cambridge English, both pre- and in-service qualifications have benefited enormously from the commitment of Cambridge English to research, and from the iterative processes of review and revision. At the same time, Cambridge English has always remained conscious of the fact that their teacher training qualifications depend to a great extent for their continued effectiveness on shared understanding across a broad-based professional community. And despite increased standardisation in every aspect of the qualifications, with all that implies, the Cambridge English external consultants, assessment staff, Principal Examiners and Chief Assessors have continued to consult and to listen to the views expressed by all the stakeholders, so that when changes do occur, they are received with an awareness that they are the result of the most extensive and attentive processes of consultation.

CELTA is perennially successful — there is no limit, it seems, to the demand for the entry-level training it provides. In a short space of time, the Delta Modules have become as well established as their unitary predecessor, and they have succeeded in reversing the slow decline of Diploma-level qualifications. TKT has rapidly acquired reputation and currency and goes from strength to strength. ICELT maintains its more limited appeal in particular parts of the world. Overall, the teaching qualifications offered by Cambridge English Language Assessment have never ceased to respond to changing contexts and the opportunities offered by new technologies at the same time as they have continued to adhere to principles that John Haycraft and his colleagues would have no difficulty in recognising.

Acknowledgements

For help and guidance received in the writing of this chapter I am indebted to Monica Poulter, Teacher Development Manager at Cambridge English Language Assessment, and her colleagues in the Archive Room, to David Carr, Director, Teacher Training at International House, London, and to Hazel Orchard, former Deputy Director, RSA, whose own brief history of the RSA years was an invaluable resource.

References

Blakeston, R. (2003) *Teacher Training: The Legacy of John Haycraft, in 50 Years of International House*. London: International House.
Edwards, C. (1997) Selecting candidates for teacher training courses, *ELT Journal* 51 (3), 251–262.

Gower, R. and Walters, S. (1983) *Teaching Practice Handbook*. Oxford: Heinemann.
Gower, R., Phillips, D. and Walters, S. (1995) *Teaching Practice Handbook*. Oxford: Macmillan.
Harmer, J. (1984) *The Practice of English Language Teaching*. London: Longman.
Haycraft, J. (1987) *Development of International House*. London: International House.
Haycraft, J. (1998) *Adventures of a Language Traveller: An Autobiography*. London: Constable.
Scrivener, J. (1994) *Learning Teaching*. Oxford: Macmillan.
Thaine, C. (2004) The assessment of second language teaching, *ELT Journal* 58 (4), 336–345.
Thornbury, S. and Watkins, P. (2007) *The CELTA Course*. Cambridge: Cambridge University Press.

Section 2
Development and assessment

Preface

Although development and assessment are often considered to be in opposition, with assessment being 'a necessary evil', this section has been entitled 'Development **and** assessment' to emphasise that these two concepts need to work in tandem and that a relevant focus on each aspect can be mutually beneficial. Indeed, all assessment, whether formative or summative, should encourage learning but, as previously noted, even assessors may feel some discomfort in the role. This is particularly the case in the context of in-service training, when practising teachers can feel their skills called into question rather than valued. Simon Borg and David Albery (Chapter 3) explore the approach to assessment in the Delta syllabus by first discussing a set of key principles of effective teacher development programmes. The importance of valuing teachers' experience is illustrated by the first two principles, which emphasise the need to build on teachers' prior knowledge and to present in-service training as developmental rather than aimed at highlighting any deficiencies in the participants' practice. Other principles foreground the specific nature of teachers' knowledge, in which context-specific personal experience mediates public knowledge about theoretical or practical aspects of teaching and learning. While acknowledging this personal knowledge, the role of effective in-service training is also to encourage teachers both to reflect on their practice and to experiment with other approaches, some of which may be used indirectly by tutors on the in-service course. In the case of Delta, tutors are free to deliver the syllabus in the most appropriate way for their context but Borg and Albery note that the key principles they present are highly likely to be evident in Delta courses as a result of the tutor training and induction process. Additionally, the assessment requirements formally acknowledge prior experience through the Professional Development Assignment (PDA) and promote diversification by means of the Experimental Practice Assignment. All the Delta assignments ask candidates to write a post-lesson reflection while the background essay that forms part of every assessed lesson promotes investigation of theoretical and practical aspects of teaching and learning that may eventually become part of teachers' personal knowledge. Formative feedback forms the basis of teachers' individual action plans established after the PDA and continues throughout the course.

The Delta assessment procedures outlined above are formalised in candidates' portfolios, which collate the five assignments completed during the course: the PDA and four Language System Assignments (LSAs). Portfolios are a feature of assessment procedures in a variety of educational contexts, and Neil Anderson (Chapter 4) begins the discussion of their role by pointing out that they have been particularly helpful when assessing young learners as they cause less anxiety than more formal tests. The word 'story' appears again in the context of portfolios as they recount teachers' development in terms of both thinking and practice. Although in artistic contexts portfolios contain a sample of the artist's best work, a teaching portfolio may also contain examples of lessons that were less successful. Anderson notes the distinction between learning portfolios for assessment and those for employability, with the latter displaying examples of teachers' knowledge and skills. Anderson describes the items that are typically included in portfolios: a statement of the teacher's philosophy together with samples of lesson plans, materials and tests, teacher reflections and learner feedback. In the case of an assessment portfolio, there may also be feedback from a supervisor. One criticism of portfolios is the time they take to prepare but Delta candidates are not required to include any additional items other than the five set assignments. Anderson discusses two cases of Delta portfolios in detail, with extracts from contributions by each specific candidate as well as their tutors, the external assessor for the final LSA and the moderator, whose role is to consider the portfolio as a whole in order to determine the final grade. This last stage highlights the role of portfolio assessment in presenting a more considered and extensive profile of a teacher than can be obtained from a single teaching event.

Two of the key principles of good in-service training identified by Borg and Albery are those of promoting reflection and encouraging collaborative learning. They point out the latter can take different forms, including sharing reflections on practice. Shared discussions of this kind have equal value in pre-service training, albeit with at least initial guidance from a tutor about focus and appropriacy. Peer-assessment of this informal kind is a feature of CELTA courses along with self-evaluation. Jo-Ann Delaney (Chapter 5) draws on the metaphor of a 'dirty mirror' to consider how these evaluative tools are used on CELTA courses. She points out that most teacher training courses would claim to be aimed at developing reflective practitioners since reflection is seen as a way of helping to link theory and practice. Delaney notes that reflection is so well established as a tenet of teacher education that it is difficult to question it, while pointing out that novice teachers not only lack the experience to evaluate their own and others' teaching but also expect the tutor-as-expert to provide an evaluation. Assessing reflective practice can be even more problematic; what of teachers who are highly reflective but unable to modify their practice appropriately and fall into the category of 'reflective but ineffective'? Delaney makes the case for caution before describing the different ways in which self- and peer-evaluation are incorporated into CELTA courses. In addition to ongoing reflection activities, which could occupy up to 20% of the time on a course, trainees are asked to write a self-evaluation entitled 'Lessons from the Classroom', which is formally assessed and forms part of the final evaluation and grade. Trainees' perceptions of these reflection-focused tasks play an important role in the training and assessment process and Delaney goes on to describe a small-scale study that investigated how trainees view self- and peer-evaluation and the role of the tutor. She cites the term 'impostorship' to describe novice teachers' doubts about their critical abilities, while one of Delaney's participants adds the label 'betrayer' when referring to giving negative feedback to a fellow trainee. Tutors questioned in the study were more pragmatic and accepted that trainees tended to support one another when making peer-evaluations; overall, the consensus was that final decisions about grading were based on trainees' performance in class rather than on their self-evaluations.

The assessment of performance is a key element in the Cambridge English Teaching Qualifications. Although there are many other aspects of teaching other than classroom performance, it is clearly an essential component in teachers' professional repertoire. The question that arises is how to assess events that are, by their nature, dynamic and ephemeral and, with large-scale assessments, how to standardise judgements between assessors. The ways in which these issues are addressed in the Cambridge English Teaching Qualifications are discussed by Evelina D. Galaczi and Marie Therese Swabey (Chapter 6) with particular reference to CELTA. Drawing on a framework developed to test language proficiency, they consider five parameters of assessment: assessment criteria, assessment process and conditions, assessor characteristics, training and standardisation and grading and awards. They note that, in large-scale international assessment systems such as the Cambridge English Teaching Qualifications, the issues of 'rater effect' and assessor variability are of prime importance. To this end, assessors are supported in their task by rating scales, scoring criteria and performance descriptors. Galaczi and Swabey report that a survey of CELTA tutors and assessors showed a very high level of confidence in understanding and applying the assessment criteria for both the practical and written components of the course, despite some tensions between competing criteria. They suggest that the existence of detailed assessment criteria for CELTA, Delta and TKT: Practical encourages objectivity, including among novice assessors who might otherwise be influenced by the judgements of more experienced mentors. The survey included questions about double marking and internal and external assessments, which are also features of the Cambridge English Teaching Qualifications and which were praised in the survey for their value in increasing objectivity. Galaczi and Swabey note that visits to CELTA courses by an external assessor are tightly structured to ensure conformity and that all assessors take part in regular online standardisation. However, they report that the latter move away from face-to-face standardisation was not universally welcomed by participants in the survey, who lamented the loss of an opportunity for professional exchange.

Standardisation meetings for both CELTA and Delta were one of the ways in which the Cambridge English Teaching Qualifications promoted professional exchange. It has often been said that 'teachers plough a lonely furrow' and that professional development opportunities are infrequent unless specifically linked to a new initiative. One important way in which the Cambridge English Teaching Qualifications have promoted professional development has been in the training and approval of a cohort of trainers. In a review of the formalisation of the training process, Marie Morgan (Chapter 7) addresses the general question of professionalism in ELT and notes that lack of status for teachers and teacher trainers is not unique to this field. Different models of training teachers, and by extension teacher trainers, are outlined to provide context for the approach taken in the Cambridge English Teaching Qualifications. Morgan notes that the CELTA Trainer-in-Training programme was introduced to standardise the way in which teachers made the transition from teacher to trainer. In addition to the knowledge and skills that are necessary in teaching, trainers are required to extend their range and become competent in supervising novice teachers and giving oral and written feedback as well as developing their organisational and time management skills. Trainers-in-training also need to develop their counselling skills and be prepared to deal with any negative and emotional reactions from trainees, often the most taxing part of a trainer's work. The trainer-in-training programme is closely supervised and participants complete a portfolio of tasks, including planning and delivering a training session on a 'live' CELTA course and assisting at tutorials with trainees. The outcome of the training process is assessed, and successful participants are approved as trainers and able to work initially as assistant tutors alongside more experienced colleagues. Morgan notes the tension involved when a teacher who is often highly experienced is required to become a 'novice', but a small-scale survey of trainers suggests that they consider the effort involved is worth the eventual reward of trainer status.

3 Good practice in INSET: An analysis of the Delta

Simon Borg
ELT Consultant
David Albery
University College London, Centre for Languages and
International Education

Introduction

This chapter draws on the international teacher education literature to identify and discuss a set of principles which are seen to underpin effective in-service teacher education (INSET), in language education and teacher education more generally. It then applies these criteria to an analysis of the Diploma in Teaching English to Speakers of Other Languages (Delta), a qualification for practising teachers offered by Cambridge English (see Part 2 of the chapter for a description). Overall, the analysis presented here allows for teacher assessment on the Delta to be considered in relation to good practice in INSET more generally. For the purposes of this chapter, INSET refers to courses and other forms of training that teachers receive after their pre-service training and which would typically involve the individual either currently working as a teacher or having worked as a teacher. We regard INSET as part of teacher development. Delta is regarded here as INSET because those who take courses leading to the award would already, normally, have worked as English teachers and will usually have pre-service qualifications.

Principles for INSET

We will now discuss a set of principles for effective practice in INSET.

1. Acknowledge and build on teachers' prior experience, beliefs and knowledge

Constructivism (for discussions in teacher education see, for example, Johnson 2006; Richardson 1997) is a theory in which learning is seen to emerge via the interaction between existing knowledge and new experience. What participants already know, then, mediates their encounters with new ideas and filters the extent to which these encounters result in learning (i.e. a change in knowledge, beliefs, attitudes or behaviours). This is an important issue in INSET, where teachers will often have substantial practical experience as well as entrenched beliefs about teaching and learning grounded in that experience. Attempts to promote learning in INSET are likely to be more productive when this prior experience and knowledge is acknowledged and built on, and where useful connections are made between what teachers already know and new ideas (Loucks-Horsley, Stiles, Mundry, Love and Hewson 2010). This often requires awareness-raising activities in which teachers have opportunities to examine their current practices, knowledge and beliefs — it cannot be assumed that teachers come to INSET fully aware of these issues (see Borg (2011) for an illustration of this) and, without this awareness, teachers will find it difficult to change (see Freeman (1989) and Wright and Bolitho (2007) for an interesting discussion of the role of awareness in teacher learning). INSET often has limited impact because it attempts to impose new ideas and practices on teachers without addressing the underlying filter of prior experience and knowledge which can block learning.

2. Position INSET as a developmental activity, not a deficit-oriented one

INSET is often presented, intentionally or otherwise, as a deficit-oriented activity — i.e. one which seeks to remedy deficiencies in teachers' knowledge and classroom practices. A more productive perspective on INSET sees it as a development activity which values what teachers know and do and uses these (in line with the constructivist position outlined above) as the basis of further learning. If we accept this position, the message to teachers who attend INSET, then, is not 'you are not doing a good job and we are going to tell you how to improve' but 'we value what you know and want to provide space for you to reflect on this and to consider additional perspectives'. The ultimate goal is the same of course — promoting change in teachers — but while the former strategy can limit the potential for learning by ignoring what teachers already know and do, the latter approach provides more scope for productive learning which builds on what participants bring to INSET. Educational change, as Wedell (2009) discusses, is more likely to succeed when it adopts this perspective. The other drawback of a deficit orientation is that teachers will often resent the suggestion that what they are doing is inadequate; particularly if this message is seen to come from someone who they feel does not understand their context. Creating resentment in teachers, of course, is not an ideal platform for promoting teacher learning.

3. Develop theoretical and practical knowledge in an integrated manner

This principle addresses the relationship between theoretical knowledge (defined as formal knowledge derived from sources external to the teacher — e.g. academic research) and practical knowledge in learning to teach (see Tsui (2011) for a discussion of different types of teacher knowledge). Both are important components of the knowledge base for teaching and we are not suggesting that one be promoted at the expense of the other. The issue to consider here, rather, is how these two dimensions of teacher knowledge can be promoted productively, and our position here is to suggest an integrative approach to doing so. What this means is that teachers should experience theory in a way that relates to practice; this does not imply that attention to theory should precede a focus on practice; in fact, many critiques of the role of theory in teacher education (e.g. Korthagen and Kessels 1999) do centre around the failure of theory, when encountered in a decontextualised manner, to contribute to productive teacher learning. An integrated approach to theory and practice in INSET implies that teachers have opportunities to (a) consider the implications of theory (e.g. of second language acquisition theory) for practice and (b) evaluate theories in the light of their own practices. Teachers often complain that INSET is 'too theoretical'. This should not be interpreted to mean that theory is not relevant to teachers' work; rather, the problem relates to the manner in which teachers experience theory and is thus essentially an issue in the design of INSET. Crandall's (2000) analysis of developments in language teacher education in the 1990s highlights one trend as 'the development of concrete, relevant linkages between theory and practice through the teacher education programme' (2000: 216). School-based INSET (as opposed to INSET which is provided through courses or workshops which occur away from classrooms — see Craft 2000) can provide excellent conditions in which productive links between theory and practice can be established, but such links can also be fostered through carefully designed INSET workshops and input sessions.

4. Recognise both public and personal forms of teacher knowledge and their contributions to teacher learning

The previous principle focused on theoretical knowledge which derives from sources external to teachers and which is typically generated through research or scholarly work conducted by individuals who are not classroom practitioners. This kind of knowledge goes by many names in the literature — e.g. public theory, formal knowledge, propositional knowledge and received knowledge (see Fenstermacher (1994) for a detailed discussion). It is an important component of teacher knowledge but can overshadow the value that teachers' personal theories have in shaping their thinking and classroom practices. Personal theories are understandings of teaching and learning that teachers develop through their experience of working in classrooms. Linking back to Principle 1 above, all teachers on INSET courses possess personal theories of this kind and it is important to (a) acknowledge these, (b) give teachers opportunities to articulate them and (c) create spaces where they can be reflected on and reviewed. It is also important to value teachers' personal theories rather than to dismiss them as being less important or meaningful than external theory. There is, after all, substantial evidence in the literature on teacher education generally and teacher cognition specifically (e.g. Borg 2006) that what teachers do in the classroom is shaped by their personal theories (which may be informed by public theories) rather than by external knowledge in an unmediated form. The challenge here for the design of INSET is how to acknowledge teachers' personal theories whilst at the same time engaging teachers with the received knowledge that may be on the 'teacher training syllabus'.

5. Provide opportunities for teachers to learn collaboratively

Contemporary perspectives on professional learning stress its social nature (Johnston 2009) and opportunities for collaboration are seen to be one characteristic of effective professional development initiatives (Walter and Briggs 2012). In his analysis of the limited impact of INSET in South Korea, Hayes (2012) does in fact highlight the lack of opportunities for collaborative learning as one of the factors. Darling-Hammond (2013: 150) also notes that 'teaching improves most in collegial settings where common goals are set, curriculum is jointly developed, and expertise is shared. In fact, research shows that student gains are most pronounced where teachers have greater longevity and work as a team'. INSET can thus be enhanced by opportunities for teachers to learn collaboratively rather than only individually. Collaborative learning can take many forms but what these have in common is a belief in the value that accrues to teachers through the process of talking to each other about their work, articulating their beliefs and being aware of those held by their peers, and engaging in group assignments which hinge on effective and open communication and sharing. To take a more concrete example, teachers on INSET may be required to write reflectively about their teaching and beliefs, without, though, having space to share their reflections in a group setting (see the example in Borg 2011), and this can promote a rather insular view of learning. Discussion is another key element in an approach to INSET which values collaborative learning (Wright and Bolitho (2007) dedicate a whole chapter of their book to 'talk in training courses'); it is important though that discussions do not become tokenistic and that real value is attached both to their process and outcomes. This implies a certain level of facilitation skills among teacher educators. It also raises questions about the value of discussions during INSET sessions which are guided towards a pre-determined conclusion rather than allowing for an open consideration of perspectives. On INSET courses where teachers complete assignments, some attention to how these can incorporate a social element provides further scope for promoting the view that professional learning is a social activity. Of course, collaborative learning on INSET does not imply that teacher educators do not have a role to play; in fact, their role as facilitators and contributors to interactions has a major influence on the extent to which collaborative learning will be productive.

6. Avoid methodological prescriptivism

One dimension of being a professional is autonomy, and while this can have various meanings, one important sense of the term is the ability to make informed decisions about classroom methodology. While at pre-service level some direction in helping prospective teachers understand what to do is justified, in INSET methodological prescriptivism runs counter to contemporary notions of what it means to be a professional. INSET, therefore, should not seek to impose (and to assess teachers against their ability to reproduce) specific pedagogical strategies but rather to expose teachers to options and to help teachers acquire the knowledge and skills through which they can make informed decisions about the value of particular strategies to their own contexts. Of course, very often the purpose of INSET is to introduce a specific way of teaching; even in such contexts, though, it is difficult to justify an approach which presents the methodology being promoted as undeniably more effective than alternatives. As a form of continuing professional development, INSET can broaden teachers' awareness of methodological options and support the development of the knowledge and skills teachers need to evaluate them in a critical and informed manner. Prescriptivism works against such goals and a move away from prescriptivism towards more enquiry-based approaches to teacher learning was in fact one of the major shifts in teacher education highlighted in the seminal collection of papers in Richards and Nunan (1990).

7.   Promote reflective practice

Assumptions about the benefits of a reflective orientation to teaching and professional development are built into many of the points discussed so far. We are not suggesting that reflection is the solution to every challenge teachers face (see the critical analysis in Akbari 2007); we would argue though that reflective practice — seen as a critically thoughtful mentality that pervades the way teachers approach their work — provides a sound foundation for continuing professional development that extends beyond the confines of INSET. (Farrell (2007) provides a book-length treatment of reflection in language teaching.) Reflection should not be seen as a separate component or session in INSET nor a procedure (e.g. journal writing) — it is, rather an approach which underpins INSET as a whole and which shapes the way teacher learning is promoted. It implies a constantly thoughtful attitude by teachers to the ideas and experiences they encounter during (and beyond) INSET. Teachers will not necessarily come to INSET equipped with the skills, knowledge and dispositions required for productive reflection and thus INSET will need to consider ways in which it can support the development of these. For example, asking teachers to write self-evaluations or journals can be a useful reflective activity but if this is a novel activity for teachers, they will not know how to engage productively in such learning opportunities. Promoting reflective practice in INSET also means that teachers are encouraged to articulate and question the rationale for their methodological choices in language teaching. Again, while many teachers in INSET will have clear ideas about how 'best' to teach languages, many will never have been required to articulate the basis of their views and to discuss these with other teachers. Reflection can also be enhanced, then, by the social dimension of professional learning discussed above. And linking to Principle 3 above, reflection can also provide a strategy through which theory and practice in INSET can be integrated (Orland-Barak and Yinon 2007).

8. Provide opportunities for active and experiential learning

Reflective practice is based on the analysis of experience. In INSET, teachers will, as noted above, bring with them prior experience of language teaching (and learning) that can provide the basis for reflection. INSET, itself, though, can create additional forms of experience for teachers to reflect on and learn from. One option is further experience of teaching in the form of teaching practice (although in its extended form this is more often associated with pre-service teacher education — Gebhard 2009). A second kind of experiential work may involve teachers assuming the role of language learners while the teacher educator demonstrates an activity. Micro teaching is another form of experiential learning which can occur in INSET. One final example of experiential learning in INSET is where teachers (collaboratively) engage in a task such as planning a lesson or designing some materials. What these examples have in common is that they generate experiences that can provide the basis of subsequent analysis and through which teachers can discuss specific pedagogical strategies and the ideas behind them, and which can support the development of teachers as reflective practitioners. Experiential learning — as a form of active or participant-centred learning — contrasts with approaches to INSET which are exclusively transmissive in nature — i.e. where teachers are expected to learn received knowledge 'passively'. Such an approach to INSET has limited potential to promote meaningful changes in teachers' beliefs, knowledge and practices and to support the development of professionals who are lifelong learners.

In contrast, as highlighted in the study by Waters and Vilches (2010), INSET which involves teachers in understanding and working with ideas is seen to be more effective in promoting such changes.

9. Model 'good practice' through the way trainers work

Loughran and Russell (1997) argue that one principle for constructivist teacher education is that teacher educators should model in their own practices the approaches to teaching and learning participants are being encouraged to adopt. In INSET teachers are influenced not just by the content they engage with but also by the way teacher educators behave. A principled approach to INSET will thus be characterised by teacher education practices which reflect the behaviours and kinds of thinking that teachers on the course are being encouraged to develop. For example, if teachers on INSET are encouraged to be reflective practitioners, then it is reasonable to expect teacher educators to illustrate this in their own work. Or if teachers are being encouraged to teach in a way that is responsive to their learners' needs or to use formative assessment, then such notions should also be evident in INSET. (The guiding principle here is that obvious mismatches between what teachers are encouraged to do and what their teacher educators do should be avoided. This also applies to any forms of assessment which are used on INSET — these should be consistent with the principles of the course.) This implies that teacher educators need to be fully aware of the principles that underpin their INSET courses as well as aware of the extent to which their own behaviours and ideas are consistent with these. This principle connects more broadly with issues related to the professional development of teacher educators — an issue which, while gaining increased attention, remains a largely unexplored one in our field (but see Hayes 2004; Malderez and Wedell 2007; Wright 2010). Borg (2013) presents case studies of two Delta trainers for whom 'practise what you preach' was a principle that shaped their work.

10. Elicit formative and summative feedback and use this to inform course delivery and design

Summative evaluation is a common element in many INSET contexts. This typically involves asking teachers to complete a feedback questionnaire at the end of the course in which they evaluate it against specific criteria. This kind of feedback (assuming the instrument has been thoughtfully designed) provides (often immediate) reactions which can inform the design of subsequent courses but it is of no benefit to those whose course has just finished. (In terms of assessing the impact of INSET, end of course questionnaires are also limited in what they can reveal — see, for example, Goodall, Day, Lindsay, Muijs and Harris 2005). In addition to summative feedback, then, INSET should also incorporate space for the teachers to give formative feedback which can be used to inform what happens during a course. This does not imply that courses cannot be planned in advance and must be totally responsive to formative feedback from teachers — that would be unrealistic. However, collecting feedback from teachers during a course can allow adjustments to be made which, within a pre-determined framework, can improve teachers' experience. Formative feedback need not be formal — brief reactions on a slip of paper can often suffice, or, once a teacher educator knows a group sufficiently well, formative feedback can also take place through discussion (see the discussion of collecting feedback from teachers in Wright and Bolitho 2007). The length of the INSET will of course determine whether formative feedback is needed and how best to obtain it but the principle here is that formative assessment will allow teacher educators to understand teacher learning more effectively and to support this learning in a more responsive manner. And, linking to Principle 9, teachers who see teacher educators making positive use of formative feedback may also be encouraged to use it in their own teaching.

11. Provide sustained contextualised opportunities for teacher learning

Learners require repeated encounters with concepts in order to master them; teacher learning is no different and effective INSET will thus avoid 'one-shot' strategies which deny teachers the opportunity to engage repeatedly and in different contexts with the skills and knowledge they are expected to develop. Analyses of the characteristics of effective professional development have noted that sustained opportunities for learning are more likely to have an impact on teachers than shorter development activities (Garet, Porter, Desimone, Birman, and Yoon 2001). The oft-noted failure of one-day INSET workshops lacking follow-up to promote change in teachers' beliefs and practices has also been noted in the literature (see, for example, Craft 2000; Lamb 1995). In practice, then, INSET will be more effective when it gives teachers opportunities, over time, to think about, talk and write about, and apply ideas (not always in that order though — application may often be the starting point, as suggested in Principle 8 above). Sustained opportunities for teacher learning also provide ongoing constructive feedback; it is also important that these opportunities connect with teachers' actual classroom practices (see Principle 3 above), for professional development activities have more impact when teachers see the relevance of them to their actual work. The connection between INSET and teachers' actual working contexts is referred to in the literature as coherence (Penuel, Fishman, Yamaguchi and Gallagher 2007).

An analysis of the Delta

The delivery and assessment of Delta Module Two is now considered in relation to the principles of effective INSET discussed above. A description of the full qualification is in Appendix 1 of this chapter. See Appendix B of the volume for the specifications of the Module Two assessment (LSAs) and for Module Two assessment (PDA).

An overview of Delta

Delta is a qualification offered by Cambridge English for practising teachers wishing to extend and enhance their theoretical knowledge and their practice of ELT. The Delta qualification comprises three Modules:

1. Understanding Language, Methodology and Resources for Teaching
2. Developing Professional Practice
3. Extending Practice and ELT Specialism

Candidates for the qualification normally have an initial teaching qualification such as a British PGCE (Post Graduate Certificate in Education) or equivalent, a Cambridge English CELTA (Certificate in Teaching English to Speakers of Other Languages) or the Trinity Certificate in TESOL, and at least a year's post-qualification experience in the classroom. Although neither an initial qualification nor teaching experience is formally required by Cambridge English for entry to Delta, the assessment requires candidates to refer to their previous experience and, for this reason, Delta is regarded as an in-service rather than a pre-service qualification.

Courses leading to assessment in the three modules are offered by

Cambridge English-approved training centres around the world, providing INSET and teacher development for teachers while, at the same time, assessing their abilities as Delta candidates. Candidates are not required to follow courses leading to Modules One and Three, although most do. They are, however, required to follow a course leading to Module Two as assessment involves ongoing coursework, including observations of teaching and a range of written practical assignments, which are collected in a coursework assessment portfolio. (See Anderson, Chapter 4.)

Delta candidates consistently state that professional development is a key motivation for taking the qualification, but employment opportunities and other instrumental considerations (and sometimes external pressure) also rank high. Indeed, requirements for specific qualifications in certain sectors have made Delta a high-stakes qualification and progression within the ELT profession may (especially outside the state sector) depend on achieving a passing grade. The following table shows an analysis of stated reasons for taking Delta Module Two from entrants for December 2012.

Table 1 Reasons for taking the Delta

Employment in your country	84.7%
Employment outside your country	86.3%
Promotion in your country	81.5%
Promotion outside your country	78.2%
Career prospects in your country	83.9%
Career prospects outside your country	83.9%
Employer's requirement	68.5%
For international recognition	82.3%
For professional development	94.4%

The weighting given to professional and career development indicates that teachers feel a need for ongoing INSET in order to develop as teachers and that they gain professional satisfaction from the process of becoming 'better' on their own terms. It is, however, also the case that teachers all over the world, along with their employers, national governments and other institutions, need and require professional qualifications that measure teachers' abilities and assess these against a standard. It is this 'standard' that is often regarded by the profession as defining a teacher as 'good', 'able' or the opposite. Grades awarded to them by an authoritative body are important to teachers because of career advancement, institutional and national employment requirements and the need to be internationally recognisable as qualified and 'good'.

Both candidates and trainers must therefore accept the premise that, while courses leading to Delta certainly provide INSET, the presence of externally stipulated assessments and grades requires changes in practice to be overt and formalised rather than personal. Many of the principles for effective INSET established above may seem easier to put into practice in programmes that do not include formal assessment of the participants' abilities as teachers. This is because, in courses that include formal assessment, there may be a tendency for both trainers and candidates to 'work to the test', possibly compromising development. For example, teachers may be reluctant to explore any strategies or approaches which involve taking risks and potentially creating 'negative evidence' in their portfolio. Such reluctance may prevail despite the statements made in relation to candidates' teaching style that 'uniformity of delivery is not expected. There will be variation in teaching style relative to individuals and the teaching contexts in which they are operating' (Cambridge English 2014: 65). Indeed, the Delta syllabus (Cambridge ESOL 2011) specifications state that one aim is 'to increase critical awareness of approaches and methodologies and the principles underpinning these used in a range of ELT contexts' (Delta Module One Aim 2). Similarly, 'uniformity of delivery' in training methodology is not expected although trainers are required to meet minimum professional requirements and induction and training is a mandatory part of the approval process. For these reasons, the key principles of INSET outlined earlier such as collaborative learning, trainer 'modelling' and trainees' ongoing evaluation of the training process (Principles 5, 9 and 10) are highly likely to be evident in Delta training courses.

The procedures in Delta Module Two add the assessment of product to the process of INSET described earlier. Delta assignments are assessed by course tutors and an external assessor through specific criteria which are judged to be Met, Partially Met or Not Met. (See Appendix B, pages 421–438, for a full list of these criteria). The assessment criteria will often be seen by candidates and tutors alike as a measure of 'good' practice against which teachers' performance is measured. The implication of this could be that if criteria are assessed as Partially Met or Not Met, there is something 'wrong' with the teacher's practice, i.e. 'you are not doing a good job and we are going to tell you how to improve' in order to be assessed as Met in subsequent lesson observations. This could be seen as reinforcing the idea of what was referred to as 'deficit-orientation' in the discussion of Principle 2 in the first part of this paper. Even if tutors are actively seen to value teachers' knowledge and experience during training, the 'developmental activity' referred to in this discussion, they are then required to judge this against an external standard which may or may not reflect or 'build on' teachers' previous knowledge and experience; on the contrary, it may negate these. The question, then, is how this tension between personal 'developmental activity', underpinned by the principles discussed earlier, and the possible effect of external assessment is acknowledged in the Delta specifications and how it is addressed.

Cambridge English has attempted to resolve this tension by including two interweaving assessment strands in the Delta assessment structure. The first of these is the Professional Development Assignment (the PDA), which includes reading, research and reflections as well as two lessons clearly focused on development. The second strand consists of four graded Language Systems and Skills Assignments (LSAs) set at intervals during the course. Importantly, however, it is the PDA assessment strand, with its primary focus on formative assessment, which launches the course with a diagnostic lesson observation which is not assessed for summative purposes. Following feedback and discussion of this observed lesson, the candidate, in consultation with the tutor, agrees an action plan for the course, and this action plan becomes a reference point for the teacher's personal development and for the more formally assessed systems and skills assignments.

Associated with the idea of personal development as opposed to externally assessed ability is the need for tutors to acknowledge and value teachers' prior knowledge and beliefs and for teachers to identify what they believe about teaching and learning and what the impact of this is on their classroom practice. Both of these are explicitly referred to in the PDA with a significant part of the assignment asking candidates, at the beginning, and at various points during the course, to explicitly identify what their beliefs are and reflect on how these inform their teaching. In this way, the formal and external assessment of teaching (the 'Cambridge English is telling you what we believe about good teaching and requires you to demonstrate this in your practice') is balanced, in part, by acknowledging the value of teachers' own beliefs and views on their teaching practices.

Above we noted that effective INSET should include an acknowledgement of teachers' knowledge and experience and the entrenched beliefs about teaching and learning that these can give rise to and thus help remove a filter that can block learning. The idea of building on existing beliefs is implicit in the design of the PDA in which candidates are required to refer to their beliefs and practices at the start of the course and consider how these have developed as a result of exposure to new ideas (see Appendix B). The assessment criteria for the Reflection and Action part of the PDA assignment in Module Two include:

Successful candidates can focus on their professional development by:

- critically reflecting on their teaching practices and beliefs during the course of this assignment (Cambridge English 2014: 54, see also Appendix B, page 424).

The inclusion of this professional development strand therefore provides the opportunity for candidates to 'acknowledge and **build on** (their) prior experience, beliefs and knowledge' (Principle 1 discussed earlier). Delta candidates are encouraged to make useful connections between what they already know and do in the classroom and new ideas. However, as stated earlier, simply referring to teachers' beliefs and practices is not sufficient and here, as elsewhere, a full realisation of this principle relies on tutors and teachers translating the specifications and assessment criteria into practice. The need for awareness-raising activities in order to examine beliefs and practices is also acknowledged in the documentation for this part of the qualification (Cambridge English 2014: 56, see also Appendix B, pages 426–427):

The following specific suggestions might help tutors administer the Reflection and Action (part of the PDA):
Beliefs questionnaire
- Beliefs are often unconscious and candidates may need help in raising them to a level of consciousness. Questionnaires may be useful for this purpose.
- It may be useful to encourage candidates to explore the extent to which they feel their teaching reflects their beliefs.

The tentative nature of this suggestion goes some way to acknowledging the distinction between completing a questionnaire and actually demonstrating awareness-raising in practice. Overall though, the suggested procedures for supporting the PDA provide tutors and teachers with the opportunity to address the entrenched beliefs about teaching and learning that can block teachers' development during INSET. As this discussion of beliefs highlights, Delta Module Two provides a framework within which many of the principles for effective INSET discussed earlier *can* be implemented — the extent to which they *are* in practice, though, will always depend on the pedagogical practices that trainers implement.

Another element of the PDA is the Experimental Practice Assignment in which candidates research an ELT method, approach, procedure or technique with which they are unfamiliar and evaluate their experience in teaching using the specified method, approach, procedure or technique. The choice of experimental practice explored in the teaching part of this assignment is the candidate's own and the decision is made based on their interests and, again, the teaching practices that they want to develop. Importantly, in the PDA the onus is on individual teachers to choose areas of personal interest and concern within their own practice and to experiment with, reflect on, and develop these areas. The explicit reference to teachers' beliefs and their impact on practice together with the negotiation of areas to focus on for development can be interpreted as an acknowledgement by the Delta programme of the importance of 'personal forms of knowledge' (Principle 4) i.e. knowledge developed by individual teachers through their experience of working with learners in classrooms.

The fact that teachers are encouraged to reflect on their practices and beliefs throughout the course in the PDA (and also in the more formally assessed language and skills assignments to be discussed later) reflects Principle 7 discussed above. This principle posits that an effective INSET development course should 'promote reflective practice', as is supported by the requirements of Module Two. Furthermore, as mentioned previously, teachers will not necessarily come to INSET equipped with the skills, knowledge and dispositions required for productive reflection and INSET needs to develop these. Built into the PDA is an acknowledgement that a course leading to Module Two needs to give teachers the opportunity to develop their ability to reflect productively through researching methods and designing tools to monitor and develop their own teaching practices. In other words, the PDA asks teachers to learn about reflective practice and how this might practically be achieved in their own professional lives; it attempts to support the development of reflective practice in teachers. In addition, the PDA asks candidates to reflect on what areas of their teaching they feel they would like to continue to develop outside of the course and how they could go about this; an acknowledgement that reflective practice should be encouraged as part of ongoing continuing professional development (CPD) that extends beyond the confines of INSET and, in the case of Delta, beyond the confines of the assessment criteria.

The second assessment strand consists of two language systems and two language skills assignments (LSAs), three of which are internally assessed and all of which are graded from Fail up to Distinction. The specifications for the LSAs acknowledge the principle of integrating theoretical and practical knowledge in INSET (Principle 3). For each LSA, candidates write a background essay which gives them the opportunity to research areas of language, theories of language learning and different approaches to enabling learning in the classroom. Candidates are then required to apply this theoretical knowledge to practical classroom procedures, materials and techniques, both in the essay and in the second part of the LSA: the teaching. As part of the lesson plan, candidates are required to produce a commentary on the lesson they have prepared that explains the rationale for the lesson in terms of, among other things, theories of language, of language learning and different approaches to learning in the classroom. Retrospectively, they are required to reflect on their practice, which affords the opportunity to critically evaluate the theories that they researched in the background essay. The integration of the various stages is an essential part of the assignment and forms part of the assessment with specific criteria (see Appendix B). In addition, the LSAs in Module Two provide candidates with regular opportunities to put into practice the theories to which they are exposed and then to evaluate them in terms of authentic classroom experiences.

These regular opportunities to relate theory to practice in Module Two also allow for the possibility of 'sustained contextualised opportunities for teacher learning' (Principle 11). As noted above, 'INSET will be more effective when it gives teachers opportunities, over time, to think about, talk and write about, and apply ideas' and this opportunity is afforded by the fact that a course including 'live' teaching is a requirement of Module Two. It is also inherent in the fact that candidates are required to discuss their own evaluations of their teaching experiences in feedback with their tutor and in the fact that they have to research and write about ideas that they then put into practice both in the LSAs and in the PDA. While it could not be claimed that these requirements mean teachers will always see the relevance of the ideas they process to their actual classroom practice, the opportunity to do so is clearly provided in the Delta assessment design. That these opportunities are 'sustained' is ensured by the design of the Delta programme; the suggested schedule for the PDA interacts with the LSAs to create courses where there have to be regular teaching opportunities, sustained over the length of a course rather than one-off or haphazard opportunities. Furthermore, these opportunities and experiences are inter-related through the PDA in that the 'diagnostic' lesson has to be at the start of a course and the LSAs are utilised to allow teachers to assess how they have developed and where they feel they need to progress next; the process is ongoing throughout a course of whatever length.

After each of the three internally assessed lessons that form part of the LSAs, the tutor provides the opportunity for a discussion of the lesson. The candidate completes a self-evaluation of the lesson and the outcome for their learners, and this forms the basis of the post-observation discussion with the tutor. During this discussion, the tutor will provide the candidate with a summative assessment of the lesson with reference to the assessment criteria but, importantly, will provide guidance on how the candidate might develop their teaching. This 'development' may be partly seen as a formative-style focus on the assessment criteria ('you need to do x in order to achieve Met in criterion y'), but will also be more generally developmental because one important aim of Delta is for teachers to progress as professionals and not just as 'better Delta candidates'. Indeed, the fact that candidates typically begin the discussion with an evaluation of their teaching skills (regardless of assessment criteria) allows for the possibility of personal development outside the confines of the qualification. Providing formative feedback given after each of the LSAs, which are submitted at intervals during the course, illustrates how the deficit-oriented approach (Principle 2) can be avoided, as feedback includes a focus on strengths as well as points 'to consider'. The inclusion of points for development (i.e. forward looking to the next teaching opportunity whether assessed or not) provides evidence that 'contextualised learning opportunities' (Principle 11) are sustained over the duration of a Delta course.

The following extract from feedback on a Delta lesson is an illustration of formative feedback incorporating guidance with areas to work on crucially linked to learners' needs.

Extracts from tutor-assessed lesson including formative feedback

Strengths:

> ... You generally taught in a way that was appropriate for these learners — they seemed to feel the relevance of your focus, and you ensured that a potentially dry area was made engaging through some elements of personalisation and variety in interaction and task types. A good percentage of tasks involved the students working together in a meaningful way. (6a, 6b, 8c) ...

To Consider:

> Watch out for ambitious aims and timings when planning — overall, I think you had 90 minutes of material here if it had been fully exploited, and the focus on anaphora, while useful, was ill-timed and could have been lost to devote more time to strategy-building for the main focus on organising sentences and paragraphs. (5b, 5j)
>
> ... When monitoring, you tend to be hands-off, which can be appropriate but at the same time, monitoring can be seen as an opportunity to monitor and micro-teach. When working in such EAP contexts on skills-related work, it is important for the learners to go away with tangible strategies which they can apply next time they approach such a writing task. 8a, 8d ...
>
> ...
>
> ... Overall, you are clearly a highly competent teacher and you have a good sense of what is relevant for your learners. There were many strong elements to this lesson, but also some issues which prevent me from grading it as more than a pass. Aim to address these in planning and teaching similar lessons in the future as you are clearly capable of more than pass level planning and teaching.

The feedback is referenced to the assessment criteria and includes a summative grade in relation to the final standard (it is *'a Pass but not more'*). The phrase may be considered unfortunate, but candidates need and demand transparency in relation to the standard they are striving to attain so clear indicators are required. The supportive nature of these tutor comments can be compared with the more critical tone of the following extract from external assessor feedback on the same lesson provided as part of a standardisation exercise.

Weaknesses

1 There was a good variety of ways to check answers, but too many tasks to check 5h).

... 5 Feedback was not sufficiently searching, though adequate, and elicitation was limited 8d). Etc.

Another important feature of reflective practice is that methodological prescriptivism should be avoided (Principle 6). To this end teachers should be encouraged to question their methodological choices. This is promoted through the design of the LSAs. As previously stated, candidates are required to produce a 'commentary' on the materials and approaches they have chosen for the lesson they are to teach. This 500–750-word section of the lesson plan is designed to encourage teachers to critically examine their practice and make choices based on reason and beliefs; the process of doing this encourages them to question their methodology. That there is an assessment criterion for this commentary again highlights the tension between development and assessment, but the fact that the procedures require candidates to examine their methodological choices provides the opportunity for them to develop criticality in relation to the methodological choices available to them.

As stated in the discussion of Principle 8, 'reflective practice is based on the analysis of experience' both prior to the INSET and during the course itself through providing experiences for teachers to learn from. A limited number of these experiential opportunities are included in the design of Module Two in the form of 'live' lessons in which candidates plan lessons and teach learners. The tension between development and assessment remains an issue in the LSAs but despite this, the teacher has the opportunity to learn from a teaching experience through reflecting on it and relating it explicitly to their on-going personal development through the PDA, in which teachers can use the LSA lessons as examples of their development. As previously described, the PDA with its emphasis on formative assessment provides a platform for candidates to draw on and extend personal knowledge (Principle 4). The LSAs also provide opportunities for candidates to do so as there is no requirement to teach particular content and candidates are able to select the systems and skills areas they wish to focus on in relation to their current learners' needs, and to make reference to their previous teaching experience in different contexts in the background essays.

It could be argued that even the assessment criteria in the LSAs are an acknowledgement of personal knowledge in that they assess abilities such as managing the learners and classroom space, responding to learners appropriately, monitoring their progress effectively and so on; all skills that are as much informed by personal knowledge gained through experience as they are through public forms of knowledge e.g. techniques and the theories informing them. What is less apparent in the documentation is an explicit acknowledgement that this personal knowledge is to be valued equally with external theory. For example, there are no assessment criteria for the LSAs that refer explicitly to personal knowledge though there are some that appear to promote public knowledge (criterion 5k). As noted previously, Delta presents an external standard of assessment and in this context it may be difficult for emphasis to be given to the value of personal knowledge.

The degree to which the LSAs can include collaborative learning (Principle 5) is restricted in a course where work is submitted for assessment; use of shared reading, shared data, and co-operative planning may be judged to constitute plagiarism. Indeed candidates are required to sign a statement confirming that all work submitted for assessment is their own thus to some extent enforcing insularity on the candidate. However, opportunities for collaborative learning exist in the course delivery and in the PDA tasks. For example, candidates are required to observe 10 hours of teaching which may involve observing other teachers on the course or teachers in their own places of work or filmed lessons. Again, this adds to the experiential learning identified as an important feature of INSET and, in this case, is a requirement that informs teachers' development but is not assessed. While no formal tasks are prescribed, it is common practice for centres to either provide a task for these observations or for the teacher to select a focus based on their own development needs or areas of interest. The Delta Handbook emphasises that these observations should not be passive experiences, but should include 'reflections on these observations' (Cambridge English 2014: 53) and be 'used to gather data for the (teacher's) action plan' (Cambridge English 2014: 57).

Conclusion

We started this chapter by discussing a number of principles for effective INSET before moving on to analyse the extent to which Delta Module Two reflects these. Our conclusion is that evidence of these principles can be discerned in the design, assessment, and suggested procedures of this module. The assessment structure allows, at least in part, a balance between development and assessment through the promotion of reflective practice, which shifts the focus away from assessment and on to the personal development of teachers. All Delta assessments are collected together in a coursework portfolio which provides a written record of progress over the course. Comparison between tutor feedback reports at the beginning and end of the course can provide evidence of development in terms of changes in practice. Tutor summary reports, which are compulsory assessment documents, indicate that, for many Delta candidates, real developmental changes have occurred during the course, as the following summary comment illustrates.

> P has worked very hard over the course to broaden her range of procedures and techniques and to adapt her teaching manner to a more learner-centred style. She approached her PDA assignment with purpose and clarity, and achieved her goals of making her feedback more learner centred and her activities more authentic. She has been accepting of guidance from her tutors, and very supportive of her peers. She is a thoughtful and committed teacher, who sets herself very high standards, and who is very motivated to develop her skills. She has clearly benefited from the course to question her usual practice and acquire insights from her research and input sessions. She has made excellent progress, and her coursework is of a very good standard.

This candidate had clearly engaged with the course and built on her previous experience and, to some extent, changed her practices and possibly her underlying beliefs. Clearly, there can never be any guarantee that teachers participating in any professional development course, whether assessed or not, will have changed their beliefs and/or modified their practices for more than the duration of the course, or that there will be follow-through from the course to the teacher's subsequent teaching context. The importance of context is shown in the following extract from another summary comment.

> H has worked conscientiously in all aspects of the course. She had some adjustment to make in moving from her usual teaching context, a more academic environment which demanded a different approach to the more communicative methodology expected in her Delta classes. She worked hard to make this adjustment, and as her ability to analyse her lessons, her understanding of theory and principles, and her self-awareness developed, this led to a successful transition from a more teacher-centred to a learner-centred approach. She has made good use of opportunities on the course to examine her own experience in the light of the literature and to re-assess her beliefs and her classroom practice.

INSET courses can provide 'opportunities' for teachers to extend their knowledge and to reflect and build on their current beliefs and practices. Though the Delta Module Two course provides these opportunities, the fact remains that the assessment load in Delta (as in all credit-based awards) may sit uneasily with teacher development. Despite the course-based nature of the qualification, the intensity of the assessment may not allow sufficient 'space' for teacher learning and sustained development to occur. Further resolution of the tension between development and assessment, perhaps by having different pathways through the qualification with a lighter assessment load (with potentially, however, a lower number of credits) could be an option for future consideration.

References

Akbari, R. (2007) Reflections on reflection: A critical appraisal of reflective practices in L2 teacher education, *System* 35 (2), 192–207.

Borg, S. (2006) *Teacher Cognition and Language Education: Research and Practice.* London: Continuum.

Borg, S. (2011) The impact of in-service teacher education on language teachers' beliefs, *System* 39 (3), 370–380.

Borg, S. (2013) Delta trainers' cognitions and pedagogical practices, *Research Notes* 54, 3–13.

Cambridge ESOL (2011) *Delta Syllabus and Assessment Guidelines.* Cambridge: Cambridge ESOL.

Cambridge English (2014) *Delta Module One, Module Two, Module Three: Handbook for Tutors and Candidates.* Cambridge: Cambridge English Language Assessment.

Craft, A. (2000) *Continuing Professional Development: A Practical Guide for Teachers and Schools* (2nd edition). London: Routledge.

Crandall, J. A. (2000) Language teacher education, *Annual Review of Applied Linguistics* 20, 34–55.

Darling-Hammond, L. (2013) *Getting Teacher Evaluation Right: What Really Matters for Effectiveness and Improvement.* New York: Teachers College.

Farrell, T. S. C. (2007) *Reflective Language Teaching: From Research to Practice.* London: Continuum.

Fenstermacher, G. D. (1994) The knower and the known: The nature of knowledge in research on teaching, *Review of Research in Education* 20, 1–54.

Freeman, D. (1989) Teacher training, development and decision making: A model of teaching and related strategies for language teacher education, *TESOL Quarterly*, 23 (1), 27–45.

Garet, M. S., Porter, A. C., Desimone, L., Birman, B. F. and Yoon, K. S. (2001) What makes professional development effective? Results from a national sample of teachers, *American Educational Research Journal* 38 (4), 915–945.

Gebhard, G. (2009) The practicum, in Burns, A. and Richards, J. C. (Eds) *The Cambridge Guide to Second Language Teacher Education.* New York: Cambridge University Press, 251–258.

Goodall, J., Day, C., Lindsay, G., Muijs, D. and Harris, A. (2005) *Evaluating the Impact of Continuing Professional Development (CPD).* London: Department for Education and Skills.

Hayes, D. (Ed) (2004) *Trainer Development: Principles and Practice from Language Teacher Training.* Melbourne: Language Australia.

Hayes, D. (2012) Mismatched perspectives: In-service teacher education policy and practice in South Korea, in Tribble, C. (Ed) *Managing Change in English Language Teaching: Lessons from Experience.* London: The British Council, 99–104.

Johnson, K. E. (2006) The sociocultural turn and its challenges for second language teacher education, *TESOL Quarterly* 40 (1), 235–257.

Johnston, B. (2009) Collaborative teacher development, in Burns, A. and Richards, J. C. (Eds) *The Cambridge Guide to Second Language Teacher Education.* New York: Cambridge University Press, 241–249.

Korthagen, F. and Kessels, J. P. A. M. (1999) Linking theory and practice: Changing the pedagogy of teacher education, *Educational Researcher* 28 (4), 4–17.

Lamb, M. (1995) The consequences of INSET, *ELT Journal* 49 (1), 72–80.

Loucks-Horsley, S., Stiles, K.E., Mundry, S., Love, N. and Hewson, P.W. (2010) *Designing professional development for teachers of science and mathematics* (3rd edition). Thousand Oaks: Corwin Press.

Loughran, J. and Russell, T. (Eds) (1997) *Teaching about Teaching: Purpose, Passion and Pedagogy in Teacher Education.* London: Falmer Press.

Malderez, A. and Wedell, M. (2007) *Teaching Teachers: Processes and Practices.* London: Continuum.

Orland-Barak, L. and Yinon, H. (2007) When theory meets practice: What student teachers learn from guided reflection on their own classroom discourse, *Teaching and Teacher Education* 23 (6), 957–969.

Penuel, W. R., Fishman, B. J., Yamaguchi, R. and Gallagher, L. P. (2007) What makes professional development effective? Strategies that foster curriculum implementation, *American Educational Research Journal* 44 (4), 921–958.

Richards, J. C. and Nunan, D. (Eds) (1990) *Second Language Teacher Education.* Cambridge: Cambridge University Press.

Richardson, V. (Ed) (1997) *Constructivist Teacher Education: Building a World of New Understandings.* London: Falmer.

Tsui, A. B. M. (2011) The dialectics of theory and practice in teacher knowledge development, in Hüttner, J., Mehlmauer-Larcher, B., Reichl, S. and Schiftner, B. (Eds) *Theory and Practice in EFL Teacher Education*. Bristol: Multilingual Matters, 16–37.

Walter, C. and Briggs, J. (2012) *What professional development makes the most difference to teachers?*, available online: elt-marketing.oup.com/files/oup_elt/project_339/handouts/ WalterBriggs_2012_TeacherDevelopment_public_v2.pdf

Waters, A. and Vilches, M. L. C. (2010) *Tanggap, Tiklop, Tago (Receive, Fold, Keep): Perceptions of Best Practice in ELT INSET*. London: The British Council.

Wedell, M. (2009) *Planning for Educational Change: Putting People and Their Contexts First*. London: Continuum.

Wright, T. (2010) Second language teacher education: Review of recent research on practice, *Language Teaching* 43 (3), 259–296.

Wright, T. and Bolitho, R. (2007) *Trainer development*, available online: www.lulu.com/ content/554846

Appendix 1
A description of the Cambridge English Delta scheme

The Delta qualification comprises three Modules:

1. Understanding Language, Methodology and Resources for Teaching
2. Developing Professional Practice
3. Extending Practice and ELT Specialism

Each module is separately certificated and they can be taken in any order and in any combination. Some candidates prefer not to take all three modules but to concentrate on those that are most relevant to their developmental needs at a particular point in their teaching careers. Although the modules are separately certificated, they combine to form the full Delta qualification and an additional certificate is awarded on completion of all three modules.

Aims and syllabus

The following summary of aims and syllabus content for the three modules is taken from *Delta Module One, Module Two, Module Three: Handbook for Tutors and Candidates* (Cambridge English 2014):

Module One

The aim of Delta Module One is to extend and develop candidates' knowledge and understanding of:

- theoretical perspectives on language acquisition and language teaching
- different approaches and methodologies including current developments
- language systems and learners' linguistic problems, language skills and learner problems
- resources, materials and reference sources for language learning
- key concepts and terminology related to assessment.

Module Two

Delta Module Two aims to develop candidates' ability in the following areas:

- working with language learners in a variety of learning contexts
- preparation for teaching learners of English
- evaluation, selection and use of resources and materials for teaching purposes
- managing and supporting learning
- evaluation of lesson preparation and teaching
- observation and evaluation of other teachers' lessons
- professionalism and professional development.

Module Three

Module Three aims to develop candidates' knowledge of and competence in:

- a chosen specialism (e.g. Young Learners, English for Academic Purposes, English for Specific Purposes, English for Speakers of Other Languages)
- approaches to needs analysis
- curriculum and syllabus design principles
- different types of syllabus
- course design and evaluation
- assessment of learners.

(An English Language Teaching Management option is also available.)

Assessment

Module One

The emphasis in Module One assessment is on candidates explicitly demonstrating knowledge of the areas outlined in the syllabus and aims above. Assessment is not concerned with practical teaching abilities nor is there a particularly strong focus on the application of teachers' knowledge to the practical considerations of the classroom. Instead the emphasis is on the professional knowledge that teachers might reasonably be expected to have as advanced, and often experienced, practitioners.

Assessment is achieved through 2×1.5-hour written papers. There is a variety of tasks across the two papers asking candidates to:

- analyse samples of authentic and learner-generated language at discourse and sentence level and in terms of phonological features

- critically analyse published teaching and testing materials in terms of their intended uses and outcomes, and in relation to theories of second language learning and teaching
- discuss current and historical perspectives on English language teaching methodologies and on learning.

Candidates' answers are assessed by markers using guideline answers and mark schemes produced by Cambridge English. Reliability is ensured through standardisation and moderation of markers overseen by a Principal Examiner.

Module Two

The emphasis in Module Two assessment is on candidates demonstrating their knowledge of the English language, theories of second language learning, ELT methodologies and the effective application of this knowledge to a practical teaching context. Candidates are required to demonstrate not only a sound theoretical knowledge but, perhaps more importantly, an ability to teach learners of English effectively, with a clear sense of their own strengths and weaknesses as a teacher and how their practice might be further developed.

Assessment is achieved through a two-part Professional Development Assignment (PDA):

- Reflection and Action: An essay of 2,000–2,500 words in which candidates reflect on their beliefs about teaching and learning, identify strengths and weaknesses in their practice, research methods and design tools to monitor and develop their own teaching practices.
- Experimental Practice: An essay of 1,500–2,000 words in which candidates research an ELT method, approach, procedure or technique with which they are unfamiliar and evaluate their experience in teaching using the specified method, approach, procedure or technique. Candidates provide a lesson outline to enable the candidate to teach a lesson using the specified method, approach, procedure or technique.

Four Language Systems and Skills Assignments (LSAs) including a background essay of 2,000–2,500 words, a lesson plan with background information on the learners, the approaches to be followed and materials used during the lesson, the procedure for the lesson, a 40–60-minute observed lesson and an evaluation of teaching and learning as exemplified in the lesson.

Two of the LSAs focus on language skills (reading, writing, speaking and listening) while two focus on what Cambridge English refers to as 'language systems' (discourse, lexis, grammar and phonology). For each of the assignments, candidates choose one of the skills or systems areas referred to above. In background essays, candidates are required to provide an analysis of a specified area of skills or systems, a discussion of issues related to learning the chosen area and suggestions for teaching materials, procedures and techniques. The second, taught and observed, part of the LSA then focuses on the practical realisation of (part of) the area chosen and (some of) the issues highlighted in the background essay.

Three of the LSAs are assessed during a course by tutors employed by the assessment centre. The final LSA is externally assessed by a Cambridge English appointed assessor. The background essays, the lesson planning and the teaching are measured against stated assessment criteria in the following areas:

Background essay

1. Quality of writing
2. Clarity of topic
3. Analysis and issues
4. Suggestions for teaching

Lesson planning, preparation, teaching and evaluation

5. Planning and preparation
6. Creating and maintaining an atmosphere conducive to learning
7. Understanding, knowledge and explanation of language and language skills
8. Classroom procedures and techniques
9. Classroom management
10. Reflection and evaluation

Internal tutors and external assessors are standardised and moderated by Cambridge English to ensure consistency and reliability.

Module Three

Module Three is assessed through a 4,000–4,500-word assignment that requires candidates to research and write about teaching or management within a specialist area (EAP, ESOL, Young Learners etc.), research and design tests and assessments for a stated group of learners and plan, design and evaluate a syllabus and course responding to features of the specialist area and the needs of the stated group of learners. An ELT Management option is also available.

The assignments are externally assessed by examiners approved by Cambridge English.

4 The role of portfolios in language teacher assessment

Neil Anderson
International House Budapest

Introduction

Views of teacher knowledge have increasingly focused on the role of pedagogical content knowledge (Shulman 1986), in which teachers' knowledge of their subject matter is combined with their understanding of how to share it with their learners. Within this framework, a teacher's ability to plan a lesson is just the first stage in a process that involves on-the-spot decision-making as well as reflection after the event (Wallace 1991). Effective teacher assessment procedures therefore need to capture not only the teaching event itself but also the thinking behind it and the modifications to practice that arise from it.

Written tests may offer insights into certain areas of teacher knowledge but tend to be atomistic and far removed from the more holistic reality of teaching performance. Observation, while offering a direct assessment of teaching, suffers if it is limited to one or two occasions over a school year, as it often is. Mere snapshots of performance on a limited number of occasions cannot capture an adequate sample of a teacher's knowledge and performance to be valid for assessment. Such means, narrow in scope and irregular in occurrence, can be questioned as effective modes of assessment since they limit the potential for positive impact, having potentially little effect on the development of teacher effectiveness.

Maximising positive impact requires an assessment tool that samples a wide range of teaching skills, encourages self-assessment and reflection, and takes place over time, becoming less concerned with product and more with the emerging complexities of the teaching process (Freeman, McBee

Orzulak and Morrissey 2009). Teaching portfolios, pegged to appropriate content and performance standards, appear to offer one solution to this problem (Katz and Snow 2009).

This chapter will provide an overview of teacher portfolios and the uses to which they can be put, followed by a discussion of how portfolios are used in the Cambridge English Diploma in Teaching English to Speakers of Other Languages (Delta) both as an assessment tool and a vehicle for developing candidates' knowledge and awareness and improved practice.

Teaching portfolios

Defining teaching portfolios

Portfolios can take many forms, the precise nature of which is determined by their overriding purpose (Richards and Farrell 2005). In education, they have typically been associated with young learners (Brown 2003); portfolios are popular tools for learner assessment in primary and secondary education as, in bypassing formal assessment, they offer a low-anxiety means of demonstrating progress in predetermined areas to various stakeholders such as parents. A useful definition of portfolios within second language teacher education is offered by Brown and Wolfe-Quintero (1997). Noting their relative novelty in the field, they define a teacher portfolio as: 'a purposeful collection of any aspects of a teacher's work that tells the story of the teacher's efforts, skills, abilities, achievements, and contributions to his/her students, colleagues, institution, academic discipline, or community'(1997: 28).

This collection, as Richards and Farrell (2005) note, can be paper based or electronic, with the latter having the advantage in terms of allowing the use of a broader range of media including audio and video (for instance, links to videoed lessons or recorded feedback sessions with supervisors or learners). The 'aspects of a teacher's work' cited above are often referred to as artefacts. Seldin (1993) states that a portfolio should in essence summarise best practice, in a way that can be empirically verified (though as is explored later, portfolios — notably assessment portfolios — include instances of teaching failures, and reflections on these failures). Finally, it is important that a portfolio be considered as more than a collection of carefully selected artefacts; it is not simply a product but can enable a teacher, and by extension assessor, to focus on the process of teaching over time in a structured way, charting shifts in beliefs and practices (Wolf and Dietz 1998).

Types and purpose of teaching portfolios

Richards and Farrell (2005) and Tanner, Longayroux, Beijaard and Verloop (2000) suggest there are two types of teaching portfolio and Wolf and Dietz (1998: 15–18) broaden this distinction, considering there to be three primary types. Each has a distinct defining purpose though they should not be seen as mutually exclusive.

Learning portfolios

Also called professional growth portfolios (Tanner *et al.* 2000), these are driven by professional development: the primary purpose is formative, encouraging the teacher to create and select artefacts as part of a process of sustained reflection and self-assessment with the goal of improving teaching practices. There is a high degree of ownership of the contents of the portfolio, with artefacts selected by the teacher over time. They allow the teacher-compiler to showcase evidence of achievement in different teaching competencies. However, they may also include reflection on negative teaching experiences and failures, as part of evidence of the necessary critical reflection and self-assessment (Foord 2009). Structurally, these portfolios are looser and more open-ended than others in order to accommodate the philosophy of individual growth — the teacher may set their own objectives and then chart progress against these over time, supported by evidence. This allows for a greater flexibility than the other types as well as a stronger sense of personal ownership over the process, potentially leading to a higher intrinsic motivation driving the teacher through the process, and leading to positive impact: learning portfolios encourage a teacher to engage in 'a holistic assessment of one's teaching' (Richards and Farrell 2005: 102) and in doing so provide a rationale for engaging in and experimenting with tools for professional development.

Assessment portfolios

These assess teacher effectiveness; the evaluation may be used by professional organisations such as language schools and higher education institutes in order to provide certification for employment or promotion.

As such, they are more strictly standardised in terms of both contents and organisation and leave less room for teacher selection of elements. Guidelines specify not only what is to be included but also how these documents should be composed, thereby regulating contents in accordance with criteria that are applied across the cohort, increasing reliability for assessment purposes. How effectively standards have been met is judged by an assessor, with contents qualitatively measured against the criteria. As well as artefacts such as lesson plans and accompanying reflective documents, they are likely to include periodic evaluations of the teacher's work written by the supervisor. Wolf and Dietz (1998) note that, despite having stringent externally mandated guidelines, assessment portfolios offer scope for teacher choice with regard to the precise areas covered or documents selected. In summary, they can potentially provide a comprehensive view of a teacher's competences against established standards; however, they may lack flexibility in terms of the individual's ability to determine goals for development.

Employment portfolios

As the name suggests, these are compiled with prospective employment in mind, the teacher showcasing their abilities through selected documentation and reflective statements. 'Showcase portfolio' is in fact the name Richards and Farrell (2005) give this type, whereas Tanner *et al.* (2000) label them employability portfolios; accordingly, artefacts are selected to provide an unequivocally positive view of the teaching skills of the compiler. Furthermore, employment portfolios should be accessible in order to allow employers efficiently to evaluate the suitability of the teacher for further employment. With this type of portfolio, more attention is given to attractive presentation as this is likely to be judged alongside the actual content. As it is designed to showcase, it lacks the reflective and exploratory theme that the other portfolios (notably the learning portfolio) allow.

As previously indicated, a portfolio may appear to combine elements of each of these. One example is the Delta Module Two, a fuller examination of which follows in the second half of this chapter. Another is the European Portfolio for Student Teachers of Languages (EPOSTL). The EPOSTL is designed for student teachers undertaking their initial training. It is structured around self-assessment, using 193 Can Do descriptors linked to teaching competences; these are subdivided into sections such as lesson planning, methodology, resources and so on (Newby, Allan, Fenner, Jones, Komorowska and Soghikyan 2007). This emphasis on assessment — along with the fact that artefacts filed in the 'dossier' may include reports by mentors and teacher educators — suggest the EPOSTL can be considered an assessment portfolio; however, its aims emphasise reflection and professional growth, and it is explicitly stated that the descriptors should 'act as a stimulus for students, teacher educators and mentors to discuss important aspects of teacher education which underlie them and that they contribute to developing professional awareness' (Newby *et al.* 2007: 7). As such, it functions as a learning portfolio.

Contents of teaching portfolios

An important initial inclusion is a statement of teaching philosophy (Bailey, Curtis and Nunan 2001; Brown and Wolfe-Quintero 1997). This is a summary of beliefs concerning teaching and learning, including what the teacher considers helps or hinders the underlying processes. As it should come towards the beginning of the portfolio, it sets the tone for what follows. The EPOSTL, for instance, opens with a 'Personal Statement' designed to encourage initial reflections on areas of general importance in language teaching (Newby *et al.* 2007).

The main portion of a teaching portfolio is often made up of documentation that arises as part of the normal course of teaching: lesson plans, course syllabuses designed by the teacher, tests, learner feedback, summaries of objective data on teaching experience, journal entries, papers written by the teacher and so on. Selection requires careful planning: the portfolio should be representative rather than exhaustive (Kaplan 1998: 2) in providing selective evidence of the teacher's effectiveness supported by the gathered documentation (Seldin 1993). If a portfolio is in some sense a collage, then it needs to be a 'cogent collage' (Brown and Wolfe-Quintero 1997: 29) that demonstrates an underlying coherence in representing the teacher's competencies. The opening statement of teaching philosophy on its own is insufficient for promoting cogency: artefacts are to some extent dumb and therefore those included need to be supported by explanations and reflections (Richards and Farrell 2005: 106). The former indicate what the artefact is and provide a rationale for its inclusion in terms of the overall narrative goals of the portfolio. The latter elucidate the value of the artefact for the teacher.

Key advantages of portfolios as a tool for development and assessment

Green and Smyser (cited in Bailey *et al.* 2001) summarise a key advantage of teacher portfolios both as a tool for learning and a tool for assessment: '[t]he teaching portfolio as a strategy for professional development is based on the premise that the best assessment is self-assessment. Teachers are more likely to act on what they find out about themselves'. The process of assessment and the process of teacher development become closely harmonised — almost indistinguishable, in fact. As Seldin (1993) and Brown (2003) note, the chances of positive impact are consequently maximised. The act of compiling a portfolio encourages a teacher to set goals, gather artefacts as part of normal teaching documentation to support the development of these goals, and reflect on the evidence provided by these goals. In this way, a portfolio can engage the teacher in a spiral process of action research promoting professional development in areas relevant to their teaching needs as well as offering potential solutions to issues arising in the particular teaching and learning context (Burns 2009).

Closely linked to the above, and recurrent in the literature as one of the outstanding advantages of a teaching portfolio, is the provision of opportunities for reflective teaching (Tanner *et al.* 2000). The previously mentioned explanations and reflections provide explicit opportunities for teacher reflection, encouraging reflective teaching and providing written evidence of teacher reflection for the reader (Bailey *et al.* 2001). A strong ability to reflect effectively on one's own practices is a well-established goal of teacher education; it stimulates professional development in the long term by allowing the teacher to engage habitually in a process of critical reflection on their teaching leading to the improvement of future teaching decisions (Burton 2009). Portfolios facilitate the cultivation of these skills through demanding a reflective approach in a number of ways: articulation of beliefs, awareness and selection of portfolio goals, experimentation in practice, self-evaluation of the experiments and reflection on further practice (Brown and Wolfe-Quintero 1997; Tanner *et al.* 2000). Furthermore, if the opening statement of teaching philosophy is to be empirically supported, the teacher should engage in a process of critical selection in terms of finding or devising the most suitable artefacts and documents that support their beliefs. The portfolio-building process therefore involves the comparison of the ideal and the real, a crucial step in teacher development: teachers are able to critically observe and reflect on where they need to be in their teaching and where the collected data suggests they actually are (Kaplan 1998).

Finally, as portfolios are compiled over time, and sampled from a range of aspects of teaching, they provide what occasional observations, periodic student feedback and pencil and paper tests fail to offer for teacher assessment and evaluation i.e. diachronic assessment of a teacher's ability that does justice to the complexities of the teaching process. Seldin (1993) offers a useful metaphor: traditional methods of teacher assessment are flashlights, illuminating only a small area of a teacher's competences; a portfolio, by contrast, is a searchlight whose beam takes in a much broader range of abilities, beliefs and teaching skills. A more comprehensive sampling is available for assessment and there is consequently less sense of the reduction of a complex phenomenon to a single but conveniently assessable product.

In summary, an effective sample of a teacher's work is likely to demonstrate the following portfolio characteristics (PC):

- PC1: Action research driven: it encourages investigation into and experimentation with current teaching practices and beliefs.
- PC2: Reflective: multiple opportunities to justify and reflect on teaching practices and beliefs are provided.
- PC3: Assessed diachronically: evidence of teacher effectiveness is based on examining multiple artefacts over time. This assessment includes self-assessment as part of PC1 and PC2.

Issues for assessment

These three characteristics pose problems for assessment. The most common criticism of teaching portfolios is that they lack practicality, being time-consuming both to assemble and to assess (Bailey, Curtis and Nunan 2001; Brown 2003; Richards and Farrell 2005). The greater the degree of agency afforded to the teacher, the more time-consuming the artefact selection process becomes, and the less clarity there is concerning how to approach assessment. There seems to be an inherent tension between the roles of a learning portfolio and an assessment portfolio: it is difficult to consistently measure or allocate scores to a piece of work that is by nature complex and multi-layered, a series of artefacts and reflections that emphasise an individual, presumably unique learning journey (Tanner *et al.* 2000). This is compounded by the fact that much of what is included and reflected on in a portfolio is qualitative rather than quantitative and accordingly difficult to assess objectively. It is also unclear what weight the different elements of the portfolio should carry, in terms of determining a final grade (where a final grade is part of the process). A further issue concerns the assessor: if the compilation of a portfolio is supervised, it seems logical that the supervisor be involved in assessment, but it is less clear how this leads to reliable assessment across a cohort.

The issue of reliability is compounded by an essential mismatch between reflection and assessment; while the former concerns itself with the learning process, the latter examines products and attributes scores or grades to these. If assessment of reflective learning is overemphasised, it has the potential to have a negative impact on the learning that occurs; instances of this can include teachers who are being assessed focusing on a limited range of experiences seen to be most relevant to assessment, or worse still, fabricating data and material in order to meet requirements (Bolton 2010). Furthermore, set against this, if reflection is part of the teaching construct, then the ability to reflect effectively would itself seem to require some form of measurement — yet the reduction of effective reflection to discrete criteria for assessment has been challenged, appearing to run counter to the nature of reflection and devaluing its role as a tool in experiential learning (Redmond, cited in Bolton 2010).

Several questions therefore concerning the specifics of assessment need to be answered:

1. How can the tension between a learning portfolio and assessment portfolio be minimised?
2. What evaluative criteria should be used?
3. Who should assess the portfolio?
4. What elements of the portfolio should be assessed, and which should carry more or less weight?

Offering solutions

If portfolios are to be credible tools for assessment, it is important to consider these concerns.

1. How can the tension between a learning portfolio and assessment portfolio be minimised?

One solution is circumscription: a restrictive assessment portfolio offers a more practical and reliable approach to teacher evaluation: by prescribing from the outset what is to be included and when, a framework emerges for both selection and assessment of artefacts. However, this compromises a key advantage of the teaching portfolio as learning portfolio, i.e. the ownership of process it offers to the teacher. A sensible approach would be to establish a middle ground. When portfolios are used to assess teachers, Bailey *et al.* (2001: 231) recommend a two-step approach:

(i)   Determining content and evaluative criteria.
(ii) Selecting and compiling the materials to be included.

Their belief is that a teacher should be part of the decision-making for step 1 and should have total control over step 2. The extent to which this is possible will vary depending on how standardised the portfolio should be, but even so, if a portfolio is to maximise its potential for positive impact, the teacher needs to be a collaborator, if not in selecting criteria, then in adopting research 'themes' (Tanner *et al.* 2000: 21) that are pertinent to their teaching situation. Evaluative criteria can be used to both guide and assess the selection of these research themes.

2. What evaluative criteria should be used?

Kaplan (1998) notes that there is no one method for assessing the contents of a teaching portfolio. This is not perceived as a negative factor; instead it allows scope for the evaluative criteria to be determined on a situated basis, as is relevant to the goals of a given teaching context, and the role a portfolio serves in this context. It is important that the learning outcomes of the portfolio, and the criteria that will be used to assess these, be made transparent from the outset — not just to the assessor but to the teachers, who need to understand how they will be evaluated and therefore the basis for success (Richards 2008). In practical terms, the drive for transparency may necessitate orientation sessions before portfolios are implemented, or offering a portfolio guidebook to teachers (Richards 2008; Tanner *et al.* 2000). These serve to explain the purpose of the portfolio, the expected contents, standards to be achieved and the evaluative criteria to be used.

The nature of the evaluative criteria will vary, and indeed the selection of criteria helps illuminate what the institution believes to be valuable in terms of teaching competences (Kaplan 1998). At the shallower end of assessment, Tanner *et al.* (2000) refer to the use of checklists designed as a basis for giving trainee teachers feedback on their development; they could also serve as a basis for self-assessment and guidance during the construction of the portfolio. At a deeper end, criteria may be derived from outcomes that are linked to standards, and may be framed as performance indicators, i.e. 'a series of descriptions at various levels that provide specific information about what teachers know or can do' (Katz and Snow 2009: 67). This involves a more analytic approach to assessment, breaking the contents of the portfolio down into various competences for which evidence is sought — each can be judged on (for instance) a 5-point scale leading to a total score for the portfolio. Assuming the descriptors are valid and clearly written, analytic scoring helps improve the reliability of scoring portfolios (Hughes 1989) in cases where it is necessary to assign a score or judge whether teachers (as candidates of assessment) have passed a given threshold.

3. Who should assess the portfolio?

Hughes (1989) recommends two or more assessors (a third to arbitrate where necessary) for evaluating written student work and it would seem prudent not to rely on a single assessor for all the elements of a teaching portfolio. Another consideration for scorer reliability is whether the trainer supervising the construction of the portfolio is also assessing it — a problematic situation given the difficulty of separating the nature of the two roles, with supervision being collaborative and pastoral, and assessment requiring a more objective position. Ideally, these two roles will be undertaken by different individuals (Wallace 1991), though the same criteria may be used to ensure appropriate formative and summative feedback is provided.

4. What elements of the portfolio should be assessed, and which should carry more or less weight?

It is important that the evaluative criteria closely align to the kind of learning those assessed expect to be engaged with (Moon 2004). For the assessment of a portfolio, then, the criteria should focus directly on how well the teacher has demonstrated abilities in a range of areas perceived to be useful and inherent to their development in a given teaching context. Moon (2004) also argues for the separation of criteria that focus on product (e.g. a complete set of plans is included, as required) from those that focus on process (e.g. evidence of ongoing reflection and decision-making based on data gathered). A portfolio's contents may discriminate in terms of what is assessed, with some elements contributing more decisively to the final grade than others; for instance, lesson plans and lesson observations may carry more weight than the 'raw data' of action research (e.g. journal entries, field notes, research notes). However, documents that summarise and comment on this data may provide valid records for assessment purposes.

Summary of characteristics of effective teaching portfolios

Earlier, portfolios were established to be action research driven (PC1), reflective (PC2) and assessed diachronically (PC3). In light of the assessment considerations discussed above, these can be elaborated on and one more added. Portfolios should be:

- Action research driven (PC1): This scope for areas selected for inclusion may be limited/guided in the interests of greater standardisation across the cohort but not to the extent that the teacher is unable to select themes of personal relevance, ensuring the portfolio remains a personal learning journey (Tanner *et al.* 2000).
- Reflective (PC2): In being process-driven and investigative, portfolios should actively encourage reflection on beliefs and practices, and these reflective artefacts may play some role in the assessment process.
- Assessed diachronically (PC3): With clarity from the outset concerning the modes of assessment, the weight of different elements towards overall grades.
- Assessed reliably (PC4): By providing transparent evaluative criteria from the outset; involving more than one assessor using the same evaluative criteria; requiring teachers to submit the same range of artefacts for consideration even if the themes selected are personal.

The Delta Module Two portfolio

Delta Module Two, Developing Professional Practice, is intended for in-service teachers (hereafter referred to as candidates) who wish to develop their teaching abilities in a variety of areas. Candidates may be motivated intrinsically to improve through reflective practice, or have instrumental reasons — for instance, moving into educational management or teacher training. Progress is achieved through the compilation of an electronic portfolio, typically compiled over 200 hours of research and study (undertaken intensively or extensively). There are two main threads in the portfolio, both of which require completion, with the candidate collecting various artefacts as part of each:

- Thread 1: One Professional Development Assignment (PDA). This engages the candidate in action research based on their own selected themes or action points — for instance, improving clarification of language, dealing with mixed-ability classes, broadening range of drilling techniques. This is divided into Part A (Reflection and Action, or RA) and Part B (Experimental Practice, or EP). The RA includes four separate elements (stages 1–4) that take place over the duration of the course, encouraging the candidates to select action areas, investigate and experiment, reflecting on the data collected and amending their action plan for the next stage. The EP is a single more in-depth experiment with a teaching procedure or approach unfamiliar to the teacher, but of professional interest and value. For the PDA, the candidate submits the raw data of action research and reflects in an essay on the insights gained from the data and action research tools used. The PDA must be completed for the portfolio to be a success. It is assessed internally by one or more tutors who supervise the process.
- Thread 2: Four Language Systems and Skills Assignments (LSAs) including for each:
  1. A background essay based on research of a language systems or skills area.
  2. A lesson plan.
  3. A post-lesson reflection and evaluation by the candidate.
  4. Tutor assessment and feedback on three of the essays, plans, lessons and reflections (the fourth being externally assessed).

The assignments are assessed against the same 10 categories of evaluative criteria with performance indicators of Met, Partially Met and Not Met (see Appendix B of the volume). The portfolio is compiled over the duration of the course. By the end, two of these four LSAs must pass for the portfolio to pass overall. Three LSAs are assessed internally (by tutors who also supervise and provide course input), and one is assessed externally (by an assessor who is unknown to the candidate). The portfolio is then moderated externally, based on the internal and external grades given, before a final grade is decided. The grades for the final portfolio are: Pass, Merit, Distinction and Referred — the last necessitates resubmission of an LSA in order to be considered subsequently for a Pass.

With regard to portfolio types, the Delta Module Two portfolio is best described as blended. The PDA thread emphasises the development of teaching skills through applying principles of action research. As such, it contributes greatly to the portfolio's nature as a professional growth or learning portfolio. The LSA thread is also concerned with professional development — the first three receive formative as well as summative assessment, with tutor feedback on planning and teaching skills offering scope for further development. The LSA thread is more explicitly assessment focused than the PDA thread, and contributes more substantially to the final grade; in this sense, the portfolio is an assessment portfolio. This is particularly evident in relation to LSA4, which is summative and is significant in determining the final grade of the whole portfolio.

As illustrated in Table 1, these two strands — the PDA and the LSAs — interact in a way that initially appears complex:

- The course starts with the PDA: stage 1 of the RA, which is a diagnostic observation of the candidate by the course tutor.
- From this, the candidate, guided by the tutor, creates an action plan for their own development in RA stage 2; they also outline their core beliefs concerning teaching and learning. Therefore one of the first entries into a Delta portfolio is a statement of teaching philosophy, consistent with a typical learning portfolio.
- As Table 1 indicates, the PDA is an ongoing piece of action research and it occurs in stages before and after LSAs, meaning that action research of the PDA can inform decisions and performance in the LSAs, and the feedback from LSAs can provide shape and direction to the action plan of the PDA. The two strands occur concurrently and are complementary. This helps to maximise the positive impact of each thread on the other.

Table 1 The Delta Module Two portfolio contents and staging

The course	PDA		LSAs	
	Learning Portfolio: Emphasis on process, lower stakes formative assessment by one internal tutor/supervisor		**Assessment Portfolio: Emphasis on both process and product; higher stakes assessment by two internal tutors and one external tutor**	
200 hours (100 tutor facilitated, 100 independent)	**RA stage 1**	Diagnostic observation by supervisor. Feedback helps inform stage 2.		
	RA stage 2	Teacher outlines beliefs, strengths and weaknesses. Outlines action plan for action research (AR) into improving weaknesses.		
		AR implemented	**LSA1**	Essay, plan, lesson, reflection focusing on a skills or systems area. Assessed by tutor. Considered a summative product of research but feedback has formative value for future LSAs.
		AR implemented		
		AR implemented	**LSA2**	Essay, plan, lesson, reflection focusing on a skills or systems area. Assessed by tutor. Considered a summative product of research but feedback has formative value for future LSAs.

(To be continued)

(Continued)

RA stage 3	Teacher reviews findings from AR and comments on developments. A new action plan is developed informed by findings and formative feedback on LSA1 and LSA2.		
	AR implemented	**LSA3**	Essay, plan, lesson, reflection focusing on a skills or systems area. Assessed by tutor. Considered a summative product of research but feedback has formative value for future LSAs.
RA stage 4	Teacher discusses beliefs in light of development over the course and reflects on AR done. Action points for the future are outlined.		
EP	Experimental Practice assignment: a larger scale one-off experiment related to developmental interests implemented at some point prior to LSA4, usually early on in the course.		
		LSA4	Essay, plan, lesson, reflection focusing on a skills or systems area. Assessed by external assessor. Summative: it carries more weight than other LSAs and is a product of independent teacher work with minimal supervision.

Characteristics of Delta portfolios

The portfolio is constructed and assessed in a way that is consistent with the characteristics of an effective portfolio ident'ified previously.

- PC1: The Delta portfolio is action research driven. It allows candidates to be involved in choosing their agendas. The themes of action research in the PDA are selected by the candidate with guidance from the tutor; candidates are free to select both areas to investigate and the tools to use to do so. The process therefore belongs to the candidate and remains a personal learning journey; there may be evaluative criteria, but these provide structure rather than restricting scope for professional investigation. Even though the LSAs involve higher-stakes assessment, they also allow for agency on the part of the candidate, who selects two skills and two systems areas relevant both to their professional development and their learners' needs. Each LSA is extensively researched, and a lesson designed and executed in a way that implements this research, linking practice and theory.

- PC2: The Delta portfolio emphasises reflective teaching in both threads. The PDA, beginning as previously mentioned with a statement of teaching philosophy, puts a strong emphasis on developing teacher reflection through its construction — teachers (with the support of the tutor, and feedback from the LSAs) are continually engaged in critically evaluating their teaching practices, setting developmental objectives, selecting action research tools to investigate these, and reflecting on the data gathered, before re-evaluating their objectives. It allows the candidate to compare the ideal and the real. The process is supported by appended evidence — the raw material of action research: field notes, logs, completed observation tasks and so on. The LSAs also encourage reflection. Explanations are evident when the candidate justifies the value of researched activities and teaching approaches in the essay and the lesson plan commentary (a document offering rationale for decisions made). Reflections are evident in the post-lesson reflection and evaluation — an artefact that is also assessed and, as is evident in the case studies below, can carry some weight in terms of the view of the moderator.

- PC3: Assessment occurs diachronically in line with the diagram in Table 1. It begins with the informal diagnostic observation; it continues with the extended critical reflection of the PDA. However, the LSA thread provides the backbone of formal assessment, with four separate assessments that evaluate a wide range of direct and indirect teaching skills: classroom teaching areas such as management, clarification and response to emerging learning, planning, materials design, language and skills analysis, self-evaluation — these and many more areas are considered. In this way, a range of competences can be sampled, going some way to capturing the complexity of the teaching construct: a searchlight far more encompassing and informative than a flashlight.
- PC4: Reliability of assessment is attended to in various ways. There are requirements concerning what needs to be submitted and when, with a relatively fixed structure; artefacts include both the specified teacher work and tutor feedback on these (see Table 1). Assessment is based on a set of transparent evaluative criteria externally mandated in order to ensure fair and reliable assessment of a large and geographically varied cohort. The same criteria are used for each LSA; the criteria are made transparent to the candidates from before the first LSA and a portfolio guidebook is available — the Delta Handbook for tutors and candidates (Cambridge English 2014). There are multiple assessors; LSAs are evaluated by two internal and one external assessor, and then reviewed by an external moderator. Although the final LSA is the most important single assessment event, the moderator reviews the whole portfolio in order to decide if LSA4 offers a representative view of the candidate.

Case studies from Delta Module Two

To consider even more concretely the evidence provided by a portfolio when assessing teacher knowledge and development, consideration will now be given to two recent Delta Module Two candidates who completed and submitted their portfolios. In both cases, permission was obtained from the candidates and names have been changed. Table 1 should be used as a reminder in terms of the overall frame of Module Two and how it progresses. Rather than considering all evaluative criteria, the intention in the case study is to focus on a limited sampling of areas, tracking their progress through the written evidence available in both the PDA and the LSAs; lesson planning documents, candidate reflections, tutor feedback and the moderator's summative conclusions on reviewing the portfolio will all be drawn upon. For Case Study 1, the areas focused on are: a) teacher vs. student talk/use of varied interaction patterns and b) instructions. For Case Study 2, the areas are: a) efficiency of focus on target language and b) increased attention to phonology.

Case Study 1: Josh

PDA Reflection and Action Stage 1: The diagnostic observation

The process begins with a diagnostic lesson of 60 minutes, followed by a reflection and tutor feedback. Summary tutor feedback indicates Josh would benefit from working on various areas including the need to balance interaction patterns, incorporating more student-centred interactions such as pair and group work, and the reduction of teacher talk:

> You need to think about how you might better balance the amount of time given to different interactions. There seemed to be a lot of 'S' followed by 'T-Ss', with very few opportunities for sts to work in pairs or groups. This ended up feeling a little predictable (as the interactions lacked variety) and teacher-centred. Almost all interactions ultimately involved you speaking directly to a student — or them talking to you.

PDA Reflection and Action Stage 2

In the week following tutor feedback on stage 1, Josh writes a reflective statement of teaching philosophy (Bailey *et al.* 2001) before outlining key strengths and weaknesses as he perceives them; the tone of self-assessment is set early. Interestingly, a core belief stated is the value of being learner-centred and reducing teacher talk while maximising student talk. As is noted in the tutor's comments, this is not a belief that was evident in practice in stage 1. A positive interpretation of this is that a gap between beliefs and practices has been exposed — the portfolio even in this early stage is providing potential for 'the comparison between the ideal and the real ... the first step in the process of improving teaching' (Kaplan 1998: 2). Further investigation into these areas of his teaching may help close this gap. A more negative interpretation, however, would be that Josh is not so much reflecting as 'reproducing' — that is, replicating what he perceives to be the trainer's desired agenda. Balance of student/teacher talk and attention to interaction patterns becomes one of his action points, or themes (Tanner *et al.* 2000), along with the other considered here: clarity of instructions. The task for Josh now is to investigate his practices, collecting data on these and reflecting on them before stage 3 is submitted. He selects observation task templates to investigate how other experienced teachers approach interaction patterns and instructions. The task for the tutor is to decide at stage 3 whether Josh has made a serious attempt to collect data to investigate and reflect on these aspects of his teaching; or whether, in the end, he is merely going through the motions of reproducing his tutor's agenda.

LSA1/LSA2: The next entries in the portfolio are assessed products: his investigations into helping lower level learners with communication strategies (LSA1) and multi-word verbs (LSA2). These were completed during the implementation of his ongoing investigation into student-centred interactions and clarity of instructions. As the planning and teaching of these lessons runs concurrently with his PDA-based action research, an examination of his lesson planning documents and tutor feedback on the lesson offers potential insights into the level of performance in these areas for this lesson and any changes evident (if feasible at this early stage).

Interaction patterns and student vs. teacher talk: In LSA1 there is little discussion of this area in his lesson plan rationale. In outlining his lesson procedure, however, there is evidence that within and across stages he is seeking to vary interaction patterns and provide appropriate opportunities for student communication, and tutor feedback confirms this: 'You effectively varied interaction patterns between students'. In LSA2, although the lesson remains student-centred, it is clear there is work to be done on quantity/quality of teacher talk with tutor feedback noting: 'Yours tends to be the dominant and loudest voice in this group of low level learners and you could consider moderating volume, and the amount of talk, at times. Also, be careful of a tendency to echo what students say.' This criterion is not yet being fully met, as a result. There is evidence for improvement in variety of interactions and overall student-centredness but a need to work on clarity and amount of teacher talk at times. This is at least something he identifies as a weakness in his post-lesson reflection; this self-awareness is in his favour, and it is not possible that he is reproducing the assessor's agenda here as he has not yet seen the written feedback.

Instructions: In both LSA1 and LSA2 the criteria relating to instructions and task set-ups are partially met, reflecting that Josh is still struggling with this area with his lower level learners. Tutor feedback notes that it is not significantly diminishing the overall high-quality learning experience being offered, but is nonetheless a developmental priority. Over LSA1 and LSA2 there is little evidence that action research into instructions (his peer observation programme) is yet bearing much fruit in his teaching. An examination of the lesson planning documents suggests that more consideration needs to be given to instructions at the planning stage: there is little evidence in his procedure that he is putting significant thought into how best to set tasks up. Encouragingly, again, Josh shows in LSA2 a strong ability to self-evaluate this area: he identifies instructions as a key weakness and demonstrates evidence of emerging reflection-on-action skills. He cites the evidence of occasional student confusion over tasks. However, he does not yet seem clear on why instructions were problematic, attributing it to not using scripted instructions (which were themselves not evident in the plan in any case); tutor feedback notes the key issues involving factors such as his physical position (he tended to be mobile and lose eye contact with learners), the need to broaden techniques (e.g. use of demonstration) and the need to consider what language needs to be supplied or clarified before a task is undertaken.

PDA Reflection and Action Stage 3

This offers Josh the chance to summarise the key points learned so far from his action research on interaction/teacher talk and instructions, and to modify his action plan. It also provides evidence of the reflection and action completed so far: artefacts submitted are extensive and impressive in terms of the quality of reflection evident in them. Encouragingly, there is some impressive data available to support the reflection.

Interaction patterns and student vs. teacher talk: these include an analysis of the interaction patterns used based on a video observation of his own lesson. He expresses satisfaction at the improvement in the student-centred nature of his lessons but notes the need for further monitoring of this. The data supports this as a valid conclusion.

Instructions: The primary artefact is a detailed observation template on a very experienced teacher's instructions. As part of the instructions task, he has:

- anticipated the instructions the teacher would give based on their procedure
- transcribed the instructions of the experienced teacher as they occurred
- compared his version to what occurred
- considered the student response to instructions given
- reflected on the effectiveness of techniques used.

This proves to be very useful in providing evidence of reflective learning, with many techniques being noted and critically evaluated (e.g. the power of demonstration, use of the whiteboard, the need to monitor immediately, the value of being concise in wording). However, he concludes that there is still a gap between theory and practice: 'While this helped establish my beliefs about instructions, my LSA2 highlighted that this is still an area I need to work on in practice.' He therefore intends to continue to research this area, modifying the tools used. For instance, before stage 4, he plans to use the same observation task for instructions, but with the tables turned: he will be the teacher and his supervisor will anticipate his instructions, followed by a discussion of the findings. Overall, the RA stage 3 is fairly strong: action research has included some close data collection and analysis of interaction patterns and instructions; he is showing a fairly convincing ability to reflect on the data available in order to make choices for subsequent teaching. Assessment would be strengthened further if there were even more data available here e.g. further quantitative examples of recorded instances of teacher talk over time accompanied by qualitative comments on strengths and deficiencies evident.

LSA3: In this final internal LSA, Josh chooses to examine reading strategies which help learners deal with unknown lexis in texts — guessing based on co-text, choosing to ignore words and so on. It proves to be another successful lesson in terms of the quality of the learning experience offered overall.

Interaction patterns and student vs. teacher talk: There seem to be no issues at this stage concerning balance of interactions — his practice is by now much more fully reflecting his belief in keeping learning student-centred, evidence for which is available in the variety of interactions included in his procedure and supported by the tutor's view of interactions in the lesson. However, some issues concerning teacher talk recur, notably when it came to clarification of the central teaching point, with tutor feedback noting a 'tendency to lecture where you could draw more on the learners — particularly at key pedagogical moments. Watch out for this slight tendency to declaim as it is unclear to what extent it is useful for their learning (whether they are getting it).'

Instructions: The work done in the RA seems to be having a positive impact on his performance in the LSAs. He has taken to adopting strategies to help improve instructions: there is evidence in the lesson plan procedure of more extensive use of demonstration, and he has bolded concise phrases to help him with wording. This is in contrast to earlier lesson plan procedures where evidence of attention to instructions was lacking. Pleasingly, this theoretical improvement proves also to be a real one in this lesson as the criterion for instructions is fully met, with the tutor commenting: 'instructions were generally good in the lesson ... you made very good use of the whiteboard to set up the tasks. You had a clear idea of the key elements of tasks you wanted the learners to do.' This is not to say instructions were perfect — but the evidence in tutor feedback and in the lesson plan procedure is that they have improved significantly as the portfolio has developed. There is evidence of the effectiveness of PC1 and PC2 in this case study.

PDA Reflection and Action Stage 4

This is the final submission in the portfolio as LSA4 is externally assessed. In his summative reflection on the action research done Josh notes the improvements to interactions and instructions, but offers the caveat that continued monitoring is needed, and proposes means for doing so. He also makes an insightful comment into the value of reflective writing as a tool for development: 'Dedicating time to writing down post-lesson reflections and analyses proved effective ... Whilst I often think about how I can improve a lesson afterwards, or talk about it informally with peers, written analysis really exploits the ideas more fully and captures them in a way that can be reflected on long after the lesson.' He has identified how writing reflective documents for the portfolio has allowed him to engage more deeply and permanently with the learning issues at hand, helping him to make sense of the raw material of learning (Moon 2004). The power of the portfolio for promoting reflective teaching through action research seems to be evident (PC1, PC2). This positive view of Josh's action research process and the PDA as a whole could however be challenged: to what extent was it genuine independent action research as opposed to mentor-scaffolded reflection? This relates to a potential weakness inherent in the process — the dual role of the mentor in the PDA as both tutor and assessor.

LSA4: By contrast, in line with PC4, the need to safeguard the reliability of portfolio assessment, the final LSA is evaluated by an external assessor who has had no involvement in helping Josh develop. It is essentially summative: he will receive no formative feedback from the assessment and it will carry great weight in determining the final grade he receives for his portfolio. It represents a high-stakes conclusion to the portfolio and one in which Josh would hope to do justice to the solid level of achievement and development so far.

Interaction patterns and student vs. teacher talk: Josh has selected to help his pre-intermediate learners with modals of obligation. The assessor is impressed in general by Josh's lesson plan, noting that 'this is a really good and thoughtful set of materials, very thorough, and showing good understanding of where the students are, what they need and what they have been doing'. This bodes well. However, Josh seems to have taken a conservative approach to the lesson in terms of what the learners are given to do. While he gives the learners plenty to do, and demonstrates a generally facilitative role with measured, appropriate teacher talk, a key weakness soon emerges: a lack of variety in interaction — the assessor considers the lesson static and somewhat dull, with the learners conducting a series of essentially written tasks:

> They never moved, stood up, changed places or partners or groups, or did anything else for the whole 60 minutes. He needed to radically alter the dynamics. He also needed to provide activities which let the learners use the language more, orally. They really didn't communicate at all, just read out written sentences.

Instructions: These were not problematic, partly due to the paper-based nature of the tasks, and the assessor does not offer specific comments on task set-ups, instead focusing on the lack of variety mentioned above.

Overall, the lesson, while broadly useful in its focus, is perceived to be flat and static in dynamic; Josh does not appear to have done justice to himself. The external assessor is impressed by Josh's post-lesson reflection, noting that 'this is a good piece of evaluation, and shows a teacher thinking about and really understanding the main flaw in the lesson and knowing what he should have done'.

Moderation of the portfolio

As mentioned, LSA4 carries great weight in the overall evaluation of the success of the portfolio. Were it to be the only evidence considered, Josh's portfolio would seem set for a disappointing outcome. However, as mentioned in PC4, the final grade is determined by a moderator who reviews all of the evidence available in the LSAs before reaching a final conclusion. In line with PC4, the moderator is able to draw in several strands of evidence in order to come to a final decision — balanced against the conflicting evidence for the lesson itself, she factors in:

- the assessor's comments on the strong plan for LSA4
- the assessor's view that Josh's LSA4 post-lesson reflection is perceptive
- the higher level of performance in other LSAs

The moderator comments that it 'reads like a lesson that just didn't go well'. Based on the review of the portfolio, the moderator is able to confirm that Josh's external assessment is not representative of his performance across the duration of the course: in line with PC3, the portfolio is assessed diachronically, allowing for a more reliable and fairer assessment of Josh's abilities.

Case Study 2: David

PDA Reflection and Action Stage 1: The diagnostic observation

The diagnostic lesson focused on teaching intermediate learners past modals. Feedback makes it clear that David already has many very good qualities as a teacher, including thorough planning, solid management of the lesson and a sensitivity to the individuals in the class. The observer notes issues with David's approach to clarification: 'as a general rule, you are reluctant to "teach", even when it is necessary and the efficient response — have you internalised a rule that everything needs to come from the students?' The observer traces this back to the thinking at the planning stage: 'The number of times the words "elicit" and "check" occur (and the absence of "tell", "show", "demonstrate") reveals an underlying problem. Look at the verbs you use in your draft plans: are you teaching enough?' David would, it seems, benefit from deepening his understanding of when it is appropriate to teach/inform rather than elicit/check.

PDA Reflection and Action Stage 2

An issue in reflective practice is the degree to which the teacher is prepared to be honest about aspects of teaching which could be improved. David's reflective statement appears to demonstrate how a portfolio can encourage honest and thoughtful reflection on one's practices. He demonstrates an awareness of this key problem in his teaching:

> I have a tendency to 'labour' the presentation stage of systems focus lessons. I over elicit when doing guided discovery and am slow to confirm, preferring to check numerous students' opinions in a misguided attempt to avoid 'rubber-stamping' (Scrivener 2012: 347). The effect on the learners is that this stage of the lesson can take far too long, reducing pace and engagement and causing confusion … I have given primacy to an inductive approach, but have neglected that, 'many rules — especially rules of form — can be more simply and quickly explained than elicited from examples. This will allow more time for practice and application.' (Thornbury 2009: 30).

As with Josh's stage 2, it is not entirely clear to what extent this reflects a conclusion he has come to on his own or whether he is reproducing the tutor agenda. He also identifies a lack of focus on phonology in his lessons as a major weakness. Efficiency of focus on target language and increased attention to phonology have become two major themes of David's development; the progress he makes can be tracked through examining various artefacts: his lesson plans, his reflections and tutor feedback, as well as the explicit action research conducted on these areas. He comments that he intends to research techniques, experiment with what he has learned and seek learner feedback on these. PC1 is strongly in evidence.

LSA1/LSA 2: LSA1 focuses on structures for expressing past habit (would/used to/past simple). LSA2 focuses on speaking, specifically helping learners with achievement strategies. Both essays demonstrate a very strong understanding of the topic areas, and both plans demonstrate a good ability to shape this research into a lesson suited to the learners.

Efficiency of focus on target language: David's personal aim in LSA1 demonstrates how he is carrying his action research concerns into the complementary LSA strand of the portfolio: 'To improve the clarity and efficiency of my grammar presentation.' As such, he uses his lesson plan commentary to justify his test/teach/test framework and notes that 'it allows me to move directly to the target language. This efficiency will provide more time for the students to practise using the language'. The lesson receives a favourable assessment across a range of criteria (see Appendix B). Interestingly, however, tutor feedback suggests he is not striking the right balance in terms of giving and eliciting information from the learners. The tutor praises the clarification but suggests 'taking a little more time and more consistently making sure that all learners were following. Perhaps rather than explaining (which you began to do quite a lot), getting learners to tell you or testing them further through your materials'. The evidence here suggests that David is experimenting with different roles when teaching but has perhaps swung too far towards teacher explanation. By LSA2, he seems to be striking a better balance, and is praised for helping the learners with his focus on form and pronunciation of the chunks related to achievement strategies. It is clear he is aiming to tailor the level of input and focus of clarification to the learners' emerging needs; his thinking is evident in the lesson plan commentary (a reflective explanation part of the plan) where he notes 'task one provides a base-line for the learners' pre-existing level of skill, which will give the teacher information about what level of demand to put on the learners'. This suggests an emerging, more sophisticated view of the teaching roles required at a given moment.

Attention to phonology: This was particularly relevant to LSA2, the speaking lesson. David's plan demonstrates clear attention to phonological form, with an analysis of the language to be used for circumlocution.

While he is praised in execution for attention to pronunciation, there seems still to be room for improvement in terms of how he is approaching this. The tutor notes that 'it would have helped if you had drilled the sentence to ensure more accuracy before they did the practice stages and as a formative action point: drilling target language to ensure that they remember it more easily. This will also help students with accuracy.'

PDA Reflection and Action Stage 3

The portfolio shows that David is teaching to a high standard in general. He is experimenting and not shying away from trying out new areas in his teaching. After two successful LSAs, he reflects on his action research so far and, consistent with a portfolio developing over time, he notes shifts in his thinking and teaching based on his action research:

> My previous belief that 'inductive is always better' has now changed. I have tried using a more deductive approach during the presentation stage of grammar lessons, which has challenged some of my assumptions, but resulted in an increased efficiency in my classes. Timing has shown that the presentation stage is now quicker, which has resulted in more opportunities for the learners to practise the target language.

He is as yet less convinced about work on phonology, considering it a partial success: 'the observations I have organised have shown that I need to be more effective in devising specific strategies for individual learners' pronunciation issues'. He resolves to continue his investigations into phonology, particularly the identification of individual problems and the extension of his drilling techniques. Both PC1 and PC2 are strongly evident.

LSA3: As noted earlier, a learning portfolio and an assessment portfolio can provide evidence of both successes and failures. So far, David's portfolio has comprised successful essays and lessons, and a beneficial professional development thread in which he has grappled sincerely with areas needing improvement in his teaching. LSA3, focusing on helping learners listen through focusing on key words, represents David's first failure with a lesson that falls short of the standards maintained so far.

Efficiency of focus on target language/attention to phonology: Both areas can be treated together, given the primary developmental focus: for students to become better able to deal with authentic speech by identifying key stressed words and decoding weak forms in connected speech. His task then was to raise awareness of, and practise listening strategies related to, the phonological system. The tutor feels the lesson plan is of mixed quality but singles out David's rationale for praise: 'It often provides a real insight into the planning decisions you have made and how these relate to your learners and their needs. You have referred explicitly to reading and research in your background essay and clearly show how this has affected your planning decisions.' David has based his lesson focus on difficulties for these learners, and his decisions have been informed by his reading and research: this is strongly evident through his plan. However, ultimately, the tutor feels that, despite his best efforts — focusing clearly on relevant phonological features from authentic texts — the learners did not seem to leave the lesson more confident with listening; in fact, they possibly misunderstood the key point due to the nature of the procedure and materials:

> Your intention was to encourage learners to examine the weaker forms around stresses so that they didn't seem so daunting but, in fact, I think that learners were still unconvinced that they could ignore these weaker forms in 'real life' and it did matter to them ... learners seemed to get the message that it was the bottom up processing of weaker sounds that was crucial to their understanding of a listening text — I think they missed the point that they could use their knowledge of grammar to fill in the gaps that they didn't 'hear'.

The evidence in the portfolio does not suggest that David has become a less effective teacher, but in this instance, he simply tried to be too ambitious with these learners, and needed to be more careful to balance challenging learners while having clear, achievable aims. Were this occasion the only assessment event that mattered, then the outcome for David would be unsatisfactory, as the lesson was not a success. However, PC3 ensures that there are multiple assessment opportunities that can be considered in forming a picture of his teaching skills.

PDA Reflection and Action Stage 4

David's conclusions concerning his action research, and the effects this has had on his beliefs and practices, provide further evidence of a strongly reflective teacher, one who is able to learn critical lessons from both successes and failures in his action research and in the LSAs:

> I previously thought that when teaching a language point it was necessary to be fully comprehensive, including all possible aspects of the language point. I believed that this allowed the learner to be exposed to and aware of all the nuances of meaning and use. Through observation and classroom experimentation, I now feel that it is better to restrict this content to the amount that can be meaningfully practised in a session, in order not to overload the learner.

His conclusions are convincingly balanced: he notes it is important to use both inductive and deductive approaches to clarification as the situation requires. Regarding phonology, he observes that 'I now have a greater understanding of pronunciation issues specific to different first languages (L1s) and have modified the manner in which I conduct drilling in open class. I still need to develop my understanding of teaching phonology, but have now identified means by which to do this'. He recognises that the action research has not yet transformed him into a highly skilled teacher of phonology; it has instead, equipped him with the tools to continue to evolve these (and other) skills as his career progresses. This is evidence that the action research process the portfolio has promoted is facilitating a transition from 'experienced teacher' to an 'expert teacher' (Burton 2009: 299): an impressive work in progress.

LSA4: The tutors so far have been involved in David's development. In line with PC4, evaluation of LSA4 falls to an external assessor who has had no involvement so far and has no vested interest or idea of his level of performance. Whereas Josh had performed to a consistent standard until LSA4, David's performance has varied — he has shown great strengths (LSA1/LSA2), but also some flaws in lesson planning choices (LSA3); the outcome of this LSA becomes even more instrumental in determining the overall success of his portfolio. His focus — hypothetical language — also allows for some consideration of how his selected themes from his RA have had an impact on his planning and teaching in this final phase of portfolio-building.

Efficiency of focus on target language: His lesson focuses on the type two conditional with B1 level learners. His lesson plan commentary reveals his concern for 'getting down to business': 'I also decided to use an initial testing activity (stage 1, warmer) as it allows me to move directly to the target language. This efficiency will provide more time for the students to practise using the language.' His approach is inductive — as he noted in stage 4, deductive/inductive approaches should be chosen based on needs, not ritualistically. He is though, clearly concerned with increasing time spent dealing with meaningful production and moves from establishing context to examples to rules with what appears to be much greater efficiency than earlier in the course. This is borne out in the assessor's report: the assessor notes strengths in the pacing and that the clarification is a 'strength — diligent yet light in presentation'. The assessor praises the high level of engagement, realised in a variety of ways, including through personalisation and a range of activities. The chief strengths noted include his monitoring and response to learner output in terms of content and language, 'possibly the best monitoring I have witnessed; delicate, targeted, challenging; encouraging of autonomy, personalised'. It seems that the decision to clarify language up front in an efficient way, in order to allow plenty of practice and reaction to learner output, has allowed for a very strong lesson.

Attention to phonology: There is little explicit reference to this in the assessor's report except as part of the general, effective variety of the lesson, and the mention that models of language were 'careful, comprehensive, accurate'. The written evidence in the plan supports this evaluation: a stage in the procedure is dedicated to this; the language analysis offers a sophisticated consideration of the target sentence in terms of supra-segmental features. In his reflection on the lesson, David again offers a balanced view: he is pleased that the phonological focus challenged some stronger learners. However, there are clearly mixed feelings about the delivery: 'Drilling in open class, both chorally and individually, was too unfocused. I need to be more precise and to attend to individuals more. However, I compensated by giving further pronunciation, stress and rhythm instruction to individuals during the milling activity.' This is not an issue that the assessor comments on, but David's preoccupation with the effectiveness of his drilling is testimony to the importance he has attached to this developmental theme.

Moderation of the portfolio

LSA4 was a success — the assessor labels the lesson:

Very high quality in its planning and delivery, highly competent and a pleasure to watch. The teacher had a clear grasp of his aims and their match to the needs of the class, and also of the properties of the language he was aiming to teach; he had a clear idea of the range of teaching options at his disposal and chose appropriately.

With this as the final major entry in his portfolio, it is left to the moderator to decide the level of performance overall. The moderator notes that the tutors within the centre feel the candidate performed to a very high level by the end of the course, despite the single 'failure' in the portfolio; with this judgement being fully supported by the external assessor and the contents of the portfolio as a whole, the moderator can agree without reservation and notes of LSA4 that the lesson was not planned for display, but focused on learning and the needs of these learners.

Conclusion

In Case Study 2, David's portfolio is judged to be highly successful despite the lower level of performance in the internal assessment of LSA3; in Case Study 1, the centre's view of Josh is upheld despite the external assessor having some reservations in LSA4. In both portfolios, there is compelling written evidence of teachers working to improve areas of their practice and offering reflective insights into the action research process. What conclusions can be drawn concerning the Delta portfolios in relation to broader concerns with portfolio-based assessment? In the PDA, both candidates engaged in action research (PC1); in doing so, they established themes based on initial artefacts such as diagnostic tutor feedback. The development of these themes can be traced through the various artefacts: lesson plans, reflection on action research, tutor feedback. Both portfolios provide solid evidence of the power of reflective practice (PC2); reflective attention to perceived weaknesses in teaching is promoted by the complementary strands of the PDA and the LSAs. The PDA provides evidence of reflection empirically supported by the gathered data. The LSAs provide further evidence through the lesson plans and lesson reflections. Tutor feedback on both the PDA and on LSAs 1–3 is primarily formative; the candidates are able to further reflect and make adjustments to practice based on these comments. LSA4 is summative. Reliability of assessment is increased not only through the use of evaluative criteria but also by allowing the moderator to survey the perspectives of different tutors at different stages: initially, the internal tutors invested in the teacher's development, and for LSA4, the impartial external assessor.

However, it remains the case that the case studies pose some questions concerning the PDA in particular:

1. If tutor feedback on an initial diagnostic lesson drives the selection of research themes, whose agenda is being followed? There appears to be a danger that subsequent discussion of developmental needs may include reproduction of the tutor's agenda and it is necessary for tutors to exercise some caution in the early stages to help encourage the teacher to select their own themes.

2. A candidate may talk persuasively of developments made to action points but how can such assertions be assessed? There is a need for substantial 'real' classroom data as evidence to support conclusions made in the PDA if assessment is to be credible.
3. How can reliability of assessment be ensured when the tutor acts as sole assessor? There is a natural tension between these roles, with the tutor becoming less impartial as an assessor the more invested they are in the candidate's action research. This is, however, off-set by the fact that the Delta Module Two portfolio overall is externally assessed and moderated by experts who do not know the candidate.

Nevertheless, a chief strength of portfolios for assessment is evident in the Delta portfolios of these two candidates; the moderators can base their judgement on more than a single observed lesson. They are able to consider evidence of performance diachronically, drawing on teaching over multiple occasions, and examining various artefacts (lesson plans, lesson reflections, tutor feedback, external assessor feedback) to seek support for assessment ratings. This is consistent with Seldin's (1993: 3) searchlight metaphor, alluded to earlier in this chapter and now worth quoting in full:

> Earlier assessment methods, such as student ratings or peer observations, were like flashlights. That is, they only illuminated the teaching skills and abilities that fell within their beams ... but with portfolios, the flashlight is replaced by a searchlight. Its beam discloses the broad range of teaching skills, abilities, attitudes, and philosophies.

At its best, this process of illumination occurs within a framework that provides the means for sustained formative development over time, blending the function of the portfolio as both a tool for assessment and a tool for structured development through reflective action research: assessment is composed not simply of teacher knowledge, but of teacher performance and reflection in a manner that is situated and of direct professional relevance to the teacher. In this way, positive impact is maximised; the opportunities provided by written reflective practice, despite being used as a 'slogan term' by some, can be effectively blended with practical exploration of teaching issues — reflection-in-action and reflection-on-action — allowing teachers 'to critique teaching and make better-informed teaching decisions' as part of their 'lifelong professional development' (Burton 2009: 298–299).

References

Bailey, K., Curtis, A. and Nunan, D. (2001) Teaching portfolios: Cogent collages, in Bailey, K., Curtis, A. and Nunan, D. (Eds) *Pursuing Professional Development: The Self as Source*. Boston: Heinle and Heinle, 223–236.

Bolton, G. (2010) *Reflective Practice*. London: Sage Publications.

Brown, H. D. (2003) *Language Assessment: Principles and Classroom Practices*. New York: Longman.

Brown, J. D. and Wolfe-Quintero, K. (1997) Teacher portfolios for evaluation: A great idea or a waste of time? *Language Teacher* 21 (1), 28–30.

Burns, A. (2009) Action research and second language teacher education, in Burns, A. and Richards, J. C. (Eds) *The Cambridge Guide to Second Language Teacher Education*. New York: Cambridge University Press, 289–297.

Burton, J. (2009) Reflective practice, in Burns A. and Richards, J. C. (Eds) *The Cambridge Guide to Second Language Teacher Education*. New York: Cambridge University Press, 298–307.

Cambridge English (2014) *Delta Module One, Module Two, Module Three: Handbook for Tutors and Candidates*. Cambridge: Cambridge English Language Assessment.

Foord, D. (2009) *The Developing Teacher*. Peaslake: Delta Publishing.

Freeman, D., McBee Orzulak, M. and Morrissey, G. (2009) Assessment in second language teacher education, in Burns, A. and Richards, J. C. (Eds) *The Cambridge Guide to Second Language Teacher Education*. New York: Cambridge University Press, 77–90.

Hughes, A. (1989) *Testing for Language Teachers*. Cambridge: Cambridge University Press.

Kaplan, M. (1998) The Teaching Portfolio, *CRLT Occasional Papers* 11, available online: www.crlt.umich.edu/sites/default/files/resource_files/CRLT_no11.pdf

Katz, A. and Snow, M. A. (2009) Standards and second language teacher education, in Burns, A. and Richards, J. C. (Eds) *The Cambridge Guide to Second Language Teacher Education*. New York: Cambridge University Press, 66–76.

Moon, J. (2004) *A Handbook of Reflective and Experiential Learning*. London: Routledge Falmer.

Newby, D., Allan, R., Fenner, A., Jones, B., Komorowska, H. and Soghikyan, K. (2007) *European Portfolio for Student Teachers of Languages*, available online: archive.ecml. at/mtp2/fte/pdf/C3_Epostl_E.pdf

Richards, J. (2008) Second Language teacher education today, *RELC Journal*, available online:www.professorjackrichards.com/wp-content/uploads/second-language-teacher-education-today-2009.pdf

Richards, J. and Farrell, T. (2005) *Professional Development for Language Teachers: Strategies for Teacher Learning*. Cambridge: Cambridge University Press.

Seldin, P. (1993) *Successful Use of Teaching Portfolios*. Bolton: Anker Publishing.

Shulman, L (1986) Those who understand knowledge growth in teaching, *Educational Researcher* 15 (2), 4–31.

Tanner, R., Longayroux, D., Beijaard, D. and Verloop, N. (2000) Piloting portfolios: Using portfolios in pre-service teacher education, *ELT Journal* 54 (1), 20–30.

Wallace, M. (1991) *Training Foreign Language Teachers*. Cambridge: Cambridge University Press.

Wolf, K. and Dietz, M. (1998) Teaching portfolios: Purposes and possibilities, *Teacher Education Quarterly* 25, 9–22.

5 The 'dirty mirror' of reflective practice: Assessing self- and peer-evaluation on a CELTA course

Jo-Ann Delaney
Canterbury Christ Church University

Introduction

Teaching practice, either in a real or simulated context, is an integral part of most teacher education courses. An activity that plays a central role in teaching practice is the trainees' reflection on their teaching, supplemented by feedback from a more experienced tutor or mentor and, in some cases, peers. Metaphorically, reflection 'holds a mirror' up to practice, allowing the trainee to reflect on what they are doing in the classroom. The aim of this reflection is to have a positive impact on the trainee teacher's development; by noticing features of their teaching they can implement change and improve.

Reflection can be verbal or written and will usually be evaluative, as it will involve highlighting both the teacher's strengths and areas for development. The term 'evaluation' is normally used for activity on such teacher education courses and it is the term that will be used throughout this chapter. It could be argued that the trainee teacher is actually being asked to engage in 'assessment', since they are making a judgement about what they have done in a particular lesson. In this chapter, however, the term 'assessment' is reserved for the judgement made by tutors on the quality of the trainee evaluation.

Since the quality of the evaluation and its impact on practice often form part of the assessment of the trainee teacher, this chapter will consider some of the factors which affect that evaluation and question some generally accepted reflection processes. The challenges of assessing reflective practice, something which is, by its nature, private, informal and complex are discussed in the context of the Cambridge English Certificate in Teaching English to Speakers of Other Languages (CELTA), a pre-service teacher education course for English language teachers.

The role of reflective practice on teacher education courses

Most teacher education courses, including CELTA, would ascribe to the notion that they are developing *reflective practitioners*. Such practitioners are seen as able to continue their development after their formal programme of instruction because they are able to evaluate their practice and, through this, ensure it evolves. The concept has become almost an 'axiom' in language teacher education contexts (Burton 2009: 298) and tends to be an unquestioned orthodoxy in much the same way as teaching methodologies can become highly valued and unchallenged.

Formal reflective practice is most often used in the self-evaluation of teaching, where a teacher or trainee teacher considers a lesson or series of lessons and draws conclusions as to what worked well and what could have been more effective. It may also involve peer-evaluation of other teachers' lessons. The rationale for self- and peer-evaluation is that being able to evaluate one's own and others' teaching will lead to improvement, as the trainee teacher will know what to work on and possibly how to improve. Additional evaluative feedback from an experienced tutor or mentor provides further guidance as to how they can develop.

The appeal of reflective practice is easy to appreciate. In learning where there is a *practical element* or *doing*, such as teaching, reflection on that practice allows the doing to take on a cognitive aspect. Reflective practice allows *doing* to become *thinking* by taking 'the raw material of experience and engaging with it to make sense of what has occurred' (Boud 2001: 10). In order to gain a better understanding of why this may appeal to teacher educators, it is important to consider the perceived role of reflection in unifying those two pillars of teacher knowledge and teacher education: theory and practice.

Reflective practice as the bridge between theory and practice

The interplay between theory and practice does not just occupy practitioners and teacher educators; it permeates discussions of professional training in general. The knowledge/practice divide mirrors discussions about knowledge in a more general way across centuries. Aristotle's Epistēmē and Technē identified scientific knowledge (Epistēmē) to be an essential part of wisdom and to be a purer type of knowledge, whereas craft (Technē) included action and the practical ability to produce something.

A key contributor to the body of literature on reflective practice, Donald Schön, placed reflective practice within the discussion of theory and practice highlighted above and identified the 'crisis of confidence' that arose from the 'widening gap between thought and action, theory and practice, the academy and the everyday world' (Schön 1992: 119). His proposed model for reflective practice would militate against the perceived division between positivist scientific knowledge and its practical application in a professional role.

Schön initially proposed two different ways of reflecting. Reflecting 'in action', where the teacher is aware of the process of teaching as they are doing it, in situ, and is able to make judgements and adjust their practice. Reflecting 'on action' is done after practice and requires the teacher to look back on a lesson. Reflecting on action allows the teacher to draw on factors outside the moment of practice, including the views of others, theoretical reading and feedback from their students.

Others have built on or augmented Schön's approach to reflection. Kolb (1983) focused on the experiential cycle, where we take a concrete experience, reflect on it, and through this reflection form abstract concepts and generalisations. In other words we attempt to theorise practice. The theories we form from reflection on our experiences are the basis of *experiential* learning. Such learning is set in contrast to more formal learning, where we access repositories of knowledge gathered by others.

In Brookfield's (1995) model of reflection, an experience is considered from a range of different perspectives or 'lenses'. For teachers, Brookfield suggests using the teacher's autobiography, critical incident feedback from students, theoretical readings and peers' advice as possible sources of reflective material. Having these different perspectives, Brookfield argued, enhances our critical stance and provides more reflective data to consider.

Reflection as part of building a 'community of practice'

Teacher learning on teacher education courses can also be considered using the model described by Lave and Wenger (1991) of 'Legitimate

Peripheral Participation' within a community of practice. Through working with a 'master' or experienced teacher, new trainees gradually take on aspects of the teaching role and learn to participate gradually in the activity of teaching. They are provided with guidance from the 'master' and sometimes from peers. Lave and Wenger's model reflects the manner in which much professional learning takes place. Part of the gradual journey from the periphery to expertise is observing, trying out and having feedback on practice. The notion of communities of practice therefore builds on the idea of experiential learning, but foregrounds the role of social interaction. There are other people in other roles who contribute to our learning. It is through dialogue with them that we grow and develop. Part of this dialogue is reflection on our practice with input from our peers, and the 'master'.

In Lave and Wenger's model it is assumed that the relationship between the expert and the novice is benign: both work in tandem to foster the learning of the novice. One of the critiques of the paradigm is its lack of exploration of the 'unbenign' (Hughes, Jewson and Unwin 2007: 11) quality of this relationship. Lave and Wenger assume that the masters' role is one of support and that they have a vested interest in the success of their learners, which is not always the case. In addition, it must be recognised that there is not an even distribution of power in the learning communities of practice (Barton and Tusting 2005; Hughes *et al.* 2007). The master is likely to have some control over the learner's success. This control is very evident on teacher education courses where the master — the tutor — usually takes on the role of assessment and is the arbiter of who passes the course syllabus.

Some concerns about reflective practice

The acceptance of reflective practice as good practice seems universal in the literature that supports the delivery of teacher education programmes. This acceptance makes it more difficult to question. There are, however, a number of issues in both the concept and the practice of reflection that pose problems for the teacher educator. These issues are even more important when trainees are asked to reflect on their practice in the form of self- or peer-evaluation. They are not only being asked to think about their teaching, but make an evaluative judgement of it.

One criticism of reflective practice is, in fact, the way it reinforces the notion that the theory/practice divide needs to be bridged. Tomlinson (1999) explains how by emphasising reflection, Schön is actually confirming the fact that cognition is more important than action because you have to think about an action to make it of value. Schön thereby boosts 'the traditional tendency to see conscious deliberation as vital to intelligent action and capability in teaching' (Tomlinson 1999: 407). There seems to be no place in professional learning for simply *doing* or *acting*. On many teacher education programmes, including the CELTA, teachers' knowledge of procedures and teaching routines constitutes an important strand of their learning. Reflective practice questions the value of such learning without the cognitive act of reflecting on it. Criticisms of the CELTA course often focus on the notion that it provides a 'toolkit' of techniques. An insistence on the importance of reflective practice seems to support the notion that having a toolkit is somehow inadequate.

A further issue in reflective practice is raised by Brookfield in his work on critical thinking under the concept of 'impostorship' (Brookfield 2011: 222). His students, like CELTA trainees, come to his course with doubts about their ability to succeed and recognise that they are not experts in their field. They are then asked to be critically reflective about the subject matter of the course. He describes the difficulty of the student, a novice in the subject, being required to be critical. He feels that this is 'both brutal and confusing' and that by 'disclosing one's errors and owning up to one's mistakes, there's another level of emotional stress involved' (Brookfield 2011: 223).

Brookfield's discussion of impostorship also considers his own role as the perceived expert, due to his standing and title. He imagines his students' astonishment at being asked to express their critical ideas instead of the expert, their teacher, providing this criticality. From the point of view of the students, the teacher is not an impostor, but an authority. In the same way trainees may see the tutor as the expert who should provide the evaluation of the practical teaching, as the tutor has both the knowledge and experience; it is the tutor's job.

Assessing reflective practice

It is difficult conceptually to unite the idea of reflection, an evaluative and subjective process with ambiguity at its core, with the idea of assessment, a concept based in some way on a *right* answer. However, on the majority of teacher education courses, trainees' ability to reflect on their practice is assessed.

A number of concerns have been raised in different fields on the legitimacy of assessing reflective practice. Hargreaves highlights some of the difficulties, drawing on examples from the training of nurses (Hargreaves 2003). She concludes that though reflection in general can be ambiguous and those reflecting can take any direction they wish to, in professional education the pressure of being assessed has a considerable impact. The result is that trainees 'choose only those reflections that fall within a professionally acceptable frame, or [choose] to fictionalise events' (Hargreaves 2003: 200). This 'professionally acceptable frame' is very much set by the tutors and the course syllabus. Hargreaves' argument suggests an element of *untruth* about assessed reflection that is somewhat ignored in the literature. It therefore seems problematic to use what trainees say or write as a basis of trainers' assessment of them. Trainees may be making contributions that they feel are acceptable rather than saying or writing their real thoughts about their teaching.

A further issue in the assessment of reflection is the fact that trainers are relying on what the trainee says or writes; declarative knowledge (Tomlinson 1999). Only what the trainee expresses can be assessed. However, trainers cannot make the assumption that what a trainee says or writes is the limit of what they are thinking; declarative knowledge is not the sum of tacit knowledge. The knowledge that they are reflecting on may be 'entirely tacit: we may know it but not be *able* to tell it, even to ourselves' (Tomlinson 1999: 409). If trainers are relying on verbal or written output by trainees to judge their ability to reflect and evaluate, then they may not appreciate trainees who are engaging in reflection but are not able to, or may be reluctant to, express their ideas in spoken or written language.

Reflective practice activities on the CELTA course

On a CELTA course each trainee engages in reflection in the form of self- and peer-evaluation and these activities contribute to their overall assessment on the course. Each course group is organised into Teaching Practice (TP) groups, normally of four to six trainees. This group plans lessons together and carries out their required 6 hours of teaching by sharing the lesson time, each trainee teaching a part of the lesson in turn. As the course progresses, they gradually take on longer teaching slots. When they are not teaching, they are observing their peers teach. A trainer, referred to as the tutor, also observes all the teaching practice.

Once the teaching of each lesson has finished, each TP group engages in a feedback session. This may take place immediately after the lessons. Alternatively, some tutors use *delayed feedback*, where feedback is conducted the next time the course takes place. On a full-time course, this is likely to be the next day, on part-time courses, there may be a break of a few days. The arrangement of delayed feedback may be due to practical issues, such as when TP occurs late in the evening, or because the tutors feel that delayed feedback provides better opportunities for reflection.

TP feedback can be organised in a number of ways. It is likely that in the early stages, the tutor will lead the session and provide more commentary on the lessons, though this is not always the case. Many tutors may ask each trainee in turn to reflect on their lesson, evaluate strengths and weaknesses and then ask other trainees for comments. Sometimes a trainee may lead the feedback and organise the way trainees provide their comments. Towards the end of a course, the tutor might adopt a lower profile in the feedback activities, sitting to the side and observing as trainees direct their own evaluation sessions. There is no set pattern to the way these sessions are organised and it is largely a matter of tutor preference and perhaps the nature of the TP group, with some trainees being perceived as capable of working more independently from an earlier stage.

The common thread in the different ways TP feedback is organised is the expectation that trainees will provide comments that *evaluate* their own and their peers' teaching. Trainees will often provide descriptive commentary, but the expectation articulated in the course syllabus and assessment guidelines is that this should be accompanied by evaluative points that highlight the effective and less effective elements of the lesson. The nomenclature of TP feedback documentation would normally include such terms as 'strengths and areas for development', 'what worked well, what worked less well', 'strengths and weaknesses'. The self- and peer-evaluation, therefore, requires some judgements to be made.

To help with reflection and evaluation, trainees may have observation tasks to complete on their peers' teaching. These tasks may ask for a general overview, for example, 'What did the teacher improve on today?' or they may have a specific focus on an aspect of teaching, for example, 'Make a note of instructions that were confusing to students'. Trainees are also usually asked to complete written self-evaluations immediately after their individual teaching slot as well as after the TP feedback. The final, formal self-evaluation activity is the writing of an assignment entitled 'Lessons from the classroom', in which trainees provide an overview of their strengths and weaknesses as a teacher and describe what they have learned from observing others teach. Reflection activities such as those described above could constitute about 20% of the course hours.

Each of these opportunities for reflection is assessed. There are two assessment criteria for the course specifically focused on the reflective processes during the feedback on lessons. These criteria refer to trainees.

> **5m** noting their own teaching strengths and weaknesses in different teaching situations in light of feedback from learners, teachers and teacher educators
> **5n** participating in and responding to feedback
> (Cambridge ESOL 2010: 16)

These criteria are further developed in advice for trainees and trainers as to what might constitute evidence in making a judgement on trainees' reflective practice.

> **5m** noting their own teaching strengths and weaknesses in different teaching situations in light of feedback from learners, teachers and teacher educators
>   o Complete a written self-evaluation for each TP lesson noting your strengths and weaknesses
>   o Incorporate feedback from others in future TP lessons
> **5n** participating in and responding to feedback
>   o Evaluate your own lessons and your colleagues' lessons critically but constructively in TP feedback
>   o Suggest strategies for improving weak areas
>   o Respond positively to comments, suggestions and criticism made by peers and tutors on your lessons
>   o Make constructive suggestions on your peers' teaching
> (CELTA Candidate Record Book: 29)

Assessment of reflection in the 'Lessons from the Classroom' assignment is through another specific criterion. Trainees must demonstrate their learning by:

a. Noting their own teaching strengths and weaknesses in different situations in light of feedback from learners, teachers and teacher educators

(Cambridge ESOL 2010: 18)

The centrality of reflection and evaluation to the course is thus evident in the number of occasions it takes place. Its role in the formal assessment of trainees is also evident. It is to be expected, therefore, that trainees will both engage in reflection as part of their learning and be cognisant of its importance to their overall success on the course.

A pragmatic approach to assessment on a CELTA course

Tutors on a CELTA course undertake all the assessment. There is no final exam or external assessment, though each course has an external assessor who moderates the tutors' assessment and endorses final grades. To facilitate the tutors' assessment, the awarding body provides a list of criteria relating to the different aspects of the course. Each written assignment has assessment criteria and there are multiple (42 in total) criteria related to planning and teaching, including those mentioned in the previous section related to reflective practice. At the end of the course each trainee is awarded a grade (Fail, Pass, Pass B or Pass A) depending on their achievement of the criteria.

According the *CELTA Administration Handbook 2014*, trainees are successful on the course if they 'meet the course requirements' and their 'performance meets or exceeds the criteria in both assessment components' (Cambridge English 2014: 20). The Handbook also specifies that assessment is continuous and integrated, i.e. 'both assessed components contribute to the overall grade. Any one assessment can cover a number of topics and objectives in the syllabus' (Cambridge English 2014: 20). This view of assessment discourages tutors from adopting a rigid, *tick box* approach to assessment and allows them to view a trainee's performance over different aspects of the course. In relation to self- and peer-evaluation, it would allow a tutor to take a more pragmatic approach and give credit to a trainee who was unable to contribute much to the TP feedback session, but whose teaching showed evidence of having incorporated insights from the feedback into their teaching. It therefore allows the tutor to gather evidence from different aspects of the course as evidence of meeting the criteria.

Reliability of assessment is supported on the CELTA course through the rigorous trainer-in-training (TinT) programme that every tutor has to follow before they are able to work independently as tutors. (See Morgan, Chapter 7.) The TinT programme involves shadowing of a course and the gradual involvement in all of the activities: input sessions, teaching practice and feedback as well as marking assignments. During the programme trainers-in-training are monitored and assessed to ensure that they are assessing and grading according to CELTA standards. Reliability is further enhanced by the fact that every individual course is moderated by an external assessor, who scrutinises all aspects of the course assessment, including the assessment of teaching practice.

Nevertheless, the list of assessment criteria equally offers tutors the possibility of adopting a tick box approach to assessment. In this scenario, tutors could use trainees' contributions in feedback as a limiting factor in their grade. Such an approach could occur for a number of reasons. For a relatively inexperienced tutor, sticking rigidly to the criteria might offer assurance that they are assessing appropriately. Some tutors may prefer a more transparent way of assessing where they can demonstrate easily to trainees where they have been successful and where they have not. Whatever the reason, there is always the possibility for criteria to be used and interpreted differently leading to inconsistencies in the assessment process. The TinT programme and the role of the external assessor are important in minimising these inconsistencies as far as possible.

The perception of trainees: A case study

Trainees' views on the value and impact of feedback on TP and reflective practice activities on the CELTA course were gathered through a small, qualitative, longitudinal study of six trainees on a part-time CELTA course. The course ran over four months with TP running throughout the course. The trainees were interviewed at three key points: before they had started TP, halfway through the course and at the end. The study is part of a broader research project into teacher learning on the CELTA course. The findings are now discussed in relation to the issues of self- and peer-evaluation and the assessment of that evaluation. All trainees are referred to by initials (C, G, H, J, L, and M).

The role of 'impostorship'

As outlined above, a concern about asking trainees to evaluate lessons is the fact that they may feel like impostors; non experts being asked to take on the role of an expert. In this case study, trainees were unanimous in identifying a distance between themselves and the tutors in terms of experience and expertise. This distance had an impact on the way they related to feedback from the tutor as opposed to the feedback from other trainees. It also, for some trainees, made them less likely to question a tutor's view on their teaching.

The expertise of tutors was highlighted throughout the interviews. M would listen to the tutor because 'the tutor's got the experience, she's the expert', 'he or she knows their stuff'. L also felt that the tutor's expertise was 'that kind of experience that I kind of look to actually'. G confirmed that 'the tutors are certainly more experienced, so I think I'd probably respect what they had to say' and that 'each person needed to have their *proper* (emphasis added) feedback from the tutor' as opposed to trainee feedback.

The distance was reinforced by trainees' identification of themselves as non-experts without the experience needed to give views on others' teaching. L felt that opinions from other trainees would be less valued because she would think 'You don't really know.' J felt that as a group 'none of us know what we're doing' and that it would only be once she had more teaching experience that she would be able to make independent decisions about teaching in contrast to 'at the moment I'll follow the book and do what they tell me to do'.

The relationship between the tutor and trainee is not one of equality. The tutor has more experience as an English language teacher and has undergone a comprehensive tutor training programme. The role of the tutor is, of course, to support but also to assess. One of the aims of TP feedback is to allow the trainees to identify good and less successful practice in order to improve. However, the comments above reinforce the question of whether trainees are in a position to do this effectively. Returning to the metaphor of 'holding a mirror' up to practice, as one tutor commented, we may be asking them to look at a 'dirty mirror', their view blocked by inexperience and lack of expertise.

The role of 'closeness'

Trainees generally work in the same TP groups for the whole of the CELTA course. The dynamic of any TP group can vary greatly. For the trainees in this case study the relationships in TP groups were consistently described as positive. Therefore, juxtaposed against the feeling of distance between trainee and tutor is the close and cohesive relationship described between the trainee and other trainees.

The creation of the relationship of closeness was attributed to the common purpose of all the trainees to be successful on the course. The language used in the interviews suggested that the experience of the course was a difficult trial and therefore those enduring the trial together would need to support each other. M commented that it was 'such a nerve-wracking experience and we all know what we're going through'. Similarly L confirmed that she would be reluctant to comment on others' lessons because 'we're all under a lot of pressure and I don't think these people actually need me to chip in with anything else'. Two trainees used a disaster scenario rescue image: 'we were all in it together kind of thing ... We were all in the same boat'.

The group cohesion created by the fact that trainees seemed to get on well and, possibly more importantly, that they felt they were unified by a purpose, also represents a distance from the tutors. If the tutors were their assessors or judges and the trainees were struggling together, then it could be expected that there would be a difficulty in creating a community relationship while providing the feedback on teaching. This is highlighted quite emotively by G, who explains why she was reluctant to provide a negative evaluation: 'In the process I felt like a bit of a — you know, a *betrayer* of the — because we have a — we have a bond between us' (emphasis added).

The guidance in the CELTA Handbook asks tutors to assess how trainees 'evaluate ... own lessons and ... colleagues' lessons critically but constructively in TP feedback'. The case study trainees have highlighted some of the difficulties around carrying out this evaluation. If trainees are primarily concerned with the maintenance of the group relationship, then they are more likely to evaluate against the criterion of what they feel maintains a good group dynamic. Any assessment of their evaluation may then also be problematic.

Self- and peer-evaluation leading to learning

Of course, the purpose of TP feedback is not simply to assess how perceptive trainees may be about their teaching. The idea is that through reflection and evaluation trainees will be better placed to make improvements to their teaching. They are expected to incorporate suggestions from feedback into their lessons in the future. The guidance is clear that they need to 'incorporate feedback from others in future TP lessons'. This resonates with the core tenets of reflective practice in which reflection is followed by new action which can then be reflected on in turn.

In the case study trainees were initially very positive about the impact that feedback would have on their development. They felt they would learn from each other because of their perceived equality of inexperience. As they were bonded by a lack of thorough knowledge, they would be able to notice different features of lessons and feedback in a way that would be helpful to learning. M initially felt giving feedback to others would be 'good because we're all learning and we've all got our strengths and weaknesses'. L was very positive about her willingness to comment on others' lessons and the benefit of this for her learning on the course:

> I'm absolutely fine with it. I think it's a good idea really, you know everybody has a different angle on things, everybody sees things slightly differently ... I look forward to it because I think it's probably the best way to learn actually.

They also anticipated or hoped that group feedback would be something positive and that everyone would be supportive of each other. L's positive expression above was tempered by the proviso as long as 'nobody's being malicious about it'. J was also concerned that giving feedback to others would be good 'as long as you're tactful'.

They had some awareness, even initially, that a concern for being supportive of each other could act as a block to trainees' contributing to feedback fully. This was noted by H:

> I think that's a really good idea because we're all in the same boat, but I think — I wonder if people will try to be nice ... if people — they may not be quite as honest as they might as time goes on.

Once the trainees had experienced the group feedback on a number of occasions their views changed, some more than others. The most significant change reported by most trainees was that their comments on others' teaching were being constantly modified by the desire to not disturb the group's supportive nature.

By the second interview M was describing how 'we try — rather bolster each other up than give — you know, because even if you try to give constructive criticism it can come across as negative'. She was also able to give an account of the progressive change in how she behaved in feedback. From the beginning she was able to notice things that had not gone so well in other people's teaching, however she 'learned not to say those, just the positive things'. Her explanation for how she had learned this relates back to the themes of impostorship and of group cohesion:

> I think that was sort of what was implicit, I think it's very difficult as a novice maybe to give constructive criticism, and it might have come across not constructive or something. So you know, and my way, the way that I think I might have done it, is not necessarily the way that [tutor name] might have done it.

If tutors are being guided to assess this 'constructive feedback' on others, this seems to be based on the assumption that the process is unproblematic. Trainees in this study are suggesting that the actual act of giving such feedback was causing them many problems.

Trainees seemed well aware that their peers were not always being open in their evaluation. In terms of learning, this suggests that what trainees gain from the TP feedback is mainly the advice and input from tutors. L comments 'to be honest most of the peer feedback I've had has been — has been really sweet and positive and kind'. J feels that everyone is being open but still monitoring what they are saying so as not to offend. 'Obviously you've got to be quite tactful I think, if there some things — but I think everyone — yeah, everyone in our group was quite open to hearing from each of us.'

There was no criticism by trainees of their peers for acting in this manner. It seemed accepted that in order to maintain the support for each other and in recognition of the relative inexperience of trainees, not saying what they really thought in feedback was a good thing. C spoke about giving more honest feedback to the others in her group informally, outside the course feedback session. When asked whether she would give others suggestions for improving their lessons she commented that 'I would. But not in front of the observer. We'd talk outside of class.' This might suggest a role for two ways of handling feedback: a tutor-led group session and an informal peer feedback session where there is no tutor, but then also no assessment.

The TP group feedback is identified in the CELTA course syllabus as an important part of the course content. Trainees should learn to evaluate their own and others' teaching through their engagement with this group process. It is evident from the above that there are a number of limitations to the impact of the process. The distance in experience and expertise between the tutors and the trainees, as perceived by the trainees, undermines the value they assign to the feedback they get from their peers and supports the idea that the main learning comes from tutor feedback. Trainees understand and appreciate the process initially, but their desire to maintain the group cohesion prevents them from actually expressing what their evaluation of others' teaching really is. In addition, the power balance between tutor and trainee, with the tutor holding the important assessment role, means that trainees are worried about betraying themselves and the group in some way and this further limits the contributions they are making and any assessment of those contributions.

The perceptions of tutors

To gain an insight into tutors' views on assessing self- and peer-evaluation, an online survey of 14 experienced tutors was conducted. All the respondents but one had been working as a CELTA tutor for at least five years. They responded to a number of questions (see Appendix 1 of this chapter) clarifying their views in relation to the aspects of TP feedback raised by the trainees and, in addition, their views on the assessment of self- and peer-evaluation. The contributions to the survey were anonymous and the quotes given are, therefore, not attributed to individual tutors.

The value of self- and peer-evaluation

All tutors valued the opportunity for self- and peer-evaluation as part of the course. Most of the responses identified the forward-looking aspect of evaluation in improving the trainees' teaching. One tutor wished to 'encourage/challenge them further', while another said that it would 'make trainees aware of the strengths and areas for improvement in their teaching'. The comments corresponded with trainees' views that feedback would contribute to learning on the course.

For two tutors there was a strong identification of the bridge between theory and practice which Schön felt was the basis for reflective activity.

They identified that the purpose of TP feedback was to:

> Guide trainees to understand what went on in their teaching
>
> Reflect and evaluate individually and collectively on their teaching and **explore the consequences** of particular strategies. (my emphasis).

For these tutors, the feedback discussion allowed for the action (the lesson) to become thinking (reflection) and for practice to be theorised.

The impostor effect

The tutors confirmed that they structured their feedback to ensure that the majority of the contributions would come from trainees. In general, they felt that the amount of input from trainees would increase as the course progressed and the trainees became more confident. Tutors linked the stage of the course to the growing expertise of the trainees, who, they felt, could take on a bigger role towards the end of the course:

> When they are more confident about expressing their opinions and know more. In the beginning the feedback is more tutor-led, as the course progresses, trainees can do more.

It seems, therefore, that tutors do not feel that trainees are 'impostors' in the feedback process and should make a full and significant contribution to the evaluation of teaching, albeit in a gradual manner over the course.

When asked about the content of their evaluations, tutors concurred that trainees are mostly positive about their peers' teaching. The difficulty of saying something negative about a peer's teaching was recognised, with one tutor commenting that they are 'understandably reluctant to criticise their peers'. Such a view indicates that in applying the assessment criteria related to providing a critique of peers' lessons, tutors are able to take a more pragmatic view and understand the reluctance to come forward with opinions that may offend or disrupt the group cohesion.

Although tutors were committed to encouraging trainees to participate in the evaluation of lessons, there was recognition of the expertise of the tutor and an understanding of the tutor's role in providing guidance as an experienced professional. One tutor felt the purpose of feedback was:

> An opportunity for peer feedback and for the tutors to provide commentary and evaluation of the lesson and prescribe strategies, approaches etc for improvement.

Another tutor commented that trainees 'look to me as the "trained professional" to give the final say'. This acknowledgement suggests that tutors are not reluctant to act as an expert in the feedback sessions, but are committed to trainees' having a full participatory role. Trainees, however, may still find this role daunting as they are still being asked to provide knowledgeable contributions in the form of judgements on teaching.

The benefits of delayed feedback

The potential pressure placed on trainees to come up with evaluative comments immediately after a lesson is recognised by some tutors who prefer, where possible to do 'delayed feedback'. In this model, discussion of the lessons is postponed to the next session of the course so that trainees have more time and distance from the teaching event. For some courses, this decision is forced by the course timetable, where TP finishes very late or where rooms are not available for immediate feedback sessions. None of the trainees in the study experienced delayed feedback. For the group of tutors surveyed, timetable issues were the sole reason for choosing to delay feedback. Tutors who engaged in delayed feedback felt that the quality of feedback was different in a number of ways.

It has been mentioned already that asking trainees to comment in a knowledgeable manner in feedback, as 'impostors', carries with it a level of emotional stress. A common thread in tutors' views was that delayed feedback was less emotional. One tutor commented that with the delay:

There is more time for the trainee to reflect and become less attached emotionally.

Other tutors said that trainees could 'receive feedback more openly, calmly', and take 'a more dispassionate view of the lesson', 'it's less stressful'. The detachment in time from the original lesson seems to result in an emotional detachment for the trainee and a reduction in the stress of contributing to feedback. Such benefits for the trainees' emotional state were not always matched by the content of the feedback. Although tutors felt that 'trainees and tutor have time to collect, process and structure thoughts' it was also the case that 'the details are often forgotten'. In their design of a course timetable, tutors may have to make a pragmatic decision about whether they will choose a more stressful scenario where they can have more immediate and detailed commentary or provide feedback that is less emotional, but perhaps less focused. They may also consider a mixture of both.

Another way of incorporating delayed feedback into the course is through the use of written self-evaluations after the lesson. Tutors commented that this feedback was more honest and more detailed. One tutor highlighted the fact that trainees found it difficult to express themselves in writing sometimes, raising the issue about the 'declarative' ability that is assumed in the use of formal reflective practice:

> In verbal feedback trainees tend to be more defensive, less likely to listen to their peers'/tutors' suggestions. However, some trainees really struggle to express themselves in writing and write one-word answers, so they are better off trying to explain themselves.

If trainees struggle to express themselves, then any assessment of their self-evaluations may not recognise the full extent of trainees' reflections, only those which they can convert from *tacit* to *declarative*. This poses one of the challenges of assessing self- and peer-evaluation and it is this challenge that will now be discussed.

The challenge of assessing self- and peer-evaluation

The difficulty in assessing self-and peer-evaluations stems partly from the problematic nature of the content of trainees' reflections highlighted thus far. Trainees may not be able or willing to contribute effectively to post-lesson feedback and this may have little to do with their ability to reflect effectively on their teaching and implement change as a result of that reflection.

There was little sense, however, that tutors perceived the assessment to be problematic. All tutors were able to articulate a specific approach for assessing, though these approaches were very varied. Their views seemed to support the points made above about expertise and impostorship. Three tutors said they compared trainees' self-evaluation to their own notes and noted the differences. In other words, their assessment was made through a comparison of the evaluation of a novice teacher with that of an experienced tutor.

Reflecting a more pragmatic approach to the assessment of self-evaluations, two tutors commented on a less structured assessment, saying that the assessment was done 'informally, as an on-going process' and 'impressionistically — often in the moment'. They were adopting a less rigid approach and allowing trainees' comments to be seen as part of their overall performance on the course. Such an approach allows assessment to happen, but its problematic nature to be recognised.

However, equally possible is that tutors take a less pragmatic view. Two tutors commented that they were looking for 'accurate' and not 'wrong' judgements made by trainees. As one tutor commented, assessment:

> Depends on how accurate I feel they have been in pinpointing strengths and weaknesses, how balanced it is and if it shows that they have learned from input.

It may be that by focusing on a *right answer* in their assessment, which is the tutor's 'answer', tutors have unrealistic expectations of trainees and may penalise them unfairly.

Self- and peer-evaluation in the overall assessment of the trainee

Trainees' final overall grade (Fail, Pass, Pass B and Pass A) is supported through the grading of each lesson. Centres give trainees a grade for each lesson, usually phrased as 'to standard' or 'not to standard'. As self- and peer-evaluation forms part of the assessment criteria, it would be expected to contribute to the overall grade. When tutors were asked about the relationship between trainees' evaluations of teaching and their grade, there was a general feeling that it did not impact much. As one tutor commented: 'If they can teach well but are not very perceptive, I would not hold it against them.' In fact, good self-evaluations tended to work in favour of the trainee if they were 'borderline' between grades (both lesson and overall), but not to have a negative effect; it could push them into a higher grade, but was unlikely to bring them down a grade.

There was a strong sense, however, of a correlation between stronger trainees and better self-evaluations. One tutor felt that:

> Strong trainees tend to write very detailed evaluations and provide relevant suggestions/constructive criticism in both written and spoken evaluations. Weaker trainees tend to be less focused, less accurate and have fewer ideas in both.

Comments on this correlation did not specify whether a stronger trainee will contribute more effectively to feedback or whether better contributions would actually strengthen the trainee's teaching.

A final approach to assessment is expressed by a tutor who views the role of the self-evaluation in developing the trainee as more important than its role in tutors' assessment of the trainee overall:

> I am not sure that our assessment of their evaluations has as much impact as the evaluations themselves, and the points they take away from feedback.

This view recognises the potential difficulties of assessing reflective practice in its different forms, but recognises that tutors will often reach a pragmatic compromise and focus on their trainees' development.

Implications for practice

So far the assessment of self- and peer-evaluation on a CELTA course as an example of assessing reflective practice has been considered. Some difficulties about the nature of reflective practice in general and specifically in the CELTA context have been discussed. Through the insights gained on the small study of trainee and tutor experiences some tentative conclusions can be drawn.

Roles and responsibilities

In a sense, the CELTA course creates a community of practice where trainees and tutors work together to support the learning of the trainee. Tutors are usually keen to foster positive relationships with their trainees. They take care to provide supportive feedback and many tutors admit to modifying feedback to take into account the emotional state of a trainee, particularly if this feedback comments on ineffective teaching.

However, there is a challenging balance of power to manage and trainees recognise this fully. Trainees are aware that the assessment of their teaching and their overall grade is in the hands of the tutors. Trainees, therefore, also modify their feedback to support themselves and other trainees, with whom they have forged a common bond in the 'struggle' to pass the course. Tutors are aware of this, yet still feel able, in some cases, to make a judgement on the quality of the feedback offered verbally and in writing. The area where *untruths* are most prevalent is in the evaluation of peers' teaching. This is to be expected given the relationships in the group. The comment by a trainee that she felt like a 'betrayer' if she said anything negative about her colleagues' teaching is a good representation of the trainees' perspective.

A suggestion for practice would be to revisit some of the guidance on the 'participating in feedback' assessment criteria. Currently, it highlights the need to evaluate 'your colleagues' lessons critically but constructively in TP feedback' and 'make constructive suggestions on your peers' teaching'. This seems to demand too much in the context of the relationships built on the course. There may be a tacit understanding amongst tutors that trainees are overly positive about their peers' teaching, but to ensure that this is consistently recognised, some modification of the guidance would be useful.

Another suggestion would be to have some 'written only' feedback sessions where trainees only provide feedback in writing. Tutors felt that written feedback allowed trainees to be more honest and perhaps being able to write, even anonymously, might make for more open contributions. Allowing trainees to have part of the feedback session without the tutor present might also have a positive impact on their contributions.

Acknowledging expertise

Tutors have a different level of expertise and knowledge than their trainees; it is this that allows them to take on the role of tutor. Trainees see their tutors as more expert than they are and expect to hear the evaluation of their teaching from the tutor; something they consider to be the *proper* feedback. They do not always feel in a position to provide evaluative comments and see themselves as impostors in the role of experts. Tutors' comments, however, suggest that some expect trainee evaluations to be similar to the tutor's, suggesting an expectation of some expertise.

Discussions on how to manage the feedback sessions on the CELTA course are often focused on how to encourage trainees to make contributions. Materials to support observation of peers' teaching tend to be based around tasks for trainees which are used as a basis for feedback. There is a danger that trainee-led feedback becomes an orthodoxy. One tutor commented that she felt she ought to do more trainee-led feedback and that this was what was expected.

There are some possibilities for addressing this issue in practice. One suggestion would be to include some taught input on reflective practice on the course before TP starts and make explicit the implications of asking trainees to adopt an evaluative role when they are at the beginning of their teaching. This might make the role more authentic and trainees might be more willing to evaluate more honestly.

Another suggestion could be to have more focus in the training of tutors on the management of more tutor-led feedback. It might stimulate sharing of practice amongst tutors on how to lead as well as facilitate feedback. One tutor who took part in the survey felt that, currently, it was almost *taboo* to say that you preferred to provide a lot of tutor input in feedback. This does not mean that feedback would consist only of the tutor's evaluation, but that tutors could feel more comfortable about having the majority of feedback led by them on some occasions.

Assessing the impact, not the reflection

The laudable aim of developing reflective practitioners is to ensure that teachers improve their practice. Although trainees had some reservations about contributing to feedback, they did feel that the feedback sessions formed an important part of their learning on the course. Tutors also commented that there was a very positive correlation between trainees who were stronger classroom practitioners and those who were perceptive in feedback.

It seems then that there is evidence to suggest that being more perceptive about your teaching can lead to improvements in practice. The issue still remains that by including assessment of self- and peer-evaluations, tutors are assessing declarative knowledge which is considerably influenced by a number of factors highlighted in this chapter. It might be fairer to simply assess the impact on practice. The survey of tutors suggested that this is what many do, pragmatically, at present. However, the concern expressed about 'accurate' comments in feedback by some tutors suggests that there is a residual belief that trainees must 'get it right'; something that does not sit easily with the nature of reflection.

Conclusion

It is not suggested here that reflective practice should be eliminated from the syllabus of teacher education courses or from the CELTA course in particular. Trainees and tutors confirm that *thinking* about the *action* of teaching supports the improvement of practice. What is questioned is the semi-orthodoxy of reflective practice without considering issues such as the roles and relationships of the trainee teacher and the nature of declarative knowledge.

A further question for the assessment on teacher education courses is whether it is possible to really assess reflective practice through the trainees' evaluation of their own and their peers' teaching. It does not seem fair to expect them to provide expert commentary on their teaching and on the teaching of those with whom they seek to maintain a positive relationship. What is being suggested here is that as tutors continue to ask trainees to hold up a mirror to their practice, they recognise that this mirror does not provide a straightforward reflection; it is a mirror that is distorted by a range of factors and the reflection may not be a true representation of trainee thinking. Likewise any assessment of that reflection is also not straightforward.

Some tutors take a pragmatic path and follow the guidelines of the course assessment but recognise that there is some difficulty in the assessment of self- and peer-evaluation. They simply focus on classroom teaching and, if the quality of the self-evaluation can add a positive note to the trainee's grade, then it is used. Yet such a pragmatic stance poses some questions for a course that is so popular and a qualification that is so well regarded. It leaves the door open for other tutors, equally, to use the assessment criteria to make a negative judgement and perhaps lower a trainee's grade.

It would be useful to investigate this issue further and perhaps embed within the CELTA assessment guidelines a reflection of the sentiment of one tutor:

> If they can teach well but are not perceptive I wouldn't hold it against them.

Acknowledgement

The expression 'dirty mirror' applied to reflective practice on the CELTA course was first suggested to me by Dominic Braham, a CELTA tutor.

References

Barton, D. and Tusting, K. (Eds) (2005) *Beyond Communities of Practice*. Cambridge: Cambridge University Press.

Boud, D. (2001) Using journal writing to enhance reflective practice, in English, L. M. and Gillen, M. A. (Eds) *Promoting Journal Writing in Adult Education, New Directions in Adult and Continuing Education*. San Francisco: Jossey-Bass, 9–18.

Brookfield, S. D. (1995) *Becoming a Critically Reflective Teacher*. San Francisco: Jossey-Bass.

Brookfield, S. D. (2011) *Teaching for Critical Thinking: Tools and Techniques to Help Students Question Their Assumptions*. San Francisco: Jossey-Bass.

Burton, J. (2009) Reflective practice, in Burns, A. and Richards, J. C. (Eds) *The Cambridge Guide to Second Language Teacher Education*. New York: Cambridge University Press, 298–307.

Cambridge English (2014) *CELTA Administration Handbook 2014*. Cambridge: Cambridge English Language Assessment.

Cambridge ESOL (2010) *CELTA Syllabus and Assessment Guidelines*. Cambridge: Cambridge ESOL.

Hargreaves, J. (2003) So how do you feel about that? Assessing reflective practice, *Nurse Education Today* 24, 196–201.

Hughes, J., Jewson, N. and Unwin, L. (Eds) (2007) *Communities of Practice: Critical Perspectives*. London: Routledge.

Kolb, D.A. (1983) *Experiential Learning: Experience as the Source of Learning and Development*. New Jersey: Prentice Hall.

Lave, J. and Wenger, E. (1991) *Situated Learning: Legitimate Peripheral Participation*. New York: Cambridge University Press.

Schön, D. A. (1992) The theory of inquiry: Dewey's legacy to education, *Curriculum Inquiry* 22 (2) 119–128.

Tomlinson, P. (1999) Conscious reflection and implicit learning in teacher preparation, part 1: Recent light on an old issue, *Oxford Review of Education* 25 (3), 405–424.

Appendix 1

Questions used for online survey of CELTA tutors

1. How long have you been a CELTA tutor?
2. What do you feel is the purpose of TP feedback?
3. Approximately what percentage of your feedback is trainee-led and what percentage tutor-led?
4. In general, do trainees focus more on the positive or the negative about their own and peers' lessons in feedback?
5. Do you think trainees are honest about their views in feedback? Explain your answer.
6. Do you ever do delayed feedback and if so, why?
7. In what ways is trainee feedback different when it is delayed?
8. What differences do you notice between trainees' response in verbal feedback and their written self-evaluations of their lessons?
9. How do you assess trainees' verbal and written evaluations of their own and their peers' teaching?
10. How does your assessment of their verbal and written evaluations have an impact on trainees' overall grade?

6 Capturing the ephemeral: Standardising the assessment of teaching practice

Evelina D. Galaczi
Cambridge English Language Assessment
Marie Therese Swabey
Freelance teacher trainer and ELT consultant

Introduction

The evaluation of performance is a notoriously difficult endeavour, since it comprises an array of facets which interact in complex and at times unpredictable ways and involve subjective judgement. Spolsky (1995) draws a useful comparison between the measurement of sports achievements and performance assessment: in sports, some disciplines can be readily measured, e.g. how many seconds an athlete takes to run 100 metres, or how high they can jump, while others involve the subjective judgement of expert judges, as in the evaluation of gymnastics or diving routines, for example. The assessment of practical teaching ability — an exponent of the assessment of performance — is clearly in the latter category.

The assessment of teaching performance is all the more complex due to its ephemeral nature, i.e. the fact that it cannot be readily captured in permanent form and so typically has to be evaluated in real time. Unlike the assessment of writing ability, for example, where learner performance can be captured in a durable written form, evaluators of teaching practice often do not have a full record of the teaching event for post-lesson evaluation, but rely instead on real-time evaluations against a set of assessment criteria specified in assessment scales or assessment checklists. The video recording of teaching for post-lesson assessment is, of course, possible, and while it is a valuable record of teaching performance and a useful tool for self- or peer-evaluations, as shown for example by Lee and Wu (2006), in a formal assessment context it brings with it a number of complications, such as the difficulty of capturing the entirety of teacher language and actions, the work of the students as they work individually and in pairs or groups, the work on the black/white board and in the student books, the materials used, etc. The assessment of teaching performance, therefore, is typically carried out in real time, and presupposes the need for a rigorous and comprehensive evaluation system to ensure a fair and accurate assessment. Our focus in this chapter will be on the key elements which are involved in providing such a fair and rigorous assessment of teaching performance. In this endeavour we will be guided by a conceptual framework for analysing key aspects of assessment, proposed by Weir (2005) in the context of language test validation and analysis, but equally applicable as a heuristic in the discussion of standardising the assessment of practical teaching. Weir refers to 'scoring validity' in his framework in relation to those elements of an assessment system which ensure a standardised and reliable assessment. An assessment is considered reliable if two or more assessors use the same evaluation instrument in the same conditions (e.g., same teacher, same classroom, same students, same content) and come to the same/similar conclusion. Typically, when considering the reliability of an evaluation, the predominant focus is on assessor training and standardisation. This is certainly a fundamental aspect of enhancing the reliability of performance assessment, but is just one aspect of a whole array of elements involved in an assessment. In our discussion we will go beyond the procedures in place for assessor training and standardisation, which are important, but insufficient, elements of ensuring a fair assessment and will focus on a range of assessment elements which interact together to form an elaborate system for achieving and maintaining standards of assessment. These aspects of assessment (from Weir 2005) include:

- assessment criteria
- assessment process and conditions
- assessor characteristics
- training and standardisation of judges (i.e. assessors, raters, markers, examiners)
- grading and awarding.

We will situate our discussion of these five parameters of assessment within the Cambridge English Teaching Qualifications, and will use the Certificate in Teaching English to Speakers of Other Languages (CELTA) as a representative case study illustrating the procedures in place for the standardisation of the assessment of practical teaching. When relevant we will also refer to two other Cambridge English Teaching Qualifications which involve practical teaching — the Teaching Knowledge Test: Practical (TKT: Practical) and the Diploma in Teaching English to Speakers of Other Languages (Delta). In doing so, we hope to present a detailed account of the quality-assurance procedures supporting the accurate and reliable assessment of CELTA teachers, and also highlight problematic issues in the context of evaluating practical teaching which need to be acknowledged and addressed. We also hope to contribute to the teacher education literature, where descriptions and discussions of pre-service teacher evaluations are rare. The available literature (e.g. Mathers, Oliva and Laine 2008) mainly focuses on in-service teacher evaluations typically carried out by administrators such as Principals or Heads of Department or self-assessment guides for teacher's self-development (e.g. British Council 2011, 2012). Information on preservice teaching qualifications and the procedures in place for ensuring a standardised assessment seems to be less readily available.

Subjectivity of evaluating performance

Assessor subjectivity and variability have long been explored and recognised in the assessment literature as one of the inherent issues associated with the assessment of performance by human assessors. This was noted more than a century ago by Edgeworth (1890), who explored the issue of assessment reliability in the context of the British civil service examinations and pessimistically noted: 'I find the element of chance in these public examinations to be such that only a fraction — from a third to two-thirds — of the successful candidates can be regarded as safe, above the danger of coming out unsuccessfully if a different set of equally competent judges had happened to be appointed' (1890: 653). This variability in assessor judgements is not entirely surprising since assessors are individuals, each with their own set of personal attributes which they bring to the evaluation task, and which shape the way they interpret and apply the assessment criteria/scale(s), the way they make judgements, their tendency towards leniency or severity and the consistency of their rating behaviour. Our understanding of assessor variability has evolved and the so-called 'rater effects', i.e. the subjective influence which assessors may exert on a specific evaluation, have been explored in detail (Myford and Wolfe 2003, 2004) and a range of procedures for minimising assessor variability have now become commonplace.

Assessor variability has been described in the language performance literature as a 'fact of life' (McNamara 1996) and not something that necessarily needs to be (or can be!) eliminated. Instead, the current belief is that assessors should not become machines that agree all the time (which, if possible, would entail the reduction of assessment criteria and categories to superficial right/wrong features). Rather, assessors are expected to bring in their different perspectives, within limits, and some degree of variability is to be expected.

The fact that the evaluation process is affected by assessor subjectivity has obvious implications for the fairness of a performance test. At the same time, the available research has clearly demonstrated that assessors can succeed in reaching an acceptable level of agreement provided they are supported by a range of quality assurance procedures (e.g. Weigle 1994 in the context of assessing writing).

Considering the inherent variability in assessor judgements, a range of practices underlie the Cambridge English Teaching Qualifications and aim to moderate the subjective influence of assessors. One such practice is the use of *assessment scales, scoring criteria* and *performance descriptors*. Assessor variability is also minimised through an *assessment model* which uses partial double marking and standardised assessment procedures. Another method for standardising assessment of the Cambridge English Teaching Qualifications is a rigorous system of *rater training and standardisation*, as well as explicit and sound professional requirements governing *assessor characteristics*. Finally, the variability across assessors and the threat to the fairness and reliability of the evaluation is reduced through transparent and comprehensive *grading and awarding procedures*. These parameters all play a role in minimising subjectivity and ensuring acceptable standards of assessment. We now turn to discussing each in turn in the context of the CELTA qualification, with additional exemplification, where relevant, from

TKT: Practical and Delta.

The term 'assessor' will be used in the general sense of a person who has to evaluate performance. When used in the context of CELTA, a distinction will be made between two stakeholders with assessment responsibilities — 'external assessors' and 'internal course tutors'.

Achieving and maintaining standards of assessment in CELTA

Background

The CELTA course aims to assist candidates in developing essential subject knowledge and familiarity with the principles of effective language teaching, to acquire a range of practical skills for teaching English to adult learners, and to demonstrate their ability to apply their learning in a real teaching context. The certificate is awarded to candidates who have completed the course and who have met the assessment criteria for all written and practical assignments.

CELTA assessment is continuous, i.e. takes place throughout the course, and comprises two components — teaching practice and written assignments — both of which contribute to the overall grade (Pass A, Pass B, Pass, Fail). Component One involves lesson planning and teaching (6 hours in total), while Component Two encompasses classroom-related written assignments (four assignments in total). The two components are internally assessed by CELTA tutors, who assess all teaching practice and written assignments, and externally moderated by a Cambridge English approved assessor, who samples portfolios and teaching practice and who discusses and agrees the grades for all candidates with the tutor.

CELTA assessment categories and criteria

We begin our detailed discussion of the procedures in place for standardising the assessment of the CELTA qualification by focusing on the assessment categories and criteria used. Two questions play a key role here: (i) are they *valid* for their purpose, i.e. do they measure what they intend to measure? and (ii) can they be *reliably* used?

Danielson (2012: 33) notes that 'unless there is a clear and accepted definition of good teaching, teachers won't know how their performance will be evaluated, and observers won't know what to look for'. Assessment criteria, therefore, need to be explicitly based on an accepted theory or framework and to clearly and accurately conceptualise and operationalise that theory/framework. Instrumental in the conceptualisation of key professional teacher competencies is work by Shulman (1986) and Grossman (1990): the latter proposed four categories of teacher knowledge and competence: general pedagogic knowledge (knowledge, beliefs and skills related to teaching and learning in general), subject matter knowledge (teachers' knowledge of the subject they teach), pedagogic content knowledge (specific knowledge of how to teach a particular subject) and knowledge of context (understanding the particular context in which the learning is taking place and how it affects teaching and learning). Tsui and Nicholson (1999) have further developed Grossman's framework and expanded the four domains in the context of English as a foreign/second language. More recently, a framework for teacher evaluation has been proposed in the general education domain by Danielson (2008), whose 'Framework for Teaching' is used for mentoring, professional development and teacher evaluation for schools and districts. The framework breaks down the complex activity of teaching into four domains: Planning and Preparation, Classroom Environment, Instruction, Professional Responsibilities, which are in turn subdivided into smaller components.

Several recent frameworks in the context of English language teaching are also worth noting, since they attempt to provide a macro–micro link between high-level theoretical concepts, as proposed by Shulman and Grossman in the 1980s, and usable practical frameworks outlining different levels of teacher competence. One such framework is the EAQUALS European Profiling Grid (2013, also Rossner 2009), which is a framework of descriptors for profiling language teachers. It includes, among other elements, a set of 'Core Competences' (Methodology: Knowledge and Skills; Lesson and Course Planning; Interaction Management and Monitoring; Assessment) profiled across six 'phases of development' and described in detail in order to facilitate self-assessment and assessment by trainers. Another framework, the Cambridge English Teaching Framework (Cambridge English 2014a), offers a further attempt to profile the competencies underlying teaching, and does so across four developmental stages. The key categories included are: 'Learning and the Learner', 'Language Ability, Knowledge and Awareness',

'Teaching, Learning and Assessment', and 'Professional Development and Values'. The British Council CPD framework for teachers (2011) is a further example. Such frameworks provide a valuable theoretical and empirical point of reference for the assessment categories and criteria underlying the very practical endeavour of teaching practice evaluation, since they document the key features of the ability to be assessed.

The general and language-specific competencies underlying the conceptualisations and frameworks noted above are reflected in the CELTA assessment criteria, which tap into syllabus/content areas such as: the teaching and learning context, language analysis and awareness, language skills, planning and resources for different teaching contexts, developing teaching skills and professionalism. In addition, each CELTA assessment criterion is clearly and explicitly linked to a relevant CELTA syllabus/context area (Cambridge ESOL 2010: 15). Such theoretical underpinning of the assessment criteria and careful and explicit alignment between syllabus content and assessment criteria is an important aspect of CELTA assessment since it explicitly operationalises the underlying competence and enhances the validity of the assessment criteria used.

In addition to theoretical underpinnings, which contribute to the validity of the assessment, evaluation instruments also need to be reliably used. Mathers *et al.* (2008: 8) note that one way to achieve this is through 'clearly defined, non-subjective criteria that require minimal interpretation'. Transparent, unambiguous and jargon-free assessment criteria, therefore, contribute to the reliability of assessment. The CELTA assessment criteria are given as a list of statements: a total of 42 statements for the 'Planning and Teaching' component and 17 for the 'Classroom-related written assignment' component. The list in Table 1 provides an illustration of the level of detail provided in the CELTA assessment criteria which define Pass level.

Such detailed and explicit assessment categories and criteria enhance the reliability of CELTA assessment by providing an explicit yardstick for judging performances which is external to individual users and which minimises the possibility of assessors/tutors applying personal constructs and beliefs to the evaluation. Assessment criteria cannot, of course, completely remove subjectivity, but play a significant role in reducing it.

Table 1 CELTA assessment criteria (Cambridge ESOL 2010: 15–18)

Planning and Teaching: Prepare and plan for the effective teaching of adult ESOL learners

Identifying and stating appropriate aims/intended outcomes for individual lessons

Ordering activities so that they achieve lesson aims/outcomes

Selecting, adapting or designing materials, activities, resources and technical aids appropriate for the lesson

Presenting the materials for classroom use with a professional appearance, and with regard to copyright requirements

Describing the procedure of the lesson in sufficient detail

Including interaction patterns appropriate for the materials and activities used in the lesson

Ensuring balance, variety and a communicative focus in materials, tasks and activities

Allocating appropriate timing for different stages in the lessons

Analysing language with attention to form, meaning and phonology and using correct terminology

Anticipating potential difficulties with language, materials and learners

Suggesting solutions to anticipated problems

Using terminology that relates to language skills and subskills correctly

Working constructively with colleagues in the planning of teaching practice sessions

Reflecting on and evaluating lesson plans in light of the learning process and suggesting improvements for future plans

Planning and Teaching: Demonstrate professional competence as teachers

Teaching a class with an awareness of the needs and interests of the language group

Teaching a class with an awareness of learning styles and cultural factors that may affect learning

Acknowledging, when necessary, learners' backgrounds and previous learning experiences

Establishing good rapport with learners and ensuring they are fully involved in learning activities

Adjusting their own use of language in the classroom according to the learner group and the context

Identifying errors and sensitively correcting learners' oral and written language

Providing clear contexts and a communicative focus for language

Providing accurate and appropriate models of oral and written language in the classroom

Focusing on language items in the classroom by clarifying relevant aspects of meaning and form (including phonology) for learners to an appropriate degree of depth

Showing awareness of differences in register

Providing appropriate practice of language items

Helping learners to understand reading and listening texts

Helping learners to develop oral fluency

Helping learners to develop writing skills

Arranging the physical features of the classroom appropriately for teaching and learning, bearing in mind safety regulations of the institution

Setting up whole class and/or group or individual activities appropriate to the lesson type

Selecting appropriate teaching techniques in relation to the content of the lesson

(To be continued)

(*Continued*)

Managing the learning process in such a way that lesson aims are achieved
Making use of materials, resources and technical aids in such a way that they enhance learning
Using appropriate means to make instructions for tasks and activities clear to learners
Using a range of questions effectively for the purpose of elicitation and checking of understanding
Providing learners with appropriate feedback on tasks and activities
Maintaining an appropriate learning pace in relation to materials, tasks and activities
Monitoring learners appropriately in relation to the task or activity
Beginning and finishing lessons on time and, if necessary, making any relevant regulations pertaining to the teaching institution clear to learners
Maintaining accurate and up-to-date records in their portfolio
Noting their own teaching strengths and weaknesses in different teaching situations in light of feedback from learners, teachers and teacher educators
Participating in and responding to feedback

Classroom-related written assignment 1: Focus on the learner

Showing awareness of how a learner's/learners' background(s), previous learning experience and learning style(s) affect learning
Identifying the learner's/learners' language skills/needs
Correctly using terminology relating to the description of language systems and language skills
Selecting appropriate material and/or resources to aid the learner's/learners' language development
Providing a rationale for using specific activities with a learner/learners
Finding, selecting and referencing information from one or more sources using written language that is clear, accurate and appropriate to the task

Classroom-related written assignment 2: Language-related tasks

Analysing language correctly for teaching purposes
Correctly using terminology relating to form, meaning and phonology when analysing language
Accessing reference materials and referencing information they have learned about language to an appropriate source
Using written language that is clear, accurate and appropriate to the task

Classroom-related written assignment 3: Language skills-related tasks

Correctly using terminology that relates to language skills and subskills
Relating task design to language skills development
Finding, selecting and referencing information from one or more sources using written language that is clear, accurate and appropriate to the task

Classroom-related written assignment 4: Lessons from the classroom

Noting their own teaching strengths and weaknesses in different situations in light of feedback from learners, teachers and teacher educators
Identifying which ELT areas of knowledge and skills they need further development in
Describing in a specific way how they might develop their ELT knowledge and skills beyond the course
Using written language that is clear, accurate and appropriate to the task

The reliability of an assessment has additionally been shown to be enhanced by having more parts to an examination. Edgeworth's (1888) early conclusion that having more parts to an examination greatly increases its reliability and validity (provided each sample gives a reasonable estimate of the ability in question) has since been supported by a number of researchers (e.g. in the field of assessing writing, Finlayson 1951; Godshalk, Swineford and Coffman 1966; Willmott and Nuttall 1975). The six assessment components in CELTA, each supported by explicit assessment criteria, thus play a further role in enhancing the reliability of the assessment.

A recent (March 2013) survey of CELTA tutors and assessors which involved a total of 170 respondents from 40 countries also provided evidence for the beneficial role of clear assessment criteria which are easy to understand by users. In the case of the statement 'I have a clear understanding of the assessment criteria' (Figure 1) the proportion of respondents who chose 4 and 5 on a 1–5 point scale (1=Do not understand; 5=Fully understand) ranged between 91.3% and 100.0%.

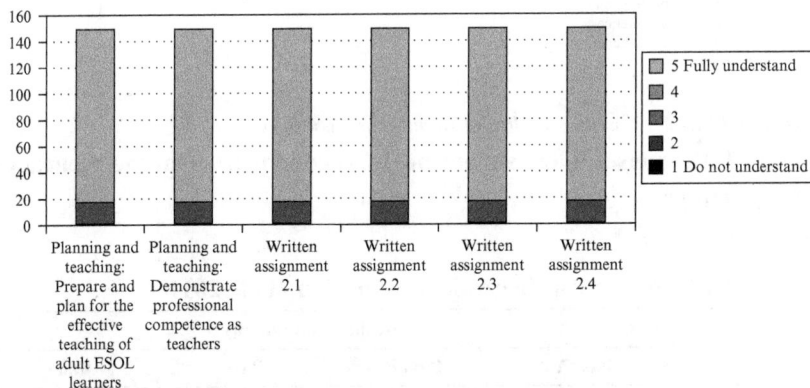

Source: CELTA 2013 survey, N=149 CELTA tutors and assessors

Figure 1 Responses to the statement 'I have a clear understanding of the assessment criteria'

When responding to the statement 'I feel confident about the accuracy of my ratings', again a strong theme emerged, as seen in Figure 2: the proportion of respondents who chose 4 and 5 on a 1–5 point scale (1=Not understand; 5=Very confident) ranged between 86.7% and 95.9%.

It would also be useful to consider at this point not just the CELTA assessment criteria from a conceptual point of view, but also in terms of their use by tutors and assessors. Table 2 provides statistical summaries of the distribution of grades for the CELTA qualification based on grade data of all CELTA candidates worldwide from 2008 to 2011, and shows a remarkably similar distribution across years. This indicates that the CELTA assessment criteria, which are the external 'yardstick' for CELTA grades, are interpreted in a similar fashion by tutors and assessors worldwide.

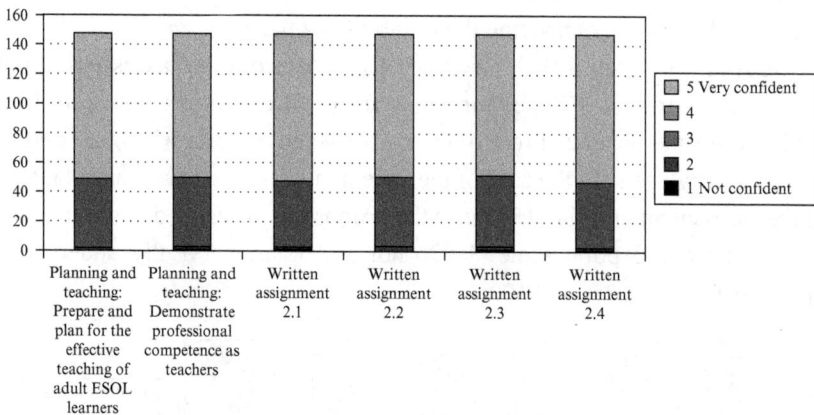

Source: CELTA 2013 survey, N=146 CELTA tutors and assessors

Figure 2 Responses to the statement 'I feel confident about the accuracy of my ratings'

Table 2 CELTA worldwide grade distribution 2008–2011

Year	Grade distribution (%)			
	Pass A	Pass B	Pass	Fail
2011	4.73	23.56	66.20	1.07
2010	4.38	22.93	68.06	3.83
2009	4.83	24.19	65.73	1.08
2008	4.93	23.96	65.68	1.11

(Data source: www.cambridgeenglish.org/research-and-validation/quality-and-accountability/ grade-statistics/)

Interestingly, defining the construct underlying an examination through a detailed list of assessment criteria, as is the case with CELTA, also brings about some caveats which need to be considered. One of them relates to the competing needs of assessment criteria to be detailed enough to capture the underlying ability they aim to tap into, but also succinct enough to be easily used by judges. In the case of CELTA, the large set of assessment criteria provides comprehensive coverage of the construct, on the one hand, but does so possibly at the cost of being over-articulated. A way forward would be to simplify the set of assessment criteria through clearer organisation and weighting.

A related issue inherent in detailed lists of assessment criteria is the need to signal the hierarchic relationship between some criteria, which would in turn indicate their relative level of importance. A list of criteria creates the impression that all are of equal importance, whereas that may not necessarily be the case. A few representative comments from the 2013 CELTA survey signal the perceived need by tutors and assessors for clearer indications about how assessment criteria are organised and weighted in a hierarchy of criteria:

> I think the criteria are clear. The only issue is that some are more important than others (to use an extreme example, 'analysing language' as opposed to 'setting up furniture'), and it is the subjective good sense and professional know-how of tutors and assessors that enables the fair and accurate application of the criteria in reality.

> I feel there are too many criteria. It would be helpful if these were cut down. This means that all criteria are given equal weight when some are obviously more important than others.

One important role of detailed assessment criteria, such as the ones found in CELTA, is that they contribute to the formative element of the assessment, since their aim is to serve not just as evaluation tools, but as learning objectives. As such, the criteria used throughout the CELTA course provide developmental feedback to prospective teachers. In order to be useful and meaningful, they need to be detailed. In contrast, the final summative grade is supported by a much briefer holistic profile describing typical CELTA teachers at grades Pass A, Pass B, Pass and Fail. The role of the CELTA assessment criteria as both assessor-oriented and trainee-oriented was commented on in the CELTA survey by a number of survey respondents. As one survey respondent noted:

> They [assessment criteria] are generally clear to tutors but not always to trainees

who are meant to assess themselves on the basis of the criteria. In other words they seem to target tutors and assessors but leave trainees nonplussed. I suggest they be worded in the form of plainly written 'I can ...' statements similar to CEFR statements that describe what learners can do in English.

The assessment criteria and scales used in TKT: Practical provide a further useful comparison here. Unlike CELTA, the TKT: Practical qualification is not based on a course, but on one assessment. As a result, the assessment is supported by a set of scales which include succinct and brief performance descriptors in a number of categories at four levels of achievement (Cambridge ESOL 2012: 66–67; see also Appendix C).

Providing a set of detailed and explicit assessment criteria and addressing some of the caveats noted above is also a means of reducing the subjectivity of personal judgements which could be passed down from an 'expert mentor' to a 'novice assessor/tutor'. Becoming a tutor and an assessor in CELTA could potentially be influenced by the personal beliefs of the mentor, as has also been noted for the Delta context by Borg (2012). Such mentor influence, although important, is balanced by the theoretically driven, comprehensive and explicit assessment criteria used, which provide reference to broader, external standards and as such minimise deeply held and possibly 'fossilised' personal and professional beliefs.

CELTA assessment model

In addition to assessment criteria, the assessment model used in performance assessment also has an impact on the standardisation and fairness of the assessment. The CELTA assessment model encompasses both *internal assessment* by a CELTA tutor and *external assessment* by a Cambridge English-approved CELTA assessor. The teaching practice and the written assignment components of the CELTA course are internally assessed by the course tutor(s) and a sample is moderated by the external assessor (Cambridge English 2014b: 17–18). Double marking is an integral part of the CELTA assessment model, which contributes to internal verification of standards and the maintenance of a centre-external common standard. As a result, CELTA assignments from a centre are double-marked by tutors and a sample is looked at by the external assessor. The multiple marking of assignments and teaching practice, albeit of a sample only, is an important positive feature of the CELTA assessment model, since it enhances the reliability of the assessment, supports the maintenance of a common standard and factors in assessments from different perspectives — that of an internal tutor familiar with the teacher and their work to date and that of an external assessor not directly familiar with the professional development of that teacher. The assessor brings both an external standardisation perspective and the independent perspective of an additional judge. Practicality considerations limit the possibility of the external assessor observing every single lesson and reading every single assignment of a prospective teacher, but when assessors visit a centre (typically for the duration of a day or equivalent time), they read a cross-section of the candidates' assessment portfolios, observe teaching practice and tutor feedback for some of the candidates teaching that day, and hold a provisional grading meeting with tutors (Cambridge English 2014b: 29–30). If the assessor and the tutor do not agree on a grade for an assignment or a lesson, they reach consensus based on evidence from the work and how it meets or does not meet particular criteria. In the rare cases when they cannot reach agreement, the candidate's grade is noted as 'grade not agreed' and the work, alongside the candidate's portfolio, is sent to be scrutinised by a Joint Chief Assessor.

In addition to the monitoring and standardisation role of the external assessor, CELTA Joint Chief Assessors monitor the assessors' reports on their centres and as such provide an additional layer of standardisation and expert judgement. The network of professionals involved in the assessment of a CELTA teacher (shown in Figure 3) illustrates the multiple sources of expertise which inform the assessment of a prospective CELTA teacher. Such an elaborate hierarchical system of roles and responsibilities (which is also present in a slightly different form for TKT: Practical and Delta) is a fundamental element in standardised assessment since it greatly minimises the subjectivity of individuals and draws directly and indirectly on the expertise and judgement of a wide network of professionals beyond the individual tutor.

In the survey of CELTA tutors and assessors mentioned earlier, the value of double marking and the collaboration and discussion between tutors and/or assessors in supporting a universal standard emerged as a strong theme. CELTA tutors and assessors commented on the beneficial aspect of the double (or even multiple) marking system used, the positive role of the assessor as an external point of standardisation and as a person aiding the

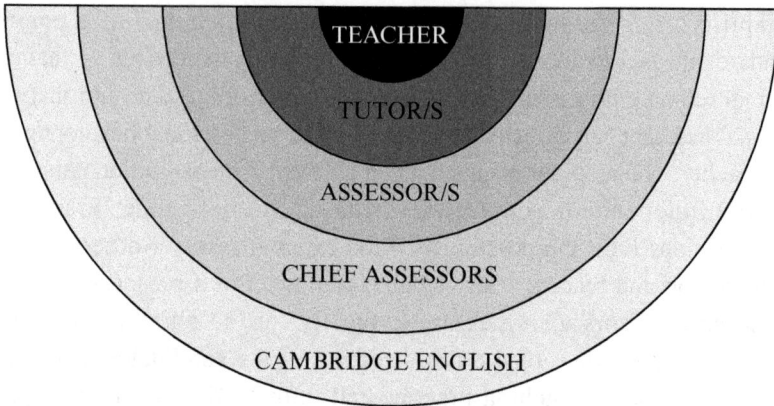

Figure 3 Network of professionals supporting CELTA assessment

professional development of tutors beyond their training and standardisation. The few representative comments below capture the views expressed by many of the respondents:

> Usually any doubts one may have are shared with other tutors so that everyone is confident that they have agreed and awarded the right grades.

> Do we ever feel 100% confident? But after quite a lot of experience and working with many different tutors, I feel quite confident of the accuracy of my ratings.

> The double marking system is clear and allows us to discuss any possible issues as a team.

> At our centre, the trainers tend to sit down before the course if they have never worked before and discuss what kinds of classroom behaviour = certain criteria, and this helps to get all the trainers on the page.

> As a tutor, I have always found the discussions with assessors very useful in confirming my grading parameters, and it has always been positive to see that we were nearly always grading along the same lines. When we weren't, it has been informative to have the assessor's perspective.

> It's very useful for centres to have an unbiased person watching their trainees as it's easy to see the progress a particular trainee has made and let that influence the tutor's overall judgement. The assessor's visit helps in this sense.

Such comments highlight the value (both perceived by assessors and tutors and supported by good practice in educational measurement) of incorporating multiple perspectives in the CELTA assessment model.

As noted earlier, CELTA assessment is continuous, takes place throughout the course and incorporates, as such, both formative and summative aspects. The continuous aspect of the CELTA assessment model is a further instance of the multiple sources of evidence used in deciding on a final grade. It enhances the quality of the assessment, as it allows for longer-term evidence about a teacher's performance to be collected and evaluated throughout multiple decision points along the way. While broadening the range of evidence used for the assessment, it also plays a formative role in the development of that teacher. Such practice ensures that different assessment perspectives are brought to bear on the assessment decisions, which combine continuous assessment and in-depth familiarity with the teacher's work on the part of the tutor, complemented by the one-off external judgements made by the assessor. It moves away from an evaluation which captures just a one-time snapshot of a teaching event as interpreted by one assessor, to an evaluation which is built on multiple evaluations both *diachronically* throughout the course by one person, the tutor, and *synchronically* at a single point in time by two people, the assessor and the two tutors, who are, in addition, accountable for their decisions in a hierarchical network of responsibilities and expertise, as shown in Figure 3.

CELTA assessment conditions

Another aspect of the standardisation of performance assessment relates to the assessment conditions involved. Detailed guidance is provided in the *CELTA Administration Handbook 2014*, which devotes a whole section to the procedures for the assessor's visit and to requirements to be followed before the assessor's visit, during and after (Cambridge English 2014b: 25–31). Before the visit the assessor is required to read through extensive documentation, which includes:

- information on the teaching practice and tutorials of the course participants
- individual descriptions of the candidates
- a proposed timetable for the visit, including adequate time for the assessor to read a cross-section of candidates' assessment portfolios, observe the teaching practice of some of the candidates teaching on the day of the visit, observe tutor feedback and meet the candidates

- the course timetable
- teaching practice schedule with details of the teaching practice arrangements for the time of the visit
- written assignment titles
- a sample candidate end-of-course report
- recommendations from the last assessor's report.

During the assessor's visit at the centre, the following documentation is made available:

- candidate assessment portfolios
- the tutor's recommended grade for each candidate for the stage of the course and a brief summarising comment
- completed selection tasks for each candidate
- lesson plans for candidates teaching in teaching practice that day (provided either when the assessor arrives or at the beginning of the observed lesson).

During the visit to the centre, the assessor matches the tutor's judgements of candidates against the samples of observed teaching practice and the evidence in the candidate assessment portfolios. Since it would not normally be possible for the assessor to examine the entire contents of each candidate's assessment portfolio, the assessor reads a minimum of four candidate assessment portfolios across the range of ability, including the portfolio of candidates who have been provisionally graded 'Fail' or potential 'Fail'. Within the time available, assessors are also required to look at a range of work across as many portfolios as possible. In addition, the assessor is introduced to the candidates and opportunity for discussion is provided. After observing the lessons, the tutor and assessor discuss and agree the standard of the observed lessons and the feedback to be given. The assessor then observes the tutor — candidate feedback session and holds a formal grading meeting with the tutors to discuss and agree provisional grades (to be discussed in more detail later in the chapter).

Such detailed descriptions of procedures and conditions before, during and after the assessor's visit are important in supporting the standard of assessment of CELTA trainees. The marking of a sample of work by the tutor and assessor, the reaching of a mark by discussion and consensus, the range of evidence gathered about each trainee in their portfolio all contribute to capturing aspects of teaching practice in a complex and non-subjective manner, and are examples of the multiple sources of evidence which underpin a CELTA assessment and contribute to its reliability and validity.

CELTA assessor characteristics

The professional characteristics of the assessor represent another important parameter affecting the fairness of an assessment. To reach analogous judgements assessors need to have comparable knowledge about their subject and comparable experience to draw on when assessing. In the CELTA scheme, prospective tutors are required to have both in-depth subject knowledge and extensive classroom experience (Cambridge English 2013: 3). This ensures that assessments of CELTA teachers are made by professionals who have a shared comprehensive knowledge base and comparable practical expertise.

Uniformity in the professional characteristics of assessors is also considered in the appointment of external assessors. External assessors are all practising CELTA tutors, which ensures that they are familiar with current procedures and are in tune with assessment standards at CELTA level. The *Assessor Application Form and Supporting Notes* document states that CELTA assessor applicants need to have a minimum of two years' experience of CELTA teacher training including experience of directing at least two courses, and evidence of continuing professional development in the field of English language teaching, for example: attendance at courses and seminars, participation in in-service training or teacher development schemes and if appropriate, regular contact with professionals involved in English language teaching beyond the institution where the potential assessor is employed.

Such minimum professional requirements for tutors and assessors contribute to the standardisation of assessment, as they ensure a uniform and adequate level of professional knowledge and experience.

CELTA assessor and tutor training and standardisation

As would be expected, assessor training is a vital element in standardising the assessment of performance, since lack of training or inadequate training can have an impact on the reliability of the assessment. The importance of assessor training has been recognised and strongly advocated in the performance assessment literature (e.g. Alderson, Clapham and Wall 1995; Coggshall 2007; Danielson 2008; Mathers *et al.* 2008).

Interestingly, some researchers have cautioned about the possible negative effects of training. In the context of second/foreign language writing assessment, for example, Weigle (1994) notes that if raters of writing scripts can be trained to show exceptionally strong agreement on ratings, it is likely that they are agreeing on superficial aspects of a text, rather than any substantive criteria. In addition, an emphasis on very strong agreement during training could force raters to ignore their own experiences and expertise, thus denying the possibility that there may be more than one 'correct' judgement of a performance. Lumley and McNamara (1995: 57) have made a similar assertion: 'in the assessment of human performance, which is a matter of some complexity, no one judgement may be said to be definitive, although there is likely to be a considerable area of overlap between judgements'. This is especially true in the assessment of teaching practice, which is a highly complex event and difficult to reduce to a set of universally agreed ratings. Thornbury (2014, personal communication) asks a further important question which needs to be kept in mind: 'How "permeable" and adaptable are the training schemes to substantive changes in beliefs, values, and practices across the profession, e.g. with regard to issues such as linguistic norms (native-speaker vs proficient non-native) and the use of the L1 in the classroom?' Assessor training which recognises different perspectives while reducing extreme differences in evaluation and is open to changes in professional beliefs, therefore, is important.

A further fundamental aspect of training and standardisation is the evidence used to make a judgement. In the context of researching classroom teaching, Ball and Rowan (2004: 5) note that the quality of data gathered during an observation (be it by a researcher, tutor or assessor) is 'dependent on the observer'. Thus, training and standardisation need to focus carefully and explicitly on the collection of *observable evidence* rather than qualitative opinion. In this vein, Danielson (2012: 34) suggests three types of evidence which can be gathered: 'words spoken by the teacher or students, such as "Can anyone think of another idea?"; actions, such as, "The students took 45 seconds to line up by the door"; and the appearance of the classroom, such as, "Backpacks are strewn in the middle of the floor."' The recoding of such *facts* is different from forming *opinions and interpretations*. It is important, therefore, for assessors to be trained in distinguishing between fact and interpretation and between low inference and high inference data — the latter being assessing learner engagement, for example, the former being recording number of turns for each learner (Thornbury 2014, personal communication). This distinction is fundamental because, as Danielson (2012: 35) argues, 'when observers disagree about a teacher's level of performance, it is essential to know whether the differences stem from a difference in the evidence collected or in how the observer has interpreted the evidence'.

Stages of CELTA tutor and assessor training

In the CELTA context, tutor and assessor training proceeds through several stages.

Becoming a tutor: Tutors-in-training

Procedures for teachers to become CELTA tutors are overseen by Cambridge English Language Assessment and teachers who meet the minimum professional requirements in terms of expertise and qualifications are approved as CELTA tutors-in-training. (See also Morgan, Chapter 7.) In order to progress from a tutor-in-training to an approved CELTA tutor, teachers need to complete a supervised training programme which includes structured and guided tasks undertaken while 'shadowing' a CELTA course. The completed tasks are included in a portfolio of work compiled by the tutor-in-training as they proceed through the course. The work in the portfolio is evaluated by the training supervisor and the external assessor who observes the tutor-in-training conducting an input session and supervising teaching practice and reads the portfolio of the tutor-in-training to assess whether tasks have been completed to a satisfactory standard. The tutor-in-training's portfolio includes the following documentation:

- the training programme, including a list of tasks
- evidence that these tasks have been carried out
- evidence of the tutor-in-training having completed at least one input session
- feedback from the training supervisor on input session(s)
- shadow-marked assignments, with copies of assignments marked by the main tutor for comparison
- feedback from the training supervisor on the tutor-in-training's marking
- shadow-written teaching practice feedback, with copies of the main

tutor's feedback for comparison

- evidence of the tutor-in-training having conducted oral teaching practice feedback on at least one occasion
- feedback from the training supervisor on the tutor-in-training's oral and written feedback.

The external assessor and the CELTA tutor supervising the training programme write reports on the progress made by the tutor-in-training. The reports include evaluations of the tutor-in-training's ability to apply the assessment criteria to a range of CELTA candidates' written assignments and practical teaching over the whole course. The reports are sent to a Chief Assessor who either confirms that the tutor-in-training can be approved as a CELTA tutor or, following recommendations made by the supervisor and/or the external assessor, recommends continued training. Tutors-in-training who complete the training programme successfully are approved as assistant course tutors. Assistant course tutors must work with a main course tutor on a minimum of three subsequent courses before they can progress to becoming a main course tutor and manage their own courses. At each stage of their progression from being a tutor-in-training to becoming a main course tutor, the new tutor's assessment of CELTA candidates' work including written assignments and lessons taught, is discussed and evaluated by the training supervisor, the main course tutor and the external assessor (Cambridge English 2013).

Such extensive training provides tutors-in-training with the necessary experience of assessing candidates' performance at each stage of a CELTA course. It is fundamental in providing a benchmark for new tutors to use when applying the CELTA assessment criteria to lessons and written assignments they assess.

Becoming an assessor: Assessors-in-training

The induction process of new assessors, described in detail in the *CELTA Guidelines for Assessors-in-Training* (Cambridge ESOL undated), includes (i) a pre-assessment meeting between the assessor-in-training and the relevant CELTA Chief Assessor, (ii) an assessment of a CELTA course including assessment of prospective CELTA teachers in situ, which is attended by the assessor-in-training and Chief Assessor, and (iii) a post-assessment follow-up discussion between the Chief Assessor and assessor-in-training.

At the pre-assessment meeting the Chief Assessor and assessor-in-training discuss all aspects of a CELTA assessment and documentation involved, namely: the role of the assessor, the regulations relating to assessments, how assessments are organised, the role of Cambridge English Language Assessment and the Chief Assessors in course assessments, the procedure for assessments, and the completion of relevant reports and forms. The Chief Assessor and assessor-in-training also discuss a number of CELTA case studies which represent some cases which assessors may come across. Three examples of case studies are given below:

What would you do as an assessor in the following situations?

1. You see a candidate's written work that contains over a dozen serious language errors (other than spelling). The work has been marked as Pass with no reference in the tutor's comments to the mistakes.
2. A possible Fail candidate has left his portfolio at home on the day of the visit.
3. You have seen evidence in Teaching Practice and assignments that a candidate's language awareness is very weak. The centre is recommending a 'Pass B' in the Week Four Provisional Grading Meeting.

Assessors-in-training do not go through any additional standardisation procedures, since they are already standardised in their role as tutors. As tutors they would have completed annual standardisation tasks and their judgements would have been validated by assessors assessing the courses they work on.

After the pre-assessment stage, the assessor-in-training shadows the Chief Assessor or delegate during an assessment visit and participates as appropriate in the following:

- discussion of the documentation provided by the centre on arrival
- discussion on selecting candidate assessment portfolios for review
- review of selected portfolios
- meeting with the candidates
- observation of Teaching Practice and Teaching Practice feedback
- grading meeting
- feedback to the centre
- a post-assessment discussion (Cambridge ESOL undated: 6).

The assessment visit allows the assessor-in-training to become involved as a participant in all stages of a CELTA assessment. After the assessment visit, the assessor-in-training is advised of the content of the final grading meeting. The assessor-in-training then completes a separate electronic assessment report, which is sent to the supervising assessor for review. Based on these three stages of the training procedure, the supervising assessor either confirms the assessor-in-training as a CELTA assessor or, if appropriate, recommends a second phase of training.

Such extensive training procedures assist assessors to become cognisant with all stages of a CELTA assessment through first-hand experience and close monitoring and support. An extensive induction process like this also helps them to apply assessment criteria to a range of teaching situations and base evaluations on evidence, thus minimising the influence of personal beliefs.

Maintaining assessor standards: Tutor and assessor standardisation

Standardisation of CELTA tutors and assessors takes place online annually and involves the assessment of a video-recorded CELTA lesson and written assignments. The benchmark grades are based on Chief Assessors' grades and detailed feedback on the lesson. The objectives of the standardisation are for tutors and assessors to (re)familiarise themselves with the assessment criteria and their application. Tutors and assessors observe the recorded lesson independently, complete an assessment sheet and award a grade. The grades are then judged as either 'Satisfactory' (i.e. they agree with the benchmark grade) or 'In need of improvement' (they were either too generous or too harsh). Once tutors and assessors have completed their assessment of the lesson and have been advised of their rating, they are then asked to read the assessment sheet completed by the Chief Assessors and to compare their assessment of the lesson with the Chief Assessors' comments. Online standardisation is monitored by Chief Assessors and the Senior Assessment Manager at Cambridge English Language Assessment, who may contact tutors and assessors to provide individual feedback if they feel it is necessary to provide additional support. It is important to note that the annual standardisation of tutors and assessors is only one part of their ongoing standardisation. The 'formal' standardisation functions alongside the ongoing standardisation that takes place every time a tutor works on a course and every time an assessor assesses a course. Such a continuous ongoing approach to standardisation addresses the fact that a tutor's/assessor's status should not be dependent on evaluating one recorded lesson of a candidate they do not know in a situation with which they are not familiar, but should be dependent on a wider range of quality-assurance processes.

The annual CELTA standardisation exercise and the multi-step training process of assessors and tutors can be considered strengths of the CELTA qualification which enhance the reliability of evaluations. At the same time, the immense complexity of assessing teaching performance and the inevitable subjectivity judges bring to the process cannot be ignored. The variability of assessor/tutor judgements in the CELTA can be seen in the percentage of tutors and assessors who agree/disagree with the benchmark performances during standardisation. Data from the most recent CELTA standardisation exercise (2013) indicate that of 437 tutors and assessors, 71.85% agreed with the benchmark grade 'Pass', 15.20% gave it a 'Pass B', 1.14% awarded a 'Pass A' and 11.90% a 'Fail' mark. While it may seem disconcerting that not all participants agreed with the benchmark, it is important to remind ourselves that in performance assessment rater disagreements are a 'fact of life'. The available academic literature on rater agreement in writing and speaking assessment, for example, has indicated that inter-rater correlations in the .75 to .85 range are the norm between trained raters (e.g. McNamara 1996), which equates to 56%–72% rater agreement.

While acknowledging the presence of assessor variability, assessment providers have a responsibility to minimise its effects. As noted earlier, in the case of CELTA, that is achieved through gathering multiple sources of evidence about a teacher's performance both diachronically (i.e. throughout the course at different points of teacher development) and synchronically (i.e. at one point in time but through a range of assessment perspectives from tutors and assessors), and by using explicit and detailed assessment criteria.

It is also important to note that agreement/disagreement with the benchmarked lesson during standardisation is just one aspect of standardisation. Beyond the standardisation process, the involvement of both tutors and assessors in making grade decisions is also an element of standardisation. Such ongoing features of the standardisation and quality assurance process supporting the CELTA enhance the reliability of the assessment. Extended survey feedback from CELTA tutors and assessors also supports this. The representative comments below are indicative of a strong theme running through the survey feedback, namely that the CELTA standardisation of tutors and assessors is seen not as a one-off event, but part of a broader process which tutors and assessors find valuable:

> When assessing a course as an external assessor I feel that I do play this [standardisation] role to some extent, especially with fairly new tutors. But it works both ways — assessing a course and discussing observed lessons with the tutors helps in my own standardisation.

> I think a good assessor should see part of their role as helping less experienced tutors develop. I know that I have learnt a great deal from getting advice and feedback from good assessors, and I've seen plenty of other tutors benefit from it too. Just recently I assessed a very inexperienced tutor who had made a few classic clangers that I made myself when I was just starting out. I sat down with the person and talked it through. It gave me a nice feeling the next time I saw them because they said the feedback had really helped and I thought their own feedback to trainees had improved since.

As noted earlier, CELTA standardisation takes place online, a reflection of the growing use of technology in the last decade and a way to address the real-world constraints of face-to-face training and standardisation, e.g. holding annual face-to-face standardisation meetings for a relatively small cadre of tutors and assessors who are based around the world in different time zones and with different levels of professional commitments is extremely resource-heavy and is a key militating factor against such an approach.

The available research on online training has highlighted several advantages of online assessor training, such as its time-saving and flexibility aspects, and more opportunity for reflection (Hamilton, Reddel and Spratt 2001). Caveats of online assessor training have also been noted, mainly the absence of discussion opportunities — a valuable process of synergy — in an online training environment.

The CELTA survey feedback indicated that many CELTA tutors and assessors consider online standardisation a limitation of the current standardisation model since it does not allow for discussion and exchange of ideas. In the words of some CELTA tutors and assessors:

> The move to having only online standardization is, to my mind, problematic. It locks trainers into binary responses, which is potentially a danger with criterion-referenced assessment. This means that tutors/assessors often have a

sense of failure or grievance with the 'correct' answer. Either way they are less likely to re-think their evaluation. Face-to-face standardisation with trainers from different centres allows for a negotiated response and I think is likely to lead to tutors/assessors re-evaluating their judgments in a more constructive way.

I miss the face to face element where open discussion was available. This discussion between members of the community I found enriching. I believe this to be especially so for tutors who work in places where they are the only resident tutor.

I consider that the standardisation where we were not allowed to discuss with colleagues was a very unnatural situation. On a CELTA course and at assessment, the actual assessment is done in collaboration not isolation.

A possible improvement on the present system would be a blended standardisation approach which combines both face-to-face and online elements. Online meetings or webinars could be used to allow some exchange of views in real time.

A further constraint of CELTA standardisation relates to the numbers of benchmarked lessons used. Only one lesson is used annually — a number which could be considered inadequate. At the same time, each benchmarked lesson becomes part of a bank of standardisation materials which can be accessed at any time and which can support standardisation and training.

The range of grades illustrated by the benchmarked samples is a further issue which has to be addressed in the context of assessor standardisation. Ideally, the bank of available material should contain several examples of all available grades. In reality, it is easier to include performances exemplifying the middle bands in a scale and more difficult to show examples of top and bottom bands. CELTA is no exception. While this uneven distribution reflects a normal curve of grade distribution, where a much larger part of the population is in the middle, there are also interesting additional considerations at play. A key consideration, for example, is the ethics of including a Fail lesson which shows a teacher in a unfavourable light. A possible way of addressing this need in the future could be through the use of parts of lessons, in addition to entire lessons, which illustrate different CELTA teachers attempting the same aspect of a lesson (e.g. giving instructions) with varying degrees of success. Such an approach which uses both whole lessons and parts of lessons could provide more focused guidance for assessors and tutors.

A further issue regarding a bank of standardisation materials is the need not just for a wide range of grades/ability levels, but also for contexts. Indeed, this issue emerged from the CELTA survey. In the words of one respondent:

> The lessons we see take place in a very different setting from my own, with very different classroom conditions and students. I would like to see a wider variety — and particularly, at least once in a while, a monolingual group. This said, it is not the only 'standardisation practice' I get as we do internal standardisation, and assessing also meets this purpose.

CELTA grading and awarding

As explained earlier, the external assessor holds a formal grading meeting with tutors at the centre to discuss and agree provisional recommended candidate grades. The CELTA assessment criteria are fundamental in deciding on recommended grades and assessment is based on performance throughout the entire course:

> In agreeing provisional and final recommended grades, it should be borne in mind that candidates cannot be judged on the basis of their performance on any particular occasion. The decision as to whether a candidate should receive a particular grade must be on the basis of the candidate's development throughout the course and their ability to meet the specified assessment criteria as documented in their portfolio. Decisions about candidates' grades should not be based solely on candidates' performance on the day of the assessor's visit (Cambridge English 2014b: 30).

This requirement reflects the CELTA ethos of continuous assessment and minimises the effect of 'exit velocity', i.e. basing the final grade on, for example, just one pass-level lesson towards the end of the course. CELTA tutors give grades for individual lessons, a practice which provides greater transparency for the assessment process. A Pass-level teacher would need to have most lessons graded at Pass standard in order to pass the course.

A final recommended grade is given at the end of the course and is based on the tutor's recommendation, a discussion with the assessor and an endorsement by the assessor. Before they are issued, the final grades are agreed by a Grade Review/Award Committee comprising the Senior

Assessment Manager responsible for the CELTA award and a number of Chief Assessors. The Grade Review/Award Committee uses the assessor's report and the centre's grade form in endorsing the final grades. In addition, portfolios of all candidates who were recorded as borderline Pass/Fail or Fail at the provisional grading meeting are scrutinised at the Grade Review/ Award meeting. The different levels of decision-making — by tutor, assessor, Grade Review/Award Committee — and the range of evidence considered at the Grading/Awarding stage is a further illustration of the procedures in place to reduce subjectivity of judgement, even if it cannot be fully eliminated.

CELTA teachers are awarded a grade of Fail, Pass, Pass B and Pass A. The current criteria for distinction between these four grades were revised in 2013 in order to expand the information given for each grade and clearly capture essential characteristics which distinguish across grades (See Appendix A of the volume). Clearly articulated levels of performance — within one qualification and across qualifications — enhance the accuracy of a judgement. Such descriptions of different levels/grades would also serve as more useful statements of learning objectives for teachers. In the words of one CELTA survey respondent:

> While they [grade descriptions] are obvious to us as tutors, they could be more defined for candidates. Even though we go over the grades on the first day of the course, if the candidates do not directly ask about them again, we don't know how much has really stuck with them or whether or not they actually know what it means to have achievements significantly higher than that required at pass-level, especially since 'pass-level' is so broad.

The development of the revised CELTA grade descriptions has been a multi-phase process which involved the production of draft grade descriptors by a group of experts, followed by a consultation with the CELTA Chief Assessors, and leading to revisions to the draft descriptors and a larger-scale survey of all tutors and assessors inviting feedback on the proposed grade descriptors. The involvement of a range of stakeholders in the drafting of grade descriptors describing teaching performance adds credibility to the assessment tools by taking into account different perspectives and ultimately contributing to its validity. There is also some food for thought here for future development, since stakeholders such as language school directors or professional recruitment agencies are rarely involved in decisions about professional standards. As Thornbury notes, 'negotiating professional standards without taking into account the expectations and needs of potential employers might undermine the utility and portability of the qualifications' (2014, personal communication).

Conclusion

We have outlined the various aspects of CELTA assessment which enhance the standardisation and fairness of the qualification and have discussed the important role of a range of procedures which support the rigour and quality of the qualification. It is also important not to lose sight of caveats and challenges in the context of CELTA and teaching qualifications in general. One of the main challenges relates to maintaining a rigorous process to ensure reliable and accurate assessments. As discussed earlier, in the context of CELTA this is addressed through the collection and integration of *multiple sources of evidence* gathered at different development points in a prospective teacher's development and from different assessment perspectives, e.g. from tutors, from external assessors and also from a wider group of Chief Assessors. And yet work remains to be done in this area. Feedback from tutors during standardisation, for example, indicates that they follow a complex process in deciding on a final grade. Sometimes the grade they give may deviate from the benchmark grade, and yet there is overlap between their judgement of individual assessment criteria and the Chief Assessors' judgement of those assessment criteria. In other words, there is agreement in terms of the smaller building blocks (i.e., detailed assessment criteria) but disagreement about the final grade. The opposite is observed as well — different tutors/assessors may give the same grade as the benchmarked grade, but arrive at it through attention to different assessment criteria. Such rating processes and results are not new and have been well documented in the literature on writing assessment (Lumley and McNamara 1995). Understanding this process in greater depth in the context of CELTA would lead to useful insights which could inform decisions about assessor agreement/disagreement.

A further challenge relates to the purely online nature of standardisation. As noted earlier, a preference for a blended online/face-to-face approach was a strong theme in the assessor and tutor survey feedback. This decision is heavily constrained by practicality considerations, but considering the complexity of assessing teaching performance, it would seem important to consider possibilities which involve discussion between assessors/tutors.

Reliable assessments are a function not just of judges giving evaluations, but also of the tools they use to form a judgement, i.e. the assessment criteria, scales and descriptors. As we have explained, CELTA qualifications are based on a detailed and explicit set of assessment criteria and a holistic grade profile. Such assessment tools have been used successfully in the assessment of CELTA teachers, but they would benefit from empirical validation (either *a priori* in the case of future assessment instruments or *a posteriori* in the case of existing ones) through a range of qualitative and quantitative empirical methodologies. Such an empirically driven approach, which would inform an area of research aptly referred to by Shavelson, Webb and Burstein (1986) as the 'measurement of teaching', has the potential to provide useful empirical insights to support assessment scales and criteria.

Finally, even though we have discussed in detail the assessment underlying the CELTA qualification, it would be beneficial to consider it in the broader context of teacher competence. Developing clear standards of teaching performance would be an ambitious undertaking in the absence of comprehensive and clear theoretical and empirical guidance from the English as a second/foreign language teacher education literature on what constitutes different levels of teaching competence. As Strong, Gargani and Hacifazlioglu (2011) contend, in the field of general education, while there is widespread agreement that the best predictor of student learning is high-quality teaching, identifying and defining effective teaching and describing it in terms of levels does not enjoy such strong consensus. Recent work by Hattie (2012) on integrating and synthesising results of individual studies from the general education field does offer a promising way forward, however. The task of defining and assessing teachers' practices is more complex in the area of second/foreign language teaching, not least because of the 'dilemma of language as content' (Freeman, McBee Orzulak and Morrissey 2009: 79), where language is both the content of learning and the medium. Defining teaching practice at different levels of ability and capturing it in a manner which is unambiguous, theoretically driven and supported by all stakeholders involved is arguably one of the biggest challenges facing not just the CELTA qualification, but all evaluation frameworks of teaching practice.

Notwithstanding the challenges associated with capturing the ephemeral nature of teaching practice, we hope that our discussion of the possibilities and limitations within one examination board will serve as a useful beginning of a dialogue among the stakeholders involved which will inform and support future work on assessing teaching practice.

References

Alderson, C., Clapham, C. and Wall, D. (1995) *Language Test Construction and Evaluation.* Cambridge: Cambridge University Press.

Ball, D. L. and Rowan, B. (2004) Introduction: Measuring instruction, *The Elementary School Journal* 105 (1), 3–10.

Borg, S. (2012) Practices and principles in language teacher education: Case studies of experienced Delta trainers, paper presented at the Cambridge English Language Assessment Seminar, November 2012, Cambridge, UK.

British Council (2011) *CPD Framework for Teachers of English*, available online: www. britishcouncil.org/continual-professional-development-framework-3.pdf

British Council (2012) *Going Forward: Continuing Professional Development for English Teachers in the UK.* London: British Council, available online: britishcouncil. org/sites/ec/files/B413%20CPD%20for%20TeachTea_v2_0.pdf

Cambridge English (2013) *Cambridge English Teaching Qualifications: CELTA Trainer in Training Guidelines.* Cambridge: Cambridge English Language Assessment.

Cambridge English (2014a) *Cambridge English Teaching Framework*, available online: www. cambridgeenglish.org/cambridge-english-for/teachers/professional-development/teaching-framework/

Cambridge English (2014b) *CELTA Administration Handbook 2014.* Cambridge: Cambridge English Language Assessment.

Cambridge ESOL (2010) *CELTA Syllabus and Assessment Guidelines.* Cambridge: Cambridge ESOL.

Cambridge ESOL (2012) *TKT: Practical Handbook.* Cambridge: Cambridge ESOL.

Cambridge ESOL (undated) *CELTA Guidelines for Assessors-in-Training.* Cambridge: University of Cambridge Local Examinations Syndicate.

Coggshall, J. G. (2007) Communication framework for measuring teacher quality and effectiveness, *Quality National Comprehensive Centre for Teacher Quality Research and Policy Brief.* Washington, DC: National Comprehensive Center for Teacher Quality.

Danielson, C. (2008) *Enhancing Professional Practice: A Framework for Teaching.* Alexandria: Association for Supervision and Curriculum Development.

Danielson, C. (2012) Observing classroom practice, *Educational Leadership* 70 (3), 32–37.

EAQUALS (2013) *Teacher Profiling Grid*, available online: www.epg-project.eu/grid/

Edgeworth, F. Y. (1888) The statistics of examinations, *Journal of the Royal Statistical Society* 51, 599–635.

Edgeworth, F. Y. (1890) The element of chance in competitive examinations, *Journal of the Royal Statistical Society* 53, 644–663.

Finlayson, D. L. (1951) The reliability of the marking of essays, *British Journal of Educational Psychology* 21 (2), 126–134.

Freeman, D., McBee Orzulak, M. and Morrissey, G. (2009) Assessment in second language teacher education, in Burns, A. and Richards, J. C. (Eds) *The Cambridge*

Guide to Second Language Teacher Education. New York: Cambridge University Press, 77–90.

Godshalk, F. I., Swineford, F. and Coffman, W. E. (1966) *The Measurement of Writing Ability*. New York: College Entrance Examination Board.

Grossman, P. (1990) *The Making of a Teacher*. New York: Teachers College Press.

Hamilton, J., Reddel, S. and Spratt, M. (2001) Teachers' perceptions of on-line rater training and monitoring, *System* 29, 505–520.

Hattie, J. (2012) *Visible Learning for Teachers*, New York: Routledge.

Lee, G. C. and Wu, C. (2006) Enhancing the teaching experience of pre-service teachers through the use of videos in web-based computer-mediated communication (CMC), *Innovations in Education and Teaching International* 43 (4), 369–380.

Lumley, T. and McNamara, T. (1995) Rater characteristics and rater bias: Implications for training, *Language Testing* 12, 54–71.

Mathers, C., Oliva, M. and Laine, S.W.M. (2008) *Improving Instruction Through Effective Teacher Evaluation: Options for States and Districts, National Comprehensive Centre for Teacher Quality Research and Policy Brief.* Washington, DC: National Comprehensive Center for Teacher Quality.

McNamara, T. (1996) *Measuring Second Language Performance*. London: Longman.

Myford, C. M. and Wolfe, E.W. (2003) Detecting and measuring rater effects using many-facet Rasch measurement: Part 1, *Journal of Applied Measurement* 4 (4), 386–422.

Myford, C. M. and Wolfe, E.W. (2004) Detecting and measuring rater effects using many-facet Rasch measurement: Part 2, *Journal of Applied Measurement* 5 (2), 189–227.

Rossner, R. (2009) Developing common criteria for comparison and assessment in language teacher education, *Research Notes* 38, 4–14.

Shavelson, R. J., Webb, N. M. and Burstein, L. (1986) Measurement of teaching, in Wittrock, M C (Ed) *Handbook of Research on Teaching*. New York: Macmillan, 50–91.

Shulman, L. (1986) Those who understand knowledge growth in teaching, *Educational Researcher* 15 (2), 4–31.

Spolsky, B. (1995) *Measured Words: The Development of Objective Language Testing*. Oxford: Oxford University Press.

Strong, M., Gargani, J. and Hacifazlioglu, O. (2011) Do we know a successful teacher when we see one? Experiments in the identification of effective teachers, *Journal of Teacher Education* 62 (4), 367–382.

Tsui, A. and Nicholson, S. (1999) A hypermedia database and English as a second language teaching knowledge enrichment, *Journal of Information Technology for Teacher Education* 8 (2), 215–237.

Weigle, S. (1994) Effects of training on raters of ESL compositions, *Language Testing* 11 (2), 197–223.

Weir, C. J. (2005) *Language Testing and Validation: An Evidence-based Approach*. Basingstoke: Palgrave Macmillan.

Willmott, A. S. and Nuttall, D. L. (1975) *The Reliability of Examinations at 16+*. London: Macmillan.

7 Developing and assessing English language teacher trainers

Marie Morgan
Freelance teacher trainer, writer and teacher

Background

In the world of English language teaching (ELT), training programmes continue to proliferate. The demand for qualified teachers has been driven by a number of factors. Firstly, more and more public and private institutions demand a higher level of certification of teachers, particularly where an educational culture has reframed their definition of 'learner-centredness' to include 'customer-centredness'. Secondly, increasing globalisation and the growth of English as a Lingua Franca, or ELF (Jenkins 2000), has also increased the need of citizens of different countries and mother tongues to communicate with others whose first language is not English even more than with 'native speakers'. Thirdly, changing global demographics have affected local ELT needs within the national school systems in some countries. A report published in *Education Week* in 2009 stated there were 4.5 million English as a Second Language (ESL) students in compulsory education in the USA (K-12 settings) between 2005–2006, an 18% increase from 2000 (He, Prater and Steed 2011). Finally, proficiency in English, as demonstrated through international exams such as the International English Language Testing System (IELTS), is increasingly demanded as part of citizenship application requirements for countries such as the UK, Canada, and Australia (www.ielts.org).

Given this continually changing landscape of expectations, English language teachers clearly require training and development to initiate and sustain their practice across time, and to respond effectively and appropriately in different contexts. Equally important is the training and development of those whose task is to train teachers.

ELT teachers and teacher trainers: Perceptions of self and of others

Grass-root concerns have often been raised about the professional status of English Language (EL) teachers. In 1974, Allen and Pit Corder noted that most people 'for the most part wandered into ELT, which was not then recognised as a specialism within language teaching' (1974: 12–18). Small-scale research on a group of Polish and expatriate teachers in Poland suggested they saw their entry into teaching as accidental or 'a second choice' (Johnston 1997). These teachers lacked 'a shared discourse of profession' (Johnston 1997: 703), which includes being 'administered by [their] members', having 'clear standards and processes for entry and licensure' and operating 'from a recognized and defined knowledge base' (Freeman 1991: 2). Yet in spite of a less than auspicious entry to the field, many individuals have made the transition from ELT teacher to teacher trainer while others have gone on to become conference keynote speakers and ELT authors of note, past and present.

Breshears (2004) asserts that within ELT, the lack of social standing — so freely granted to many other professions — is well documented in the literature. In her Canadian context, she saw the position of ELT teachers 'uncomfortably' resting somewhere between unskilled workers and highly trained professionals. Overhearing English language teaching being described as 'the lowest of the low' (Breshears 2004: 23) at an ELT conference served only to confirm her perception. Surprisingly perhaps, this sense of marginalisation does not seem to be limited to English language teachers. Beaven's findings from a small scale research project (presented at IATEFL 2013, Liverpool) reported one of the 30 ELT teacher trainer participants as stating 'it's highly skilled work ... there's no recognition whatsoever'. Interestingly, even the work of teacher trainers within mainstream education has been described as being perceived as nonspecialised and under-valued (Korthagen, Loughran and Lunenberg 2005).

It could be argued that one way in which the professional status of individual teachers, those who train them, and the field as a whole may be viewed more positively from outside (as well as within), rests on the quality of the training provided to teachers and importantly to its teacher trainers. Around the world, a number of organisations are helping to set benchmarks for the quality of training and development provision — for example, the Office of Qualifications and Examinations Regulation (Ofqual) in the UK, the Languages Council and TESL Canada. Initiatives such as the European Profiling Grid recently published by Evaluation and Accreditation of Quality in Language Services (EAQUALS) and other members of the EPG Project team (2013), and the Cambridge English Professional Development Framework (Cambridge English 2014) serve the same purpose.

The purpose of educational training standards for teachers is to ensure quality in teacher training programmes. Such standards offer a more structured approach to the professional development of those wishing to enter and progress within the field. It follows that those who *train* teachers must then undertake training that meets equally high standards. This chapter seeks to establish a link between a number of paradigms adopted in ELT trainer training with those adopted in ELT and mainstream teacher training. It will then describe one particular approach to ELT trainer training that has been offered over the last three to four decades through what are now called the Cambridge English Teaching Qualifications (formerly Cambridge ESOL, and previously the University of Cambridge Local Examinations Syndicate). The ways in which these paradigms are operationalised within Cambridge English trainer training will be discussed with reference to practitioners, and illustrated with comments collected in interviews with trainers (Morgan 2007). The procedures by which trainers-in-training are assessed within the Cambridge English Teaching Qualifications framework will also be described. The initial selection of potential trainers is a matter for individual institutions and therefore beyond the scope of this chapter although it is worth noting the view in both mainstream education and ELT that 'good teachers are not necessarily good educators' (Bullough 2005). The chapter will conclude with some reflections on becoming, behaving and being a teacher trainer, and the role the Cambridge English trainer training programmes can play in the development of ELT trainers.

Teacher training and trainer training models: Parallel paradigms

In this chapter, the terms 'trainee teacher', 'teacher trainer',

'trainer-in-training' (i.e. a teacher learning to be a trainer) will be used for both ELT and mainstream educational contexts. A distinction is drawn between 'trainee teachers' and 'novice teachers'; the former refer here to prospective teachers on a training programme, the latter to new teachers in post. Opinions differ about the use of the terms 'teacher trainer' or 'teacher educator'. Interestingly, in a study of six ELT teacher trainers with training experience ranging from nine months to 15 years, not one was prepared to accept the title of 'teacher educator' (Morgan 2007). Whether this is as a result of personal choice or conventional wisdom is open to debate.

Though the contexts may be very different, similar trends have occurred within ELT teacher training and mainstream teacher training in terms of initial pre-service training of trainee teachers. Whilst agreeing with Nunan on the need to 'exercise caution in applying research findings derived in one context to another context removed in space and time' (1992:xii), the comparison of similar processes and practices still seems of value. If EL teaching and teacher training are to move from what some have seen as a marginalised position within the teaching domain, the need to look beyond this territory to wider landscapes within education and assessment seems one way in which bridges can be built, connections made, and mutual enrichment assured, as suggested by Beaven (2004) and Morgan (2007).

The craft model

A century ago, teaching was 'mastered' primarily through experience, with no formalised theoretical professional training. Initial teacher training in mainstream education was often based on a 'craft model' (Korthagen and Russell 1995: 187). As such, it was often conducted within an 'apprenticeship' with an experienced teacher after a study of the relevant subject matter; young trainees learned 'by imitating', according to Wallace (1991: 6). The rather unfortunate phrase 'sitting by Nellie' (Randall and Thornton 2001: 35, citing Stones) — akin to Lortie's 'apprenticeship of observation' (1975) — seemed to be the dominant model in action. Embedded within this approach to teacher training lay a view of teaching as a set of routines and behaviours which could simply be copied and applied, regardless of context and individuality. Experience of teaching was assumed to be synonymous with the necessary 'expertise' to train new teachers, and no formalised trainer training was therefore required.

It is perhaps hardly surprising that the 'drift and shift' into English language teaching referred to earlier was to some extent mirrored in the role-transition from teacher to teacher trainer within ELT, notwithstanding early attempts made by some institutions to develop their own programme of training trainers, e.g. International House London (Duff 1988). As in mainstream education, it seemed that an experienced language teacher could also become a trainer of teachers, with no specific training for the role changes involved. As late as 1997, Bax (citing Aboshiha 1995) proclaimed that 'many teacher educators have little or no training themselves and are effectively picking up their skills on the job', whilst McGrath (1997: viii) noted that learning about being a teacher trainer was something of a 'selfdirected endeavour'. A similar theme was to emerge in articles discussing the transition from mainstream teacher to mainstream teacher trainer. Tracing the development of a group of first-order practitioners (i.e. school teachers) to a Higher Education environment where they became second-order practitioners (working as teacher educators), Murray and Male reinforced earlier claims made by Gilpin (2003) that 'induction procedures for teacher educators in England are highly variable in the HE [higher education] context' (2005: 28). Zeichner's personal reflection on his transition from a teacher to a 'cooperating teacher' tasked with mentoring prospective teachers also highlighted a need to 'find the support that I needed in my work as a teacher educator on my own' (2005: 3).

In the absence of a standardised procedure, professional development for teacher trainers within and outside of ELT would appear to have developed in an ad hoc manner. Within ELT, for as long as teacher training was undertaken by self-selected 'master trainers', there was also likely to be no 'formalised' consensus on how to approach the process of trainer training or how to assess its outcomes. Meanwhile, ELT trainer training may have been at risk of perpetuating a form of 'ELT-practitioner cloning', particularly in certificated programmes run on a commercial basis. Speaking of her own experience of being an ELT teacher trainer, one very experienced trainer of trainers commented that trainer training was all 'very unstructured' in the beginning, and 'initially ... the first experience of training others to be trainers was a kind of traditional apprenticeship model of passing on experiences ...' (Trainer P, personal conversation, 2006). Whether found in the training of teachers or in the training of trainers, one of the problems of the craft model is its tendency to preserve the status quo by encouraging imitation of the 'master trainer'. In mainstream teacher education, Smith also noted the danger for 'fossilization', astutely asserting that 'professional fossilization endangers professional curiosity' (2003: 203–204).

The craft model may have led to teacher trainers delivering course content to trainee teachers in the same way as they had observed in their own trainers, but this approach did not always produce standardised assessments of practical teaching. Research by Mackay (cited in Rosenberg 2002: 23) suggested that different assessors did not necessarily perceive demonstrations of the same classroom practices to be of equal importance in terms of how they contributed to effective teaching. It was argued that 'assessment may be as much a feature of the assessor as of the candidate and the way in which the lesson proceeds.' Rosenberg (2002), citing Piper's 1996 research on the RSA/UCLES CTEFLA (the Royal Society of Arts/UCLES), concluded that in spite of guidelines provided at the time by UCLES in order to achieve a standardised assessment, teacher trainers 'do not share a common set of priorities and there are differences between their espoused views and their actual practices'. In part, it may have been concerns such as these, linked to broader changing views on the nature of teaching and learning, which led to some review of the professional development of EL teacher trainers within the Cambridge English Teaching Qualifications. (See summary by Poulter 2007.)

Competency-based approaches

A shift away from 'imitation' to the establishment of criteria against which good teaching could be assessed led to competency-based teacher education. Described as the 'formulation of concrete and observable criteria for good teaching', this approach was promoted as a means which 'could serve as a basis for the training of teachers' (Korthagen and Russell 1995: 188). This approach to mainstream teacher training sought to itemise and isolate different teaching skills and behaviours to be developed and assessed by teacher trainers. This movement to a competency-based description and assessment of trainee teachers seemed to be a global phenomenon. There were similarities of focus in teacher training programmes in England, Wales, the Netherlands, and Switzerland (see Smith 2003). With content, pedagogy and organisation areas, reflective practice, and communication/group facilitation were identified as common competency areas. However, just as criticisms have been levelled at craft models, competency-based models have not been spared their critics either. Hagger and McIntyre (2000: 485) proclaim that 'long lists of "competencies" or "standards"' were produced with neither reference to rationale or explanation of the 'conception of teaching expertise which underlies the lists'.

Within some sections of the world of ELT trainer training, this trend towards 'competencies' was also reflected in an initial mapping of a pathway of professional development and recognition for those who wished to make the vertical shift from teacher to teacher trainer. The implications of this for the training of trainers meant a shift from the earlier craft model or paradigm; the trainer was now required to be more than just a 'transmitter' of good practice.

A set of competencies required by teacher trainers was developed by Cambridge English Teaching Qualifications through a consultation process, which led to the development of a trainer training programme to help calibrate a trainer-in-training's understanding of the principles of the work (see Appendix 1 of the chapter). The programme also included supervised practice in the skills necessary to operate within the shifting sub-roles required of a teacher trainer: assessor/gatekeeper; counsellor/facilitator; instructor; model; mentor; reflector; service provider; coordinator/team worker (Morgan 2007). This pathway of professional development to support the development from teacher to teacher trainer/assessor within the Cambridge English Teaching Qualifications' framework will be described below. The development and assessment of competencies in those wishing to train EL teachers also assumed shared understanding of what constitutes teaching expertise and that those training to be trainers had been identified as having demonstrated a certain level of a shared view of expertise.

The concept of 'expertise'

Critics of the articulation of competencies and the 'institutionalisation' or standardisation of the training of teachers will often mention the lack of 'commonality'. A set of effective teaching principles, behaviours and skills can be identified, but the world of teaching is so diverse that their universal application to different contexts is impossible. Consequently, reaching a consensus on such competencies may be more 'exceptions to the rule' rather than 'accepted by rule'. Related to this debate are the various interpretations of the concept of teacher expertise. Although many teachers may be uncomfortable in positioning themselves as 'experts', it is presumed that most students would expect their teachers to have more expertise than they do. Similarly, those in training to be teachers could be expected to have these expectations of their trainers, no doubt as concerned as Widdowson was more than two decades ago about those 'pretenders' ... of minimal educational qualifications and expertise claiming the status of teacher trainers' (1992: 338).

However, even if teachers or teacher trainers are unhappy at being thought of or positioned as 'experts', two useful constructs emerge from the work of Hatano and Inagaki in terms of 'routine experts' vs. 'adaptive experts' (Lin, Schwartz and Bransford undated). While both kinds of expert are said to continue to learn over a lifetime, routine experts are thought to develop competencies that they apply with increasing efficiency. On the other hand, adaptive experts have the ability to 'verbalize the principles underlying [their] skills, the ability to judge conventional and non-conventional versions of skills as appropriate, and the ability to modify or invent skills according to local constraints' (Lin *et al.* undated). It is interesting to note that adaptive expertise is discussed as a 'gold standard' in a document entitled *How People Learn* (Bransford *et al.* 2000) (a framework used by the National Academy of Science Committee published by the National Research Council, US).

When teachers become teacher trainers, they can experience some role-shift tension (Hargreaves 1972), and feel initially insecure when suddenly positioned as 'novices-assumed-experts' (Murray and Male 2005). Such tension may have implications for their ability to systematically and consistently assess the work of trainee teachers. All six ELT trainers in the study by Morgan (2007) reported experiencing challenges related to the multiple roles of assessor: gatekeeper/counsellor; facilitators, regardless of length of experience of the work. One experienced teacher trainer admitted she still 'agonised' over grading lessons and individual teachers (Trainer T, collected in Morgan 2007). Comments of this kind may not be unusual amongst teacher trainers whose work involves this continuum of developer-assessor roles. In discussing 'role sets and networks', Wright (1987:

6–9) suggests that people may experience some inner conflict where the 'personality of the individual is at odds with the role'. Teacher trainers need support in order to help them overcome such role tension and move from a 'routine' to an 'adaptive' zone of operation. Dealing with the 'real time' circumstances of a face-to-face teacher training course demands appropriate and organic responses, not simply 'efficient' ones. In addition, other bodies of knowledge may be necessary within trainer-in-training programmes to help trainers assist trainee and novice teacher trainers navigate between 'developer' and 'assessor' sub-roles.

The role of reflection

Movements in mainstream education in the 1980s leaned towards a more reflective approach towards teaching, and the increasing recognition of the cognitive processes involved in teaching. They foreshadowed Kumaravadivelu's reminder that 'in order to make any meaningful shift, we need to first go beyond the transmission models of teacher education' (2012: 7). Though dismissive of the 'overlapping dimensions' of globalised ELT today, he extols the virtue of moving away from a 'pre-selected and predetermined body of knowledge to a transformative perspective that seeks to transform an information-oriented teacher educator into an inquiry-oriented one' (Kumaravadivelu 2012: 7). There has been debate over the merits of different forms of reflection. Brookfield (1995: 8) takes a pragmatic view of this when he says that it is not inherently 'critical'. For him, it is quite possible to teach reflectively while focusing solely on the nuts and bolts of classroom process. Randall and Thornton (2001) point out that novice teachers are indeed often concerned with the 'technical' rather than the political or ideological as they seek to establish themselves in the classroom.

Building a desire, ability, and willingness to reflect in and on practice would seem to be a valuable strand within initial EL teacher training programmes — though the continuum of development that a teacher goes through must also be taken into account in terms of the expectations on focus and quality. It is possible that if reflection is also included in the final assessment of suitability to gain a qualification, a trainee teacher may simply 'compliantly reflect' in line with what they believe to be the expectation in order to meet requirements to gain certification. Furthermore, linked to notions of the continuum of novice-expert (Berliner 1988; Tsui 2003), trainee teachers and novice teachers alike may direct their reflections to immediate concerns (such as classroom management) rather than more 'critical reflection'. Novice teachers are reported as moving through somewhat predictable stages in their life cycle as a teacher from 'novice' to 'expert' (Randall and Thornton 2001: 33). This view of a progression through 'stages' of development may in itself determine the depth of reflection individuals are capable of at any point in their professional life-cycle. Trainers-in-training may likewise demonstrate a tendency to be more concerned with routine tasks than with reflecting on their own development as a trainer, or focusing on the development of their own trainee teachers. This may also have a bearing on how EL teacher trainers handle trainee teacher assessment when reflection is built into their course criteria or competencies. Behind such notions lies the assumption that teacher trainers themselves are capable of appropriate reflective depth and focus, that 'life-cycle' stages are linear, and that it is both possible and appropriate to evaluate a teacher or a trainer on the basis of their stated reflections. (See Delaney, Chapter 5.)

Just as it is widely accepted that professional development for teachers needs to be a continuing process, so too should professional development for trainers. If professional development is to be seen as part of lifelong learning and to have ongoing impact, then it is incumbent upon both the individual and the institutions for which they work that opportunities for ongoing professional development be offered, if not mandated, beyond initial training programmes for both novice teachers and teacher trainers. Linked to this is the need for teacher trainers to be aware of the concepts of the 'life cycle/stages' in their own development, as well as within trainee and novice teacher development.

Communities of practice

Beyond individual teacher or teacher trainer development, however, are the opportunities for professional development and training within more social forms of entry into larger 'communities of practitioners', if not communities of practice (Lave and Wenger 1991). The concept of legitimate peripheral participation (Lave and Wenger 1991: 11) attempts to expand beyond the traditional notions related to apprenticeship. Described as 'an interactive process in which the apprentice engages by simultaneously performing in several roles — status subordinate, learning practitioner, aspiring expert' (Lave and Wenger 1991: 23), it suggests the construction of identities within a vocational context. By participating with 'old-timers', 'newcomers' participate in the actual practices of an expert, but with limited responsibility. The study by Delaney (2007) of a group of trainers who had participated in the Certificate in Teaching English to Speakers of Other Languages (CELTA) training-in-training programme reported that having an 'expert' practitioner both to observe and to engage with in dialogue was one of the features which participants felt had played an important role in their learning. This process helped 'newcomers' develop a 'multi-membership' of the community as well as acquire the language of this community. For some EL teacher trainers, this 'multi-membership' is in evidence where they remain a teacher while also undertaking teacher training. As noted, some teacher trainers are responsible for formal assessment as well as development, acting as both 'gatekeeper to the profession ... mentor and facilitator of reflection' (Calderhead and Shorrock 1997: 17). Wenger suggests that this 'reconciliation of identity' may be 'the most significant challenge faced by learners who move from one community of practice to another' (1998: 160), for example, from the teaching community to the ELT teacher training community. The phenomenon of 'role-shift identity' may well need to form a significant part of any trainer training programme to support novice teacher trainers in this aspect of their professional development in order that they can best support trainee teachers in theirs.

Cambridge English CELTA: The training context

The current Cambridge English Teaching Qualifications have been in operation for over 40 years in various formats. CELTA is a preservice entry-level introduction to English language teaching to adults, i.e. individuals in settings other than the compulsory school sector. It is designed for people with no teaching experience or for those with some teaching experience but no recognised qualification. It is accredited by the Office of Qualifications and Examinations Regulation (Ofqual) at Level 5 on the Qualifications and Credit Framework (QCF) for England, Wales and Northern Ireland. Cambridge English also works with a range of international ELT organisations to promote the acceptance of CELTA globally. With an estimated annual candidature of 10,000–12,000, the CELTA programme is offered in over 300 centres in more than 60 countries (see www.cambridgeenglish.org/images/celta-brochure-2013.pdf). Both the CELTA (and the in-service Delta) ELT qualifications have come to be viewed as benchmarks for quality. They are increasingly named by employers around the world as one of the main qualifications for hiring teachers at pre- and in-service levels. The British Council lists the CELTA as one of two pre-service qualifications accepted for 'standard teaching roles at entry level' within their schools (www.britishcouncil.org/jobs/careers/english/teachers).

The last 25 years have seen significant development in terms of both of these teaching qualifications to bring them to this point in their evolution not only in terms of their content and structure, but also in terms of procedures by which pre-service trainee and in-service teachers are assessed. These changes reflect developments in the understanding of teaching and learning as well as the ways by which assessment of teachers' knowledge and skills can be evidenced. These changes within the Cambridge English Teaching Qualifications to both syllabus and assessment have had an impact on how teacher trainers approach the delivery of material and the evaluation of trainee teachers. They have placed increased demands on teacher trainers to ensure that they equip trainee teachers more fully to meet not only the needs of language learners but also the constantly evolving requirements of accreditation bodies tasked with quality control, as mentioned above. These changes have in turn underlined how teacher trainers themselves need to be better equipped to deliver such courses through participation in structured teacher trainer-in-training programmes. It can be argued that teaching qualifications such as those in the Cambridge English framework have therefore not only had a significant impact on increasing both the professionalism and credibility of teachers within the field, but also on the teacher trainers responsible for their delivery.

The increased clarity and specificity in the focus and manner of assessment of trainee teachers has required a similar shift in terms of assessing the suitability of those wishing to become teacher trainers. Trainers are responsible not only for helping to develop teachers' potential, but also for assessing pre- and in-service teachers' abilities to cope with increasingly sophisticated and diverse markets. As such, the role of teacher trainers as gatekeepers and 'standard-bearers and setters', and not just 'cloners', has taken on more significance in recent years.

The CELTA trainer-in-training programme

The CELTA trainer-in-training programme was developed in the 1990s in recognition of the need for greater transparency and standardisation to support training delivered in an increasing number of global contexts. In part, its mandate was to standardise the pathways and means by which EL teachers made the vertical role-shift to EL teacher trainers, thus enabling them to deliver CELTA pre-service courses to consistent syllabus and assessment criteria. Previously, the lack of structure — or indeed a complete absence of any kind of training programme for an earlier era of teacher trainers — did not always help to create a smooth transition from teacher to teacher trainer. One such CELTA trainer said of his entry into this work: 'When I first started training, I felt badly equipped and scared of being found out by the trainees (Trainer S, collected in Morgan 2007). Another trainer described feeling 'daunted. I know how to teach but I didn't know how best to communicate this knowledge' (Trainer G, collected in Morgan 2007). This is not to say that since the advent of the Cambridge English trainer-in-training programmes novice teacher trainers do not feel any anxiety: 'When I first started training, I felt overwhelmed by the amount and importance of the administrative work involved in running a CELTA course but confident about my abilities to provide input sessions and lesson planning guidance ...' (Trainer D, collected in Morgan 2007).

The CELTA trainer-in-training programme was designed to develop 'both the general skills and competencies common to all training contexts and the specific training skills relevant to contexts where formal assessment is part of that process' (Poulter 2001: 27).

Appendix 1 (taken from Cambridge ESOL 2013) shows the full list of competencies for assistant trainers and course leaders (main course tutors). The following extract indicates the span of competencies expected of a CELTA teacher trainer:

- knowledge/skills related to methodology content
- knowledge/skills related to oral and written lesson preparation, supervision, and feedback
- knowledge/skills related to assessment of written assignments and teaching practice
- knowledge/skills related to approaches to teaching and learning

- organisational skills, such as time management, prioritisation
- personal and interpersonal skills/qualities such as enthusiasm, counselling skills, reflection, tactfulness.

The development of this trainer-in-training programme at CELTA, and later at Delta level, has no doubt had a significant impact upon the standardisation of training of trainers working on the Cambridge English Teacher Qualifications. It allows for 'customising' of content, relative to any pre-existing training experiences that the proposed trainer-in-training may have. It has also provided external recognition for the status of teacher trainer, which for many is a source of personal and professional pride. As one trainer interviewed remarked, 'it's quite an achievement to actually ... teach and train English teachers, me not being a native speaker, and that's why... I actually feel quite proud of what I have achieved. Because I've always felt that ... not being a native speaker, I always have to be *better* than the others to be considered *equal* to them ... I can't tell you how proud my *mother* is!' (Trainer D, collected in Morgan 2007). Additionally, an EL teacher with over 23 years' experience prior to participation in the trainer-in-training programme noted that it had had an impact on his professional development not only as a teacher trainer, but also as a teacher. 'My own teaching has kind of morphed into ... a different style; the CELTA model allows me to see myself as a coach' in contrast with what he termed more 'traditional ESL roles' (Trainer A, collected in Morgan 2007).

The CELTA trainer-in-training programme involves some shadowing of experienced trainers (see Appendix 1 for details of competencies). In describing her experience of her own trainers as 'role models' whom she found 'very impressive' because of the 'way they conducted themselves in terms of their own lives and handling the courses they were running', Trainer T (collected in Morgan 2007), pointed to the value of this possibly maligned mode of trainer development. However, the CELTA programme does not rest here; it also lists competencies to be met by the CELTA trainer-in-training: the need to demonstrate evidence of the ability to reflect and be proactive, as well as the ability to assess teachers according to the criteria for the course. In this way, the trainer-in-training programme seeks to cluster together some of the very principles identified in the various models of teacher training discussed previously.

The trainer-in-training programme itself is divided into three stages —

pre-in-course and post-course. Trainer trainers oversee the trainer-in-training's work on tasks, and provide written and oral feedback. In many cases, they may be simultaneously delivering the CELTA course to a group of trainee teachers. Appendix 2 of the chapter shows examples of a selection of pre-course trainer-in-training tasks, trainer-in-training responses and reflection, and associated trainer trainer feedback. It is important that trainers-in-training spend a significant amount of time at the pre-course stage familiarising themselves with key documents. Responses to this stage allow the trainer trainer to ascertain the trainer-in-training's expectations, views about teaching and learning, and any concerns. For example, the trainer-in-training's responses in Appendix 2 include a comment that pitching input appropriately might be an area to focus on. This is commented on by the trainer and is proved subsequently to be an area requiring attention. (In Clarifying Language 2 the trainer-in-training predicts that pedagogical approaches, TTT (Test, Teach, Test), TBL (Task Based Learning), functional, notional and integrated approaches will all be covered in one session. This shows he was as yet unaware of the amount of input a trainee teacher can meaningfully engage with in a single training session.) For trainers-in-training there is often an unspoken tension between becoming what Murray and Male (2005) describe as 'experts-become-novices' and 'novices-assumed-experts'. On the one hand, they come to the training programme and process with substantial teaching experience behind them, and yet are now learners again. On the other hand, within a short space of time, they must also demonstrate to the trainer trainer, and ultimately to trainee teachers, that they have the required skill set to deliver a course successfully and evaluate trainee teachers' practical classroom skills.

During the in-course stage of the programme, trainers-in-training work under supervision and with support (see Appendix 3 of the chapter). Engin (2013) notes the influence of Vygotsky's concept of the Zone of Proximal Development in trainer talk with trainee teachers on CELTA courses. In that context, she saw an overlap with scaffolding which she feels is effective if 'contingent on the learner' and 'appropriate to the learner at a particular time in the interaction and to move learning forward' (Engin 2013: 13). This process is also at work in the CELTA trainer-in-training programmes in terms of an 'expert other' helping to guide a 'learner' through effective support. This support is incrementally removed as the trainer-in-training comes to the end of their programme, mirroring perhaps Glaser's 'change of agency' stages during the acquisition of competence or expertise (1996: 305). Trainers-in-training are expected to question and reflect on their practices, and, significantly, to design some methodology sessions to be delivered on a live face-to-face course as part of the while-phase of their training (see Appendix 3). They must also prepare pre- or post-session worksheets for trainee teachers to complete so that trainers-in-training create some of their own sessions rather than simply continue to replicate and deliver 'set pieces' created by their own trainers. As such, this may well lay the foundations for 'adaptive expertise'. The following comment suggests the early emergence of such adaptation: 'an input session that I've done, and I think "yeah, this is great" … three courses down and suddenly I'm thinking "you know what, I need to change this; it's not working". And so there's that constant refinement …' (Trainer M, collected in Morgan 2007).

Throughout the while-stage, a focus on the assessment of trainee teachers is clearly acknowledged within the competencies listed in Appendix 1. A range of tasks is set for the trainer-in-training and these will indicate to their training supervisor, and to an external moderator, the extent to which the trainer-in-training is able to accurately assess both written and practical components of a trainee teacher's work. This is achieved by a combination of tasks, e.g. shadowing experienced trainers in a live training situation over the duration of one or more courses; shadow marking written assignments; writing shadow feedback notes on teaching practice lessons — including the allocation of an overall grade. Appendix 3 shows partial examples of this.

Trainers-in-training are also expected to participate in tutorials for candidates during which the trainee teachers are given indications as to their progress at that stage of the course in terms of an overall grade at either Pass, Pass B or Pass A level. CELTA candidates are not always successful in meeting the Pass criteria. It is therefore critical that trainers-in-training are given guidance about commenting on weak performance. The trainee teachers need to be very clear about their relative status, strengths and weaknesses, and what steps to take to overcome the latter. These messages may have significant impact on their confidence and willingness to continue to try to meet the course criteria, or even on their willingness to remain on a course. It is often within this area that most trainers-in-training and novice teacher trainers find difficulty. No amount of observing others or reading articles on how to give constructive feedback can adequately prepare a teacher trainer for what can be the most challenging aspect of this component of course delivery. Speaking of the sometimes 'violent, emotional or critical reaction of trainees' to her feedback, a highly experienced teacher trainer summed up this dilemma: 'It has taken me many years to get over the trauma of having to deal with such incidents … and I feel it never really gets any easier' (Trainer T, collected in Morgan 2007). No matter how experienced, it seems the reality of working with trainee teachers is always 'new'; sometimes experience cannot change that perception. Similarly, 'routine' expertise may be equally unhelpful if teacher trainers continue to work in formulaic ways when giving feedback and handling potentially emotionally charged situations.

Some trainers find an unexpected impact on their own teaching as a result of the attention they have to pay when observing assessed trainee teacher lessons. For another trainer, 'as I sat through those TPs and had to come up with some kind of observations, I realized the things I had to pay attention to, not just in observing but also in monitoring my *own* teaching' (Trainer A, collected in Morgan 2007). For another equally experienced classroom teacher, the process of becoming a teacher trainer meant she 'had to now think about what I did and *why*, and break it down into stages of what you do first to be able to then communicate that'. For her, the process of 'observing other trainers … was really, really useful' in helping achieve this articulation (Trainer G, collected in Morgan 2007).

Final acceptance as a CELTA teacher trainer is formalised. The trainer-in-training programme has also rightly functioned as 'gatekeeper' to ensure that those not yet considered ready (or suitable) to work as teacher trainers on courses leading to Cambridge English Teaching Qualifications will not be approved. As one experienced teacher trainer, commented: 'It shouldn't be anyone who's allowed to train teachers. You've got to show, got to be able to prove that you're good at it, you gotta earn your … you prove your mettle, and earn your stripes' (Trainer M, collected in Morgan 2007).

Trainers-in-training must collate and submit a portfolio of their work as part of the assessment at the end of their trainer-in-training programme. This includes a reflective piece about the process they have experienced based on data collected during the programme and written as part of the post-stage work (see Appendix 3). The format of this portfolio is suggestive of what

Richards and Farrell call the 'showcase portfolio' (2005: 99). It is designed to allow the individual to show themselves at their best, and can be used as part of an appraisal or as part of an application. In many cases, the vertical role-transition from teacher to trainer on successful completion of the CELTA trainer-in-training programme can lead to some form of 'promotion' and change of status.

Conclusions: Becoming, behaving and being a teacher trainer

The previous discussion has described the trainer-training programme for the Cambridge English CELTA qualification and similarities between the life cycle of a trainee teacher and a new trainer-in-training have been suggested. Looking back, it seems that much has changed for the better since the days when teacher trainers for CELTA or Delta courses were left to 'learn on the job' and assimilate what they could from watching others in 'unstructured' ways. It is important to acknowledge, however, that just as learners often learn 'different and other' to what is taught, so too do teacher trainers. Input does not always equal uptake, and many teacher trainers have honed their skills to a very high level without the aid of any training programme at all. Interestingly, recent small scale research on a group of Delta trainers by Borg (2012) suggests that, in spite of advances in the ways in which the professional development of teacher trainers seem to have been addressed through trainer-in-training programmes, practices are still informed to a large extent by models of training demonstrated by trainers' own Delta trainers or trainer trainers. This raises a note of caution that the Cambridge English trainer-in-training programmes, at both pre- and in-service level, should not be seen as the end of the process of entry into the realms of teacher training but the beginning. Training new teachers is no longer limited to the transmission of knowledge but includes an understanding of some of the beliefs about and processes involved in teaching and learning. So too, the training of new teacher trainers needs to encourage more than mere replication of existing practices in order to maximise impact on their professional development. Common ground between ELT and mainstream education suggests that much could be gained from collaborative projects. Within their own teaching domain, Calderhead and Shorrock (1997: 208) suggested 'in the interests of improving the quality of initial training, the expertise of teacher educators, in both schools and higher education, needs further exploration. The basis of this expertise needs to be made more explicit, and to be open to critical discussion.' The same can be said of the Cambridge English Teaching Qualifications 20 years on from the introduction of the trainer-in-training programmes. One experienced teacher trainer and trainer of trainers working within these qualifications commented about the process of CELTA training that 'a lot of it is done by what I would call observation and mentoring and there's very little instruction in *how* to do things. I mean, people learn how to give feedback by watching somebody else give feedback ... The system just becomes self-perpetuating with *very little outside input or influence ...*' (personal conversation, 2006; emphasis added). Even experienced teacher trainers can find themselves struggling to handle some course elements, particularly feedback, and the gamut of personal, emotional, and cognitive challenges experienced by some trainee teachers. It may be time to revisit these programmes through the experiences of individuals who have not managed to successfully demonstrate the required competencies and/ or through analyses of experiences which have caused teacher trainers themselves to feel less than fully equipped to offer appropriate support. This may mean moving beyond the field of ELT and drawing on expertise from other domains in a more formalised way, for example, from mainstream education, or specialised training organisations. It is interesting to note that many experienced CELTA and Delta teacher trainers anecdotally report having taken various courses such as Neuro-linguistic Programming, basic Counselling Skills (see Granich 1995), or even Non-Violent Communication. Some publications have long recognised the value of investigating how people train in other domains (e.g. the interview by Woodward (1990) with Turner, a person who trained people how to ride horses).

The trainer-in-training programmes have helped teachers start working as new CELTA trainers with more structure, confidence, and clarity about the means and focus of assessment. Over and above these instrumental gains, however, may lie other, less expected impacts. For one trainer reflecting on her development came the realisation that being a trainer is 'not about finely crafted input sessions and professionally produced materials', a view she had at the start of her trainer-in-training programme. Instead, she has come to see training as being about 'taking trainees through an organic process of learning and development so that they are able to see how all the "pieces fit" and at the same time can relate to the process as individuals' (Trainer T, collected in Morgan 2007).

As the Cambridge English Teaching Qualifications move forward, and as our thinking about what is required to undertake the work of being a teacher trainer on the courses evolves, it may be of benefit to undertake further exploration of trainer-in-training programmes. Research could highlight any recurring themes or motifs which novice teacher trainers experience as difficult, which in turn could identify what additional support can be given to sustain their ongoing professional development and minimise any 'burn-out' or indeed 'drop-out'. In addition, specialised modular courses for training the trainers-of-trainers could provide input on providing structure and guidance to trainers-in-training; this is an area that remains unexplored within the Cambridge English Teaching Qualifications. The introduction of the CELTA Blended Online programme has brought a new technology-based format for some elements of course delivery. Course content is delivered online in this programme and moderated through forums managed by CELTA teacher trainers with the practical teaching component remaining face-to-face. The very nature of teacher training within this course has shape-shifted, and may continue to do so even more in the future as technology makes more things possible in terms of virtual assessments. In addition to the need to be trained in e-moderation in order to deliver this blended programme, it is likely that this transition, much as any other, will bring with it other challenges for CELTA teacher trainers to manage. It will likely have different impact on their professional development and assessment as trainers.

The journey to 'becoming' a trainer, whether working on CELTA, Delta or the CELTA Online programme, has been made more explicit and transparent with the development of a range of trainer-in-training programmes. Individuals who have undertaken or delivered these programmes have gained in terms of their professional development, and their ability to handle some of the simultaneous sub-roles required of trainers. The trainer-in-training programmes have helped with 'behaving' as a teacher trainer through explicit articulation of teacher trainer competencies and the tasks required to demonstrate them. As one trainer remarked about training, 'It's not what you say … it's what you *do*' (Trainer S, collected in Morgan 2007). Yet beyond becoming and behaving as a teacher trainer is the lived reality of 'being' a teacher trainer and all that that encompasses in terms of professional and personal identity. As Wright and Bolitho (2007: 234) suggest, 'developing as a trainer is about personal development and transformation of perspectives and behaviour'. For one trainer, and many others it seems, 'what happens when you're training people is ... you meet ... yourself' (Trainer S, collected in Morgan 2007). And as Wenger would remind us, 'the work of identity is always going on' (1998: 154).

References

Allen, J. P. B. and Pit Corder, S. (1974) *Techniques in Applied Linguistics: The Edinburgh Course in Applied Linguistics*. Oxford: Oxford University Press.

Bax, S. (1997) What are we training trainers to do? Evaluating teacher education sessions within a context-sensitive framework, in McGrath, I. (Ed) *Learning to Train: Perspectives on the Development of Language Teachers*. Hemel Hempstead: Prentice Hall, 153–161.

Beaven, B. (2004) How eight English language teacher trainers made the transition from teaching to training, unpublished PhD thesis, University of Exeter.

Beaven, B. (2013) *Learning and Growing as a Teacher Educator*, paper presented at IATEFL Conference Liverpool, UK, April 2013.

Berliner, D. (1988) The development of expertise in pedagogy, paper presented at the Charles W. Hunt Memorial Lecture, American Association of Colleges for Teacher Education, New Orleans, LA, February, 1988.

Borg, S. (2012) Practices and principles in language teacher education: Case studies of experienced Delta trainers, paper presented at the Cambridge English Language Assessment Seminar, November 2012, Cambridge, UK.

Bransford, D., Brown, L. and Cooking, R. (2000) *How People Learn: Brain, Mind, Experience and School*. Washington, DC: National Research Council (US), National Academies Press.

Breshears, S. (2004) Professionalization and exclusion in ESL teaching, *TESL Canada Journal*, available online: www.teslcanadajournal.ca/index.php/tesl/article/view/1038

Brookfield, S. (1995) *Becoming a Critically Reflective Teacher*. San Francisco: JosseyBass.

Bullough, R.V. (2005) Being and becoming a mentor: School-based teacher educators and teacher educator identity, *Teaching and Teacher Education* 21 (2), 143–155.

Calderhead, J. and Shorrock, S. B. (1997) *Understanding Teacher Education: Case Studies in the Professional Development of Beginning Teachers*. Washington: Falmer Press.

Cambridge English (2013) *Cambridge English Teaching Qualifications: CELTA Trainer in Training Guidelines*. Cambridge: Cambridge English Language Assessment.

Cambridge English (2014) *Cambridge English Teaching Framework*, available online: www.cambridgeenglish.org/cambridge-english-for/teachers/professional-development/teaching-framework/

Delaney, J. (2007) Communities of practice and teacher education: The contribution of the CELTA trainer training programme, *Research Notes* 29, 19–24.

Duff, T. (1988) The preparation and development of teacher trainers, in Duff, T. (Ed) *Explorations in Teacher Training: Problems and Issues*. Harlow: Longman, 110–117.

Engin, M. (2013) Trainer talk, *English Language Teaching Journal* 67 (1), 11–19.

Evaluation and Accreditation of Quality in Language Services (2013) *European Profiling Grid*, available online: egrid.epg-project.eu/

Freeman, D. (1991) What is a burning issue in the profession today? *TESOL Matters* 2 (2), 4.

Gilpin, A. (2003) Teaching about teaching: The knowledge base of professional practice in education, in Murray, J. (Ed) *New Teacher Educators' Needs: Perspectives from Research and Practice*, report of the symposium for the Teaching Training Agency, London, May 2003, 4–15.

Glaser, R. (1996) Changing the agency for learning: Acquiring expert performance, in Eriksson, K. A. (Ed) *The Road to Excellence: The Acquisition of Expert Performance in the Arts and Sciences, Sports and Games*. New Jersey: Laurence Erlbaum Associates, 303–311.

Granich, V. (1995) *Counselling and the CTEFLA: Trainer Roles in Pre-service Teacher Training*, report for UCLES of 1995 Conference held at the Australian TESOL Training Centre, Sydney, Australia, 18–27.

Hagger, H. and McIntyre D. (2000) What can research tell us about teacher education? *Oxford Review of Education*, 26 (3–4), 483–494.

Hargreaves, D. H. (1972) *Interpersonal Relations and Education*. London: Routledge Kegan and Paul Ltd.

He, Y., Prater, K. and Steed, T. (2011) Moving beyond just good teaching: ESL professional development for all teachers, *Professional Development in Education* 37 (1), 7–18, available online: dx.doi.org/10.1080/19415250903467199

Jenkins, J. (2000) *The Phonology of English as an International Language*. Oxford: Oxford University Press.

Johnston, B. (1997) Do EFL teachers have careers? *TESOL Quarterly* 31 (4), 681–712.

Korthagen, F. and Russell, T. (1995) Teachers who teach teachers: Some final considerations, in Russell, T. and Korthagen, F. (Eds) *Teachers Who Teach Teachers: Reflections on Teacher Education*. London: Falmer Press, 187–192.

Korthagen, F., Loughran, J. and Lunenberg, M. (2005) Teaching teachers — studies into the expertise of teacher educators, *Teaching and Teacher Education* 21 (2), 107–115.

Kumaravadivelu, B. (2012) *Language Teacher Education for a Global Society: A Modular Model for Knowing, Analyzing, Recognising, Doing and Seeing*. Routledge: New York.

Lave, J. and Wenger, E. (1991) *Situated Learning: Legitimate Peripheral Participation*. Cambridge: Cambridge University Press.

Lin, X., Schwartz, D. and Bransford, J. (n.d.) *Intercultural Adaptive Expertise: Explicit and Implicit Lessons from Dr Hatano*, available online: aaalab.stanford.edu/papers/Hatanos_Intercultural_Expertise%5B1%5D.pdf

Lortie, D. (1975) *Schoolteacher: A Sociological Study*. Chicago: The University of Chicago Press.

McGrath, I. (1997) Introduction, in McGrath, I. (Ed) *Learning to Train: Perspectives on the Development of Language Teachers*. Hemel Hempstead: Prentice Hall, vii–viii.

Morgan, M. (2007) Becoming, behaving and being: Exploring aspects of professional identity with six teacher educators from the Cambridge ESOL CELTA scheme, unpublished MA dissertation, Institute of Education, University of London.

Murray, J. and Male, T. (2005) Becoming a teacher educator: Evidence from the field, *Teaching and Teacher Education* 21 (2), 125–142.

Nunan, D. (1992) *Research Methods in Language Teaching*. Cambridge: Cambridge University Press.

Poulter, M. (2001) Not cloning but training the trainers: A special issue of summaries from Developing Trainers in ELT — strategies, issues, perspectives, held at the University of Leeds, 10–12 November 2000, *IATEFL Teacher Trainers and Educators SIG Newsletter*, 27–29.

Poulter, M. (2007) Teacher training and development — Future directions, *Research Notes* 29, 2–4.

Randall, M. and Thornton, B. (2001) *Advising and Supporting Teachers*. Cambridge: Cambridge University Press.

Richards, J. C. and Farrell, S. (2005) *Professional Development for Language Teachers: Strategies for Teacher Learning* (2nd edition). New York: Cambridge University Press.

Rosenberg, C. (2002) Exploring CertTESOL tutors' beliefs on effective teaching, *ELTED* 7 (Winter), 23–43, available online: www.cdelsbham.ac.ukELTED/Vol17/rosenberg. pdf

Smith, K. (2003) So, what about the professional development of teacher educators? *European Journal of Teacher Education* 26 (2), 201–215.

Tsui, A. (2003) *Understanding Expertise in Teaching: Case Studies of Second Language Teachers*. Cambridge: Cambridge University Press.

Wallace, M. J. (1991) *Training Foreign Language Teachers: A Reflective Approach*. Cambridge: Cambridge University Press.

Wenger, E. (1998) *Communities of Practice: Learning, Meaning and Identity*. Cambridge: Cambridge University Press.

Widdowson, H. (1992) ELT and EL teachers, *English Language Teaching Journal* 46 (4), 333–339.

Woodward, T. (1990) People who train people, *The Teacher Trainer* 4 (1), 25–27.

Wright, T. (1987) *Roles of Teachers and Learners*. Oxford: Oxford University Press.

Wright. T and Bolitho, R. (2007) *Trainer Development*. Milton Keynes: Lightning Source.

Zeichner, K. (2005) Becoming a teacher educator: A personal perspective, *Teaching and Teacher Education*, 21 (2), 117–124.

Appendix 1

CELTA Trainer-in-training competencies

Reprinted with permission from the *Cambridge English Teaching Qualifications: CELTA Trainer in Training Guidelines* (Cambridge English 2013: 16–17)

By the end of the training programme the trainer-in-training must show evidence of the following:

- an understanding of a variety of principles and approaches to teaching and training and the ability to put these into practice appropriately
- readiness to work flexibly and co-operatively within a team
- sensitivity to trainee needs and ability to adapt the programme accordingly
- good organisational/presentational skills (relating to course delivery and course administration including record keeping and maintenance of candidate files)
- a knowledge of trainer roles and responsibilities as detailed in the *Administration Handbook*
- a readiness to respond positively to feedback from fellow trainers and trainees
- enthusiasm and motivation for their work
- awareness of their strengths and weaknesses as a trainer
- an awareness of strategies for continuing professional development.

In relation to the CELTA course, the trainer-in-training must be able to do the following:

- design input sessions and implement these in relation to the five syllabus units using a variety of modes of delivery
- design pre-session and post-session input tasks
- pitch the level of input appropriately and make informed decisions as to what to select or exclude in all aspects and at all stages of the course

- provide appropriate guidance for teaching practice with regard to content and preparation for the lesson
- give feedback on teaching practice appropriately and sensitively (according to different personality types and different stages of the course) and effectively (using different modes e.g. group work, eliciting)
- write clear and focused teaching practice feedback sheets
- give clear, accurate and sensitive feedback to candidates on all aspects of the course
- evaluate and assess candidates appropriately.

This requires:

- knowledge of, and familiarity with, the standards of the award
- the ability to evaluate on an ongoing basis with reference to the assessment criteria throughout the course and at final grading
- the ability to recognise significant strengths and weaknesses in teaching
- design of appropriate observation tasks for peer observation and the observation of experienced teachers
- ability to plan, set and evaluate a range of written work
- ability to apply the award's requirements and regulations
- ability to select candidates through appropriate interview skills
- ability to show an awareness of the role of the assessor.

Giving feedback involves a number of skills, for example:

- giving feedback on the lesson plan
- giving constructive criticism on the lesson
- prioritising
- relating feedback on an individual lesson to overall progress
- providing an appropriate balance between progress made and action points
- summing up and leading candidates to the identification of action points
- listening skills
- appropriate intervention during feedback
- managing peer feedback
- being tactful
- time management
- counselling skills.

The following competencies are required for the role of the main course tutor. An ability to:

- design a course programme in accordance with the *Syllabus and Assessment Guidelines* booklet
- set up a rota for teaching practice, observation and monitoring in accordance with the regulations
- co-ordinate, direct and support the work of others
- prepare for the assessor's visit in accordance with the regulations
- liaise and correspond with Cambridge English regarding completing and returning documentation.

Appendix 2
Pre-course training-in-training tasks — task, response, feedback cycle

As part of a series of pre-course tasks, trainers-in-training must familiarise themselves with a number of documents and the requirements of a CELTA trainer. Oral and/or written feedback is then given by the training supervisor(s) responsible for the trainer-in-training.

A trainer-in-training produced the following in response to this selection of pre-course tasks. The responses are reprinted here with permission of the trainer-in-training.

Task: CELTA Trainer competencies

Look at the published list of trainer-in-training competencies (see Appendix 1) and comment on which ones you feel are established, and which would be new(er) areas of competency for you to achieve.

Trainer-in-training responses:

Looking at the TinT competency list on page 16 by section, I believe that I already possess many of the competencies listed.

"By the end of the training programme the trainer-in-training must show evidence of the following"

From this section, I feel that I do have a good understanding of a variety of principles and approaches to teaching and training and their practical application. I enjoy working in a team and through my teaching experience I am sensitive to the needs of learners. I have experience of adapting my delivery to match different people, and I have good organizational and presentational skills already. I am an enthusiastic and motivated worker and I am also aware of CPD strategies.

I have studied the handbook so I have knowledge of the trainer roles and responsibilities, and I am ready to respond positively to feedback. Both of these will require further work as will being aware of my strengths and weaknesses as a trainer. However, I think through the support of the training staff and my own efforts I am confident that this can be achieved.

"In relation to the CELTA course, the trainer-in-training must be able to do the following"

From this section, I also believe that I am competent in most of the skills needed. However, I think I will have to further hone my skills. I have some experience of designing input tasks but this is something I will have to work on and I look forward to improving on with the aid of the feedback of the trainers. With respect to pitching the level of the input, and providing appropriate guidance and feedback on teaching practice, I believe that the experience I already have in this regard will serve me well. However, the different background and skills sets of the trainees compared to my usual learners will require a readjustment of my approach and a sensitivity to this change.

I believe that my experience as a Cambridge and IELTS examiner will serve me well with respect to applying a standard, following evaluation criteria, as well as doing pre-course interviews. I have additional interview experience from previous jobs.

"Giving feedback involves a number of skills"

As regards the sub-section on feedback skills, I am used to giving feedback to learners and my experience teaching TESOL, acting as a practicum teacher, and also teaching examination preparation classes such as CAE, FCE and PET will serve me well in this area.

"The following competencies are required for the role of the main course tutor"

Finally, page 16 also deals with the competencies required of a main course tutor. This section is not relevant for me at this point, but I would hope that this is something I could move towards after obtaining sufficient experience following my training period.

In conclusion, I believe I have many of the competencies listed and I am confident that I will be able to achieve the level required of me with respect to the others with the support and guidance of the trainers on the programme.

Trainer trainer feedback:

Competencies

You discuss current strengths and weaknesses, and you come across as confident in your abilities to undertake this kind of work. This confidence is an important factor in presenting an informed and professional persona as a trainer, and should stand you in good stead over the coming months. Willingness to reflect with specificity and to take on board feedback from your own reflections and those of colleagues is also a critical factor here; it models what we expect trainees to do in relation to tutor/learner feedback.

You may want to revisit your point about pitching content appropriately in terms of what is relevant in a pre-service entry level course as this will be directly linked to your ability to choose and design input sessions. Consider also how the feedback required within CELTA — based on what you know to date — may be the same/different to the practicum feedback you have previously been engaged in delivering. There are likely to be some core generic skills involved in feedback regardless of context, but the CELTA context may also have signature features which distinguish it from other feedback processes.

Task: Predicting course content

Task

Look at some of the methodology/input sessions to be delivered in the course timetable, and predict which key points will be covered by the trainer during these sessions.

(Note: this is an important part of benchmarking the appropriate level/ depth and breadth at which the pre-service sessions should be delivered to trainee teachers. This is particularly important since not all CELTA trainers-in-training have themselves taken the CELTA course as their first initial ELT training programme. The right-hand column is completed during the training programme as an on-going task; it offers the trainer-in-training and supervisor the chance to assess the former's ability to accurately gauge the level at which to pitch pre-service methodology sessions.)

Trainer-in-training responses (In left-hand columns in italics):

Name of session:	Receptive Skills
Predicted points	Main areas covered in session
Focus on Listening and Reading with reference to frameworks such as pre and post reading and listening, activation of background knowledge, grading of materials, types of listening and reading (e.g. gist, scanning etc.)	

(To be continued)

(Continued)

Name of session:	**Vocabulary I**
Predicted points	Main areas covered in session
Word types, level of words (word appropriacy by level), ways of defining words, focus on context and co-text, ways of practising and remembering words	

Name of session:	**Lesson Planning and Lesson Plans**
Predicted points	Main areas covered in session
Realisable aims, pedagogically sound tasks, correct sequencing of tasks	

Name of session:	**Language Analysis I**
Predicted points	Main areas covered in session
Second Language Acquisition, teaching methodologies and theories of teaching	

Name of session:	**Phonology I**
Predicted points	Main areas covered in session
Segmental phonemes, focus on syllables, weak/strong stress, schwa	

Name of session:	**Clarifying Language I / Language Analysis II**
Predicted points	Main areas covered in session
Tense and aspect	

Name of session:	**Restricted and Authentic Practice Tasks**
Predicted points	Main areas covered in session
Lesson staging, PPP approach to language teaching, focus on importance of using authentic materials	

Name of session:	**Ways of Checking Meaning**
Predicted points	Main areas covered in session
Eliciting, concept checking, dangers of assuming understanding	

Name of session:	**Clarifying Language II**
Predicted points	Main areas covered in session
Different pedagogical approaches: TTT, TBL, functional, notional, integrated approaches	

Name of session:	**Oral Error**
Predicted points	Main areas covered in session
Balance between fluency and accuracy; distinction between a mistake and an error.	

Trainer trainer feedback:

Predictions

You have some sense of what might be covered in methodology sessions; it will be interesting for you to return to these predictions as we go forward, especially in relation to gauging the 'depth' of knowledge (or lack thereof) that is appropriate for entry level training. This is often challenging for new trainers when combined with the limitations of session timings they must work within.

Meanwhile, look again before the course starts at the following sessions on your chart — LA Sessions I and Oral Error Correction on the current timetable. See if their titles suggest any specifics that might be included in the sessions. Consider also the sessions on LA II and Restricted/Authentic Practice Tasks from the standpoint of CELTA and its focus on a practical, hands-on approach to principles and their application to practice.

Appendix 3
In-course training-in-training tasks — task, response, feedback cycle

Trainers-in-training must plan and deliver a number of methodology/ input sessions to the group of trainee teachers during a live course. These sessions are initially discussed with the training supervisor. The sessions are observed by the supervisor who then writes feedback notes on their final planning and delivery. The trainer-in-training writes up a self-evaluation and reflection, which is given to the training supervisor. An oral feedback session is then held, at the end of which the trainer-in-training receives the written feedback notes from their supervisor.

Task: Session planning and delivery

Testing and international ELT exams

(Note: the materials and content produced by the trainer-in-training are not included here. This was the final session to be planned and delivered by the trainer-in-training at the end of the training-up programme. Note also that the training supervisor is now also giving feedback on the quality/ accuracy and focus of the trainer-in-training's own reflections and evaluation of the session. This is due to this being the final piece of in-course work on this particular programme.)

Trainer-in-training's own self-evaluation

Summary

This observed session has been the one I feel happiest about up until this point, and it's good that it is the one in the last week, as it makes me think that I'm making some progress with respect to doing the input sessions. I think the session had a lot of strengths, although of course some things could have been done differently. I'll highlight these below.

Strengths

In terms of strengths, I feel this was a very interesting and fun session for the trainees. They got a lot of useful information about testing, and by delivering it through involving them in forms of testing, they were able to have experiential learning and fun. I managed to include a range of interaction types (pair, group, jigsaw) as well as a range of delivery methods (OHP, handouts, board), all of which I think kept the trainees engaged. I tried to avoid telling the trainees too much but elicited from them whenever I could, and I was surprised how well this worked. I also appreciated some very pertinent and helpful questions from the group.

Weaknesses

As regards weaknesses, I think I could have handled my materials better. I had quite a large amount of material, and the challenge of keeping track of sets for the trainees, myself, the trainer, and the other trainer in training stretched me to the limit! As a result, I ran into a few hitches during the session where I had trouble putting my hands on the material I wanted to give out. The room set-up, which I decided to leave from the previous session, caused some trouble for me as I found that just trying to use one of the two boards for both OHP and writing, meant it became a little busy on the board at times. I wanted to point the OHP at the board and not wall though as it meant all the trainees could see it. In retrospect, I needed a bit of a different set-up. One other weakness I noted was that I hadn't made a note of all of the answers to my various questions on the different handouts, despite the fact I know all of the answers, I think it's good practice to keep a record of them all to hand, as in the moment it is easy to forget (particularly in a higher stress observed situation).

Conclusion

In conclusion, I feel this session went well, and I am broadly happy with it. For the next time I do it, however, I want to make sure to have a different set-up for the OHP, a tighter organization of my materials, and finally be a bit more careful with the timing for some of the activities to improve the session further.

Trainer trainer feedback

This was an effectively planned session, X. The session met its aims of raising awareness about different kinds of informal and formal tests. The session needs a few small adjustments before you deliver it again to balance out some content areas, and develop the focus of eliciting questions. Congratulations on a session which gave the trainees some important information, and engaged them in a number of tasks.

Planning

You planned for variety through different groupings, including a jigsaw task. You collected together some useful examples of certain exam task types, together with some informative supplementary handouts. These provided the trainees with an overview of the Cambridge suite, some reference to the TOEFL test, and the IELTS exam. The use of colour-coding was helpful for the jigsaw; make sure you have your handouts organized so they are all given out by session end, and that you provide the observing tutor with a full pack along with your plan at session start. We discussed the need to add in some information about TOEFL to show alongside the Cambridge suite handout for the next time you run this session.

Your decision to try out some loop input was a good one in relation to testing. You have begun to plan so that you can engage learners in participative tasks in both teacher/student roles, which is good development to see. For the next session, give more consideration to the kind of eliciting/questioning techniques you use so that they have more focus.

Delivery

The session had variety in terms of work in groups and pairs. You seemed to enjoy the session, although on occasion somewhat lost sight of your role in relation to the group — for example, it's important that other organizations, accrediting bodies etc. are portrayed in neutral terms. This is important not only for the local context, but also in light of your role as a trainer representing an international body. Unguarded comments can come back to haunt us.

The session had a sense of pace, and you moved through activities setting time limits and other task parameters clearly. You used nomination to bring in different trainees and monitored the room, though tended to do this more for one side of the class/one individual at times (trainee Y, in this case). You encouraged discussion and questions, most of which you answered clearly and accurately. However, make sure that you have to hand the answers to the questions you set trainees on worksheets, etc.

You used the OHT to set up and check tasks, which also provided some variety in terms of aids in the session. Deal with the font size and/ or projection point to ensure that the content can be clearly read/seen from the back of the room for next time. The initial 'test' was an effective way to start the session, and it was important that you returned to this; the whole session was then largely based round a Test-Teach-Test framework. For the next session, adapt this worksheet to broaden out the range of task types to include things such as circling/underlining, etc.; this can help feed into discussions of exams or tests done at lower levels where production is limited. The supporting handouts for the jigsaw task were useful to support the activity, and were well presented.

In terms of presenting information about the CAE [Cambridge English: Advanced] in this session, consider giving a broader overview of the whole suite first, so that trainees know where this exam sits in the suite. These terms may or may not be familiar to members of the group, but the trainees can be helped to make connections to the TP classes/learners and to [this school's] class levels they have observed. On occasion, you tended to either echo or accept some responses which perhaps were not quite on track although at others you gave more appropriate responses such as 'close, try again'. When it is clear that trainees do not have specific content knowledge, there comes a point at which eliciting may not work at all.

Self-evaluation

You made a number of relevant points in your reflections about the session, particularly in regard to organization of room, equipment, and materials. It's good to hear that you felt the development in this session since the first one you delivered, and that you are starting to consider the various layers required of trainers when delivering input sessions beyond simply the content itself.

Points to work on

- Make sure that you have the answers to your own tasks to hand, and that handouts are organized and distributed in timely manner. This is important as it reflects what is expected of the trainees.

- Keep working on monitoring so that you check-in more with different groups. This may mean different room layouts to facilitate moving around the room on a chair, sitting with groups, etc.
- Consider the kinds of questioning techniques you will use as you plan sessions to give extra focus/precision to them.
- Monitor your own responses to questions so that you do not inadvertently say something 'off the cuff' which might detract or distract.

Task: Designing two written assignments to be given to trainee teachers

Trainer trainer feedback

(Note: the trainer-in-training's assignment design is not included here.)

Language-related task

Strengths

- You have included the marking criteria, which is important.
- You state the word limit as well as the manner in which the assignment is to be answered. This is good to see.
- It's good you mention reference books, though you need to be more explicit in your rubric and tell trainees to include these in the assignment. This has taken on more importance of late due to plagiarism issues.
- You include meaning, form, and pronunciation as part of your rubric, necessary in an assignment like this.
- You attempt to put this into a larger frame beyond sentence analysis by suggesting that trainees reference the framework; see below.

Points to consider

- When would this assignment be suitable to hand out/take in, taking into account the skill set trainees would be required to have to complete it?
- You need to provide examples of the tasks you want the students to do with an assignment of this nature to avoid unnecessary resubmissions/ confusion. In some centres, this includes a detailed answer to a sample sentence in which every facet of the assignment is clearly demonstrated; this is very good practice when LRT assignments are done as a single assignment rather than conflated or indeed for other assignments which

are complex in any way.

- How could you support the trainees to tackle the issue of 'meaning'? Notice that you later go on to mention the important word 'context'. How could this be incorporated into the analysis task itself?
- How much of the form do you expect them to analyse in each sentence? How could you flag this clearly and simply to the trainees in the rubric/ handout?
- Which features of pronunciation do you want them to look at? Again, this is linked to the timing of the assignment, but is always something to bear in mind when writing assignment rubrics, TP notes/feedback.
- Notice that language analysis goes beyond tense work; an LRT assignment like this which focuses on analysis in isolation really requires inclusion of some lexical items, and some functional exponents, even 'small but significant' words like discourse markers. This would help trainees to recognize that language is multifaceted.
- How valuable is the reference to a framework here? Again this seems linked to issues related to level, new or unknown language, etc.
- How long do you think this task would take trainees, and would they be able to manage to complete it effectively/successfully in the word limit? Did you try out your own tasks with them in mind?

Overall, you are on the right track with this assignment, X. However, when writing assignments — as with just about every aspect of working with trainees — you need to be much more explicit with each of the steps for the trainees, provide exemplifications of what you want them to do in these tasks as part of the handout, and also remove possible different interpretations (e.g., by removing 'you can divide …' and indicating how to lay out this content).

Task: Shadow marking of written assignments (Lessons from the classroom)

Trainer trainer feedback

(Note: the trainer-in-training's comments, the trainee teacher's response to the assignment, and the training supervisor's feedback of the trainee teacher's assignment are not included here.)

Your grading for the assignment was accurate, X. Well done ☺

You have made appropriate and sufficient comments in-text which confirm and also question some of the content provided by the candidate, which is necessary in this case. You also picked up on some of her typos etc., which is important. In some cases, though not this one, candidates may have to resubmit a whole paper for this reason alone, even where content is accurate.

You have summarized the areas related to the criteria for this assignment. Use the checklist of criteria at the top of the page to also indicate which of the criteria have been met, partially met, or not met — we often use a series of check marks, crosses, and half check marks for this or you could devise an equally transparent way that tutors and candidates will be able to easily interpret.

It is good that you follow the criteria sections/foci in your summarizing comments on the cover sheet, and the points that need to be resubmitted are clear for the candidate.

Start getting into the habit of signing/dating your shadow marking as you'll be doing this in real time for candidates' eyes very soon now. Note also that we indicate the resubmission date on the bottom of the sheet; tutors usually agree on this so we give the candidates the same new deadlines to meet.

Good work, X.

Section 3
Focus on the assessment of specific criteria

Preface

The next section of this volume addresses a number of specific criteria across the Cambridge English Teaching Qualifications and how they are interpreted and used in practice. Coverage of all the criteria would require a volume of encyclopaedic proportions so the ones selected are, somewhat regretfully, the areas that tend to present candidates with the greatest challenges, in other words, criteria identified as the main reasons for failure. First and foremost is the language itself, both in terms of candidates' own English language proficiency and in their ability to analyse and present the target language appropriately in their planning and teaching. Another area of weakness flagged in examiners' reports is that of responding to learners, due in part to the stress of being observed but also because of the drive to 'teach the plan' instead of adapting flexibly to perceived needs. The last chapter in this section considers how assessment criteria are derived from underlying constructs, in this case the constructs underpinning knowledge about teaching.

One aspect of language teaching that is constantly questioned is how proficient someone needs to be in a language in order to teach it effectively. Despite the support in the field for the concept of 'expert user', it has yet to replace 'native speaker' in the popular imagination. Indeed, it remains true that, in many parts of the world, institutions promote their language teaching programme on the basis that they employ only native speakers. In his history of the Cambridge English Teaching Qualifications (Chapter 2), Pulverness referred to the preliminary language examination for the RSA Certificate and noted its emphasis on the skills of comprehension and composition. That test was withdrawn many years ago but the question of the language competence of prospective teachers and how to assess it is increasingly relevant. In a discussion of the procedures for CELTA courses, Jenny Johnson and Monica Poulter (Chapter 8) begin with a reminder of how the position and role of English has changed. They review key aspects of the native/non-native speaker debate as well as the issue of varieties of English and the concept of 'standard English'. For language teachers, the dilemma of language as content highlights the importance of their own language competence. All applicants for CELTA courses are required to take part in a detailed selection procedure and may well be encouraged to improve their language skills before considering taking the course. An extensive survey of CELTA trainers presents issues in candidate selection and discusses trainers' decisionmaking processes with reference to the weighting given to different aspects of applicants' performance.

The pre-course screening task for CELTA is designed also to assess applicants' language awareness, in particular their grammatical knowledge and, to a limited extent, their knowledge of meta-language, and language awareness is a key focus of assessment in all the Cambridge English Teaching Qualifications. Martin Parrott (Chapter 9) discusses the approach to assessment of language teachers' knowledge base taken in each qualification. Views of what language is are subject to change in the same way as language itself and Parrott begins with a brief review of these changes. He notes that the term 'language awareness' is itself problematic, with interpretations ranging from a narrow focus on grammatical systems to a view encompassing also the application of that knowledge to the planning and delivery of language lessons and then to a broader view of language as it is used socio-culturally. Parrott reports that a survey of language teachers added the notion of a 'feeling for language' that would include the ability to modify language effectively to promote understanding and explain the connotation of similar words. Parrott reviews the weighting given to the assessment of language awareness in the different Cambridge English Teaching Qualifications and notes the way that, in written examinations, test design is modified across the qualifications to reflect the target candidature. Language awareness in practical teaching is assessed at all stages of the lesson from planning, including selecting appropriate materials and anticipating learners' difficulties, to teaching the lesson and the post-lesson reflection or commentary.

Parrott makes the point that, in the assessment descriptors for Delta, language awareness is closely aligned to teachers' 'spontaneous responses in the classroom' and an ability to respond flexibly. This theme of flexibility and its assessment in the Cambridge English Teaching Qualifications is discussed further by Rosemary Wilson (Chapter 10). In an earlier chapter (Chapter 5), Delaney considered the role of reflection-on-action in teacher education and, by extension, assessment. Wilson notes that a key attribute of teacher flexibility is reflection-in-action or the ability to make real-time context-specific decisions based on learner needs. Sensitivity to learners brings into play affective factors that are in some ways inseparable from individual personality. Wilson emphasises that an assessment system needs to focus on specific actions rather than personal qualities but acknowledges that learners are likely to do the exact opposite. A brief review of the Cambridge English Teaching Qualifications shows that the extent to which candidates are expected to demonstrate flexibility increases with the target level of the qualification. At pre-service and early in-service levels, the emphasis is on careful planning while at Delta level, the criteria include an ability to adapt plans and be responsive to learners' feelings. Wilson reviews assessor feedback that provides concrete examples, linked to specific criteria, of actions taken in effective lessons. As well as modifying the planned lesson, these included using learners' names and asking referential or real questions rather than display ones or using humour. Teachers' personal qualities are often included in assessor comments and Wilson cautions that assessors must take care to distinguish between the person and their skills as a teacher.

The criteria discussed so far have identified specific instances of behaviour that demonstrate knowledge or skills. Flexibility, for example, is demonstrated by being prepared to move away from the lesson as planned while language awareness is demonstrated by the way in which language is selected, analysed, presented in context and checked. The relevant descriptors were based on the underlying concepts in each case. In practice-based assessment such as in CELTA or Delta, candidates' actions are sampled in real time and judgements made about their general competence. In other forms of assessment where performance cannot be judged directly, test procedures will reflect abilities rather than sample them. This is the case in the Teaching Knowledge Test (TKT), which in its original form is a written examination designed to test knowledge of a range of concepts about language teaching and learning. The construct or set of abilities that TKT aims to test is strongly influenced by the Grossman's model of teaching knowledge, as Mary Spratt (Chapter 11) explains. When applied to ELT, for example, Grossman's model distinguishes between general pedagogic knowledge such as motivation and organisation of learning, subject matter knowledge such as language systems and pedagogic content knowledge such as strategies for language learning and teaching. Spratt suggests how Grossman's model aligns with the three modules that make up TKT and points out that, as the test was designed for an international candidature, knowledge of specific context could not be tested. Spratt emphasises the accessibility of TKT while noting that aspects of knowing-in-action and teacher cognition cannot be tested in a paper-based objective test. A range of sample test items drawn from each of the three modules is discussed to illustrate the knowledge that is tested as well as different task types, including multiple-choice questions and matching exercises. Spratt makes the point that TKT is not a course-based assessment and that some of the necessary limitations of an objective test format may well be counteracted during preparation courses for the test. TKT preparation courses may also be encouraged to include practice-based components such as micro-teaching following the more recent introduction of TKT: Practical.

8 Teachers' language competence: Issues of appropriation and appropriacy

Jenny Johnson
Eastbourne School of English
Monica Poulter
Cambridge English Language Assessment

Introduction

The landscape of English language teaching has undergone dramatic changes over the last 50 years. The number of English speakers worldwide is increasing rapidly (Crystal 2003, 2010; Graddol 2006). There are now three or even four non-native speakers of English to every native speaker (Crystal 2010). The number of teachers of English is also increasing and it has been estimated that over 80% of the world's teachers of English are non-native speakers of the language (Canagarajah 1999, cited in McKay 2002: 41). Over the range of highly diverse global contexts, the language competence of these teachers ranges from basic to highly proficient. Many of these teachers will still themselves be language learners and, while effective in their own contexts, they may express anxiety with respect to their own language competence. As Murdoch observes: 'for the non-native teacher, language proficiency will always represent the bedrock of their professional confidence' (Murdoch 1994: 254), while Medgyes insists that 'non-native speakers are ill at ease with using English accurately and appropriately' (Medgyes 1992: 343). Such teachers may be restricted by their own language ability or insecurity to teaching at lower levels and only in specific contexts. Other teachers will be regarded as having a 'native-speaker' or 'near-native-speaker' command of English and may therefore have a potentially wider range of professional choices. In between these two extremes are teachers with a very good command of English, who are able to bring a richness of experience to language learning and teaching which compensates for any 'deficiencies' in their own language use and language experience. As Medgyes argues, 'NESTs (native English speaker teacher) and non-NESTs can be equally effective, because in the final analysis their respective strengths and weaknesses balance each other out' (1992: 347).

The growth in English language learning and teaching has been matched by research into and understanding of language as social and cultural practice, and a questioning by a number of linguists of the construct of the 'ideal' native speaker and the parallel construct of a native standard language (Davies 2003; Pennycook 1994; Phillipson 1992; Widdowson 1994). Regional differences may affect not just accent but lexical and structural uses, as may a speaker's age, occupation and class (Kramsch 2003). Native speaker use may include features which, according to the standardised code, are 'incorrect' and therefore potentially confusing for language learners. In the same way as non-native-speaker teachers, native-speaker teachers can also be placed on a continuum of language proficiency: some will need to develop their own language competence in relation to accepted standardised usage and many will need to extend their language expertise to respond to the linguistic demands of unfamiliar teaching contexts.

The issue of teachers' linguistic competence touches on broader aspects of social and cultural identity and is not restricted to the distinction between native and non-native speakers. However, in both cases, an assessment framework needs to provide benchmarks to ensure that prospective teachers demonstrate the appropriate language competence — as well as guidelines to encourage consensus as to what is considered appropriate. This chapter will consider how pre-screening procedures are used in the application process to determine the standard of teachers' language competence required for entry onto courses leading to the Cambridge English Certificate in Teaching English to Speakers of Other Languages (CELTA). A survey conducted in order to gather data on centres' decisions and trainers' attitudes and practices in relation to applicants' language ability will be analysed and discussed. The data gathered through the survey will also be briefly discussed in relation to shifting notions of 'standard' English and the ownership of English. A suggestion will be made for greater clarity in defining language competence in relation to teaching skill and levels being taught.

The language debate

Discussion of the assessment of teachers' linguistic competence needs to be situated within the wider debate on the role of native-speaker norms in language teaching and learning. 'Nativeness' has been the target because of the historic prestige of the native-speaker variety, spoken by elite, socially dominant groups for so long. Indeed, Chomsky's 'idealized native speaker' (Cook 1999: 187) is an 'authority on the language' (Braine 2010: 3), because 'native speakers ... are people who know their language perfectly' (James cited in Cook 1999: 189). Enthralment to the native speaker has been maintained and intensified by 'gatekeeper' institutions (Jenkins 2007: 239), which disseminate examinations, coursebooks, and methods worldwide.

While language students resolutely maintain their belief that 'their goal should be to sound as much like a native speaker as possible' (Jenkins 2004), the ethics and acceptability of the dominant native-speaker model have been questioned and debated by many linguists. Kachru (1992) and more recently Kirkpatrick (2007) dispute its validity in relation to the evolution of varieties of English, or World Englishes. Phillipson introduced the constructs 'linguistic imperialism' and the 'native-speaker fallacy', highlighting the interests of Inner Circle, as opposed to Outer Circle English Language Teaching (ELT) professionals (Kachru 1992). Pennycook (1994) refuted native-speaker norms from the viewpoint of cultural politics, language and power. Widdowson (for example 1994, 2003) discusses the 'spread' of English and the shift in 'ownership' and their consequences. Some Outer Circle scholars have pointed out that English is now no longer the possession solely of Inner Circle speakers, and can and should move away from the state of 'cultural carrier' of Western values and be appropriated as a tool for communication and progress (see for example Kachru 1992: 67; Kumaravadevilu 2006: 19; Rushdie 1991 in Crystal 2003: 184).

In countries where the English variety has been influenced by the local language(s), a continuum often exists between extreme broadness of accent/ dialect, perhaps difficult to comprehend for other users of English, and a more neutral version of the variety, more likely to be intelligible to all speakers of English. Language carries identity: Kirkpatrick's 'identity communication continuum' swings from the language/accent we use to communicate with the world at large and the language/accent we use to express our identity amongst those close to us (Kirkpatrick 2007: 10, 172–173). To communicate successfully with an outsider to our speech community, we front intelligibility, veering towards the more 'standard', 'educated' end, or acrolect (Trudgill and Hannah 2002), of our cline of performance (see McKay 2002). However, if we front our identity within our own speech community, we will adopt the 'broad' version (the basilect), which those close to us will comprehend but which may be unintelligible to many outside that community. Furthermore within traditionally 'English speaking' Inner Circle countries, individual language use varies, depending on age, background, education, regional and social context. The variety spoken by someone from London will be different from that spoken by someone from New York or Sydney, while the broadest regional varieties within one country, for example Glasgow or London in the UK, Texas or Philadelphia in the US, can be almost unrecognisable as the same English.

Given the above complexities, questions arise about which variety of English teachers should teach and whether the teacher's own language should be assessed in relation to the construct of 'standard' English, especially since there is a perceived lack of a consensus definition of what standard English actually is. Strevens' definition of standard English is a 'non-localised dialect' of English, with no particular accent, which is 'universally accepted as the appropriate educational target in teaching English' (Strevens cited in McKay 2002: 51). Trudgill and Hannah (2002: 110) define standard English as 'the variety of the English language which is ... normally spoken by 'educated' speakers of the language ... It refers to grammar and vocabulary (*dialect*) but not to pronunciation (*accent*)'. It is significant that 'no particular accent' is associated with standard English here; many people would call it 'the Queen's English' or 'Received Pronunciation' (RP), as spoken by the educated elite in the 1940s and 1950s and on the BBC. The view that RP may be 'standard English' is a myth: RP is in fact spoken in its pure form these days by less than 3% of 'native' English speakers (Crystal 1995; Walker 2011). Over the last few decades there has been a shift in the acceptance of different accents, dialects and regional varieties, and indeed of different 'Englishes'. This change is not only in ELT but also in the world at large: attitudes to 'standard' English have changed, there is more acceptance of variety of regional linguistic features and accent and what may previously have been viewed as 'incorrect' is now regularly heard on radio and television and seen in written media.

There remains, however, the pragmatic necessity for a 'neutral' norm, a broad area of common, intelligible ground, both for communication and as an albeit wide-ranging, 'standard' from which to operate, particularly in ELT, where English has become a global language. Train (2002: 15) raises the question of 'what role the native language or hyperstandard language plays or should play in pedagogical contexts', implying that all language models will be 'compared' in some way to a native 'norm'. Gnutzmann points out the pedagogic necessity of having 'some linguistic guidelines (for learners) to orient themselves ... which they do not necessarily have to conform to' (Gnutzmann 1999: 165). Train (2002: 21) raises an 'inclusive model of language instruction', originally proposed by Perez-Leroux and Glass, where the textbook may serve as 'the local standard' that defines accuracy, with the teacher's role being to raise students' 'linguistic sensitivity' and awareness of different varieties, and to act as informant regarding how the textbook norm differs from language use in the real world. Train suggests the use of critical language awareness activities; for example if the teacher's own use of language differs from the textbook, this can be exploited for discussion in the classroom to reconcile the teacher's own linguistic variety with the notion of a linguistic norm as found in the textbook. The implications for assessment are that the teacher may need to make decisions about what language models to teach where textbook models differ from their own usage, a 'do as I say not do as I do' approach. The teacher's own language use becomes an assessment issue where they are unable to recognise the discrepancy between their own language use and the textbook norm. Tiplady (2012) recommends a consciousness-raising approach which focuses on trainee error through comparison with usage shown through concordance in an attempt to raise awareness and involve the trainees actively in their own language improvement.

As Smith and Rafiqzad state: 'there seems to be no reason to insist that the performance target in the English classroom be a native speaker ... a person speaking any variety of educated English, although phonologically non-native, can expect to be intelligible to his listeners' (Smith and Rafiqzad 1979: 380). Intelligibility rather than conformance to a standard norm then becomes the basis for assessment of language proficiency and acceptance onto courses. In a review of lessons taught by CELTA candidates and filmed by Cambridge English for tutor and assessor standardisation, which included a range of lessons taught by native and non-native speakers, the only instances of comprehension difficulties occurred with native-speaker accents. The following is an example of one instance. The teacher teaching a group of students in Turkey (mostly Turkish) introduces the lesson:

Today we are gonna start by talking about summer (pronounced /sʊmə/)
No response from students.
Teacher continues *ok the /sʊmə/, you know the /sʊmə/* (Teacher writes 'summer' on the board.)
Students in unison: *Oh summer* /sʌmə/
Teacher responds /sʊmə/ *yes*, (in response to students' protests) *No, no English* /sʊmə/ *from the North of England so it's* /sʊmə/

This example illustrates that the learners' difficulty in understanding the teacher stemmed from their own learning and cultural experience — the importance of learner acceptance of the teacher's language will be discussed later in this chapter in the analysis of trainer responses to a survey on levels of language competence required for the CELTA.

Teachers' linguistic proficiency

A unique feature of language teaching is that the target language is both subject matter and (perhaps ideally, but not always) the primary means of instruction. If the medium of instruction serves as language content, the importance of teachers' own language proficiency becomes critical. The CELTA was originally designed with native-speaker teachers in mind, as is reflected in the 1988 RSA/Cambridge CTEFLA syllabus statement that candidates 'should have a standard of English, both written and spoken, equivalent to that of an educated native speaker for whom English is a first language. Oral competence is particularly important.' The current criterion states that candidates must 'have an awareness of language and a competence in both written and spoken English, which will enable them to undertake the course and prepare for teaching a range of levels. The recommended candidate language level is C2 or High C1, Grade A or B on the [Common European Framework of Reference for Languages] CEFR' (Cambridge English 2014b: 9). The revisions to this rubric mirror both changing attitudes towards language and the change in the target candidature and reflect the movement away from the 'educated native speaker' as candidate for CELTA and as model and target for English teachers towards the concept of 'proficient' or 'expert' user of English.

The European Profiling Grid (Evaluation and Accreditation of Quality in Language Services 2013: 3), a framework developed by EAQUALS (Evaluation and Accreditation of Quality in Language Services) lays out teachers' language training and qualifications, key teaching competences and enabling competences. It suggests that a teacher with a C1/CAE level of English would be able to provide 'correct models of language form and usage, for all levels except C2 on almost all occasions'. The implication is that an appropriate level for English teachers' linguistic skills that would enable them to teach internationally, is C1/C2 level within the CEFR.

Although teachers with this suggested language level may still lack confidence in their linguistic skills, the problem may be one of self-perception more than of reality. A study of non-native-speaker teachers on CELTA courses found that, rather than being 'disempowered' in any way by reason of their non-nativeness, these teachers' high level of linguistic competence, ensured by strict entry criteria and rigorous selection procedures, meant that they were at an advantage over native-speaker candidates, whose linguistic skills, i.e. knowledge *about* language, were less well developed (Johnson 2011).

Nevertheless both native and non-native teachers participating in initial teacher training may reveal aspects of their own language use which are considered 'incorrect' in relation to Standard English as defined by Strevens and Trudgill and Hannah earlier in this chapter, hence the need to set standards for linguistic competence. In the next part of this chapter, the data from a survey on language proficiency sent to all CELTA centres will be analysed and discussed. The survey was conducted in order to investigate the procedures used by CELTA trainers to screen applicants for suitable language competence, and to gather information about their stated decision-making processes in relation to varying levels of language competence.

Assessment of CELTA applicants' linguistic competence

The data gathered by Cambridge English indicates that CELTA candidature now includes a considerable number of candidates for whom English is not their first language though this does not mean that these candidates do not have native-speaker competence. There are 341 CELTA centres situated in 70 countries across the world. Given the variety of contexts in which CELTA is offered, the increasing number of native and non-native speakers applying for courses and the need to establish transparent and reliable language assessment standards, Cambridge English stipulates that centres must ensure that those entering the course do so with an acceptable standard of language competence. The selection procedures that form part of course approval require centres to establish that applicants meet the recommended standard (C2/C1 on the CEFR). This is a standard that while not 'error free' is regarded as 'good enough'. No distinction is made between native and non-native speakers in terms of acceptable English language level.

Detailed responses were received from 190 trainers working in a total of 56 different countries worldwide, with a number of trainers working in more than one country. A large proportion of trainers worked in predominantly monolingual learner contexts, with the rest working in predominantly multilingual contexts or a mixture of both. Many trainers worked in contexts where both trainees and learners in practice groups included speakers of a variety of first languages, but interestingly, in some cases, the balance has shifted dramatically to provision in contexts with trainers, trainees and learners in practice groups nearly all sharing the same nationality and first language such that the majority of those taking part in the training programme are non-native speakers of English. The majority of trainers who took part in the survey were themselves first-language speakers of English (85.3%); most had worked as CELTA trainers for more than six years and the majority more than 11 years and so had substantial experience of selecting trainees.

In the following analysis of the survey data, in order to maintain anonymity, the contexts the trainers are working in have not been provided. However, the comments have been selected from the full range of CELTA contexts.

A number of centres required applicants whose first language is not English to have a recognised language qualification in order to meet the Cambridge C1 guideline, e.g. *Cambridge English: Advanced (CAE)* at Grade A or Grade B, IELTS at 7.0 or above. A number of centres asked for a higher language level than required e.g. IELTS 8 or 8.5 or C2 level English. One centre was able to adopt a strict selection procedure as all their applicants are employed by the centre:

We require a C2 level of English for admission to the CELTA course. Sloppy applications can result in a rejection just as English errors can, so we clearly justify rejections that have **over 5 mistakes as being unacceptable for the course**. Since we run the CELTA as an in-service course and all of the candidates are our staff members, it makes it easier to handle issues such as this (emphasis added).

A number of respondents expressed a desire for Cambridge English to provide a standardised selection test:

I do think it would be useful to have a test that provides proof that the nonnative speaker is an advanced speaker of English — definitely a written test. The spoken can be determined by the interview.

Would it be an option for Cambridge [English] to create and have available a standardised language level test, possibly adapted in some way so as to fit the CELTA requirements e.g. the writing task could be similar in format to one of the prose-based assignments?

More stringent guidelines from Cambridge [English] would be appreciated. Perhaps an official language competence test from Cambridge English, for example, with a clear threshold grade for acceptance or rejection.

However, there was also considerable scepticism about reliance on paper tests and no centres relied on paper qualifications alone:

We simply don't trust paper qualifications to take on the full responsibility of allowing someone onto the course. We set more store by the pre-interview task and interview components.

Centres adopted a wide range of selection procedures and made use of several assessment tasks to provide a comprehensive picture of applicants' knowledge and skills, including 'soft skills', as well as applicants' language level. Assessment tasks included pre-interview screening tasks, interviews (face-to-face, by telephone or by Skype), submitted written tasks and onthe-spot tasks to assess written and spoken English. Most centres assessed spoken competence and listening comprehension informally with two-way intelligibility an important factor. The face-to-face interview was considered to be crucial and where not possible is now replaced by (mostly) Skype interview.

Table 1 shows the type and proportion of tasks used. The following is a typical example of selection procedures:

Candidates submit a task the day before the interview — task contains writing/ proofreading & error correction/explicit grammar focus and learner problems/ learner errors and pronunciation. Majority of interviews are small group and face to face.

The on-the-spot writing task is sometimes given to the candidates if we are still unsure if their language is good enough after the pre-interview task and the oral interview.

Table 1 Type and proportion of tasks used

Answer options	Response percentage	Response count
Pre-interview task to screen for interview	97.3%	181
Face-to-face interview	94.1%	175
Skype interview	75.3%	140
Telephone interview	58.1%	108
Interactive spoken task to test speaking and listening skills	28.5%	53
Spoken task focusing on intelligibility	15.1%	28
Submitted written task	72.6%	135
On-the-spot written task	71.0%	132
On-the-spot error correction tasks	48.4%	90
Language qualification, e.g. C1 grade A, English A level, Linguistics degree	62.4%	116
Other		44

Most trainers felt that the required language proficiency level for CELTA applicants is clearly specified and that the range of recommended assessment procedures was sufficient, though the inclusion of numerical scoring criteria by centres and requests for a standardised language level test set by Cambridge English are evidence of a desire from some trainers for a more 'black and white', i.e. easily justifiable, selection procedure.

The trainers emphasised the key part played in selection by the interview and the weighting given to competence in spoken language. In general, trainers highlighted the importance of intelligibility as applicants, once accepted onto the course, would be required to present accurate models of language:

The key, for me, is that they should be a good model for students; … I wouldn't want candidates to be teaching incorrect things to students.

Relatively error-free speech was expected but the ability to self-correct was seen as essential. Similarly, an error-free pre-interview written task was expected as this showed applicants' ability — and willingness — to monitor and correct their written language:

> If they have submitted inaccurate writing, they must have been able to self-correct the majority of this, either in resubmission or during the interview. Their spoken English must be at the very least better than that of the Upper Intermediate students they will be teaching.
>
> Where errors are evident, we need to see the ability to self-correct, edit work and identify problem areas.

Many trainers stressed that the over-riding criterion for acceptance in terms of language level was whether applicants would be able to participate successfully in all aspects of the course:

> While the candidate may have a few minor slips, it is important that candidates have a level of English that would allow them to participate in input sessions and teaching practice to an appropriate level. This is important from their learners' perspective but also for the trainee and what they get out of the course.

In some contexts, trainers noted a clear discrepancy between applicants' knowledge about language and their own linguistic competence, as the following comment from a trainer working in the Middle East illustrates:

> In Country X by far the most common reason for me to reject a CELTA application is on grounds of language proficiency. Almost all applicants have an excellent awareness of the English language and teaching experience, but as non-native speakers accuracy and appropriacy of the language is always of concern. If the grammatical errors in their written English are small and they can correct them in the interview — I would probably accept a candidate. But errors which distort meaning and they find difficult to correct — suggests a rejection. I have rejected applicants whose spoken English contains many errors of grammar and pronunciation. I have also rejected applicants who are obviously struggling to understand me — perhaps by consistently answering my questions wrongly!

Overall, the majority of trainers (63.4%) state that, when selecting trainees, only minor spoken and written linguistic errors are acceptable and, again, self-awareness and self-correction is crucial:

> The key with language ability is that potential trainees are aware of their own language level and can identify and self-correct.
>
> If the candidate was unable to correct their language we would see that as a red flag.
>
> We ask applicants to correct any errors in their written work. We may still accept some errors (but not basic ones).

If applicants evidence persistent language errors, for example, the use of articles, the majority of trainers (80%) would accept them but suggest they undertake remedial action before the course:

> We ask the candidate to revise the language before he/she starts the course. We offer some references to assist the candidate.
>
> Remedial tasks can be identified for such a candidate. These should be given out prior to the course with the warning that these features will have to be taught to students.

As previously noted, the trainers who took part in the survey were working in a wide range of countries, with a number working in more than one country, sometimes with highly contrasting linguistic and educational characteristics, such as the trainer who has worked in 'Thailand, UAE, Serbia, China, Armenia, Latvia, Slovenia, UK'. However, most trainers stated firmly that their decisions to accept or reject an applicant on the basis of linguistic competence were not influenced by the context in which the trainee was likely to be teaching. This reflects the international currency of the certificate, as noted by many of the trainers, as well as the particular nature of English language teaching as a field of work:

> This is a qualification which is internationally recognised and meant to equip candidates for teaching in a range of different contexts.
>
> CELTA enables successful candidates to work anywhere in the world regardless of where they may take the course.
>
> We have no guarantee where our applicants will be working in the future.

There were, however, cases where a trainee's intended teaching context was taken into consideration at the application stage:

> I have an X applicant at the moment who I am waiting to interview by Skype. Her teaching context is in X and that is going to remain the case. Knowing this,

I would take minor pronunciation, grammatical and appropriacy of use issues into consideration before deciding whether or not to accept them.

As part of the survey, trainers were presented with five short texts written by prospective CELTA trainees and asked to say whether, based on that evidence, if representative of the applicant's general standard, they would accept them onto a course.

Example 1

When I left my school, which would probably be a high school in British system, it had been very clear to me for a long time that I would like to study English after a language stay, which should increase my chances later on, for my English class was rather unambitious, and not as instructive as I had hoped, in spite of a highly competent teacher… If I am able to improve sufficiently and pass the CELTA, I can teach during my studies, earn money and more importantly experience, latter is crucial on (name of country's) job market.

Only a minority of trainers (11.9%) would accept this applicant, with the majority either rejecting them or undecided. Basic errors were identified and the style described as 'unclear and convoluted' but, more importantly, the applicant's ability to succeed on a CELTA course was questioned: 'a wide variety of errors with both grammar and lexis. I think this person might struggle on the course to give students an accurate model'. A large number of trainers felt they would want further written evidence or they would offer the applicant the chance to correct or rewrite the text or would be likely to base their decision on the person's oral skills. One trainer pointed out the difference between the language skills necessary in everyday life and those needed for language teaching with the following comment: 'they cannot provide accurate and appropriate models of written language. Although, I can accept that they may be a high level user who can work quite effectively in English, this requires a different set of competences than teaching English'.

Example 2

I have been teaching English for many years. I used to teach different students in different stages. I worked for the intermediate and secondary stages. I used to teach mixed ability classes. I use different techniques and strategies, I read more and more about up to date methods to apply inside my classrooms and that is why I am looking forward to apply for CELTA course. This course is important for teachers wanting to promote in their jobs as well. In my opinion, a teacher who passes this course will be able to teach English language more successfully. This is because of the extensive training he gets in this course.

Again, only a minority of trainers (15.9%) would accept the applicant on the basis of this evidence. The writer's sentence structure was criticised, in particular the lack of cohesion, and one comment noted that the applicant would need 'to show ability to write ... complex sentences and subordination'. Although clearly considered a 'weak candidate', some trainers would once again offer the applicant the chance to resubmit the task and, as before, the interview would play a key role in a final decision, despite the caveat from one trainer that the applicant 'would struggle with TP [Teaching Practice] at upper-intermediate level'. One response that referred to the issue of future teaching context raises issues that will be returned to later in the chapter: 'I wouldn't recommend that this person do a full-time CELTA course but it would depend on the context e.g. if the candidate intended to teach refugees.'

Example 3

Occasionally, I work with teenagers and kids who want to continue their education in British schools and universities. I enjoy interactive nature of teaching because it allows sharing my various interests with other people while passing the knowledge of the language. After 1 year of teaching, I regard my experience as a mainly positive although some areas still require improvement. For example, I may struggle on the planning stage because I cannot always determine the most effective way to present a certain grammar or vocabulary point ... Also, however good the course book may be there are always some drawbacks and I understand the necessity to adapt it to the needs of students. That is why I want to get acquainted with the ways of producing or compiling the tasks of my own and in general be able to meet the demands of a particular class.

The majority of trainers (74.7%) stated that they would accept this applicant but assessments of the text varied considerably; some were extremely positive, others more critical. The following two comments illustrate typical opposing views:

> This is an extremely well-written piece — and is easy to read. It demonstrates considerable insight and ability. Quite possibly a native speaker or one close to native speaker standard. The style is quite colloquial, but also enthusiastic.
>
> Accept on condition that they are able to identify and self-correct. I would send this application essay back and politely remind him/her that they should consider the appropriate use/register of their written work.

As in the previous examples, many trainers stated that they would want to see evidence that the applicant could self-correct the errors of article usage and, as always, the role of the interview would be crucial in reaching a decision, with typical comments such as 'I would place more importance on a candidate's spoken language'.

Example 4

> Personally I do not think that good teachers are born. I think that good teachers are made because our performance in the classroom depends on our expertise, training and knowledge of the subject than in our personality. Also, I think a English teacher should be constantly updating his or her knowledge, because the language is constantly changing. In my country is very mentioned the term 'vocation', specially in the educational field. At the same time, I think that someone with 'vocation' and no knowledge is as useful as someone with knowledge and no vocation, a good teacher should be a mix between knowledge and willingness to teach and learn.

Decisions about this applicant were fairly evenly divided between acceptance (44.4%) and rejection/undecided (55.6%) but even those trainers stating they would accept the applicant qualified their decision with the need for evidence of the ability to self-correct. Comments on the text were again split between those pointing out that the meaning was unclear — 'intelligibility i.e. what does she/he want to say is questionable' and those listing structural errors but considering the overall text comprehensible. Some comments demonstrated that trainers were reflecting on their own decision-making processes: 'Seems I conflate my consideration of language skills with the quality of the ideas expressed, to some degree. Which I wasn't really aware of. Interesting.' Context was not mentioned but one solution offered was to suggest that the applicant should take the CELTA course on a part-time basis rather than as a full-time, intensive course, presumably so that there would be time for their language skills to develop.

Example 5

I would like to enhance my knowledge by doing special supplement on the teaching of adults. The CELTA is the most widely recognised, the most respected and well-known training course. Majority Language schools in X require teachers who only have CELTA qualification. As experienced teacher I can also benefit from learning up-to-date methodology, as well as staying competitive in the job market. I have lots of questions concerning the learning process from students point of view, for example, are there any techniques to learn easily verb patterns. When we put two verbs together, the second verb is usually in the infinitive or -ing form. Which pattern we use depends on the first verb, so how to group them for easy memory storage?

The majority of trainers (73.5%) would reject the writer of this last example. The need for further evidence, the importance of self-correction and the role of the interview to 'probe' the applicants' language skills were all mentioned but, in the case of this applicant, rejection was influenced by the difficulties they were likely to encounter in the classroom because '[i]t's clear they are not proficient in English and so not able to provide accurate models for all levels of learners'. A range of structural errors were listed — 'articles, vocabulary, punctuation, prepositions, word order' — but quite a number of trainers commented that more careful proof-reading would remedy the situation. In contrast, other trainers noted the 'good range of vocabulary, generally high level of accuracy but some systematic error'.

Overall, trainers commented that written tasks formed only part of the selection process and stressed that applicants should be given multiple opportunities to demonstrate their language skills. Self-awareness and self-correction were the key elements in many cases: 'Candidates' own awareness of weaknesses is also vitally important. Better "yes I know I have some problems" rather than "no it looks fine".'

The importance that trainers involved in selection give to the identification of error is evidenced in all the extracts above as well as in trainers' responses to questions in the survey. The emphasis given to applicants being able to identify and correct error relates to two concerns. Firstly the 'ethical' responsibility that trainers have to ensure that trainees, once accepted onto the course, can meet the assessment criteria relating to language — specifically:

> 2b identifying errors and sensitively correcting learners' oral and written language
> 2d providing accurate and appropriate models of oral and written language in the classroom
> 2f showing awareness of differences in register
> In their written work candidates need to use 'written language that is clear, accurate and appropriate to the task' (Cambridge ESOL 2014: 15–18).

Secondly, responsibility to learners — whether learners would be disadvantaged by the teacher's level of English. There were numerous responses forefronting the learner in the debate, suggesting that insistence on language standards is customer-driven as illustrated by the following responses:

> Personal language skills to allow them to model language accurately and provide feedback to learners on their language.
>
> Language proficiency requirement is justified on the grounds that as trainee teachers they must be able to reliably produce correct models of language in speech and writing. Learners are likely to copy their models, so these models must be accurate.
>
> We would justify rejection if we felt that learners would be unhappy being taught by someone with a strong accent who makes repeated errors in their own use of language.
>
> If an applicant makes language errors, they would have to convince us that they have appropriate strategies to avoid badly misleading learners in the classroom. This applies to non-native speakers and to native speakers who have declared personal difficulties such as dyslexia.

One centre justified demanding a higher level of language proficiency because of the levels of the learners in teaching practice classes:

> Our justification for this is that due to the language competence of learners in X, and therefore TP students on our courses, they need to be better than the learners they are potentially going to be working with. C1 is not an uncommon level of proficiency for TP students in X to have attained.

If trainers can make pragmatic decisions to raise the standard of language competence required to meet learner needs, the question arises whether it is equally justifiable to apply some flexibility if candidates are undertaking the training to work in a specific and known context where their level of language competence will be adequate for learner needs. The following response indicates a desire to do so while still insisting that errors must be 'minimal':

> Many of our candidates who are non-native English speakers are immigrants and will teach English in (X). However, we also have several NNS who will return and teach in their own countries. For such teachers, **being able to teach English effectively is good for ELT in general** so a near-perfect grasp of language seems to set the bar a bit too high. But they must be very fluent and prove they are both able to study in English to keep up with the demands of the course and to be able to effectively teach with minimal errors in language (emphasis added).

Although the data was collected from the full range of CELTA centres, very little reference was made to language variety. There was, however, a cluster of comments all in relation to one context which suggest, with one exception, that the standard of English required was measured against an internationally accepted standard of educated English:

> Occasional minor slips and inconsistencies, influence of (X) English usage may be evident.
>
> Fluent speaker with a minimum of errors those being some uses of (X) English. If someone was an excellent speaker but whose written work contained serious grammatical errors, that candidate would not be accepted e.g. over using present continuous and lack of present perfect and an over use of past perfect.
>
> Typical (X) English ... complex and verbose ... so no problem.
>
> Here in X where articles are a problem area ... I would reject the application and suggest that they take a remedial writing course and then re-apply.
>
> The qualification is an international one and therefore qualifies candidates to work anywhere in the world, in theory, so they must be able to provide internationally acceptable models of English. In the past this has presented problems for me when dealing with for example X candidates who are considered to have a high standard of English in their own community, however, can't provide models that would be accepted internationally.

All other comments in the data relate to the notion of error in relation to a native or near-native-speaker standard.

Intelligibility with specific reference to applicants' 'accents' was mentioned by a number of respondents — 'they need to be able to model correctly in terms of pronunciation …'. Most trainers accepted that an internationally intelligible model allowed for a variety of native and nonnative accents but there were concerns about 'pronounced' or 'strong' accents:

> A grey area is pronunciation — sometimes we have candidates who have strong traces of [first language] L1 pronunciation who speak and write fluently but who are difficult to understand (this applies to native speakers with strong regional accents as well).
>
> Particularly difficult … is when the candidate has good and accurate English, but a pronounced accent … this is something we often make efforts to discuss and standardise.

One trainer accepted applicants with very strong accents as long as their written work was acceptable. The response implied that the candidates would be working in their own contexts where their accent would not be problematic.

Following the survey, one trainer provided a further example of a native-speaker pronunciation issue — a native speaker with phonological features in their language which some would describe as non-standard or even incorrect. The example given was of a candidate who identified 'finger' and 'thumb' as beginning with the same initial sound — which indeed they did for him. For this trainer the issue was not the person's use of English but the lack of awareness of features of his own pronunciation, unlike the teacher in the extract quoted earlier who drew attention to his pronunciation of 'summer' as an acceptable model. In this second case, there was the possibility that learners might imitate him without being informed that this was a feature of his own pronunciation that could have less than positive connotations. The trainer commented that this lack of awareness could even lead to future correction of the learner by different teachers.

Conclusions

This chapter has discussed issues related to language standards for teaching purposes. Challenging notions of standard Englishes is highly relevant from a socio-political perspective and may lead over time to challenges to linguistic prescriptivism and to the acceptance of forms previously considered as non-standard. However, despite the current debates about native-speaker identity, standard Englishes and the ownership of

English, there is as yet little evidence from the CELTA survey data reported in the chapter that this is currently the case in the context of international teacher training courses. The data suggests that for teachers and learners in formal language learning settings, competence is measured in relation to a generally recognised standard of educated English and achievement of this standard is a necessary and desired goal — for example to pass examinations, or perform well in academic settings. Therefore, while language improvement and formative assessment of the teacher's own language competence can be included in training courses, assessment of the teacher's own language pre-course must of necessity include a summative judgement on whether the teacher has 'good enough' language for the purposes of modelling and correction, and satisfying learner expectations.

The comments in the survey highlight the thought and care that CELTA trainers put into the selection procedure and their commitment to allowing applicants to show their language skills to best effect. Views were generally nuanced, demonstrating a pragmatic and realistic approach to the wide variations in the requirements for English language teachers in different national contexts.

In a survey that collected over 40,000 words of text, two succinct comments stand out, one reflecting what might be considered the layman's view: 'An English teacher has to be very good at English', and another reflecting the realities of the role: 'Regardless of the qualification the candidates must be able to stand up and teach in front of a class.'

Being 'very good at English' and being 'able to stand up and teach' are inextricably linked, especially where English is the medium of instruction. Trainers take a holistic approach to pre-course assessment weighing the teacher's own language competence with other factors such as their language awareness, interpersonal qualities and previous teaching experience. However, the current stated language entry requirement appears to act as a barrier to candidates who make errors which are considered unacceptable by some trainers but 'minimal' by others, and precludes entry onto the course for those below C1 but who would have the language and teaching competences for their intended context of work. One possible solution, which would need wide consultation given the view expressed by some survey respondents that standards should be 'maintained', could be to establish a clearer relationship between language competence and teaching skills and the levels at which the teacher can operate. The Cambridge English Teaching Framework (Cambridge English 2014a) provides scope for this discussion. The teacher's language level is described at four different levels, and is conceptualised not as one entity, but is broken down into a range of key functions the teacher can perform at specified learner levels. For example, a proficient teacher is described as at 'least B2' and:

- uses classroom language which is consistently accurate throughout the lesson
- responds accurately and appropriately to their learners' output most of the time, in both planned and spontaneous situations
- provides accurate examples of the language points being taught at A1, A2, B1 and B2 levels of the CEFR
- recognises almost all errors that their learners make.

Clearer and more comprehensive reporting of teachers' language competence, and acceptance that qualification at initial training may (but not necessarily) be limited to specific levels, may widen access and provide clarity for CELTA trainers operating in the borderland between what is and is not an acceptable standard for teachers. At the same time it is also important that trainers and trainees, while of necessity working with standard English models, do not imply that these models devalue other varieties of English. Even greater emphasis should be given on training courses, not only to the need for continued language development in relation to the teacher's own level and/or variety of English, but to awareness-raising and recognition of the huge variation in language use worldwide and the relevance of that variation for teaching and learning.

References

Braine, G. (2010) *Nonnative Speaker English Teachers: Research, Pedagogy and Professional Growth.* New York and Abingdon: Routledge.

Cambridge English (2014a) *Cambridge English Teaching Framework*, available online: www.cambridgeenglish.org/images/172992-full-level-descriptors-cambridge-english-teaching-framework.pdf

Cambridge English (2014b) *CELTA Administration Handbook.* Cambridge: Cambridge English Language Assessment.

Cambridge ESOL (2014) *CELTA Syllabus and Assessment Guidelines.* Cambridge: Cambridge ESOL.

Cook, V. (1999) Going beyond the native speaker in language teaching, *TESOL Quarterly* 33 (2), 185–209.

Crystal, D. (1995) *The Cambridge Encyclopedia of the English Language*. Cambridge: Cambridge University Press.

Crystal, D. (2003) *English as a Global Language*. Cambridge: Cambridge University Press.

Crystal, D. (2010) *Is the control of English shifting away from British and American native speakers?* Video interview, Macmillan Global website, available online: www.macmillanglobal.com/blog/author-blog/new-david-crystal-global-english-interview-videos

Davies, A. (2003) *The Native Speaker: Myth and Reality*. Clevedon: Multilingual Matters.

Evaluation and Accreditation of Quality in Language Services (2013) *European Profiling Grid*, available online: egrid.epg-project.eu

Gnutzmann, C. (1999) English as a global language: Perspectives for English language teaching and for teacher education in Germany, in Gnutzmann, C. (Ed) *Teaching and Learning English as a Global Language: Native and Non-native Perspectives*. Tubingen: Gunther Narr, 157–169.

Graddol, D. (2006) *English Next: Why Global English May Mean the End of English as a Foreign Language*. London: British Council.

Jenkins, J. (2004) Beware the natives and their norms, *The Guardian*, available online: www.guardian co.uk/education/2004/jan/22/teflwordsandlanguage

Jenkins, J. (2007) *English as a Lingua Franca: Attitude and Identity*. Oxford: Oxford University Press

Johnson, J. (2011) To what extent do disempowering discourses (Brutt-Griffler and Samimy, 1999), which set up the non-native speaker teacher as inferior to the native speaker teacher, exist in 4-week, initial ELT teacher training courses such as CELTA and Trinity Cert TESOL? unpublished Master's dissertation, University of Sussex.

Kachru, B. (Ed) (1992) *The Other Tongue: English Across Cultures*. Urbana and Chicago: University of Illinois Press.

Kirkpatrick, A. (2007) *World Englishes*. Cambridge: Cambridge University Press.

Kramsch, C. (2003) The privilege of the non-native speaker, in Blyth, C. (Ed) *The Sociolinguistics of Foreign-Language Classrooms: Contributions of the Native, the Near-Native, and the Non-Native Speaker*. Boston: Heinle, 251–262.

Kumaravadevilu, B. (2006) Dangerous liaison: Globalization, empire and TESOL, in Edge, J. (Ed) *(Re-)Locating TESOL in an Age of Empire*. London: Palgrave Macmillan, 1–26.

McKay, S. (2002) *Teaching English as an International Language: Rethinking Goals and Approaches*. Oxford: Oxford University Press.

Medgyes, P. (1992) Native or non-native: Who is worth more? *ELT Journal* 46 (4), 340–349.

Murdoch, G. (1994) Language development provision in teacher training curricula, *ELT Journal* 48 (3), 253–265.

Pennycook, A. (1994) *The Cultural Politics of English as an International Language*. Harlow: Longman.

Phillipson, R. (1992) *Linguistic Imperialism*. Oxford: Oxford University Press.

Smith, L. and Rafiqzad, K. (1979) English for cross-cultural communication: The question of intelligibility, *TESOL Quarterly* 13 (3), 371–380.

Tiplady, C. (2012) Exploring consciousness-raising as an approach to error correction in the context of non-native trainee teachers' classroom language, unpublished Master's dissertation. Manchester: University of Manchester.

Train, R. (2002) The (non)native standard language in foreign language education: A critical perspective, in Blyth, C. (Ed) *The Sociolinguistics of Foreign-Language Classrooms: Contributions of the Native, the Near-native, and the Non-native Speaker*. Boston: Heinle, 3–40.

Trudgill, P. and Hannah, J. (2002) *International English: A Guide to the Varieties of Standard English*. London: Arnold.

Walker, R. (2011) *Pronunciation matters!*, talk at IATEFL Annual Conference, 18 April 2011, Brighton, UK.

Widdowson, H. G. (1994) The ownership of English, *TESOL Quarterly* 28 (2), 377–388.

Widdowson, H. G. (2003) *Defining Issues in English Language Teaching*. Oxford: Oxford University Press.

9 Language awareness: Research, planning, teaching and beyond

Martin Parrott
Teacher, teacher trainer, writer and ELT consultant

Introduction

The notion that the constituents of language are simply grammar, lexis, phonology and graphology was challenged as far back as the mid twentieth century. At that time, the term *communicative competence* was coined (Hymes 1964), and the model of this later proposed by Canale and Swain (Canale and Swain 1980) had an immediate and far-reaching impact on what are seen as the goals of language learning. Applied linguistics in the 1980s and early 1990s seemed preoccupied with defining communicative ability in terms of its component skills and knowledge. Attempts were made to move beyond grammar, lexis, phonology and graphology; much discussion centred on trying to define and evaluate the role of sociolinguistic, pragmatic, textual and organisational factors in effective communication (e.g. McCarthy and Carter 1994). The term 'grammar' itself was expanded (consciously or unconsciously) by some applied linguists to embrace these additional factors, including, for example, semantic meaning and pragmatic use (Rea-Dickens 1991).

Even the conventional view of grammar as focusing largely on form and meaning in the structure of sentences and, in particular, of the verb phrase, was being challenged (Lewis 1993) as attention was increasingly paid to the collocational and grammatical characteristics of words: rather than seeing grammar as a system of patterns into which words are slotted, attention turned to how the internal grammatical properties of particular words or classes of words (as well as their meanings) determine and restrict what can precede or follow them. The developing sophistication and availability of language corpora in the 1990s and in the first decade of the current century not only facilitated research into this but allowed language researchers to examine the validity of the 'rules' that are used in the language classroom and, in some cases, to modify or reject these; to explore how language is used in different contexts, leading, for example, some to suggest that there is a grammar of spoken English that is in some significant respects different from a grammar of written English (e.g. McCarthy 1998). This chapter focuses in part on how far the Cambridge English Teaching Qualifications reflect the range of features that language comprises and, to some extent, particular views of what language is, and how knowledge of this is assessed. It also explores different aspects of awareness and how this is assessed. (See Appendix 1 of this chapter for a summary of assessment of language knowledge and awareness in Cambridge English Teaching Qualifications. Full details of criteria referred to can be found in Appendix B).

If the meaning of the term *language* is open to interpretation, the term *awareness* is perhaps still more problematic. At one end of the continuum, it is used as a synonym for *Knowledge About Language* (KAL). For example, the Cambridge English Teaching website, a teacher development resource which exists independently of the Cambridge English Teaching Qualifications, offers an online course entitled Grammar for Teachers: Language Awareness and the eight units which constitute the course are as follows: Nouns and pronouns, Adjectives, conjunctions and prepositions, Verbs and adverbs, Present tenses, Future forms, Past tenses, Perfect forms and The passive. International House, a worldwide language teaching organisation, provides another example, offering its schools a resource simply called *Language Awareness Course*. Of the 14 units which constitute the course, 11 have familiar grammatical labels (Tense, Auxiliaries and operators, Future forms etc). An introductory unit is entitled *Describing Language* and the final two units explore the interface between grammar and lexis (The Noun Phrase, Language as Lexis). Homework includes tasks which require participants 'to analyse authentic texts ... and to critique coursebook treatments of language' but the main thrust of the course is clear: 'it aims primarily to further develop participants' declarative knowledge of language'. In a book interestingly entitled not *Language Awareness* but *About Language*, Thornbury (1997) supports this narrow interpretation of the term. He discusses language awareness from different perspectives, concluding that in second language education it 'is the knowledge that teachers have of the underlying systems of the language that enables them to teach effectively'. (Although the teacher's own linguistic competence obviously informs and contributes to this 'knowledge', and indeed to other aspects of language awareness, the nature of this competence and how it is assessed is beyond the scope of this chapter). (See Johnson and Poulter, Chapter 8.)

For others, the term *language awareness* has a broader perspective. In a collection of papers, many of which make similar observations, Bigelow and Ranney comment that 'transfer of KAL to instruction does not happen automatically' (Bigelow and Ranney 2005: 196) and argue that teacher education programmes need to integrate focus on language systems with their practical application. A decade ago Bolitho, referring to pre-service trainee teachers, argued that they 'need to be able to analyse language (analogising, contrasting, substituting, etc.) in order to be able to plan lessons, to predict learners' difficulties, to answer their questions, and to write and evaluate materials', adding that, 'only if they are able to think for themselves about language will they be able to do this' (Bolitho, Carter, Hughes, Ivanic, Masuhara and Tomlinson 2003: 255). For many, language awareness encompasses not only knowledge of language systems but also its practical application in planning and teaching lessons. For Andrews, this embraces qualities of 'alertness' and 'intuition'. In a study of the qualities of three 'good language teachers' (GLTs), he notes that 'two important features of Marina's planning, both of which are indicative of the nature of her TLA [teacher language awareness], are her alertness in spotting opportunities for focusing on language content and her ability to recognise how and in what ways the textbook treatment of content needs to be supplemented' (Andrews 2007: 137). He also notes that 'in focusing on form, whether grammar or vocabulary ... all three GLTs appear to have an intuitive understanding of the importance of "input enhancement"' (Andrews 2007: 130).

Others, in their consideration of language awareness go beyond *both* knowledge of language systems *and* the practical application of this. Arndt, Harvey and Nuttall take a view of language awareness explicitly 'broader' than Thornbury's view: 'the knowledge that teachers have of the underlying systems of the language that enables them to teach effectively'. For them language awareness is 'based in the main on language seen within its sociocultural dimension, that is, how people actually use language' (Arndt, Harvey and Nuttall 2000: 11). They later argue that teachers need Critical Language Awareness (CLA): 'CLA entails, as part of a general sensitivity to language — the particular understanding of how underlying ideology, beliefs and attitudes are encoded in text; how socio-historical contexts and socio-cognitive processes are inevitably bound up together in the production and interpretation of text' (Arndt *et al.* 2000: 218). To some extent this echoes both Bolitho's advocacy of 'a model of teacher education which promotes independent critical thinking' (Bolitho *et al.* 2003: 255) and Andrews' advocacy of 'an appropriate balance between establishing the necessary foundation of a basic knowledge about language and arousing the kind of sensitivity to the diversity and complexity of language that is essential to any thinking L2 teacher' (Andrews 2007: 185). Critical thinking and reflection are obviously closely related and, for many, reflection is a key component in language awareness. Andrews identifies 'the willingness of these GLTs to engage in reflection about the content of learning' (Andrews 2007: 130) and argues 'that a combination of ... language-related self-reflection and focused collaborative activity ... represents the most effective way of helping L2 teachers to achieve enhanced levels of language awareness and the development of pedagogical strategies for dealing with language that are of direct relevance to their specific teaching context' (Andrews 2007: 189).

But many of those working in the field of ELT have an instinctive feeling that *awareness* could — or should — embrace more than knowledge, application of knowledge in planning and teaching, critical language awareness and reflection. Some 60 practising English teachers, all of whom have obtained at least one Cambridge English Teaching Qualification, were asked to write one or two short sentences beginning *Language Awareness is* ... (Parrott, informal survey, December 2012). Their classroom experience ranged from one to 30 years and the group comprised teachers in and from different parts of the world who do and do not speak English as a first language. The survey provided a huge variety of responses: knowledge of grammatical systems figured substantially, but so too did reference to lesson planning, sensitivity and decision-making in the classroom, and vaguer but no less convincing references to a 'feeling for language'.

It is often easier to recognise — and sometimes to describe — this 'feeling for language' than to explain or define it. Some people are unable to perceive that there is a difference in the meaning of the word *should* in the following sentences: 'He should be there now' and 'He should try to lose weight'. Others, guided perhaps by no more than an instinctive sensitivity to language and meaning, are able to identify the difference, sometimes almost instantly, and may be able to put it into words or to illustrate it with further examples. People with this latter skill would generally be recognised to have good language *awareness*. Equally, the language *awareness* of teachers who notice and modify their language effectively when they are not understood, or who respond in a satisfactory way to unexpected questions such as 'What's the difference between *said* and *claimed*?', would generally be applauded. To some extent this 'feeling for language' is embraced in Andrews and McNeill's assertion that 'language awareness also encompasses awareness of language from the learners' perspective and awareness of the learners' interlanguage, both its present state and its potential developmental path' (Andrews and McNeill 2005: 174). Andrews and McNeill see 'sensitivity, perception, alertness and vision' as being essential to teacher language awareness (2005: 175), and their list of characteristics of the language awareness of 'good language teachers' includes not only several uses of 'awareness' and 'willingness' but also 'a love of language' (2005: 174).

The following section concentrates on knowledge about language and its practical application. The subsequent section looks at critical awareness, reflection and 'feeling for language', focusing in particular on Delta.

Knowledge about language and its practical application

Abstract knowledge of language systems

Teacher training course programmes frequently group together sessions which focus on aspects of grammar, lexis, phonology and discourse under the general heading *language awareness*. Characteristically, these sessions aim to help course participants acquire or develop knowledge and understanding of specific aspects of language systems, especially those aspects of grammar such as modal verbs, the present perfect or the passive voice that are foregrounded in General English courses.

Teachers and prospective teachers of English need this explicit knowledge (sometimes referred to as *explicit* knowledge, *declarative* knowledge or *meta*-knowledge) of how the language works. It helps them to make sense of aspects of what they are teaching, it helps them to plan, teach and evaluate lessons which focus on aspects of language systems and to respond constructively to problems which may arise in any lesson. The terminology they learn along with their knowledge enables them to access reference materials. It is unsurprising that developing this knowledge is a substantial component of most ELT training programmes, and that a command of this knowledge figures in the assessment. It is, perhaps, a weakness that none of the Cambridge English Teaching Qualifications at present includes an explicit and comprehensive set of descriptors as to what this knowledge comprises and it might, at present, be difficult to mount a convincing defence against the charge that a candidate's gaps in knowledge may not be exposed, especially in CELTA and ICELT, where there is no formal examination and candidates may have some measure of choice in the language areas they research and teach. All reference to criteria in the discussion below are taken from the relevant syllabus or handbook.

Teaching Knowledge Test (TKT)

The name of the award leaves no doubt as to the central importance of knowledge, and knowledge of language systems is tested most explicitly in Module 1 *Language and background to language learning and teaching*. Five of the 13 sections in the test focus on language systems, accounting for 25 out of a total of 80 marks. For example, candidates are asked to match underlined words/groups of words in a given text with given lexico-grammatical terms, to match underlined subordinate clauses in complex sentences with functional labels ('their meanings'), to choose a correct lexical or phonological term from a list of three to identify instances of language use, to match phonemic symbols with sounds and to match example sentences with given communicative functions. Although the syllabus includes lexis, phonology, grammar and 'functions', the test is weighted towards the first three of these. Nonetheless, the 2007 Examination Report on TKT Module 3 Task 3 notes: 'This kind of task is not concerned so much with meaning in isolation, but with the meaning that words take on in discourse' and exhorts candidates and course providers to look at language from a broad perspective.

With the exception of TKT:Practical (see below), TKT answer papers are 'objectively' marked, making use predominantly of matching or multiple-choice testing formats. Candidates need to consider and select from a limited range of options in response to a very specific task. Thus, while the focus may be sophisticated (identifying the communicative function of examples of spoken discourse, for example), its completion requires a particular kind of cognitive approach: TKT qualifications are often taken by a wide range of teachers at various stages in their careers. But the 'level' of the qualification is determined more by its format than a particular target audience. The exercise below is typical of how language knowledge is tested in TKT.

3

It's a very **difficult** question. I'm not **sure** if I've done it **right**.

Which of the 3 words is **NOT** an adjective?

A	difficult
B	sure
C	right

(TKT Sample Paper 2011 Module 1)

It could be argued that in order to select the only 'correct' answer, the candidate needs simply to understand the difference between an adjective and an adverb — or at most to identify that 'right' functions as an adverb rather than as an adjective in the target sentence. The task does not require the teacher to consider the reality that there are different kinds of adjective and different kinds of adverb, and that the distinction between them is by no means always clear. Candidates need to approach such tasks at a simple level — the level at which distinctions may be conveyed to learners. Candidates whose approach to language is more intellectual, more exploratory and perhaps more original are not given the opportunity to display their knowledge. A glossary of terms is provided for TKT and for prospective candidates much preparation may consist of learning these. The terms are explained in the glossary and, while for some candidates learning these may be enlightening, for others they may present a frustratingly narrow view of language, but one that is necessary in order to pass the test.

TKT: Knowledge About Language (KAL)

TKT: KAL is described in handbooks published by Cambridge English variously as an *extension* or *specialist* module. Unlike the other modules of TKT which require a B1 level in the Council of Europe Common European Framework of Reference for Languages, TKT: KAL candidates need a level of at least B2. Although the syllabus is divided into four parts, dealing respectively with lexis, phonology, grammar and discourse, as in the case of TKT Modules 1–3, the test is weighted towards the first three of these.

The test attempts to place the tasks in a teaching context (so for example an exercise which requires matching spelling errors to rules that are broken is couched in terms of *teacher's advice* and an exercise which requires matching multi-word verbs in given contexts to definitions of different multi-word verb types is couched in terms of 'the teacher ... selecting sentences to exemplify different types'. Nonetheless what is being tested is very clearly an expanded version of what is tested in TKT Module 1: knowledge, understanding and terminology (see above). As the TKT: KAL Handbook states: 'It tests knowledge about the systems of the English Language that aid a teacher in planning and delivering their lessons.'

Delta Module One

This explicit testing of knowledge of language systems is not confined to TKT. Delta Module One (Understanding Language, Methodology and Resources for Teaching) comprises two written examination papers. The aim of the module is to 'extend and develop candidates' knowledge and understanding' (Cambridge English 2014: 10). One of the six bullet points which expand this aim is *language systems and learners' linguistic problems*. Candidates need to 'demonstrate understanding of key features of language systems ...' but there is no systematic itemisation of what constitutes these 'key features' beyond a reference to 'Understanding of spoken and written discourse ... which contribute to successful communication, e.g. register, cohesion, organisation, range of grammar and lexis' (Cambridge English 2014: 10) and '[f]eatures of language systems' (Cambridge ESOL 2011: 3).

In many ways what is tested is an expanded version of what is tested in TKT: KAL: despite the inclusion of *discourse* in the TKT: KAL syllabus, the assessment is focused essentially elsewhere. In Delta a wider range of language systems is tested and more depth is required from the candidate. In TKT, candidates choose the answer they think is correct and fill in their answers on a marksheet that is computer readable. The practicability that this format offers is offset by limitations imposed. There is no room for discussion or exploration of subtlety or ambiguity. Delta, on the other hand, is aimed at teachers who normally hold a first teaching qualification (e.g. CELTA) and have subsequent classroom experience. It thus presupposes a degree of range and sophistication in knowledge and understanding of language systems. The rubric *match* or *choose* that is commonly found in the TKT tasks is replaced by *comment on* in Delta. Candidates are required to provide their own definitions, examples and illustrations. For example, a text is provided and candidates are required to 'identify … features … characteristic of its genre' and provide examples. Their attention is directed to short extracts from the passage and they are asked to comment on aspects of lexis and syntax requiring them to identify the features, to understand their meanings and uses in general and to explore how they are used in the given context. For example:

c

Comment on the **use** of **relative clauses** and **relative pronouns** in the following extracts

- *BookCrossing, where 791,837 people in over 130 counties come to share their passion for books.* (lines 1–2)
- *A book registered on BookCrossing is ready for adventure.* (line 10)
- *… by others, who then do likewise* (lines 41–42)

(Delta Module One Paper 1 June 2010)

At first sight this task differs hugely from the TKT task discussed previously: it seems that candidates can respond individually and display their own knowledge and understanding. The Examiner's report notes that 'This task … acted as a good discriminator between those candidates who knew about relative clauses and those who did not, although even those who had a good knowledge lost marks because they did not consider the discoursal use of the relative pronouns *where* and *who* in terms of anaphoric reference or the fact that the second extract [contains] an example of a reduced relative clause'. However, the guideline answers which are used by examiners in marking the paper and the sample provided in the report of a 'good' answer, reveal that, although this task is significantly more open than the multiple-choice format of TKT tasks, there is still a finite number of points for which candidates can be rewarded. Familiarity with the way in which the paper is marked and with the number and kinds of points that are expected is essential to candidate success. The sample 'good' answer closely follows the style of short bullet points found in the guideline answers.

Delta Module Two

Two of the five assignments in Delta Module Two (Developing Professional Practice) focus on language systems. Candidates plan, teach and evaluate a lesson (see Lesson Planning and Teaching below), but also need to present a Background essay (2,000–2,500 words) exploring 'an area of language systems and consider[ing] related teaching and learning issues'. Candidates are expected to explore the area ('of the grammar, lexis, phonology or discourse systems of English') extensively and in depth: the following comment from an external assessor very clearly demonstrates the level of sophistication that can be rewarded: 'the first problem of tenor and mode was valid and well-exemplified. There was good reference to other languages and specific examples in her final three issues of arbitrary co-occurrence, non-transparent meaning and stress-related (or L1 transfer) problems'.

The Delta syllabus clearly flags up the importance of discourse and phonology, and course programmes often focus heavily on these areas, which may be less familiar to course participants than lexis and grammar. While some candidates choose to focus on tried and trusted aspects of grammar and lexis in their background essays and taught lessons, others seize the opportunity to push the barriers: the candidates who do well in this part of Delta are often those who have the experience, knowledge and confidence which allows them to research and tackle the more challenging aspects of phonology and discourse.

CELTA and the Young Learner (YL) Extension to CELTA

As previously observed, CELTA (and the YL Extension to CELTA) involve no externally assessed examination. However, as in Delta Module

Two, candidates are required to research, analyse and discuss language systems in written tasks and in their lesson planning. Whereas Delta is an inservice qualification for experienced teachers, CELTA and the YL Extension are intended as pre-service qualifications and this largely defines the level of knowledge required. Many candidates will be researching and analysing English language systems for the first time.

Language analysis and awareness is one of the five topics into which the CELTA syllabus is divided and one of the four *Classroom-related written assignments* is to focus on 'an aspect of the language system of English'. Centres are responsible for designing tasks in which candidates identify 'significant features of the form, pronunciation, meaning and use of language items/areas and the use of relevant information from reference materials'. *Language awareness* features as one of six topics in the syllabus of the YL Extension to CELTA. As well as 'Language description for teaching English to young learners', reference is made to teaching English through topics, tasks and activities and successful candidates need to demonstrate that they can 'identify and be aware of some significant differences between their own language and a foreign language' and can 'make practical use of reference books which will help them to develop their understanding, knowledge and awareness of language'. Although the two written assignments for the YL Extension focus on classroom teaching, young learners and learning contexts, course providers need to ensure that candidates complete a language analysis task as part of their preparation and planning for teaching.

The assessment in CELTA and the YL Extension to CELTA (and ICELT, see below) is essentially holistic. *The Assessment Guidelines* itemise competences that candidates need to evince but unlike Delta, where in each of the four assessed lessons each criterion needs to be marked as 'Met', 'Partially met' or 'Not Met', these criteria can be used more flexibly to guide tutors/assessors to implement the overall grade profiles.

Teachers often look back at the content of CELTA course programmes on which they received their initial training — or indeed at the programmes of today's courses — and comment on how prominently grammar (and to a lesser extent, lexis) feature in the language awareness strand of the course. It is sometimes argued that this is far too narrow and that the developments in our understanding of language and communication that arose from — and following — the work of Hymes, have effectively been ignored. A number of points need to be made in response to this criticism, however. The first is that CELTA is very much a special case; it is taken primarily by young adults seeking a 'toolkit' and qualification to enable them to begin teaching. CELTA courses do their best to prepare candidates for the circumstances they are likely to be working in, and this usually means using the most widely available published course materials: materials which have a very conservative linguistic content. Teachers who seek a career in ELT will very often move on to further study and qualifications (Delta, Master's degrees), where any simplistic certainties that may have provided them with an initial 'crutch' are questioned, and where their understanding of what constitutes language and communication will broaden and deepen.

A further but more important point is that it is the course providers and not Cambridge English who are responsible for course programmes. Although this is perhaps less prominent than some would wish, the CELTA syllabus does in fact qualify the label 'Grammar' as follows: grammatical frameworks: rules and conventions relating to words, sentences, paragraphs and texts (Cambridge ESOL 2010: 4). This may seem an odd interpretation of grammar, but it clearly suggests that attention should be paid to syntax and textual cohesion. This is at least a nod in the direction of acknowledging the influence of the work of Hymes and his followers.

ICELT

ICELT, like CELTA and Delta, is continuously assessed. It differs from CELTA in that it assumes prior experience and that candidates are working as teachers during the course. It is often run within or by an institution for its own teaching staff and its focus, consequently, may be on learners of a particular type such as primary, secondary or English for Academic Purposes. In terms of 'level' it falls somewhere between CELTA and Delta. A number of teachers who have obtained ICELT go on to extend and consolidate the knowledge obtained through studying and teaching to obtain Delta.

The syllabus comprises seven units. In content there is considerable overlap between the first six of these and the content of CELTA and YL Extension courses. Unit 1 *Language knowledge and awareness* includes 'Concepts and terminology used in English language teaching for describing form and meaning in language and language use'. It contains, however, no detailed breakdown of the topic as in the CELTA syllabus (where Grammar, Lexis, Phonology are given separate sub-sections and are then further subdivided).

ICELT is in many ways unique among the Cambridge English Teaching Qualifications. Candidates' own language skills are assessed in every component of the course and very detailed criteria are provided for the assessment of both spoken and written competence. Teachers whose first language is English may obtain the qualification but it is primarily adapted to the needs and context of teachers whose confidence and accuracy in using English may benefit from support; there is an assumption that course participants will want to validate their own language competence. This — and the focus on identifying, analysing and evaluating use of language in the classroom by both learners and teachers — gives ICELT a particular flavour which distinguishes it from other Cambridge English Teaching Qualifications in terms of its language awareness content.

As with CELTA, the implicit view of what constitutes language can be criticised for being narrow and for ignoring advances in our understanding of what constitutes language and communication. However, like teachers who have obtained CELTA, those with ICELT who seek a career in ELT will generally move on to further (more 'advanced') study and qualifications.

Lesson planning

In the process of planning lessons, teachers combine their knowledge and understanding of language systems with their knowledge and understanding of the learners and of the range of materials and approaches at their disposal. The term *language analysis* is often used as a sub-category of language *awareness* to describe the processes of identifying relevant aspects of meaning, form, phonology and use of the language that will be dealt with in a lesson, of narrowing down these aspects to what will or will not be included and of making decisions about how far reference may or may not be made to other instances of language which are similar in terms of form or use. The process of anticipating difficulties that learners may have and of planning how to respond to these difficulties is also often considered under the heading *language analysis*. All these decisions depend on and are informed by the teacher's understanding of the learners: their level of English, their age, cognitive skills and attention span, their needs and preferences, and the impact of their first language and previous learning experience on their approaches to learning.

A different kind of language awareness (as opposed to language *analysis*) is involved in other aspects of the planning process. Teachers select materials which will aid their learners' understanding and use of the language they are teaching, identifying instances of the language which illustrate the aspects they want learners to focus on in the lesson (and, crucially, identifying — in order perhaps to avoid them — instances which do not). They also identify opportunities which the material offers to generate learners' use of the language. It is an aspect of language awareness, again, which enables teachers to evaluate and make decisions about the accessibility or difficulty of these materials in terms of language present elsewhere in them. And language awareness again comes into play as teachers determine contexts which naturally (or, in the classroom, *conveniently*) give rise to use of the target language. *Language awareness* is moreover key in selecting teaching approaches: is there an underlying logic in the language which lends itself to an inductive process where learners will be able to work out its meaning and/or aspects of its form from context? Or would it be more efficient to provide rules and examples and then to move on to some kind of practice? Is there a level of cognitive complexity or discoursal subtlety which demands a repeated process of exposure and directed noticing over many lessons and suggests the use of examples in written rather than spoken text? Are there sociological determinants which suggest the need for varied instances within spoken contexts? Are there phonological difficulties which merit activities that help learners to develop their pronunciation? Are there difficulties in manipulating the structure which require scaffolding from the teacher and in what form? Inexperienced teachers (on CELTA or YL Extension courses) may largely rely on a coursebook to make these decisions for them. But, they would be expected, with increasing confidence and experience (in the case of Delta), to make independent decisions more adapted to their own learners' profile of abilities and needs, the coursebook becoming not only one resource among others, but one to be used critically, the teacher omitting, supplementing and adapting its contents.

TKT: Practical, CELTA (including the YL Extension), ICELT and Delta Module Two

These assessments all require candidates to plan and teach lessons which focus on aspects of language systems. A practical lesson plan template is provided for TKT: Practical, which includes a substantial section under the heading Language Analysis. This is subdivided into Form, Meaning, Phonology, Anticipated Problems and Solutions and the *Handbook for Teachers* provides examples of completed templates with detailed comments on these from the Principal Assessor. The other assessments are less prescriptive in terms of how the lesson plan is presented but the Syllabus and Assessment guidelines for each qualification make it clear that candidates need to demonstrate ability in similar areas. The degree of skill expected naturally increases from TKT: Practical to the course-based awards CELTA (and ICELT) to Delta.

Written assignments in CELTA, ICELT and Delta require candidates to go beyond research into language systems and abstract discussion of these. For example CELTA Assignment 2.1 (Focus on the learner) involves 'identifying learners' language needs' and 'selecting appropriate material and or/resources to aid the learner's/learners' language development'.

In their background essays (two of which focus on language systems), Delta candidates need to 'identify and discuss common learning problems and key teaching issues in a range of learning contexts' (Cambridge English 2014: 59). Two of the assignments in Module Two focus on language systems and 'Planning and preparation' is one of 10 assessment categories. This is further broken down into 11 points. These include: 'relevant analysis of target language in terms of meaning, use, form and phonology (5c), anticipat[ing] and explain[ing] potential problems in relation to the lesson's aims and learning outcomes, the learners and the learning context, and the equipment and resources to be used (5f), and suggest[ing] appropriate solutions to the problems outlined in 5f (5g)'.

Comments from external assessors make it clear how important language awareness is in the assessment of lesson planning. Summarising these, the 2009 Principal Moderator's report notes:

> Strong candidates gave relevant and accurate information about the language ... focus of the lesson. They had a good understanding of the area that they were teaching which they were able to transfer to the classroom. The inclusion of

239

a detailed language ... analysis sheet in the plan was generally an accurate indicator of whether the candidate would meet this criterion. These candidates also carefully planned the presentation/clarification stage of the lesson with concept questions to check learner understanding. They had given thought to exactly *how* they were going to conduct feedback in terms of the language ... aim, *how* they would check what the students had learnt at the end of the lesson and *what* record the learners would take away with them.

TKT and Delta Module One

While there is no direct assessment of lesson planning in TKT: KAL, YL and CLIL, candidates preparing for the TKT: YL Module are advised to 'look at the language demands of the lesson' beforehand, and to 'decide what kind of support is needed so that learners can understand and produce the language' and in teaching a lesson, to 'note any common strengths and problems young learners have in understanding and using key language'. In becoming 'familiar with supplementary materials' they are also advised to ask themselves questions such as 'Is the language load manageable and relevant?'. In the TKT: CLIL Module, language awareness skills and knowledge relevant to test preparation form part of the assessment. For example, candidates have been asked to 'match the language problems a teacher can face when writing a CLIL test with the possible support strategies listed'.

Although the focus in the TKT test is knowledge rather than its application, as the following two items from TKT Module 2 illustrate, this knowledge is both relevant to lesson planning and is sometimes directly linked to it:

38

To assess whether students know when to use *used to* for past habits, it would **NOT** be appropriate for

    A   students to write about what they did as a child, responding to prompts e.g. clothes, toys.

    B   students to write sentences about a man who has become famous, contrasting his old and new life.

    C   students to tell a story about something funny which happened to them as a child.

(TKT Sample Paper 2011 Module 2)

78

Which activity can be used to practise questions using *some* and *any*?

    A   Work in pairs. You each have a picture of some children in a playground, but your pictures are not the same. Talk together and find the differences. When you have finished, compare your pictures.

    B   Look at this picture of a room in a house for one minute. You are not allowed to write anything down. When your teacher tells you, turn your picture over, then write down the answers to the questions you will be asked on a separate sheet of paper.

    C   You have a map with a route which starts at the station and ends at the library. Student B has the same map without a route. Give directions to help him/her to draw the same route as yours. You are not allowed to show him/her your map.

(TKT Sample Paper 2011 Module 2)

The first of these tasks requires candidates to consider and to evaluate the language-generating potential of different classroom activities, taking them beyond the straightforward skill, for example, of matching a term to a definition. The kind of thinking involved closely replicates the processes teachers go through in selecting or devising testing (and practice) activities in planning their lessons. The second task extract is from a list of seven learning aims, three of which focus on practising aspects of language systems. Candidates need to think about a range of purposes for the three listed activities; again this task both tests — and perhaps develops — the candidates' skill in identifying the learning potential of different activities, thus replicating a process teachers carry out in planning their lessons.

In Delta Module One Paper 1, Tasks 3 and 4 focus on skills used in lesson planning; the format of the tasks is much more open than those in TKT, and the response required is more developed and in greater depth. Task 3 requires candidates to study material, usually an extract from a coursebook or resource book, and to identify language features learners at that level 'would need to use to support the activity successfully'. A short section of Task 4, which presents candidates with a piece of authentic material and requires them to identify features of the text which are characteristic of its genre and then to comment in detail on the form, meaning and use of language in a number of specific extracts, is given on page 233. Despite the reservations expressed with regard to the atomistic and formulaic approach that the marking process encourages, the knowledge and analytical skill assessed in this task provides the basis for more practical, applied analysis in the stage of determining how authentic material can be used, for what purpose and with whom.

Teaching

Further kinds of language awareness are required in classroom teaching. Language awareness comes into play 'in the moment' when teachers give explanations and supply models of language, however thoroughly they may have prepared for this.

Language awareness in the classroom is often thought of primarily in terms of how far teachers notice mistakes, and the decisions they make about whether, when and how to respond. However, even in terms of monitoring and responding to learners' language, more than this should be expected of an experienced and competent teacher. Is what the learners said or wrote what they intended? What *did* they intend? Are they simplifying or distorting their messages because they lack language? Are they avoiding language they are unsure of? To answer these questions, teachers need to focus on the full range of linguistic possibilities within the context of use, on what the learners have already studied and on what competence they have previously demonstrated. And it can be yet more challenging for the teacher to identify and diagnose learners' comprehension difficulties due to linguistic gaps. Teachers respond to learners' output, not only on-the-spot in the classroom, but also in responding to homework or in analysing any recordings they have made.

In the classroom, language awareness also helps teachers to monitor and regulate their own use of language. Judgements about what their learners know enable them to make decisions about the speed and the degree of complexity with which they speak and about choosing whether and when to provide written rather than spoken models or instructions.

Naturally the degree of spontaneity and sophistication expected from candidates in terms of language awareness in teaching, varies according to the level of the qualification.

TKT

Although among the TKT extension Modules only TKT: Practical involves working in the classroom as part of the assessment, aspects of knowledge applied to classroom use or learner output figure in a range of the Modules.

In TKT: Module 3 *Managing the teaching and learning process* Part 1 (*Teachers' and learners' language in the classroom*), candidates need to categorise mistakes in learners' language use and to evaluate different correction strategies (see 20–26 below) and identify the communicative purpose of their spoken utterances (see 34–40 below).

20–26

For questions **20–26**, match the mistakes on each line of the student's letter with the types of mistake listed **A–H**.

Mark the correct letter (**A–H**) on your answer sheet.

There is one extra option which you do not need to use.

Types of mistake

A	wrong spelling
B	wrong verb pattern
C	missing auxiliary
D	wrong noun form
E	wrong word order
F	wrong tense
G	wrong preposition
H	wrong punctuation

Dear Susan and Nick,

20 I'm writing to give you some informations about Theo's travel arrangements.

21 He leaves, Athens on December 13th on flight number

22 OM 197, arriving to Melbourne at 11.20am the next day.

23 In case you have problems to recognise him I've enclosed a recent photograph.

24 He's quite tall with brown long hair. He's got green eyes.

25 He going to wear a dark blue T-shirt, jeans and black trainers for his trip.

26 Please let me no if there is anything you would like him to bring from Greece.

Yours sincerely

Giorgos

(TKT Sample Paper 2011 Module 3)

34–40

For questions **34–40**, match the underlined words in the following transcript of a student's classroom conversation with the functions listed **A–H**.

Mark the correct letter (**A–H**) on your answer sheet.

There is one extra option which you do not need to use.

Functions

A	changing topic
B	agreeing
C	asking for an opinion
D	asking for clarification
E	giving clarification
F	hesitating
G	correcting
H	disagreeing

A student's classroom conversation

Katia: So, how long have you lived here, then?

Lydia: (**34**) <u>In this town?</u>

Katia: Yeah.

Lydia: I was born here, so I know it (**35**) <u>err, erm</u> … like the back of my hand.

Katia: Like the back of …?

Lydia: (**36**) <u>It's an expression that you use when you know something really well</u>. I like it.

Katia: (**37**) <u>Yeah, it's a good one</u>. 'Like the back of my hand', I must remember that.

Lydia: (**38**) <u>Anyway</u>, how about you? How long you have lived here?

Katia: (**39**) <u>'Have you lived here'</u> you mean.

Lydia: Oh yeah, that's right.

Katia: About three years. It's a really nice town.

Lydia: It's so boring. (**40**) <u>You can't mean that</u>.

(TKT Sample Paper 2011 Module 3)

The first of these tasks tests knowledge and skill which is a precondition for knowing how to respond in practical terms to learners' written output while the second tests a more general sensitivity to learners' language use. And while the matching format of these exercises could be criticised for narrowing down the possibilities and making the task easier, there is also a sense in which the presentation of alternative possibilities plays a developmental role in raising candidates' awareness.

Matching activities also focus on teachers' classroom language. Candidates are asked to identify the function of examples of classroom language, to identify the role the teacher is assuming and to evaluate the appropriacy and effectiveness of their language use (see 7–13 and 62–67 below). One example has been extracted in both cases.

7–13

Match the teacher's instructions to an elementary class with the teacher trainer's comments listed **A–H**.

Example of '**teacher's instructions**': Gina, do you know a synonym for the word 'pullover'?

Teacher trainer's comments

A	Well done for deciding on the order for the class to do things before giving instructions.
B	Decide which interaction is most appropriate for the task instead of relying on the students.
C	It's better to nominate one particular student as this eventually gives everyone a chance to participate.
D	This is a good, clear instruction for a vocabulary task for an elementary group of learners.
E	The grammatical language in this statement is above elementary level.
F	This statement is demotivating to learners. Try to be more encouraging.
G	Try not to change your mind when giving instructions to lower levels, and make them as short as possible.
H	The student is unlikely to know this term for a lexical category at this level.

(TKT Sample Paper 2011 Module 3)

62–67

Match the advice on correcting given to a trainee teacher with the correction strategies listed **A–G**

Example of '**Advice on correcting**': Write common mistakes on the board and see if students can spot mistakes.

Correction strategies

A	use a correction code
B	employ the technique of error correction
C	over-apply the rule
D	give delayed feedback
E	reformulate the sentence
F	allow opportunities for self-monitoring and group correction
G	encourage peer correction

(TKT Sample Paper 2011 Module 3)

The first of these tasks tests — and perhaps raises awareness of — how teachers use language in the classroom and of pitfalls that may arise. The second tests — and perhaps raises awareness of — suitable responses to learners' spoken output.

In preparation for this module, candidates clearly need to develop their sensitivity to language used by themselves, other teachers and by learners in the classroom. In TKT:YL and CLIL candidates are also required to match examples of teachers' language to their functions. In the *TKT: KAL Handbook for Teachers*, detailed guidance is given to candidates preparing for the test, which includes analysing the linguistic context of texts for classroom use and the linguistic causes of problems for learners in lessons and in homework (Cambridge ESOL 2012: 7–8).

Naturally it is in the *Practical* module of the TKT suite that practical skills in relation to knowledge of language systems are assessed in 'real' circumstances. The assessment involves five 'teaching criteria'. These include 'focus on language; form, meaning and pronunciation and include appropriate practice', 'use English appropriately e.g. when explaining, instructing, prompting learners, eliciting, conveying meaning' and 'monitor learners and provide feedback on language and tasks including oral and/or written correction'.

CELTA and ICELT

Successful candidates at CELTA Pass level need to demonstrate a range of factors relating to their own use of language, learners' use of language and how they respond to this 'convincingly and consistently in their six hours' assessed teaching practice' (see Appendix 2 of this chapter). The ICELT (*Teaching* Component) requirements are broadly similar.

The ICELT *Language for Teachers* component is assessed through four written tasks (six if this component is offered as a stand-alone course) 'designed to improve [candidates'] use of English for teaching purposes' (Cambridge ESOL 2004: 3). These tasks include analysing and discussing learners' use of language in an observed lesson, marking and correcting learners' written work and commenting on this process, recording themselves teaching a lesson and analysing and commenting on their own use of language during the lesson.

The *Methodology* component of ICELT is considered in Critical awareness, reflection and 'feeling for language' below.

Delta

As an in-service qualification, which assumes that candidates already have an initial teaching qualification or relevant experience, Delta requires evidence of a sophisticated degree of knowledge of language systems and of the ability to apply this not only in the lesson planning process but also in the classroom and in response to learner output. While the assessment criteria (see Appendix 3 of this chapter) resemble those of CELTA in scope, the wording clearly highlights how much more is expected of candidates at this level: the requirements are qualified repeatedly with the terms 'accurate and appropriate'; candidates need not only to 'notice' but also to 'exploit' learners' output 'judiciously'.

Comments from external assessors' reports on observed teaching make it clear how important language awareness is in the assessment of practical teaching (see Table 1).

Table 1 Comments from external assessors' reports

	Distinction	Fail
Information	• Useful information was provided on the use and usefulness of lexical phrases and the rationale for them. Her staging of the tasks developed their understanding of meaning and use well.	• The information given about the target language was not always as precise as it could be.

(To be continued)

247

(Continued)

	Distinction	**Fail**
Responsiveness to learner output	• Feedback included some good on-the-spot responses and her concept checking, although sometimes unplanned, was good. • The candidate was attentive to learner output. • She listened well and developed students' linguistic knowledge in accordance with their needs; e.g., students needed the phrase 'to be effective' and she was able to feed this in and deal with meaning and check it.	• There was no adaptation to emerging learner needs. • Learners' questions were evaded, misconstrued and incorrectly answered. • … teacher missed some good and also 'usefully' inaccurate use of language by learners — responding to this would have benefited the whole class and help clarify some of their confusion.
Teachers' own language		• She had a tendency to speak too loudly for the situation and oversimplify her language so it was unnatural and partially grammaticised.

Reviewing areas of weakness noted by external assessors in Module Two, the June 2010 Principal Moderator's Report makes it clear how high expectations are of a teacher at this level. A note almost of exasperation creeps in at times: 'when candidates actually *do* focus on the language learners will need … this is often at the level of individual structures rather than considering, for example, the *overall* structure of a written text or dialogue' (Cambridge ESOL 2010: 6); 'where published materials did not provide a scaffolding, candidates did not approach the material with a sufficiently critical eye to identify missing linguistic elements' (Cambridge ESOL 2010: 6).

Critical awareness, reflection and 'feeling for language'

Any review of Cambridge English Teaching Qualifications needs to be realistic not only about what and how much can be learned within the course hours available, but also about what is appropriate given the level of the course and the experience of the course participants, and what it is practical to assess given the modes of assessment available. 'Critical awareness' as defined by Arndt *et al.* (2000) is not formally assessed in the Cambridge English Teaching Qualifications although relevant questions inevitably arise in course discussion of language and context. There are other qualifications available to teachers and, indeed, many teachers who have obtained Delta move on to a Master's course in Teaching English to Speakers of Other Languages (and in related disciplines), where this may receive a more targeted focus.

In Delta Module Two 'Reflection and evaluation' forms one of the ten categories of assessment: candidates submit a written document to the assessor which is assessed using the following criteria:

Successful candidates demonstrate that they can effectively:

- reflect on and evaluate their own planning, teaching and the learners' progress as evidenced in the lesson
- identify key strengths and weaknesses in planning and execution
- explain how they will (would) consolidate/follow on from the learning achieved in the lesson

(Appendix B of this volume)

In lessons targeting aspects of language systems, the candidates' *reflection and evaluation* will normally comprise a critical evaluation of their own language awareness in planning and teaching the lesson. Where an assessed lesson has been difficult to grade, evidence of insight in this will often help the assessor come to a decision.

Nowhere, however, is reflection such an integral part of the assessment as in ICELT. The four written classroom-related assignments of the *Methodology* component all involve analysis and evaluation of their own teaching. The *Planning beyond the lesson* assignment, for example, is based on having taught and evaluated a language-focused lesson. Candidates need to 'plan for the next three or four lessons and give a rationale for [their] plan'. Detailed guidelines for this are provided.

Delta is the highest level Cambridge English Teaching Qualification. It is also the most varied and complex in terms of assessment, comprising a written examination (Module One), written assignments and assessed practical teaching (Module Two) and an extended written assignment/project based on 'an independent investigation leading to the design of a course programme' (Module Three). Although 'feeling for language' is developed throughout the Cambridge English Teaching Qualifications, it is in Delta that this is most clearly demonstrated and validated.

In Delta the importance of responsiveness to learners' needs during lessons is made especially clear: 'Candidates should be reminded that their focus when teaching their lessons should be on the learners rather than on an inflexible implementation of their plan.' 'Candidates should therefore feel reassured that if their lessons take unexpected turns, they should not become unduly distressed but rather stay calm and simply respond to what is happening as they would do under normal teaching circumstances' (Cambridge English 2014: 65). Unexpected examples of awareness emerge in assessed lessons. They can bring an appreciative smile to the observer's face and, especially if they emerge regularly or consistently, the observer may find them significant in applying the criteria which distinguish between different levels of Pass in the Cambridge English Teaching Qualifications. The 2009 Delta Module Two *Coursework report* notes: 'The fact that so many of the candidates faltered when faced with learner questions about language or gave wrong information at the language clarification stage of the lesson suggests that centres need to spend more time systematically working on the improvement of their candidates' language awareness.'

Some of the criteria assessors use in assessing lessons (e.g. 'purposefully engage learners') generally elicit short comments that may not distinguish the candidates who achieve a high level Pass overall from those who don't (or those who fail). However, the criteria relating to language systems, and especially those relating to the teacher's spontaneous responses in the classroom, elicit lengthy descriptive and evaluative detail to justify decisions.

Indeed, the *Grade descriptions* for this component of Delta (Cambridge English 2014: 61) are particularly revealing. Whereas at Pass level 'The candidate's preparation and delivery lead to effective learning', the following is expected of a candidate who achieves 'Pass with Merit': 'Planning and execution reflect a good [Distinction: 'highly developed'] awareness of learners ... and the ability to provide, and to respond flexibly and effectively to, learning opportunities during [Distinction: 'throughout'] the lesson.'

The Delta Handbook (Cambridge English 2014: 65) states that 'much of real teaching emerges in the interface between the planned and the unexpected'. Is it, in this interface that the awareness that goes beyond knowledge, that the 'feeling for language', the 'magic' perhaps is recognised and rewarded?

Conclusion

This chapter has addressed different meanings and interpretations of the words *language* and *awareness*, and has attempted to show how the different Cambridge English Teaching Qualifications interpret these terms and test these qualities.

Some, such as TKT, focus very much on knowledge about language, whereas the others extend this to its practical application in planning and teaching lessons. The issue of 'feeling for language' has been addressed, in particular with regard to how this is validated within Delta.

Andrews and McNeill (2005: 174) include 'a love of language' among the features of language awareness that they identify. The enthusiasm with which course participants respond to the *Language Awareness* component of their Cambridge English courses and the joy with which they engage with language in their lessons amply demonstrate the 'love of language' that many teachers have and pass on to their learners. Mercifully, as yet no attempt has been made to pin this down, to measure it, define its essence and package it as a component in teacher education or teacher assessment.

References

Andrews, S. (2007) *Language Teacher Awareness*. Cambridge: Cambridge University Press.

Andrews, S. and McNeill, A. (2005) Knowledge about language and the good language teacher, in Bartels, N. (Ed) *Applied Linguistics and Language Teacher Education*. New York: Springer.

Arndt, V., Harvey, P. and Nuttall, J. (2000) *Alive to Language*. Cambridge: Cambridge University Press.

Bigelow, M. H. and Ranney, S. E. (2005) Pre-service ESL teachers' knowledge about language and its transfer to lesson planning, in Bartels, N. (Ed) *Applied Linguistics and Language Teacher Education*. New York: Springer, 179–200.

Bolitho, R., Carter, R., Hughes, R., Ivanic, R., Masuhara, H. and Tomlinson, B. (2003) Ten questions about language awareness, *ELT Journal* 57 (3), 251–259.

Cambridge English (2013) *Cambridge English Teaching Qualifications: CELTA Trainer in Training Guidelines*. Cambridge: Cambridge English Language Assessment.

Cambridge English (2014) *Delta Module One, Module Two, Module Three: Handbook for Tutors and Candidates*. Cambridge: Cambridge English Language Assessment.

Cambridge ESOL (2004) *ICELT: Syllabus and Assessment Guidelines*. Cambridge: Cambridge ESOL.

Cambridge ESOL (2010) *CELTA Syllabus and Assessment Guidelines*. Cambridge: Cambridge ESOL.

Cambridge ESOL (2011) *Delta Syllabus and Assessment Guidelines*. Cambridge: Cambridge ESOL.

Cambridge ESOL (2012) *TKT: Practical Handbook*. Cambridge: Cambridge ESOL.

Canale, M. and Swain, M. (1980) Theoretical bases of communicative approaches to second language teaching and testing, *Applied Linguistics* (1), 1–47.

Hymes, D. (1964) Two types of linguistic relativity, in Bright, W. (Ed) *Sociolinguistics*. The Hague: Mouton, 114–158.

Lewis, M. (1993) *The Lexical Approach: The State of ELT and a Way Forward*. Hove: Language Teaching Publications.

McCarthy, M. (1998) *Spoken Language and Applied Linguistics*. Cambridge: Cambridge University Press.

McCarthy, M. and Carter, R. (1994) *Language as Discourse*. Harlow: Longman.

Rea-Dickens, P. (1991) What makes a grammar test communicative? in Alderson, J. C. and North, B. (Eds) *Language Testing in the 1990s: The Communicative Legacy*. New York: HarperCollins, 112–135.

Thornbury, S. (1997) *About Language*. Cambridge: Cambridge University Press.

Appendix 1

Overview of language awareness assessed in Cambridge English Teaching Qualifications

	Knowledge of language systems and language use	Lesson planning: analysis of target language and identification of potential difficulties for learners	Lesson planning: analysis of language in materials and activities for classroom use	Teaching: effectively implementing materials and activities to support learning of aspects of language systems	Teaching: language awareness in responding to learners' output	Teaching: teachers' awareness of their own use of language in the classroom
TKT	Module 1 requires candidates to match terms and concepts to examples of these.	Module 2 requires candidates to identify solutions to possible difficulties learners may face with target language.	Module 2 requires candidates to identify and analyse grammatical exponents in teaching materials.			Module 3 requires candidates to match examples of teachers' language to their communicative/ pedagogical function and to evaluate their effectiveness …
TKT (KAL)	This test requires candidates to match terms and concepts to examples of these.				Matching exercises require candidates to identify the correction strategies appropriate to different kinds of mistake.	Matching exercises require candidates to identify the function of examples of teachers' language.
TKT (Practical)		A template is provided for this.		This forms a significant part of the assessment of practical teaching skills.	How candidates respond to learners' output forms a significant part of the assessment of practical teaching skills.	Candidates need to adapt their own language appropriately in the classroom.

(To be continued)

(Continued)

	Knowledge of language systems and language use	Lesson planning: analysis of target language and identification of potential difficulties for learners	Lesson planning: analysis of language in materials and activities for classroom use	Teaching: effectively implementing materials and activities to support learning of aspects of language systems	Teaching: language awareness in responding to learners' output	Teaching: teachers' awareness of their own use of language in the classroom
TKT (YL)	Candidates are required to match language with its communicative function.	Candidates are advised to focus on this.	Candidates are required to focus on this by adapting materials and tasks in response to children's language needs.		Candidates are required to identify suitable scaffolding strategies to support children's output of target language.	Candidates are required to identify the communicative and pedagogical purposes of examples of supportive teacher talk.
TKT (CLIL)		Candidates identify language required to achieve the cognitive demands of the task.	Candidates demonstrate knowledge of language used in different text types and knowledge of how to adapt language used in materials.		Candidates identify ways to respond to and support learner output.	Matching exercises require candidates to identify the function of examples of teachers' language.
CELTA	Knowledge, understanding and analysis of language systems need to be demonstrated in written assignments and lesson plans.	Skills in this area must be demonstrated in the planning of assessed lessons.	Candidates are required to select, adapt and/or design materials appropriate to the learners and the lesson.	This forms a significant part of the assessment of practical teaching skills.	How candidates respond to learners' output forms a significant part of the assessment of practical teaching skills.	Candidates need to adapt their own language appropriately in the classroom.

(To be continued)

(Continued)

	Knowledge of language systems and language use	Lesson planning: analysis of target language and identification of potential difficulties for learners	Lesson planning: analysis of language in materials and activities for classroom use	Teaching: effectively implementing materials and activities to support learning of aspects of language systems	Teaching: language awareness in responding to learners' output	Teaching; teachers' awareness of their own use of language in the classroom
CELTA YL extension	Knowledge, understanding and analysis of language systems need to be demonstrated in Written Task 1: *Language analysis within teaching practice.*	Skill in this area must be demonstrated in the planning of assessed lessons.	Candidates are required to select, adapt and/or design materials appropriate to the learners and the lesson.	This forms a significant part of the assessment of practical teaching skills.	How candidates respond to learners' output forms a significant part of the assessment of practical teaching skills.	Candidates need to adapt their own language appropriately in the classroom.
ICELT	Knowledge, understanding and analysis of language systems need to be demonstrated in written assignments and lesson plans.	Skill in this area must be demonstrated in the planning of assessed lessons.	Candidates are required to select, adapt and/or design materials appropriate to the learners and the lesson.	This forms a significant part of the assessment of practical teaching skills.	How candidates respond to learners' output forms a significant part of the assessment of practical teaching skills. Task 2 requires candidates to write an analysis of learners' spoken output and Task 3 requires them to write an analysis of learners' written output.	This forms a significant part of the assessment of practical teaching skills. Task 4 requires candidates to write an analysis of their own use of English in the classroom.

(To be continued)

255

(Continued)

	Knowledge of language systems and language use	Lesson planning: analysis of target language and identification of potential difficulties for learners	Lesson planning: analysis of language in materials and activities for classroom use	Teaching: effectively implementing materials and activities to support learning of aspects of language systems	Teaching: language awareness in responding to learners' output	Teaching: teachers' awareness of their own use of language in the classroom
Delta	Module One requires candidates both to name examples of language systems and to explain and exemplify relevant terms. Module Two requires candidates to demonstrate knowledge, understanding and analysis of language systems in extended written assignments and lesson plans.	Skill in this area must be demonstrated in the planning of assessed lessons.	Module One contains tasks which require analysis of language in given materials. Module Two (Language Systems Assignments) requires candidates to select and/or produce suitable materials and to discuss/analyse their language content.	Module Two: this forms a significant part of the assessment of practical teaching skills.	Module One requires candidates to analyse a learner's written response to a given task in order to identify key strengths and weaknesses. Module Two: How candidates respond to learners' output forms a significant part of the assessment of practical teaching skills.	Module Two: candidates need to adapt their own language appropriately in the classroom.

Appendix 2

CELTA assessment criteria relating to language awareness from the *CELTA Syllabus and Assessment Guidelines* (Cambridge ESOL 2010: 15–16)

- adjusting their own use of language in the classroom according to the learner group and the context (2a)
- identifying errors and sensitively correcting learners' oral and written language (2b)
- providing clear contexts and a communicative focus for language (2c)
- providing accurate and appropriate models of oral and written language in the classroom (2d)
- focusing on language items in the classroom by clarifying relevant aspects of meaning and form (including phonology) for learners to an appropriate degree of depth (2e)
- showing awareness of differences in register (2f)
- providing appropriate practice of language items (2g)
- using appropriate means to make instructions for tasks and activities clear to learners (5f)
- using a range of questions effectively for the purpose of elicitation and checking of understanding (5g)
- providing learners with appropriate feedback on tasks and activities (5h)
- maintaining an appropriate learning pace in relation to materials, tasks and activities (5i).

Appendix 3

Delta assessment criteria relating to language awareness from the *Delta Handbook* (Cambridge English 2014: 60)

- listen and respond appropriately to learner contributions (6d)
- use language which is accurate and appropriate for the teaching and learning context (7a)
- adapt their own use of language to the level of the group and individuals in the group (7b)
- give accurate and appropriate models of language form, meaning/use and pronunciation (7c)
- give accurate and appropriate information about language form, meaning/use and pronunciation and/or language skills/subskills (7d)
- notice and judiciously exploit learners' language output to further language and skills/subskills development (7e)
- use procedures, techniques and activities to support and consolidate learning and to achieve language and/or skill aims (8a)
- exploit materials and resources to support learning and achieve aims (8b)
- deliver a coherent and suitably varied lesson (8c)
- monitor and check students' learning and respond as appropriate (8d).

10 Thinking on their feet: Assessing teachers' flexibility and responsiveness in the language classroom

Rosemary Wilson
Consultant, Cambridge English Language Assessment

The act of teaching has been conceptualised in a number of ways. One view is to see it as a scientific activity in which findings from academic research are applied to the classroom situation. In the case of language teaching, for example, the audio lingual method of teaching languages was based on studies of behaviourism. Another view draws on theoretical models to inform practice, as is exemplified by the case of communicative language teaching, which was based on the theory of communicative competence. A third view sees teaching as both an art and a craft and dependent on each teacher's personal attributes and professional skills. In this third view, teachers shape and redirect their planned lessons through interactive decision-making, monitoring their teaching to evaluate what is happening, recognising that different courses of action are possible, deciding what action to take and then evaluating the results of that action. Described in this way, language teaching can be seen as a 'dynamic process characterized by constant change' (Richards 1998: 11) or an 'improvisational performance' (Yinger in Richards 1998: 114) and even a 'simple, daily miracle' (Stevick in Richards 1998: 43). This conceptual view of teaching is instantiated by specific actions on the part of the teacher and it is these actions that can be observed and evaluated in the context of teacher assessment. This chapter will describe how the Cambridge English Teaching Qualifications approach the assessment of teachers' flexibility within planned lessons as well as their responsiveness to learners' spontaneous reactions and comments, with particular reference to instances cited in assessment reports in support of a judgement of effectiveness or otherwise.

The concept of interactive decision-making builds on the notion of reflection-in-action (Schön 1983), in which professionals bring past experience to bear on a new situation. The repertoire of examples and actions that professionals have accumulated allows them to have 'a reflective conversation with the materials of the situation' (Schön 1987: 31) and apply their professional knowledge to the new context. Contextual knowledge is a key component in the decision-making process; of specific relevance in language teaching is knowledge about the level of the class, the age of the learners, their motivations and learning styles and sociocultural factors such as cultural values (Richards 1998). The decision-making process is also based on a consideration of appropriate patterns of interaction between teachers and learners and the specific kind of support needed (Fradd and Lee 1998).

Kumaravadivelu (2006) sees interaction as an interpersonal activity that creates a classroom atmosphere in which teachers and learners can reach mutual understandings and express themselves. The interactive decisions that the teacher makes can provide opportunities for conversational exchanges in which learners have the freedom to express their views, with 'the outcome measured in terms of personal rapport created in the classroom' (Kumaravadivelu 2012: 28). This focus on 'context-specific community building in the [language teaching] classroom' (2012: 29) reflects the move away from a behaviourist approach to a more ecological one. It echoes one of the tenets of Allwright's exploratory practice, which stresses the role of the quality of life in a language classroom in promoting effective learning (Allwright 2003). This focus on classroom life is equally relevant in other areas of teaching. A study of secondary school subject teachers and their Year 7 pupils (11–12 years old) found that 'teachers and pupils ... agreed that effective learning was most often associated with the teacher's willingness to allow students the space to engage with learning activities in their preferred ways' (Cooper and McIntyre 1996: 156). The study highlighted the need for flexibility, responsiveness and 'thinking on their feet' (1996: 157) as well as the importance of catering to the affective dimensions of teaching and learning. From an insider perspective, a study that asked prospective and experienced teachers about the characteristics of effective and ineffective teachers found that both groups characterised ineffective teachers as disorganised and discouraging of student questions (Walls, Nardi, von Minden and Hoffman 2002), highlighting the way in which careful preparation and planning allow for real-time flexibility.

More objective studies have also identified the role of the affective dimensions of the classroom. For example, in a large-scale synthesis of meta-analyses of quantitative studies of effective teaching in general education, Hattie (2003) identified five dimensions of excellent teachers, including the ability to guide learning through classroom interactions, monitor learning and provide feedback and give attention to affective attributes (2003: 6). The affective dimensions of teaching and learning have also been investigated from the learners' perspective; for example in a study of the relationship between teachers' emotional quotient and their success as rated by their students, the most important factor identified was the quality of the interpersonal relationships (Ghanizadeh and Moafian 2010). The authors note that this is not surprising given the shift to humanistic and communicative settings, particularly in private language institutes for adult students, such as the ones in the study, where 'the teacher's support, empathy and cooperation are indispensable elements' (2010: 430), and they advocate developing these qualities as part of teacher preparation courses. Some of these qualities have been found to develop over time; a study of the development of professional teaching identities on postgraduate Teachers of English to Speakers of Other Languages (TESOL) courses noted that, with increasing experience, the teachers learned to listen to what their learners said and react in a genuine way (Kanno and Stuart 2011). Non-verbal behaviour can also be important; Dewaele (2011) reports on a study that found that teachers who fidgeted or frowned at specific points during a class received lower evaluations from their students based purely on this behaviour. Dewaele notes that in other cases, the reason why chemistry either does or does not develop between a group of learners and their teacher may be less easy to identify and less susceptible to modification. As Singh and Richards (2006) suggest, teaching is an occupation in which it is difficult to separate the person from the craft.

Good teachers tend to be described by their personal qualities rather than by their knowledge and skills and developing these qualities is one of the key challenges of a teacher education programme (Piwowar, Thiel and Ophart 2013). In assessing teacher performance, it is necessary to 'separate the person from the craft' and focus on the 'actual **instantiation** of knowledge in a particular set of movements at a particular moment and particular place' (Woods and Çakir 2011). When assessing teachers' flexibility and responsiveness, the focus will necessarily be on their interactive decision-making — the decisions that are made about events that occur in the course of the lesson. Some will be unexpected events, such as the technical failure of a piece of equipment, but relevant to this discussion is the way that teachers have anticipated and respond to learners' understanding and participation; learners may ask questions about meaning, form or phonology, have difficulty completing a task or become so involved in a task that it takes longer than planned (Tsang 2004). An 'improvisational performance' develops from the interaction between the lesson plan, the learners' responses and the teacher's interactive online decision-making and draws on their personal, practical knowledge in terms of their knowledge of the subject matter — in this case the target language — their knowledge of instruction and their knowledge of context (Golombek 1998, 2009).

The importance of context cannot be underestimated as classrooms are 'loaded places' (Miller 2009). Teaching is a situated activity, with geographical and cultural context having an effect not only on learners but also on teachers. In the specific case of English language teaching, increasing teacher mobility has meant that learners from a particular non-English-speaking background are taught by teachers from another non-English-speaking background, as exemplified by many of the classes in English for Speakers of Other Languages (ESOL) in the UK. The classroom practices of these teachers will be influenced by their own cultural heritage, for example in terms of their beliefs about the role of the teacher or the importance of individualisation (Sun 2012). Cultural background may create discrepancies between the way that teachers and students view teaching and learning. In a study of language students and teachers, students favoured grammar teaching and immediate correction of oral mistakes whereas their teachers favoured a more communicative approach with a focus on meaning rather than on form (Brown 2009). Interestingly, the author notes that 'the teachers' responses were guided by what the field at large might consider appropriate for communicative classrooms' (2009: 54), suggesting that they may have been adhering to certain methodological approaches without fully considering either context or learner needs.

Context, learner needs and the role of the teacher are key factors in planning teaching approaches and individual lessons but they are also the factors that require teachers to make real-time interactive decisions. Their ability to do so is affected not only by their prior planning and preparation but, importantly, by their previous experience and practical skills. When judging teacher performance, expectations about the degree of flexibility and responsiveness are different for novice and more experienced teachers and should be reflected in the assessment criteria. The approach to assessing this aspect of teachers' practical classroom skills in the Cambridge English Teaching Qualifications will now be described. References to assessment criteria are from the relevant syllabus and handbook criteria.

Assessment of practical teaching in Cambridge English Teaching Qualifications

Cambridge English provides qualifications for teachers at a range of levels from new entrants to language teaching to more experienced teachers. The assessment procedures for each qualification include reference to aspects of classroom practice that can be categorised as 'classroom atmosphere' and 'response to learners'. The following examples of aspects of classroom performance across the levels of the qualifications indicate the increasing level of practical skill that is expected and guidelines against which assessors are asked to fine tune their judgements.

CELTA

The Certificate in Teaching English to Speakers of Other Languages (identified by its previous acronym CELTA) focuses on learners, teachers and the learning context in Topic One. Course participants or 'candidates' are expected to be aware of their learners' 'broad range of learning needs', interests, learning styles and previous learning backgrounds as well as relevant cultural factors and to establish a 'good rapport' whilst involving the learners fully in activities. Assessment is conducted by course tutors, with a sample of practical and written assignments moderated by an external assessor. The assessment of practical teaching is continuous across a series of teaching episodes of increasing length at different levels (a total of 6 hours) and skill level is benchmarked against the stage of the training programme. At entry level, candidates are expected to adjust their language appropriately, provide clarification when necessary and give feedback on learners' use of English. 'Professional competence in the classroom' is assessed by candidates' ability to 'interact naturally with learners before, during and after the lesson' as well as to 'maintain eye contact'. Being directive or not and deciding when to intervene are also assessed as an aspect of teaching skills but there is no reference to dealing with learners' interventions or the unexpected. This is mainly due to the emphasis on carefully planned and controlled lessons but is also an acknowledgement that knowledge and skills are limited at this level.

TKT

The Teaching Knowledge Test (TKT) is not course based and is taken by teachers with different levels of professional experience in one or more contexts who wish to validate their teaching knowledge and skills formally. TKT: Practical is one of the four core modules and requires candidates to teach for 40 minutes over one or two classes, assessed by an externally approved assessor who may or may not also be the candidate's course tutor. The criteria are very similar to those for CELTA, in that they are expected to 'establish good rapport', involve the learners in activities, 'maintain a positive learning atmosphere' and make appropriate decisions about intervening or standing back. Given the short length of the assessed lesson or lessons, the emphasis is on a tightly controlled procedure that is set out in the lesson plan. This should include precise details of activities and instructions for each stage with the aim of learners staying 'on task' rather than making spontaneous interventions.

ICELT

The In-Service Certificate in English Language Teaching (ICELT) is aimed at practising teachers with appropriate local qualifications and at least 500 hours' relevant teaching experience by the end of the training course. ICELT courses tend to focus on a specific local teaching context, for example teaching young learners or teaching English for Academic Purposes. Practical teaching is assessed by the course tutors over a minimum of four lessons at two different levels and a sample of practical and written assignments is moderated by an external moderator. As with CELTA and TKT, the assessment guidelines require pass level candidates to establish rapport and to 'foster a constructive and safe learning environment' but, for the first time, reference is made to the unexpected in the criterion 'adapt plans and activities appropriately in response to the learners and to *classroom contingencies*' (italics added), recognising that teachers with a certain level of previous experience will be able to draw on the knowledge and skills they have already acquired. The descriptor for the award of Merit states that, to achieve it, there must be 'strong and consistent evidence' of flexibility, again the first reference to this quality.

Delta

The highest level of qualification offered within the Cambridge English Teaching Qualifications framework is the higher level in-service qualification known as Delta (from a previous acronym). It is aimed at teachers with an initial teaching qualification — in many cases CELTA — and teaching experience. The qualification is modular with the assessment of practical teaching (Module Two) being the only module that requires candidates to follow a course. Unlike the other two modules that are assessed by an examination (Module One) and an extended assignment (Module Three), the practical teaching component is assessed through a portfolio of coursework based around four practical teaching assignments, one of which is externally assessed. Teachers at this level would normally have a range of classroom experience and this is reflected in the assessment criteria. When assessing candidates' ability to create and maintain 'an atmosphere conducive to learning', the criteria suggest that there is an expectation of increased flexibility and responsiveness at this level. Teachers should 'where necessary adapt (the lesson plan) to emerging learner needs' and 'respond appropriately to learner contributions', which are specifically denoted as learners' spontaneous contributions to the topics discussed and not target language. By responding 'naturally and appropriately … if necessary incorporating learners' contributions into the lesson', teachers will thus demonstrate that they are listening to what learners are saying. Flexibility is not mentioned in so many words but the assessment criteria include the example of changing the pattern of interaction 'as the learning and *affective needs* of learners change' (emphasis added). This first reference to the affective aspects of teaching and learning is reinforced by the criterion requiring candidates to 'respond appropriately to the atmosphere in the class and changes in this atmosphere throughout the lesson', reflecting the view that the quality of life in a classroom is an important factor. These highly specific criteria encourage assessors to identify and note specific instances of behaviour that exemplify the quality under consideration. For each of the four criteria listed under 'creating and maintaining an atmosphere conducive to learning' and the first criterion under classroom management, assessors are required to judge how successful the teacher has been. Extracts from Delta external assessment reports are now considered in order to identify the range and type of actions that Delta assessors note to support their judgements.

Assessor feedback

The issue of interactive decision-making and the qualities of flexibility and responsiveness are explicitly addressed in section 6 of the Delta assessment criteria (see Appendix B) and implicitly assumed in criterion 9a, which focuses on teachers' flexibility with regard to the planned lesson. In section 6, candidates need to demonstrate that they can:

6a) teach the class as a group and individuals within the group, with sensitivity to the learners' needs and backgrounds, level and context, providing equal opportunities for participation

6b) purposefully engage learners

6c) vary their role in relation to the emerging learning and affective needs of learners during the lesson

6d) listen and respond appropriately to learner contributions.

In section 9 on classroom management, the first criterion requires candidates to: 9a 'implement the lesson plan and where necessary adapt it to emerging learner needs'. Examples of how this adaptation may occur are supplied:

Candidates may, for example, adapt the timing, the focus of a particular stage, the interactions in an activity, choose to omit/supplement an activity/stage, or include an unplanned activity/stage in response to emerging linguistic, motivational or learning needs during the lesson (9a Gloss: Teaching assessment criteria: with integrated explanatory notes).

This is particularly important in this context as the Delta practical teaching assessment requires an extremely detailed lesson plan — in some cases 'excessively long' (Cambridge ESOL 2012: 3) — linked to a fully referenced background essay. Apart from being understandably keen to keep to their plan after the time and effort that they have invested in it, candidates are frequently under stress during an external assessment. This is acknowledged in published advice to candidates, which reminds them:

> Despite the stress of an external assessment, take time to listen carefully to your learners' output and respond helpfully and constructively ... Be unafraid to depart from the plan if the situation warrants it (Cambridge ESOL 2012: 20).

For each of these five criteria, assessors judge whether the criterion has been met, partially met or not met and are asked to add narrative as supporting evidence. Comments range from a generic shorthand such as 'nice manner' or 'no real response to emerging needs' to accounts of specific interventions. The following discussion is based on a small sample of reports for candidates from each of the four grade bands (Pass with distinction, Pass with merit, Pass, Fail).

Teach the class as a group and individuals within the group

It is clear from assessors' comments that the use of learners' names — nomination — plays a key role both in establishing rapport and responding flexibly to learners' comments and actions. Positive comments such as 'nominated effectively to ensure an equal spread of participation' or 'good range of interactions, use of student names' highlight the role of nomination in promoting and managing interaction. An absence of nomination had the opposite result:

> Learners were involved but quieter ones were not nominated (in fact nomination was rarely used) ...
>
> There were more opportunities for the candidate to nominate as stronger/more vocal learners tended to dominate during whole-class activities.
>
> She could have used nomination more given the length of the plenary stages ...
>
> ... made good use of their names when speaking with them (although lack of nomination meant those less willing to shout out contributed much less).
>
> Only used nomination in feedback, and that to a limited selection of learners.

These comments suggest that using learners' names increases interaction by involving all members of the class as well as enabling teachers to respond to individuals in a personal way. Undirected questions tended to have a detrimental effect on interaction if responses were not carefully managed: 'Tended to hurl elicitation questions into the air and rely on one dominant Brazilian learner to answer.'

Listen and respond appropriately to learner contributions

The contributions referred to in this section are comments about topics under discussion or spontaneous interventions not related to the target language. Positive comments often referred to the thought that a teacher gave to a comment or to the response being real or genuine rather than tokenistic.

> Considered all contributions thoughtfully and positively. Praised and 'used' learner contributions.
>
> ... listened and responded to the content of student contributions.
>
> She also asked real questions in order to move on ... e.g. *was it a good story? Why?*
>
> ... skilfully exploited interest in the situation/context created through asking lots of real questions and responding encouragingly to their answers.

Less effective interactions were sometimes limited to comments on form rather than content: '... did not respond to content of what learners were saying and focused exclusively on surface error or appeared to miss what learners were saying and did not respond'.

Teach ... with sensitivity to the learners' needs

There is clearly an overlap between a comment made for clarification of a concept or form and a comment about content. However, the Delta assessment form distinguishes between learner contributions, which can be of any kind, and learner needs, which are related to the lesson aims. As mentioned above, criterion 9a assesses candidates' flexibility in terms of deviating from their lesson plan to respond to learner needs. There is a certain irony in the fact that, given the emphasis on preparation and planning, the distinguishing factor of effective teachers is frequently their flexibility in adapting their original plan, as assessors' comments show:

> Plan implemented appropriately, used as a guide rather than a straitjacket. Flexible enough to allow for adaptations as required by the learners.
>
> The plan was effectively implemented. However, a real strength was the way the teacher naturally responded to particular problems that emerged ... indicating a willingness to teach the learners not just the plan ... It was a real pleasure to watch a teacher successfully juggle both a ... plan with clearly listening and reacting to learners ... A very responsive teacher — distinction level in this lesson with regard to that.

When teachers stick resolutely to the plan, for whatever reason, learners' contributions tend to be ignored: '... there was no adaptation to meet emerging needs, particularly when it became evident that learners lacked the strategic resources to manage their conversations'. In other cases, teachers may respond too flexibly so that the lesson loses focus: 'The candidate tended to be distracted by learners' comments and questions ...' and '... became easily distracted by some learners' questions.'

Vary their role in relation to the emerging ... affective needs

Praise and humour are often mentioned in assessors' comments, either to note their presence or their absence: 'Good use of praise', 'good use of humour', 'there was not a lot of humour in a lesson that offered quite a lot of scope for it however'.

The person or the craft

The point has been made previously that teaching is a profession in which it is difficult to separate the person from the craft. The assessment criteria in section 6 do not include a specific reference to 'rapport' but assessors' reports frequently use the opportunity offered by criteria 6a and 6b to remark on the impact of the person with comments such as 'warm, natural rapport', 'friendly and efficient manner', 'she was also very obviously fun', or 'professional manner', which are reactions to the person. At times, the tension between the person and the craft is clear: 'Though there was a lovely rapport there was no actual focus on content in the lesson.'

Reports on lessons that were awarded a Fail grade not infrequently included positive comments about the teacher's manner and interpersonal skills, perhaps again the result of a blurring of person and craft. All the comments that follow are from lessons that failed to meet the required standard.

Established a positive atmosphere, responding well to individuals and to the group as a whole.
The candidate has a warm manner and good rapport with the class.
Was clear (the teacher) knew the class well ... has an encouraging manner.
Good rapport created and maintained.
There were certainly some reasonable strengths on display ... the atmosphere was positive ...

An analysis of a sample of reports on unsuccessful external assessments notes that the overarching criterion 'creating and maintaining an atmosphere conducive to learning' (section 6) is not problematic for candidates and is unlikely to be one of the grounds for failure (Cambridge ESOL 2012). Delta candidates already have classroom teaching experience, in some cases a substantial amount, and tend to have developed an easy manner and the skills of interacting with a group so that the person and the craft have become inextricably entwined.

As previously noted, the assessment of practical teaching on the Delta involves both internal and external assessments and the assessment criteria are the same for all four assessments. Delta course tutors are expected to offer support for the internally assessed assignments due to their formative nature but it 'should decrease as the course progresses so that the final externally assessed ... assignment is planned independently' (Cambridge English 2014: 67). The assessment reports from the three internally assessed lessons, plus the materials (background essay, lesson plan and related materials) for one of these lessons are submitted to Cambridge English along with the external assessment report and the candidate's independent post-lesson evaluation (300–500 words), an additional document that provides candidates with an opportunity to justify any adaptations they made to their plans. If there is a difference between the recommended grade for the internal assessments and the grade awarded by the external assessor, the coursework is moderated.

Methodological challenges in assessment procedures

This overview of the procedures in Delta for assessing teachers' flexibility and responsiveness in class highlights one of the challenges present in teacher assessment as it is generally practised: the tension between a tutor's roles as trainer or mentor and the role as assessor. This tension may confound the confusion between the person and the craft even further since the tutor will be familiar with the candidate in different contexts and will be aware of the way in which they have developed — or not — during the training programme. The tutor may even be a colleague from the same institution and may well be aware of informal feedback from the candidate's learners. These factors contribute to the 'halo effect', first suggested in the 1920s by the psychologist Thorndyke, in which the overall positive opinion of an individual influences the evaluation of their specific attributes. In this framework, a tutor-assessor may rate more highly the performance of teachers whom they consider to be confident and competent in other aspects of their professional lives. The opposite 'horns' effect may also negatively influence the judgement of a lesson. The use of external assessment in the Delta, as well as the involvement of course assessors and moderators in CELTA and ICELT, provides 'checks and balances, which blend emic, or insider, judgments of the trainer with etic, or outsider, corroboration of the assessor' (Freeman, Orzulak and Morrissey 2009: 81). Freeman *et al.* (2009) agree that 'the challenge of complex assessments [is] to judge the activity of teaching through the person who does it' (2009: 87). A further complication is that, in a language lesson, 'methodology becomes content and vice versa' (2009: 85) so that assessment procedures need to separate linguistic knowledge from language for teaching from knowing how to teach language, all of which are presented through the craft of the same person.

In any assessment procedure in which individuals are evaluated by professionals in the same field, an aspect of assessment that may need more consideration is the flexibility and responsiveness of assessors themselves. In the case of the Delta, assessors are former or practising English language teachers with many years' experience and their own preferences for teaching styles. These individual preferences are mediated to a greater or lesser extent by the standardisation process that assessors are required to undergo but the person-craft dimension is as true for assessors as it is for the teacher being assessed. Indeed, the advice to both internal and external assessors is that care should be taken 'not to import their own prejudices concerning 'best practice' in the classroom' (Cambridge ESOL 2012: 9) so that the response reflects a professional judgement rather than a personal one such as 'all the disadvantages of a PPP format'. As policies and procedures in teacher assessment are developed, it is important to maintain the checks and balances that allow both the person and the craft to be judged appropriately.

References

Allwright, D. (2003) Experimental practice: Rethinking practitioner research in language teaching, *Language Teaching Research* 7 (2), 113–141.

Brown, A.V. (2009) Students' and teachers' perceptions of effective foreign language teaching: A comparison of ideals, *The Modern Language Journal* 93 (1), 46–60.

Cambridge English (2014) *Delta Module One, Module Two, Module Three Handbook for Tutors and Candidates*. Cambridge: Cambridge English Language Assessment.

Cambridge ESOL (2004) *ICELT: Syllabus and Assessment Guidelines*. Cambridge: Cambridge English Language Assessment.

Cambridge ESOL (2010) *CELTA Syllabus and Assessment Guidelines*. Cambridge: Cambridge ESOL.

Cambridge ESOL (2012) *Delta Module Two Principal Moderators' Report December 2012*. Cambridge: Cambridge ESOL.

Cooper, P. and McIntyre, D. (1996) *Effective Teaching and Learning: Teachers' and Students' Perspectives*. Bristol: Open University Press.

Dewaele, J-M. (2011) Reflections on the emotional and psychological aspects of foreign language learning and use, *Anglistik: International Journal of English Studies* 22 (1), 23–42.

Fradd, S.H. and Lee, O. (1998) Development of a knowledge base for ESOL teacher education, *Teaching and Teacher Education* 17 (7), 761–773.

Freeman D., Orzulak, M.M. and Morrissey, G. (2009) Assessment in second language teacher education, in Burns, A and Richards, J. C. (Eds) *The Cambridge Guide to Second Language Teacher Education*. New York: Cambridge University Press, 77–90.

Ghanizadeh, A. and Moafian, F. (2010) The role of EFL teachers' emotional intelligence in their success, *ELT Journal* 64 (4), 424–435.

Golombek, P. R. (1998) A study of language teachers' personal practical knowledge, *TESOL Quarterly* 32 (3), 447–464.

Golombek, P. R. (2009) Personal practical knowledge in L2 teacher education, in Burns, A. and Richards, J. C. (Eds) *The Cambridge Guide to Second Language Teacher Education*. New York: Cambridge University Press, 155–162.

Hattie, J. (2003) Teachers make a difference: What is the research evidence? paper presented at the Australian Council for Educational Research Annual Conference, available online: www.education Auckland.ac.nz/uoa/home/about/staff/j hattie/hattie-papers-download/influences

Kanno, Y. and Stuart, C. (2011) Learning to become a second language teacher: Identities in practice, *Modern Language Journal* 95 (2), 236–252.

Kumaravadivelu B. (2006) *Understanding Language Teaching: From Method to Postmethod*. Mahwah: Lawrence Erlbaum Associates.

Kumaravadivelu B. (2012) *Language Teacher Education for a Global Society: A Modular Model for Knowing, Analyzing, Recognizing, Doing and Seeing*. Oxford and New York: Routledge.

Miller, J. (2009) Teacher identity, in Burns, A. and Richards, J. C. (Eds) *The Cambridge Guide to Second Language Teacher Education*. New York: Cambridge University Press, 172–181.

Piwowar, V., Thiel, F. and Ophart, D. (2013) Training in-service teachers' competencies in classroom management: A quasi-experimental study with teachers in secondary school, *Teaching and Teacher Education* 30, 1–12.

Richards, J. C. (1998) *Beyond Training*. Cambridge: Cambridge University Press.

Schön, D. (1983) *The Reflective Practitioner: How Professionals Think in Action*. New York: Basic Books.

Schön, D. (1987) *Educating the Reflective Practitioner*. New York: Basic Books.

Singh, G. and Richards, J. C. (2006) Teaching and learning in the language teacher education course room: A critical sociocultural perspective, paper presented at the RELC International Conference, Singapore April 2006, available online: www.professorjackrichards.com/wp-content/uploads/teaching-learning-in-education-course-room.pdf

Sun, D. (2012) Everything goes smoothly: A case study of an immigrant Chinese language teacher's personal practical knowledge, *Teaching and Teacher Education* 28, 760–767.

Tsang, W. K. (2004) Teachers' personal practical knowledge and interactive decisions, *Language Teaching Research* 8 (2), 163–198.

Walls, R. T., Nardi, A. H., von Minden, A. M. and Hoffman, N. (2002) The characteristics of effective and ineffective teachers, *Teacher Education Quarterly* 29, 39–48.

Woods, D. and Çakir, H. (2011) Two dimensions of teacher knowledge: The case of communicative language teaching, *System* 39, 381–339.

11 TKT: Testing knowledge about teaching

Mary Spratt
Freelance teacher trainer, writer and
consultant

The Teaching Knowledge Test (TKT) was introduced by Cambridge ESOL in 2005 for practising or trainee teachers of English to Speakers of Other Languages. The test is designed to 'test knowledge about the teaching of English to speakers of other languages' (Cambridge ESOL 2012) and at the time of its introduction differed from other Cambridge English Teaching Qualifications in that it contained no practice-based assessment but three paper-based modules:

1. Language and background to language learning and teaching
2. Lesson planning and use of resources for language teaching
3. Managing the teaching and learning process

Each module requires candidates to answer 80 objective format questions set in different kinds of matching and multiple-choice tasks. Unlike the other Cambridge English assessments for teachers, TKT does not require candidates to do a preparatory course though it is believed that the vast majority of candidates taking TKT choose to do so. Candidates may also take TKT as part of a broader teacher development programme.

This chapter explores the design of TKT in terms of the construct it aims to test and the task types it uses. The *Dictionary of Language Testing* defines a construct as:

> The trait or traits that a test is intended to measure. A construct can be defined as an ability or set of abilities that will be reflected in test performance, and about which inferences can be made on the basis of test scores. A construct is generally defined in terms of a theory; in the case of language, a theory of language. A test, then, represents an operationalisation of the theory. (Davies,

Brown, Elder, Hill, Lumley and McNamara 1999: 31)

In its *TKT Handbook*, Cambridge English Language Assessment states that TKT aims:

- to test candidates' knowledge of concepts related to language, language use and the background to and practice of language teaching and learning
- to provide an easily accessible test in teaching English to speakers of other languages, which is prepared and delivered to international standards, and could be used by candidates to access further training, and enhance career opportunities
- to encourage teachers in their professional development by providing a step in a developmental framework of qualifications and tests for teachers of English.

(Cambridge ESOL 2012: 5)

The first of these aims gives the construct which TKT is designed to test. It clearly shows us that TKT is not intended to assess candidates' teaching ability, performance in classroom situations or proficiency in the English language, i.e. that it aims to test candidates' declarative or received knowledge rather than their procedural knowledge. Wallace defines received knowledge as 'the vocabulary of the subject and the matching concepts, research findings, theories and skills which are widely accepted as being part of the necessary intellectual content of the profession' (Wallace 1991: 14) and procedural knowledge as 'here the trainee will have developed knowledge in action, and will have had, moreover, the opportunity to reflect on that knowledge-in-action' (Wallace 1991: 14). Figure 1 illustrates Wallace's notion of how the two types of knowledge might work together:

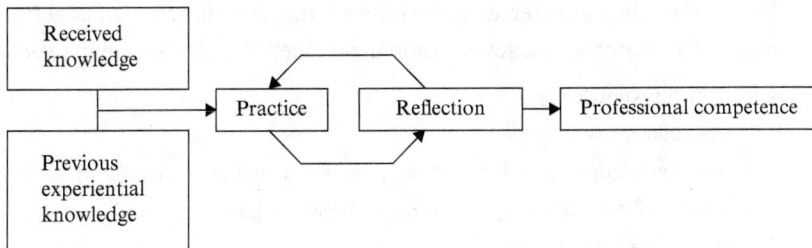

Figure 1 Reflective cycle

In the 1980s and 1990s various authors attempted to identify the components of received teaching knowledge. Grossman (1990) proposed the following four components:

- General pedagogic knowledge
- Subject matter knowledge
- Pedagogic content knowledge
- Knowledge of context

General pedagogic knowledge involves the general principles of teaching and learning which are applicable across subject disciplines. Subject matter knowledge involves the understanding of the facts and concepts of a subject discipline as well as its substantive and syntactic structures. Pedagogic content knowledge involves the representation of the subject matter through examples, analogies etc. to make it more comprehensible to students, and involves knowledge of context, the knowledge of educational aims, students and other content (Grossman 1990). Table 1 outlines what these components might cover when applied to English language teaching.

Table 1 Grossman's components applied to English language teaching

Contextual knowledge	School Students Wider educational context
General pedagogic knowledge	Management of resources Management of learning
Subject matter knowledge	Language system
Pedagogic content knowledge	Language processing and production Language learning strategies Language teaching strategies

(Tsui and Nicholson 1999)

There are other similar descriptions of the components of teaching knowledge, for example, the seven components identified by Shulman (1986):

- Subject matter knowledge
- Pedagogic content knowledge
- Curricular knowledge (knowledge of the programme and the materials which have been designed for the teaching of a particular topic at a particular level)
- General pedagogic knowledge
- Knowledge of educational aims
- Knowledge of learners

- Knowledge of other content (content outside the scope of the subject that teachers are teaching)

These descriptions of teaching knowledge focus on its declarative or received nature. But, as Figure 1 (Wallace 1991) illustrates, there is another dimension to teaching knowledge, that of 'previous experiential knowledge' i.e. its situated and experiential nature. This latter was explored particularly by Schön whose conception of professional knowledge was of 'knowing in action' (Schön 1983). He proposed that practitioners finding themselves in situations that are ill-defined, messy and full of uncertainties (e.g. the classroom) make sense of these through reference to 'experience, trial and error, intuition and muddling through' (Schön 1983: 43). He also proposed that this kind of knowledge is developed through reflection, i.e. looking at a problem or phenomenon during or after action, and from that arriving at a new understanding.

Schön's conceptualisation of teaching knowledge focuses on the practitioner knowing what to do in a given situation. It identifies procedural knowledge in a teaching context, and has been very influential in English language teaching and teacher education in particular. It emphasises reflection and the role of context, and raises the question of what role received knowledge plays in 'knowing-in-action'.

More recently, attention has focused on the concept of teacher cognition rather than teaching knowledge as the main driver of teacher activity in the classroom. Borg defines teacher cognition as 'the beliefs, knowledge, theories, assumptions and attitudes that teachers hold about all aspects of their work' (Borg 2006: 49). Tsui indicates the role cognition plays:

> ... teachers' personal conceptions of teaching and learning play a very important part in their management of teaching and learning. These personal conceptions are influenced by their personal life experiences, their learning experience, their teaching experience, their academic background as well as the opportunities for professional development, including professional courses ... there is a dialectical relationship between teachers' knowledge and their world of practice. As teachers respond to their contexts of work and reflect on their practices, they come to a new understanding of teaching and learning. The knowledge that they develop in this process constitutes part of the contexts in which they operate and part of their world of practice. (Tsui 2003: 65–66)

What these writers are saying is that declarative knowledge about teaching is an element influencing a teacher's behaviour and decisionmaking in the classroom, and making up cognition, but only one element. Before going on to discuss the reasons why TKT chose to test teachers' declarative knowledge rather than knowledge in action or all elements of teacher cognition, it is useful to consider how the Grossman model of teaching knowledge might apply to TKT to see what kinds of declarative teaching knowledge the test covers (see Table 2).

Table 2 Grossman model of teaching applied to TKT

TKT content	Grossman model
Module 1	Subject matter knowledge
Describing language and language skills	Knowledge of context
Background to language learning	Pedagogic content knowledge
Background to language teaching	
Module 2	General pedagogic knowledge
Planning and preparing a lesson or sequence of lessons	Pedagogic content knowledge
Selection and use of resources	(Subject matter knowledge)
Module 3	General pedagogic knowledge
Teachers' and learners' language in the classroom	Pedagogic content knowledge
Classroom management	(Subject matter knowledge)

(Subject matter knowledge is bracketed above to indicate that it underpins the other types of knowledge)

This mapping shows us that all components of the Grossman model appear to be present across the three TKT modules, though a construct validation exercise would be needed to see how well and to what extent it tests these components. Knowledge of context is less present than the other components, though there is some focus on general rather than specific context in TKT Module 1. Leinhardt and Smith (1985) make the distinction between situated and context-free knowledge. The distinction would seem relevant here. For example, in 'knowledge of students' (categorised by Grossman as part of knowledge of context), it is possible to distinguish between knowing that students have varying motivations, learning styles, learning experiences and other characteristics on the one hand, and knowing, on the other, how to react to the particular characteristics of particular students. The former, which are tested in TKT, would be part of context-free and declarative knowledge, whereas the latter belongs to situated context and procedural knowledge.

The mapping also shows a movement through from Module 1's focus on background knowledge to Modules 2 and 3 getting closer to the classroom as they focus on lesson planning, use of resources for language teaching, classroom language and the management of the teaching and learning process. The overlapping nature of the components within the modules reflects what is said in the literature about areas of knowledge not always being discrete but dynamically interactive, e.g. Tsui and Nicholson (1999: 219) state that 'in the actual analysis of the teaching act, these knowledge dimensions are often less distinct than they appear to be'.

Another general point evident from the mapping is that in its coverage of knowledge of context, general pedagogic knowledge, and pedagogic content knowledge as well as subject matter knowledge, TKT moves well beyond the early conception of teaching knowledge which was that of subject knowledge only.

We have seen that TKT tests various components of declarative teaching knowledge. The test, in as much as it is a pencil and paper test, does not test procedural knowledge or knowing-in-action, and with its focus on the facts and received knowledge about English Language Teaching (ELT) rather than on teacher beliefs or assumptions, it does not test all the elements of teacher cognition. There are several reasons why TKT was designed to focus on declarative rather than procedural knowledge or all the elements in cognition. Firstly, declarative knowledge is amenable to testing through pencil and paper, not requiring the sometimes complex and costly logistical and administrative support needed to assess teachers' procedural knowledge through observing them in the classroom. Pencil and paper tests are cheaper and easier to administer than performance-based tests. This puts TKT within the reach of the many teachers working in situations without extensive funding or continuous professional development (CPD) support. Pencil and paper tests involving the use of objective tasks such as those used in TKT are also cheap to process and mark, allowing for high levels of test reliability to be achieved while keeping test fees down.

A test of declarative knowledge thus allows TKT to achieve its second aim 'to provide an easily accessible test in teaching English to speakers of other languages, which is prepared and delivered to international standards' (Cambridge ESOL 2012: 5). In contrast, 'knowing-in-action' and the beliefs and assumptions which form part of teacher cognition both tend to be individual and context-bound. They may also only be visible in the classroom and hard for an observer to identify or evaluate, and therefore likely, if tested, to be prone to unreliable results.

But, in focusing on declarative knowledge rather than knowledge in action, teacher beliefs and assumptions or specific context, TKT could risk being seen as recreating the 1970s view of teacher education in which a teacher-in-training was considered to need to learn subject knowledge and methodology and then apply these in the classroom. This approach to teacher education has since been generally rejected by trainers because it emphasises a gap between the what and the how of teaching, rather than recognising that the two are often inseparable; it also fails to recognise what the teacher brings to their own learning and the role of context in shaping and developing teaching knowledge. As Freeman says, 'the notion of context moved from backdrop to interlocutor in the creation and use of teachers' knowledge'. Freeman (2002: 15) and Freeman and Johnson argue that 'the core of the new knowledge-base must focus on the activity of teaching itself; it should centre on the teacher who does it, the contexts in which it is done, and the pedagogy by which it is done. Moreover this knowledge base should include forms of knowledge representation that document teacher learning within the social, cultural and institutional contexts in which it occurs' (Freeman and Johnson 1998: 397). These writers see a risk that through certain kinds of teacher education, language educators may encourage teacher-learners to substitute declarative knowledge for knowing-in-action. For them context is the location in which and the means through which learning to teach takes place.

How do these arguments reflect on the design of TKT? Firstly we need to make a distinction between the TKT test, and TKT preparation courses, i.e. between what is tested in the TKT test, and how that is communicated, learned and situated on a preparation course. Institutions can offer courses preparing teachers specifically for the test or include the test as an element in a teacher training course as they choose. Knowing-in-action, knowing specific contexts and teacher cognition can play an important role in teacher education, helping trainees to become aware of the impact of formal knowledge on their teaching, to evaluate, operationalise and adapt it, and facilitate the possibility that TKT preparation and other development courses will bring about change in teaching practices.

For this reason, TKT preparation courses can usefully feature teaching practice, micro-teaching, class observation, feedback, the use of portfolios and reflection, so bringing all aspects of teacher cognition into play, and bridging the Sea of Teacher Learning between Seminar Island and School Land so usefully identified by Waters and Vilches:

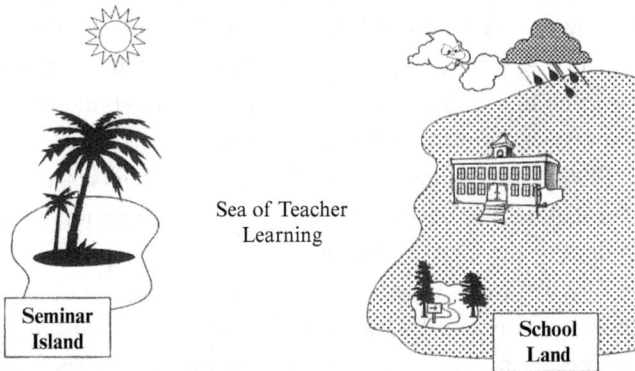

Figure 2 Waters and Vilches (2000) © Oxford University Press

Secondly and interestingly, findings from a study by Valazza (2008) in Uruguay indicate that teachers who have taken a TKT preparation course then the TKT test, see TKT as having had a strong impact on their teaching, bridging the gap between declarative knowledge and procedural knowledge. The same study indicates that the organisations for which these teachers worked also believed that TKT had not only increased teachers' knowledge about teaching but improved their practice too (see also Valazza, Chapter 12).

Finally, while knowledge can be classified into declarative and procedural, it is also true that these represent a cline with some knowledge sitting in both camps. We may know, for example, that *must have* in the sentence *he must have lost his keys* expresses a deduction about the past. This is clearly knowledge of facts, declarative knowledge. Knowing how best to react in class to a student who is known to be acutely shy is equally firmly procedural knowledge, but what kind of knowledge does lesson planning, for example, represent? Teachers can know about the general progression of lessons but may not know how to build that progression into shaping a lesson plan. As Woods says: 'Increasingly … the distinction between declarative and procedural knowledge is being blurred, for example, Leinhardt (1989: 146) states "situated knowledge can be seen as a form of expertise in which declarative knowledge is highly proceduralized and automatic"' (Woods 1996: 192). Subject matter knowledge, the focus of TKT Module 1, can be unambiguously placed into declarative knowledge, whereas General Pedagogic Knowledge and Pedagogic Content Knowledge, the main focuses of Modules 2 and 3, may sometimes sit less comfortably as one kind of knowledge rather than the other. There is an important overlap in which the one can enable and enrich the other. As Borg says 'action and experience shape, and are not only shaped by, teachers' cognitions' (2006: 166). In terms of TKT preparation courses, this is another argument for making use of all elements in teacher cognition and reflection as ways to deliver the course, showing the shortcomings of just 'teaching for the test'. TKT's focus on general pedagogic knowledge and pedagogic content knowledge as well as subject knowledge require a familiarity with and reflection on classroom practice as the task types used in TKT will show.

All the task types used in TKT are objective and include multiple choice, matching and odd one out. To answer, candidates simply have to write the letter of the response that they think is correct on their answer sheet. They are not required to produce a written answer. The syllabus for Module 1 is outlined in Table 3.

Table 3 TKT Module 1

Part	Title	Areas of teaching knowledge
1	**Describing language and language skills**	Concepts and terminology for describing language: grammar, lexis, phonology and functions Concepts and terminology for describing language skills and subskills, e.g. reading for gist, scanning

2	**Background to language learning**	Factors in the language learning process, e.g.
		• motivation
		• exposure to language and focus on form
		• the role of error
		• differences between L1 and L2 learning
		• learner characteristics, e.g.
		  – learning styles
		  – learning strategies
		  – maturity
		  – past language learning experience
		  – learner needs

(To be continued)

(Continued)

Part	Title	Areas of teaching knowledge
3	**Background to language teaching**	The range of methods, tasks and activities available to the language teacher, e.g. • presentation techniques and introductory activities • practice activities and tasks for language activities and skills development • assessment types and tasks • appropriate terminology to describe the above

This task focuses on Part 1 of Module 1:

For questions 20–26 look at the questions about phonology and the three possible examples listed A, B and C.

Choose the example which matches the term.

Mark the correct letter (A, B or C) on your answer sheet.

20   Which of the following contains a contraction?

A   USA

B   can't

C   bye

21   How many phonemes does *place* have?

A   two

B   three

C   four

22   How is *butcher* written in phonemic script?

A   /bʊtʃə/

B   /bʌtʃə/

C   /buːtʃə/

23   Which of the following is true of connected speech in English?

A   The first syllable of each word is always stressed

B   Structural words are never stressed

C   Content words are usually stressed

24   Which of the following contains a diphthong?

A   /meɪl/

B   /mæd/

C   /mɔː/

25   How many weak vowel sounds does *banana* have?

A   one

B   two

C   three

26 Which of these words is a minimal pair?

A   think/thinking

B   she/ship

C   cut/cat

This task consists of seven multiple-choice questions on two aspects of phonology: stress and sounds. To answer the questions, candidates must understand several subject-related terms: contraction, phonemes, phonemic script, connected speech, structural words, content words, diphthong, weak vowel sounds, minimal pair. They must also be able to understand what these terms mean in practice by recognising examples of the terms. Clearly, there is nothing at all in any of the questions that relates to classroom practice. The task is about knowledge of the English language. As such, it fits firmly within the category of subject matter knowledge, i.e. understanding the facts and concepts of a subject discipline. It also fits Tsui and Nicholson's allocation of phonology to subject matter knowledge and that part of received knowledge that Wallace defines as 'the vocabulary of the subject and the matching concepts' (Wallace 1991: 14). The knowledge tested in this task is factual, unrelated to beliefs or judgements. This is true of all the components of Module 1, as can be seen in the syllabus above. It is concerned with identifying or naming different kinds of task types, motivation, error, learner needs etc., or recognising the meaning of related terminology. This focus on facts lends itself to testing through the use of objective format tasks.

The syllabus for Module 2 is outlined in Table 4.

Here is a task from Module 2, Part 1:

For questions 21–29, match the information from a lesson plan with the lesson plan headings listed A–E.

Mark the correct letter (A–E) on your answer sheet.

You need to use some options more than once.

Lesson plan headings

A   Lesson aim(s)

B   Anticipated problems

C   Procedure

D   Aids/resources

E   Personal aim(s) of the teacher

Table 4 TKT Module 2

Part	Title	Areas of teaching knowledge
1	**Planning and preparing a lesson or sequence of lessons**	Lesson planning: • identifying and selecting aims appropriate to learners, the stage of learning and lesson types • identifying the different components of a lesson plan • planning an individual lesson (or a sequence of lessons) by choosing and sequencing activities appropriate to learners and aims • choosing assessment activities appropriate to learners, aims and stages of learning.
2	**Selection and use of resources**	Consulting reference resources to help in lesson preparation Selection and use of: • coursebook materials • supplementary materials and activities • teaching aids appropriate to learners and aims.

Information from a lesson plan

21 Copy of tapescript (teacher's book) and coursebook cassette.

22 Students might not want to talk about their childhood during the lead-in stage.

23 Tell students to listen a second time and answer the detailed comprehension questions.

24 Give students practice in the subskills of prediction, listening for gist and listening for specific information.

25 Students may not know several words in the listening, e.g. whisper, uniform, scary.

26 Reduce teacher talking time and involve students more, especially when answering questions.

27 Students copy down the new words from the board.

28 Class set of dictionaries.

29 Develop fluency skills.

This task has nine multiple-matching questions focusing on the area of lesson planning. To answer the questions, candidates must understand the meaning of the terms used in the options e.g. anticipated problems, procedure, personal aims as applied to the conventions of lesson planning. They must also be able to recognise what goes on in a teaching context, as understanding of the terms is tested through what they mean in practice, and recognise the function of different components of a lesson plan. The task taps into a knowledge of lesson plans and their components, which is part of general pedagogic knowledge as these are tools used across subjects. It also taps into pedagogic content knowledge as it focuses on how this is realised in English language teaching. The task appears much closer to the classroom than the task above from Module 1. This reflects TKT's move across the modules from subject matter knowledge to pedagogic considerations. Through using an objective format matching task, the task can focus on facts related to the practice of language teaching. It is this knowledge of established teaching practices and routines that is the focus of Module 2, as well as recognition of a primary purpose or function of materials or aids. There is no focus on beliefs, assumptions or specific context which might require testing through the use of more open-ended tasks, or lead to a prescriptive application of teaching methodology.

The syllabus for Module 3 is outlined in Table 5.

Table 5 TKT Module 3

Part	Title	Areas of teaching knowledge
1	Teachers' and learners' language in the classroom	Using language appropriately for a range of classroom functions, e.g. • instructing • prompting learners • eliciting • conveying meaning of new language • identifying the functions of learners' language • categorising learners' mistakes.
2	Classroom management	Options available to the teacher for managing learners and their classroom in order to promote learning, e.g. • teacher roles • grouping learners • correcting learners • giving feedback appropriate to the learners and aims.

Here is a task from Part 1 of Module 3. It focuses on teacher instructions, and uses the objective test format of multiple matching:

For questions **7–13**, match the teacher's instructions to an elementary class with the teacher trainer's comments listed **A–H**.

Mark the correct letter (**A–H**) on your answer sheet.

There is one extra option which you do not need to use.

Teacher's instructions

7 Okay, let's take a break, 15 minutes, no, no, sorry, ten minutes, no five, we've got a lot to do!

8̱ This is very difficult, but I hope you can do it.

9̱ Today we are going to look at the form and use of the zero conditional.

1̱0̱ Gina, do you know a synonym for the word 'pullover'?

1̱1̱ So now, can you all look at this exercise, and match the words to the animals?

1̱2̱ You can do this alone, in groups or pairs. It's up to you.

1̱3̱ Let's check the answers. Who can tell me what's wrong with number one?

Teacher trainer's comments

A Well done for deciding on the order for the class to do things before giving instructions.

B Decide which interaction is most appropriate for the task instead of relying on the students.

C It's better to nominate one particular student as this eventually gives everyone a chance to participate.

D This is a good, clear instruction for a vocabulary task for an elementary group of learners.

E The grammatical language in this statement is above elementary level.

F This statement is demotivating to learners. Try to be more encouraging.

G Try not to change your mind when giving instructions to lower levels, and make them as short as possible.

H The student is unlikely to know this term for a lexical category at this level.

This task has seven multiple-matching questions. It clearly contains minimal reference to subject matter knowledge but to a mixture of general pedagogic knowledge and pedagogic content knowledge. To answer the questions, candidates are helped by a knowledge of classroom practices and knowledge based on some experience of teaching. This is not Schön's knowing-in-action but the task is framed through classroom interventions and opinions evaluating them. It is moving towards the point, mentioned before, where declarative and procedural knowledge blend. The questions themselves, however, focus on awareness of aspects of instructions and the effect instructions can have. We see once again an objective task used to identify facts, this time in aspects of instructions. The objective multiple-matching format allows for a range of common but incorrect identifications to be brought into play.

Examples of the rubrics for the other tasks in this Module 3 paper (see Cambridge ESOL 2012) show how the focus on facts in teaching practice is maintained throughout the tasks in the module, thus lending itself to the use of objective format tasks.

- For questions **1–6**, match the examples of teacher language with the functions listed **A**, **B** and **C**.
- For questions **14–19**, read the instructions to a class on the following page and fill in the missing instructions from the options listed **A–F**.
- For questions **20–26**, match the mistakes on each line of the student's letter with the types of mistake listed **A–H**.
- For questions **27–33**, match the underlined mistakes in a student's writing with the types of error listed **A–H**.
- For questions **34–40**, match the underlined words in the following transcript of a student's classroom conversation with the functions listed **A–H**.
- For questions **41–47**, match the learner comments with the different teacher roles listed **A**, **B** or **C**.
- For questions **48–54**, look at the classroom management terms and three possible descriptions listed **A**, **B** and **C**. Choose the description which matches the term.

The tasks considered above show how TKT focuses primarily on declarative knowledge of subject matter and general or specific pedagogic knowledge related to teaching practices. It cannot be claimed that the tasks test how to teach, nor do they test knowing in action, reflection, a live classroom context, beliefs or assumptions. They test declarative knowledge through use of objective task formats. These formats have the practical advantage mentioned previously of allowing the test to be inexpensive and thus available to a large candidature. Since they require candidates to select answers rather than produce them, the formats also make the test available to teachers whose proficiency in English may not be high. This enables TKT to achieve the third aim mentioned in the *TKT Handbook*: to encourage teachers in their professional development by providing a step in a developmental framework of qualifications and tests for teachers of English (Cambridge ESOL 2012: 4).

To conclude, this chapter has examined the concept of teaching knowledge and the task types that underlie the design of the TKT test. It has shown that TKT tests different kinds of declarative teaching knowledge. The discussion has suggested that this view of teaching knowledge lends itself well to the use of objective format tasks, and that these two elements of TKT's design provide the basis for an objective, reliable, inexpensive test that is accessible to a wide range of teachers internationally. It has also suggested that knowing-in-action, context, and the beliefs and assumptions in teacher cognition provide invaluable tools for the shaping, content and delivery of TKT preparation courses, thus linking the different views of teaching knowledge and preparing the ground for change in the teacher and the classroom, as illustrated in Figure 1, the diagram of the reflective cycle (Wallace 1991).

References

Borg, S. (2006) *Teacher Cognition and Language Education: Research and Practice.* London: Continuum.

Cambridge ESOL (2012) *TKT All Modules.* Cambridge: Cambridge ESOL.

Davies, A., Brown, A., Elder, C., Hill, K., Lumley, T. and McNamara, T. (1999) *Dictionary of Language Testing.* Cambridge: Cambridge University Press.

Freeman, D. (2002) The hidden side of the work: Teaching knowledge and learning to teach. A perspective from North American educational research on teacher education in English language teaching, *Language Teaching* 35 (1), 1–13.

Freeman, D. and Johnson, K. (1998) Reconceptualizing the knowledge-base of language teacher education, *TESOL Quarterly* 32 (3), 397–417.

Grossman, P. (1990) *The Making of a Teacher.* New York: Teachers College Press.

Leinhardt G. (1989). Math lessons: A contrast of novice and expert competence, *Journal for Research in Mathematics Education,* 20 (1): 52–75.

Leinhardt, G. and Smith, D.A. (1985) Expertise in mathematics instruction: Subject matter knowledge, *Journal of Educational Psychology* 77, 247–271.

Schön, D. A. (1983) *The Reflective Practitioner.* London: Basic Books.

Shulman, L. (1986) Those who understand knowledge growth in teaching, *Educational Researcher* 15 (2), 4–14.

Tsui, A. (2003) *Understanding Expertise in Teaching.* Cambridge: Cambridge University Press.

Tsui, A. and Nicholson, S. (1999) A hypermedia database and English as a second language teaching knowledge enrichment, *Journal of Information Technology for Teacher Education* 8 (2), 215–237.

Valazza, G. (2008) Impact of TKT on language teachers and schools in Uruguay, *Research Notes* 34, 21–26.

Wallace, M. (1991) *Training Foreign Language Teachers.* Cambridge: Cambridge University Press.

Waters, A. and Vilches, M. L. C. (2000) Integrating teacher learning: The school-based follow-up development activity, *ELT Journal* 54 (2), 126–134.

Woods, D. (1996) *Teacher Cognition in Language Teaching.* Cambridge: Cambridge University Press.

Section 4
Assessment in context

Preface

In the discussion of TKT, the point was made that an objective test designed for an international candidature is not able to focus on specific contexts. In similar vein, CELTA was originally aimed at applicants whose first language was English and whose value was often seen as the portability of their language and culture to other contexts, a reflection of the original 'IH 4-week course' where teachers were trained in central London and then sent off to language schools abroad. In the present era, the globalisation of English language learning and teaching has meant that English language teachers are not only more than likely to be speakers of English as a second or foreign language but also to take a Cambridge English Teaching Qualification course in their country of origin run by trainers who share their first language. The next section of this volume foregrounds context both in terms of geographical location and specific teaching context.

Spratt (Chapter 11) described the development of TKT and noted that it was designed to be an accessible test for an international candidature. Candidate numbers indicate that TKT has indeed found a niche in a variety of countries and perhaps nowhere more so than in Uruguay. Following an initial survey of TKT candidates in Uruguay, Gerardo Valazza (Chapter 12) reports the views of TKT candidates, course tutors and employers after eight years of TKT administration. The focus of this second survey was again on the impact that TKT and its related training courses have had on the ELT sector in Uruguay. Valazza notes that potential impact is a key feature in the design of the Cambridge English language tests and is equally relevant in the case of a large-scale test for teachers such as TKT. The survey highlighted the attraction of obtaining an international qualification but also showed that teachers felt that preparing for and taking TKT had had a positive effect on their teaching skills despite the lack of a practical teaching component at that time. The more experienced teachers, including those already qualified in their national system, commented that they had a better understanding of the principles underlying their practice and could reflect on their teaching more effectively. Course tutors welcomed the availability of an international qualification of this kind in more rural areas of Uruguay while employers reported that offering TKT courses had improved the quality of their teaching staff as well as raised the profile of their institutions.

Valazza alludes to the fact that some of the respondents in the survey had also taken a TKT specialist module such as TKT: KAL *(Knowledge About Language)* or TKT: CLIL *(Content and Language Integrated Learning)*. The development of this latter specialist module is described in detail by Kay Bentley (Chapter 13), beginning with an account of the origins of CLIL itself. The term CLIL was originally coined in a European context to cover the teaching of school subjects in an additional language. Bentley points out that the title prioritises 'content' as the aim is for the language to be acquired through learning the subject content. The development of TKT: CLIL was guided by the 4Cs framework that was devised to help teachers and which identifies the components of CLIL as content, communication, cognition and culture. Bentley notes that CLIL not only includes a range of disciplinary areas from science to history but has also been adopted at all levels of education, thus adding to the complexity of developing a suitable test. In addition, teachers working with CLIL may either be subject teachers teaching through an additional language or language teachers who are teaching a specific academic subject. From this respect, Bentley notes that neither category of teacher may have the necessary training or resources to be fully effective. Given this complex context, TKT: CLIL aims to test knowledge about CLIL in four ways: understanding of a CLIL approach, awareness of language issues, knowledge of CLIL methodology and knowledge of suitable resources. Bentley illustrates the approach taken in TKT: CLIL with sample test items that follow the same format as in TKT. As with TKT, there is no practical component to the test but Bentley suggests that preparing for and taking the test stimulates discussion and professional development.

In contrast to the international focus of TKT and TKT: CLIL, the Inservice Certificate in English Language Teaching (ICELT) is an in-service qualification designed to meet the needs and conditions in local contexts. In previous chapters, some of the criteria applicable in ICELT have been discussed (by Parrott in Chapter 9 and Wilson in Chapter 10). ICELT is designed to be followed part time over an extended period and in many cases is not suitable as a short retraining or refresher course. In contrast, CELTA provides institutions that want to upskill their teaching staff with a programme that is designed to be delivered intensively, most often over a 4-week period. Peter Watkins, Bill Harris and Alan Pulverness (Chapter 14) draws together contributions from three course tutors about their experiences of running CELTA and ICELT courses in different contexts. Watkins begins with a note of caution as to the appropriacy or otherwise of international or UK-based training programmes for very different contexts. While there can be no one way of teaching that suits every context, Watkins notes that the umbrella term of communicative language teaching (CLT) is broad enough to encompass a range of styles of teaching. He points out that the CELTA criteria, for example, cater to context-specific needs in terms of learner needs, learning styles and cultural factors and highlight the importance of selecting appropriate materials and activities. In the same way, participants on an in-service teacher training course also have a history of learning and teaching and so require similarly culturally sensitive treatment. Watkins describes two CELTA courses, one run in Sudan and one in Russia, and an ICELT course run in Pakistan. On both CELTA courses, most if not all the participants had prior teaching experience and some had been teaching for many years. The move from grammar-translation and a transmission mode to a more communicative approach was initially a challenge for all the participants, as was the related re-evaluation of their traditional roles as providers of knowledge. Feedback on both courses was extremely positive with comments from participants such as 'life-changing'. In contrast to the CELTA courses, which were offered in Sudan by the British Council and in Russia by the local education ministry, the ICELT course was run for and by a Pakistan teachers association. Unlike the two CELTA courses, which used UK-based trainers, the ICELT course was set up and run by local trainers in order to provide context-specific training and support. The part-time nature of ICELT allowed the participants to develop their practice with their own students with positive results in terms of participants' renewed enthusiasm for teaching.

In the three cases described by Watkins, Cambridge English Teaching Qualifications were selected by different organisations as standalone training courses. The qualifications are also offered by some universities in the UK and elsewhere as part of their English language teaching degree programmes: CELTA at undergraduate level and Delta at postgraduate. The task of integrating the syllabus and assessment requirements of another provider with those of the institution requires careful thought, as Simon Phipps (Chapter 15) describes in the case of the MA TESOL at Bilkent University in Turkey. An overview of different approaches to teacher education, also described by Morgan (Chapter 7), highlights the tension between academic and practice-based courses and whether practice supports theory or theory informs practice. Phipps notes the key role played by teacher beliefs in teacher learning, as discussed by Borg and Albery (Chapter 3) and the difficulty of assessing teachers' personal knowledge base, together with the further complication in language teacher education of the dilemma of language as content. In the case of the MA TESOL at Bilkent University, the challenges inherent in teacher assessment were increased with the need to design a syllabus and assessment procedure that met the requirements both of their Master's degree and of Delta. Phipps describes how directly linked Delta assessment tasks constitute a proportion of the MA course, thus enabling participants to gain Master's credits at the same time. However, the practice-focused courses are preceded by more theoretical courses in second language acquisition to provide a basis for the applied tasks. Delta assignments are graded using the appropriate criteria and the grade converted to a numerical figure for the purposes of the MA while assignments for the Master's course reflect a more traditional academic approach. Phipps suggests that this integration of theory and practice, supported by assessment procedures that focus on theory and practice both jointly and separately, can develop teachers' classroom skills while at the same time meeting their professional needs for a Master's-level qualification.

In his account of the design of teacher education programmes, Phipps makes reference to the role of context and its related constraints. Courses such as the Cambridge English Teaching Qualifications, which are delivered in a wide range of different contexts, need to ensure not only that the syllabus addresses the issue of context but that the assessment procedures are also designed to be sensitive to the context in which individual participants are working, particularly in terms of their classroom practice. David M. Palfreyman (Chapter 16) examines a sample of Delta assessment reports to investigate to what extent assessors refer to the influence of cultural factors in lessons. Palfreyman notes that the term 'culture' as referred to English language teaching can refer to the wider geographical culture as well as to the sub-culture of the status of English and the micro-culture of a particular school or class. In addition, teaching a language involves teaching a target culture, to a greater or lesser extent. Palfreyman notes that the assessment criteria for the Cambridge English Teaching Qualifications include reference to cultural awareness and that guidelines for Cambridge English language tests also stress the importance of avoiding cultural assumptions. The sample of reports that Palfreyman discusses include lessons taught in the UK and elsewhere by teachers of different cultural backgrounds but in all cases the assessor was British. Assessor comments focus on cultural considerations at varying stages of lessons. Reference is made to the selection of materials or of discussion topics as being culturally appropriate or otherwise as well as to teachers' cultural sensitivity to students' learning styles or differences in gender or age. In the latter case, Palfreyman points out that what the UK-based assessor considers inappropriate can be culturally acceptable in the non-UK context. The reverse situation is highlighted by another comment in which the assessor expresses disquiet at a teacher's language but notes that the students do not seem to be disturbed, a reminder that assessors need as far as possible to put themselves in the place of the learners.

This last section emphasised the situated nature of teaching as well as teachers' interest in feeling part of an international teaching community. The case studies illustrate ways in which universal principles of language-as-communication and learner involvement can be applied in more traditional educational systems, including in the teaching of subjects other than language, while at the same time operating within a culturally appropriate framework. The different accounts suggest that learners benefit as much as teachers from changes in classroom practice. As one of the CELTA participants in Russia commented: 'Today we had a lesson for 60 minutes and they didn't notice it at all!'

12 Impact of TKT in Uruguay 2005–2012

Gerardo Valazza
Instituto Cultural Anglo-Uruguayo

Introduction

The requirements of educational systems, and in particular of examinations, can have a positive or negative impact on learners, teachers and the learning and teaching processes and their results. In recognition of this, Cambridge English Language Assessment explicitly integrates impact research into their test design routine procedures and refers to their approach to understanding the effects and consequences that result from the use of tests and examinations as *impact by design*. Saville (2012: 4–8) provides an account of the development and application of this model for investigating the impact of language assessment and explains that impact by design 'starts from the premise that assessment systems should be designed from the outset with the potential to achieve positive impacts and takes an *ex ante* approach to anticipating the possible consequences of using the test in particular contexts'. As further explained in Cambridge English Language Assessment's *Principles of Good Practice: Quality management and validation in language assessment* (2013: 31–32), impact by design is based on the following four maxims proposed by Milanovic and Saville (1996): plan, support, communicate and monitor and evaluate (see Table 1).

It could be argued that the rationale underpinning this model for investigating the impact of language assessment within educational contexts is equally applicable to the study of the impact of teaching qualifications. The results of the assessment of teaching knowledge and skills can have far-reaching implications at both the micro level of the immediate teaching and learning context but also at the macro level of educational systems more broadly. It is therefore important to integrate impact research into the test design routine procedures of teaching qualifications as well.

Table 1 Four maxims of impact by design

Maxim 1	PLAN
	Use a rational and explicit approach to test development
Maxim 2	SUPPORT
	Support stakeholders in the testing process
Maxim 3	COMMUNICATE
	Provide comprehensive, useful and transparent information
Maxim 4	MONITOR AND EVALUATE
	Collect all relevant data and analyse as required

It is in the light of such theoretical understanding that the present research study should be interpreted. It stems from a desire to understand the impact that the Cambridge Teaching Knowledge Test (TKT) is having in Uruguay, more precisely with a view to answering the following three questions:

a) What is the impact of TKT upon teachers and schools in Uruguay after eight years of uninterrupted administration of this teaching qualification?

b) How does impact relate to the stage of development of the teacher, i.e. more vs. less experienced and qualified vs. unqualified?

c) What strategies could be adopted to raise the profile of TKT in Uruguay so that it contributes even further to the learning and professional development of English language teachers and the educational system in general?

In addition to answering these questions it is hoped that the results of the present study will also contribute to furthering our understanding of the impact that assessment can have upon teacher learning for both novice and expert teachers.

National educational reform initiatives and TKT

The beginning of the 21st century has seen large-scale educational reform in many countries with English being increasingly taught from very early ages, often as part of very ambitious national education projects. In line with its educational mission and in order to cater for this changing scenario, Cambridge English Language Assessment has expanded its activities and focus to include 'the teaching, learning and assessment of the English language across the different levels of national education from Primary to Higher Education' (Randall 2010: 2).

A concomitant result of this educational reform has been a greater need for English language teachers worldwide, which has in turn led to Cambridge English Language Assessment developing TKT in order to cater for the needs of a new generation of teachers who either do not meet the minimum language requirements for existing teaching qualifications such as CELTA or Delta, or perhaps cannot commit themselves to lengthy and intensive preparation courses (Ashton and Khalifa 2005: 5–7).

With a view to offering test takers and test providers maximum accessibility and flexibility, 'the content of TKT has been designed to be relevant to teachers in a variety of teaching contexts, and at any stage of their teaching career' (Harrison 2007: 31). It draws from three of the four components of teaching knowledge identified by Grossman (1990): general pedagogic knowledge, subject matter knowledge and pedagogic content knowledge. The fourth component, i.e. knowledge of context, is not assessed by TKT, but it could be argued that the contextual differences are catered for by the courses that candidates take in order to prepare for the teaching qualification. (See Spratt, Chapter 11.)

TKT in Uruguay

TKT is a modular teaching qualification consisting of *three core modules* and *four specialist modules*. The focus of each of these modules is as follows:

- TKT Module 1: Language and background to language learning and teaching
- TKT Module 2: Lesson planning and use of resources for language teaching
- TKT Module 3: Managing the teaching and learning process
- TKT: KAL (Knowledge About Language)
- TKT: CLIL (Content and Language Integrated Learning)
- TKT: YL (Young Learners)
- TKT: Practical.

TKT Modules 1, 2 and 3 were introduced in Uruguay in February 2005 and by the end of 2012 a total of 3,268 modules had been administered.

At the time this study was being conducted, there was a network of four Cambridge English TKT authorised centres in the country which made entries to the whole range of the TKT modules.

Three years after the introduction of TKT Modules 1, 2 and 3 in Uruguay a first study was conducted by the Instituto Cultural AngloUruguayo (Anglo) to investigate the impact of this teaching qualification upon teachers and language schools in the country (Valazza 2008: 21–26). The present study is therefore the second investigation that has been conducted to measure the impact of TKT in Uruguay.

Main characteristics of the present research study

The present research study is underpinned by the same rationale as the first study conducted by the Anglo in 2007. It regards theory as emergent and can therefore be described as interpretive or naturalistic (Cohen, Manion and Morrison 2000: 22–23). It is characterised by a concern to understand the individual's perception of reality rather than to reach conclusions that can be generalised and transferred to other contexts.

In the same way, as a study of teacher learning, it follows a *hermeneutic research paradigm* (Freeman 1996: 360), which, instead of regarding teaching as 'externally assessable behaviour', aims to 'understand and interpret actions from the perspective of participants', i.e. from the perspective of the teachers themselves. It is precisely by exploring teachers' inner perceptions of their own reality that the reliability of the results will be increased. Reliability is understood, not as the generalisability of the findings, but as the correspondence between the data as they are recorded by the researcher and what naturally occurs in the setting under investigation (Cohen *et al.* 2000: 119).

Research design

The following data collection instruments were used to gather information for the present study:

- Two different questionnaires administered to TKT candidates and TKT trainers by email in October–December 2012. A total of 140 teachers and 27 trainers completed the appropriate surveys.
- Face-to-face interviews with key decision-makers from organisations

running TKT courses in Uruguay. A total of seven interviews were conducted in December 2012.

The questionnaires mostly consisted of closed questions but open-ended questions were also included in order to enable respondents to express their views as precisely as possible. The questionnaires were designed and the data was collected using SurveyMonkey. The face-to-face interviews were structured and questions were sent to respondents in advance so that their answers were as complete as possible. Additional questions were asked during the course of each interview to delve further into the issues raised by each respondent.

Validity and reliability of the research study

The following measures were taken in order to increase the validity and reliability of the findings:

- Data was collected from three different types of stakeholders, i.e. TKT candidates, TKT trainers and key decision-makers in institutions running TKT courses, so that the findings could be triangulated to increase the accuracy of the conclusions that have been drawn.
- In contrast with the study carried out in 2007, for which all the data was gathered by means of questionnaires only, interviews were also used on this occasion. It is suggested that the use of this additional data collection instrument has contributed to the validity and reliability of the results because the issues that have arisen have been analysed in more depth and with greater accuracy.
- In order to reach as many TKT candidates and trainers as possible, questionnaires were administered by means of email. Given the fact that the distribution lists used contained contacts from the complete network of TKT course providers, the data collected is representative of the whole range of teachers, trainers and institutions involved with TKT all over the country.

Threats to the validity and reliability of the study

A possible threat to the validity of the findings of the present study may be the fact that the 140 teachers who took part in the survey completed 335 TKT modules out of the total of 3,268 modules administered in Uruguay from 2005 to 2012. In other words, these teachers account for 10% of the total number of TKT module entries in Uruguay since 2005, which naturally leads to the question of how representative of the total population of TKT candidates from 2005 to 2012 this sample may be. Similarly, given the fact that the total population of TKT trainers in Uruguay from 2005 to 2012 is unknown, the sample of 27 trainers who answered the corresponding questionnaire may not accurately represent the opinion of this group of stakeholders. However, it could be argued that these two threats are somewhat mitigated by the fact that the data collected from TKT candidates and TKT trainers has been triangulated with the data gathered from key decision-makers from the four centres authorised to make TKT entries and from the most prominent TKT course providers in Uruguay. Finally, it is important to reiterate that the purpose of the present study is not to attain generalisability or transferability of the findings to other contexts. The main aim has been to collect data that makes it possible to draw some conclusions regarding the impact of TKT upon teachers and schools in Uruguay.

Analysis and discussion of data

TKT candidates' profile: Age

The TKT candidates' survey was completed by 140 teachers, of which 85% are female and 15% are male. As far as age distribution is concerned, the younger the teacher, the more appealing TKT seems to be to them. Figure 1 shows this very clearly. It indicates the number of respondents for each of the age ranges used in the study.

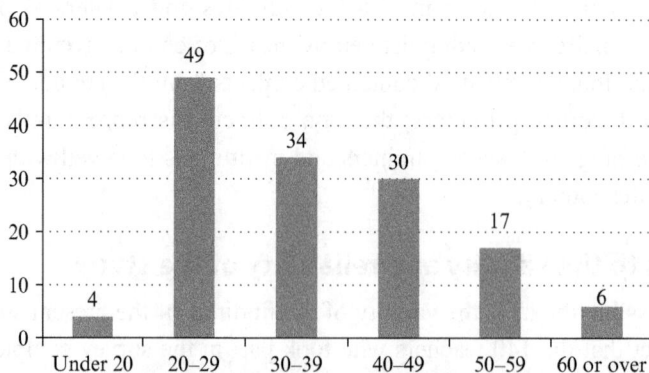

Figure 1 Age of the teachers who answered the TKT candidates' survey

Grouping the age ranges together shows that 53 respondents (38%) are younger than 30 and 87 (62%) younger than 40 years of age. It should be noted that as TKT was first administered in Uruguay in 2005, these teachers may in fact have been up to eight years younger when they sat for the different modules. The relatively young age of the candidates is consistent with some of the data gathered through the interviews. Five out of the seven decision-makers who were interviewed highlighted that TKT currently seems to be most appealing to young teachers who want to start a career in teaching or have been in the teaching profession for a relatively short period of time. However, this should not be taken as an indication that more experienced teachers do not sit for TKT or do not find it useful. On the contrary, as explained later, the opposite seems to be the case.

TKT candidates' profile: Teaching experience

As far as the TKT candidates' work experience is concerned, the scenario is very heterogeneous, with the biggest group (48 respondents; 34%), having taught for 16 years or more. Candidates with one to two and six to 10 years of teaching experience were the next group (25 respondents each; 18%) followed by candidates with three to five years' experience (23 respondents; 16%) (see Figure 2).

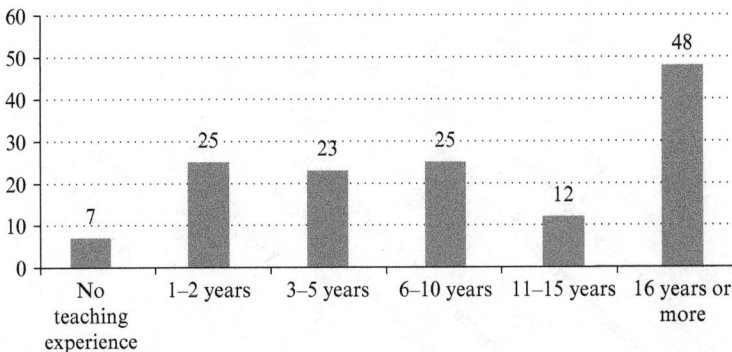

Figure 2 Teaching experience of the teachers who answered the TKT candidates' survey

TKT candidates' profile: Working context

From the data gathered through the administration of the candidates' questionnaire, TKT seems to appeal to teachers from a range of different educational sectors. Seventy-five out of the 140 respondents (54%) indicated they worked in *private language institutes* at the time of the survey, 74 (53%) expressed they worked at *private schools*, and 59 (42%) claimed to be working as *private teachers*. In comparison, the number of teachers who claimed to be working in *the state school sector* was smaller. Considered together, the number of candidates who worked in either *primary or secondary state schools* at the time of the survey totalled 27 (19%). If the private and state *primary* school sectors are considered together in comparison with the private and state *secondary* school sectors, the figures indicate that 58 of the teachers (41%) worked in *primary* school and 50 (36%) in *secondary* school at the time they completed the questionnaire. In other words, whereas there seems to be a significant difference between the number of TKT candidates in the private and state school sectors, TKT seems to be equally appealing to primary school and secondary school teachers. The breakdown of responses is shown in Figure 3.

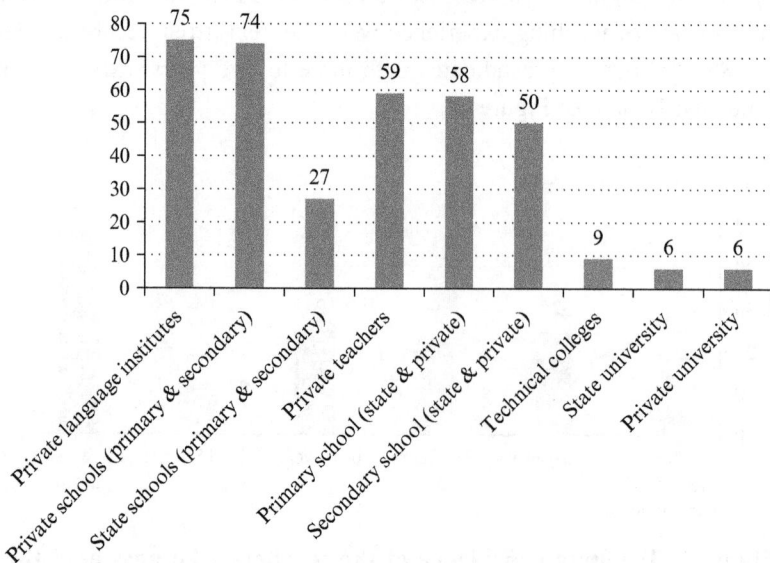

Figure 3 TKT candidates' teaching context

Candidates' reasons for taking TKT

The most popular reason for taking TKT was 'to obtain an internationally recognised teaching qualification', the response selected by 80 out of the 113 teachers (71%) who answered this question of the survey. It was followed by 'to improve my knowledge of teaching' (76 responses; 67%), and 'to improve my teaching skills in the classroom' (57 responses; 50%). It is worth highlighting that, even though six out of the seven TKT modules existing at the time of the survey test *teaching knowledge* and TKT: Practical only started to be administered in Uruguay in 2011, half the candidates who completed the survey expected TKT to have a positive impact upon their *practical teaching skills* in the classroom. This aspect of the impact of TKT is highly relevant and is therefore discussed in more detail in the section that follows.

Other reasons for doing TKT indicated by the candidates were: 'I needed formal training as a language teacher' (43 responses; 38%), 'to improve my English' (28 responses; 25%), 'to increase my chances of getting a better job' (26 responses; 23%) and 'my employer asked me to sit for TKT (14 responses; 12%). The impact of TKT upon the candidates and how this impact seems to be affected by the stage of development of the teacher are discussed in the section that follows.

The impact of TKT on candidates

Candidates were required to gauge their perceptions of how much TKT has helped them to develop as professional teachers with regard to a number of given criteria, choosing from the following 4-point Likert scale: 'Very much', 'To some extent', 'A little' and 'Not at all'. A total of 113 teachers answered this question. Table 2 shows the percentages of 'Very much' and 'To some extent' responses for each of the set criteria. These percentages are presented separately in the table but if taken together they indicate the overall *positive* impact for the purpose of the present analysis.

Table 2 Impact of TKT upon candidates

Impact criteria	Very much	To some extent
I have developed a better understanding of the theoretical principles underpinning my teaching	41%	32%
I feel more confident when discussing aspects of teaching and learning languages	42%	28%
I have become more aware of positive aspects of my teaching	41%	26%
I feel more confident about my teaching skills	43%	22%

(To be continued)

(*Continued*)

Impact criteria	Very much	To some extent
I plan my lessons more thoroughly	33%	32%
I can plan for and meet my students' needs more effectively	25%	40%
I feel better equipped to evaluate teaching materials	32%	32%
I can identify my students' needs more precisely	32%	31%
I have become more aware of problems in my teaching	34%	28%
Now I reflect on my teaching more than I used to	34%	28%
I have more ideas for the classroom	33%	28%
I can understand articles and books about teaching and learning languages more easily	35%	21%
I feel my students can learn more from my lessons	27%	29%
I find teaching more enjoyable	33%	20%
I feel my students enjoy my lessons more than they used to	23%	28%

Two observations can be readily made from the data in the table. Firstly, in general terms it could be argued that the impact of TKT is perceived as positive by the candidates. If the 'Very much' and 'To some extent' responses are taken together, 11 of the 15 criteria were positively rated by between 60% and 73% of the respondents, and the remaining five were all rated positively by over 50% of the 113 candidates who answered this question. Secondly, it seems that TKT has not only had a positive impact with regard to the candidates' understanding of teaching knowledge but also with regard to the development of their practical teaching skills. This is discussed further in the section that follows.

A positive impact on teaching knowledge and practice

As in 2007, the findings of the present study would seem to indicate that candidates perceive the impact of TKT as positive both from a *theoretical* as well as a *practical* point of view. The three criteria that received the highest ratings in 2007 have also been rated at the top and in the same order in the present study. These criteria are now considered in more detail. Consistent with the fact that TKT is a test of teaching knowledge, the two criteria that have received the highest ratings when the 'Very much' and 'To some extent' responses are considered together are 'I have developed a better understanding of the theoretical principles underpinning my teaching' (73%)

and 'I feel more confident when discussing aspects of teaching and learning languages' (70%). These two criteria had also received the highest ratings in 2007 (86% and 85% respectively).

The following six criteria receiving the highest ratings with regard to impact are all related to *practical* aspects of teaching: 'I have become more aware of positive aspects of my teaching' (67%), 'I feel more confident about my teaching skills' (65%), 'I can plan for and meet my students' needs more effectively' (65%), 'I plan my lessons more thoroughly' (65%), 'I feel better equipped to evaluate teaching materials (64%)' and 'I can identify my students' needs more precisely' (63%). This alleged positive impact of TKT upon practical aspects of teaching has also been highlighted by the decision-makers who were interviewed as part of the present research study. The decision-makers' perceptions about the impact of TKT on candidates are discussed below.

Impact on more vs. less experienced teachers

Analysing the impact of TKT in relation to the candidates' teaching experience leads to some interesting conclusions. In the first place, the group of teachers who seem to have rated the impact of TKT most positively has been those with six to 15 years' experience. This group consists of 37 of the 140 teachers who completed the survey (26%) and between 60% and 82% of these candidates rated 11 out of the 15 criteria positively. Table 3 shows the highest scores for this segment.

Table 3 Impact of TKT on candidates with 6–15 years' experience

Criteria rated most positively: Candidates with 6–15 years' experience	Very much	To some extent
I have developed a better understanding of theoretical principles underpinning my teaching	52%	30%
I feel more confident when discussing aspects of teaching and learning languages	46%	33%
Now I reflect on my teaching more than I used to	30%	46%
I have become more aware of positive aspects of my teaching	39%	36%
I feel more confident about my teaching skills	52%	21%
I plan my lessons more thoroughly	42%	30%
I can plan for and meet my students' needs more effectively	24%	46%

The less experienced (up to five years in teaching) as well as the most experienced (over 16 years) groups also rated most of the impact criteria positively. In the former case (55 teachers; 39% of the total) between 60% and 67% of the candidates rated 11 out of the 15 criteria positively. In the latter group (48 teachers; 34% of the total) between 60% and 72% of the respondents had a positive opinion of 10 of the 15 impact criteria. The highest scores for these two segments are shown in Tables 4 and 5.

Table 4 Impact of TKT on candidates with up to five years' experience

Criteria rated most positively: Candidates with up to five years' experience	Very much	To some extent
I have developed a better understanding of theoretical principles underpinning my teaching	40%	27%
I feel more confident when discussing aspects of teaching and learning languages	46%	19%
I have become more aware of problems in my teaching	42%	23%
I feel more confident about my teaching skills	38%	27%
I can understand articles and books about teaching and learning languages more easily	42%	21%

Table 5 Impact of TKT on candidates with over 16 years' experience

Criteria rated most positively: Candidates with over 16 years' experience	Very much	To some extent
I have developed a better understanding of theoretical principles underpinning my teaching	41%	31%
I feel more confident when discussing aspects of teaching and learning languages	31%	38%
I have become more aware of positive aspects of my teaching	53%	13%
I feel better equipped to evaluate teaching materials	34%	31%
I can plan for and meet my students' needs more effectively	41%	22%
I can identify my students' needs more precisely	19%	44%

If the percentages of 'Very much' and 'To some extent' responses are considered together for each of these three groups, the following results are obtained.

Each of the three groups rated most positively the same two criteria and in the same order: in first place, developing a better understanding of theoretical principles, and secondly, feeling more confident when discussing aspects of teaching and learning languages. However, some differences can be noticed if the criteria that were rated most positively from the third to the fifth place in each case are compared:

- The most experienced group highlighted a positive impact on their increasing awareness of effective aspects in their teaching as well as on two criteria extending beyond the teaching activity itself: feeling better equipped to evaluate materials and being able to plan and meet students' needs more effectively.
- The group with six to 15 years' experience highlighted a positive impact on three criteria directly linked with the teaching activity: their becoming more reflective practitioners, becoming more aware of positive aspects of their teaching and gaining confidence in their teaching skills.
- The group with up to five years' experience rated more positively their becoming aware of problems in their teaching, gaining more confidence in their teaching skills and being able to understand articles and books about teaching and learning more easily, which would seem logical given the fact that this is the least experienced group of teachers.

Candidates who have taken the TKT specialist modules

Twenty-seven (19%) out of the 140 teachers who completed the TKT candidates' survey indicated that they had taken at least one of the specialist modules (TKT: KAL, TKT: CLIL, TKT: YL and TKT: Practical) in addition to Modules 1, 2 and 3. It is interesting to note that there are representatives from all levels of teaching experience in this group: eight stated that they had been teaching for between one and five years, 14 for between six and 15 years and five for 16 years or more. Most interestingly, this is the group of teachers who had the most positive opinion about the impact of TKT. Taken together, their 'Very much' and 'To some extent' responses reached a total of 1,242, i.e. 20% higher than the group with six to 15 years' experience (see Table 6). This is also evident if this group's ratings for each of the impact criteria are compared. Table 7 shows the results for the criteria that received the highest ratings.

Table 6 Impact of TKT for each of the three groups

Number of years of teaching experience	Total number of positive responses
6 to 15 years	1,031
Up to 5 years	948
Over 16 years	936

Table 7 Impact of TKT upon candidates who have taken at least one specialist module

Criteria rated most positively by candidates who have taken specialist modules	Very much	To some extent
I have developed a better understanding of theoretical principles underpinning my teaching	63%	33%
I have become more aware of positive aspects of my teaching	46%	42%
I feel more confident when discussing aspects of teaching and learning languages	58%	29%
I plan my lessons more thoroughly	46%	38%
I have more ideas for the classroom	42%	38%
Now I reflect on my teaching more than I used to	38%	42%
I feel better equipped to evaluate teaching materials	38%	42%

Impact on qualified vs. unqualified teachers

Finally, it would seem that both qualified and unqualified teachers regard the impact of TKT as positive. Out of the total of 140 teachers who took part in the survey, 109 (78%) described themselves as qualified teachers and 31 (22%) as unqualified. The overall impact scores for these groups are similar, 968 and 985 respectively. Tables 8 and 9 show the highest ratings in each case.

Table 8 Impact of TKT upon qualified teachers

Criteria rated most positively by qualified teachers	Very much	To some extent
I have developed a better understanding of theoretical principles underpinning my teaching	39%	34%
I feel more confident when discussing aspects of teaching and learning languages	39%	31%
I have become more aware of positive aspects of my teaching	38%	30%
I feel more confident about my teaching skills	40%	25%
I plan my lessons more thoroughly	28%	37%

Table 9 Impact of TKT upon unqualified teachers

Criteria rated most positively by unqualified teachers	Very much	To some extent
I feel more confident about my teaching skills	60%	10%
I feel more confident when discussing aspects of teaching and learning languages	55%	15%

(To be continued)

(*Continued*)

Criteria rated most positively by unqualified teachers	Very much	To some extent
I have developed a better understanding of theoretical principles underpinning my teaching	50%	20%
I plan my lessons more thoroughly	55%	10%
Now I reflect on my teaching more than I used to	55%	10%

Overall, it would seem that, from the TKT candidates' own perception of the impact of the teaching qualification upon their professional development as teachers, TKT has made a valuable contribution in the case of all teachers, regardless of their teaching experience or stage of development. Some differences across the groups with different levels of teaching experience are noted, however, especially the fact that candidates who have been teaching for between six and 15 years seem to have the highest opinion of the impact. Woodward (2013) refers to the period of between seven and 18 years of teaching experience in a teacher's professional life as a stage of 'active experimentation'. After 'stabilisation' takes place at between four and six years of teaching, teachers like to experiment in the classroom and are keen on developing professionally. It is most interesting to note that teachers at this stage in their careers would seem to value the contribution of TKT most highly. As far as the qualified vs. unqualified teachers dichotomy is concerned, candidates' perceptions seem to be very similar with both groups regarding the impact as mostly positive.

The impact of TKT according to decision-makers

Harrison (2007: 31) highlights the point that two of the most positive effects of TKT are 'the potential for increased access to professional development for teachers' and the fact that TKT courses 'can be designed to suit local conditions and teachers' needs.' There is some evidence to support these two assertions in the data collected from the decision-makers who were interviewed as part of the present study. Firstly, the introduction of TKT in Uruguay has resulted in the development of a wide range of face-to-face, blended and online preparation courses and materials which have given many teachers throughout the country the opportunity to access professional development of a high standard. According to the information gathered from the interviews in this study, TKT preparation centres have developed courses which range from as short as 30 hours over a period of three months to a maximum of 80 hours in a period of eight months. This flexibility with regard to course length and delivery has meant that many teachers, especially in provincial areas, have accessed professional development opportunities that had previously been denied to them. The following quotation from one of the decision-makers interviewed supports the view that TKT has increased accessibility to professional development opportunities: 'We started offering TKT courses because many teachers in the primary and secondary school sectors are not qualified. There are not enough teacher training courses in our country to generate the number of qualified teachers that are needed.'

Secondly, decision-makers highlighted that given the fact that the linguistic requirements for teachers to complete TKT are not as high as the requirements for other 2 to 4-year teacher training courses offered by private language schools, private universities and the state education sector in Uruguay, TKT has given many teachers with a lower command of English an opportunity to prepare for and obtain internationally recognised teaching qualifications and continue developing as professional practitioners. One of the decision-makers interviewed indicated: 'To do the training courses in private institutes they need Proficiency or at least C1 and 99% of the people I get for TKT are B2 level. Those teachers feel that there is something for them.'

Decision-makers have also highlighted the fact that TKT has been a stepping stone for some teachers, motivating them to continue seeking further professional development opportunities after obtaining TKT:

> Trainees start to love the profession after TKT and do other teacher training and development courses. They keep on studying after TKT and enrol on other courses.

> I think TKT opens doors for teachers to continue developing, to keep on studying. Students who have taken TKT would like to go on studying. Afterwards they try to go on a course like CELTA, or they go into courses like IPA[*]. I would like to offer them something else. Maybe the other modules ...

In addition to highlighting the positive impact of TKT with regard to the accessibility of teacher training and development, decision-makers also pointed out some of the positive effects of TKT upon the teachers that have prepared for the qualification: 'teachers step into the classroom feeling more confident', 'TKT opens the teachers' minds and they see what the profession is really about', 'we have seen our teachers develop, change their minds and approach their teaching differently' and 'when trainees come to us they have no knowledge or experience about teaching and when they leave they can get a job'.

Decision-makers were also asked for their opinion with regard to the impact that offering TKT courses has had upon their own organisations. In the section that follows, their perceptions in this respect are reported.

The impact of TKT on organisations

TKT seems to have a positive impact on organisations as well. Three of the seven decision-makers pointed out that TKT has increased the reputation of their organisation in the local community. One of these pointed out that students and their parents like the idea of there being teacher trainees in their classes preparing for a Cambridge English Teaching Qualification. The other two decision-makers both mentioned that their institute is now not only regarded as a language institute but as a teacher training course provider as well, which has added value to the organisation.

Two of the decision-makers have run TKT courses for the teaching staff in their own institutions. One of these is based in the interior of the country and highlighted the fact that, prior to preparing for and taking TKT, there were no qualified teachers in their organisation. In addition, TKT apparently helped to develop a better rapport between the teachers and the decision-maker, who, after delivering the course herself, is respected not only for 'being the boss' but for her knowledge of and experience in teaching as well. The second decision-maker who has run TKT courses in-house indicated that 'the recognition of the certificate added to the quality offered by the institution.'

Finally, two of the decision-makers pointed out that they have incorporated the option of sitting for TKT within their own pre-service teacher training courses. Although these courses comprise about 1,000 hours of training and lead towards diplomas in English language teaching that are already very well reputed in the Uruguayan context, decision-makers still decided to add the option of sitting for TKT to these courses because they felt that obtaining a Cambridge English Teaching Qualification within the course would add value to it.

The impact of TKT on trainers

A further dimension that is investigated in the present study is that of the impact of TKT upon teacher trainers. When TKT Modules 1, 2 and 3 were initially administered in Uruguay in 2005, it might have been predicted that it would give some teachers an opportunity to start working as teacher trainers, thus contributing to their own professional development. In the paragraphs that follow, some of the evidence in this respect is discussed.

The TKT trainers' profile

Out of the 27 trainers who completed the survey, five (18%) are male and 22 (82%) are female; 12 (44%) gave their age as in their 40s, seven (26%) in their 30s, five (19%) in their 50s, two (7%) in their 20s and one (4%) as over 60 years old. The majority of the trainers, 17 (63%), stated that they had been teaching for more than 20 years at the time they completed the survey. One (4%) had been teaching for between three and five years and there were three trainers (11%) in each of the following groups of teaching experience: 6–10 years, 11–15 years and 16–20 years.

It is interesting to note that about a quarter of the trainers (26%) indicated that they had been working in teacher training for less than two years and about another quarter (26%) had been working as teacher trainers for six to 10 years. Taking into account that three trainers (11%) had apparently been training teachers for between three and five years, the findings show that overall 17 trainers (63%) had less than 10 years' teacher training experience when they completed the survey. Considering that TKT was first introduced in Uruguay eight years ago, the trainers' experience in teacher training may be an indication that they started working in teacher training as a result of TKT. In the paragraphs that follow some more evidence is provided in this respect.

Starting to work in teacher training

Although most of the trainers who participated in the study (70%) had some experience in making presentations and delivering workshops for teachers before they started preparing candidates for TKT, only 13 of them (48%) stated that they had previous experience working as teacher training *course tutors*. This data can be interpreted as an indication that some of the trainers who completed the survey may have started working in teacher training as a result of TKT. Two of the decision-makers who were interviewed provide some clear evidence in support of this hypothesis. One of them explicitly stated that TKT had given her the opportunity to get involved in teacher training for the first time. She explained that some of the students at their language institute had already taken exams such as Cambridge English: Advanced and Proficiency and wanted to start a career in teaching. TKT had therefore not only given her the chance to start working in teacher training, but had also enabled the language institute in question to respond to these students' requests. A second decision-maker explained that although she had already been helping teachers informally before she learned about TKT, the test had provided her with a clear framework to offer a formal teacher training course. A further contribution that this decision-maker highlighted is the recognition and reputation that a Cambridge English Teaching Qualification had offered her. These findings indicate that TKT has made a valuable contribution to the professional development of some teachers who have seen this qualification as the chance to take the leap and start working as teacher trainers. In addition, when asked why the trainers had decided to start preparing candidates for TKT, 76% indicated that they had regarded it as an opportunity for professional development and 84% claimed they had liked the challenge.

In the section that follows the TKT trainers' perceptions with regard to the impact that preparing candidates for TKT has had on their own teacher training and teaching skills are analysed.

Developing teacher training and teaching skills

As in the case of TKT candidates, TKT teacher trainers were asked to indicate how much TKT had helped them to develop as teachers and teacher trainers with regard to a number of given criteria, choosing from the following 4-point Likert scales: 'Very much', 'To some extent', 'A little' and 'Not at all'. The results are shown in Table 10.

Table 10 Impact of TKT upon TKT trainers

Impact criteria	Very much	To some extent
I feel more confident when discussing aspects of teaching and learning languages	36%	56%
I feel more motivated to continue developing my skills as a teacher trainer	60%	28%

(To be continued)

313

(Continued)

Impact criteria	Very much	To some extent
I can identify trainees' needs more precisely	44%	40%
I feel trainees can learn more from my lessons	44%	40%
I have become more aware of problems in my teaching	40%	44%
I have developed a better understanding of the theoretical principles of ELT	32%	52%
I can plan for and meet trainees' needs more effectively	52%	28%
I have gained more confidence as a teacher trainer	48%	32%
I find teacher training more enjoyable	40%	40%
I have become more aware of positive aspects of my teaching	40%	40%
I have earned more prestige as a teacher and teacher trainer in my area	36%	44%
I feel trainees enjoy my lessons more than they used to	32%	48%
Now I reflect on my teaching more than I used to	32%	44%
I feel more confident about my teaching skills	44%	28%
I feel more motivated to further my studies of ELT	40%	32%
I feel better equipped to evaluate teaching materials	44%	24%
I can understand articles and books about teaching and learning languages more easily	28%	28%

The results show that the TKT teacher trainers' own perceptions of the impact of preparing candidates for TKT is very positive. Taking the 'Very much' and 'To some extent' responses together, 12 out of the 17 criteria were rated positively by over 80% of the respondents, 15 were rated positively by over 70% of the trainers and only one criterion received a positive rating below 60%. The two criteria that received the highest ratings in the present study are connected with general issues such as feeling confident when discussing aspects of teaching and learning and feeling more motivated to develop their skills as a teacher trainer. These were very highly rated at 92% and 88% respectively. The fact that these two criteria received the highest ratings may also provide some evidence in support of the hypothesis that some of the trainers who took part in the study had started working in teacher training very recently. Another criterion providing evidence in this respect may be the fact that 84% of the respondents claimed that TKT has helped them to develop a better understanding of the theoretical principles in ELT.

A further observation that can readily be made is that TKT seems to have had a positive impact on trainers not only with respect to their role as teacher trainers but also on their role as teachers. As regards the former role, trainers claim that TKT has helped them to identify trainees' needs more precisely (84%), maximise the learning potential of their training (84%), plan for and meet trainees' needs more effectively (80%), gain more confidence as trainers (80%) and find teacher training more enjoyable (80%). For their role as teachers, trainers indicated that TKT has contributed to their becoming more aware of problems (84%) and positive aspects in their teaching (80%) and that they have become more reflective practitioners (76%).

TKT preparation materials

Candidates and trainers seem to have made use of a wide range of resources to prepare for TKT. The most frequently used resources by the 133 teachers (95%) and by the 25 trainers (93%) who answered the corresponding questions in the surveys are indicated in Tables 11 and 12.

Table 11 TKT preparation resources most frequently used by candidates

Preparation resource	Number of teachers	Percentage of teachers
The corresponding *TKT Handbook*	59	44%
TKT past papers	54	41%
The TKT Course (CUP)	53	40%
The Cambridge English official website	34	26%
The TKT and TKT: CLIL glossaries	31	23%
The Cambridge English teacher support website	17	13%

Table 12 TKT preparation resources most frequently used by trainers

Preparation resource	Number of trainers	Percentage of trainers
The TKT Course (CUP)	22	88%
TKT past papers	21	84%
The corresponding *TKT Handbook*	19	76%
The TKT and TKT: CLIL glossaries	16	64%
The Cambridge English official website	15	60%
The Cambridge English teacher support website	13	52%

For the trainers the most commonly used resource has been *The TKT Course* (Spratt, Pulverness and Williams 2011), probably because it provided them with a comprehensive preparation resource that covers the complete range of skills tested in Modules 1, 2 and 3. In the case of the candidates, it is interesting to note that the most useful resource seems to have been the corresponding *TKT Handbook*s. These provide the candidates with information about the rationale behind TKT, the testing focuses of the different modules and sample papers for each of the tests.

Future impact of TKT in Uruguay

In the light of the results of the present research study it is suggested that TKT has a positive impact upon teachers, teacher trainers and organisations running TKT preparation courses in Uruguay. However, it would seem that the *private* ELT and mainstream education sectors are benefiting from its impact more evidently than the *state* education system. Whereas a total of 127 teachers out of the 140 respondents (91%) claimed to be working within the private sector, only 34 candidates (24%) indicated they worked within the state education system at the time of the survey.

The state education authorities have very ambitious plans for English language learning within the national state education system in Uruguay in the next 15 years. The aim is that by the year 2030 students will leave the national educational system at 6th grade of secondary school with a B2 level of English in the Common European Framework of Reference for Languages (CEFR). As a result, different English language learning projects are being implemented simultaneously at primary and secondary school level throughout the country and at present there is a shortage of English teachers within the national state education system. Considering the positive impact that TKT seems to be having within the professional development of teachers in the private ELT and mainstream education sectors, the adoption of TKT within the state education system might be able to contribute towards the realisation of the ambitious English language learning goals that have been set for the year 2030. Adopting TKT in this way might in turn have a positive impact upon the private sector as well because it is likely that the recognition of TKT would increase nationally, thus motivating more teachers to prepare for and sit for the different TKT modules. For the private ELT and mainstream education sectors, it is expected that TKT candidature will continue to grow given the existing national interest in learning English in Uruguay. It should be noted that with a total candidature of close to 14,000 examinations in 2012 and a total population of about 3.2 million in the country, the penetration of Cambridge English examinations in Uruguay was of one exam in every 230 inhabitants in 2012.

Conclusions

The findings from the present study indicate that TKT is serving and will probably continue to serve an important purpose in the ELT sector in Uruguay in a number of respects. Firstly, TKT seems to attend to the needs of teachers at different stages of development as professional ELT practitioners. From young people who are about to start a career in teaching to teachers with over 15 years of experience in ELT, the majority have all described their perceptions of the impact of TKT upon their teaching knowledge and practice positively. In this sense, it would seem that TKT is performing a significant role by awakening the vocation for teaching in young students of English, who later pursue their studies by taking other courses for teachers, and by helping more experienced teachers to develop their teaching knowledge and skills further.

Secondly, an additional benefit of TKT seems to be that it caters for practising teachers whose command of English is below the levels of C1 or C2 in the CEFR and who therefore cannot apply to teacher training courses with more demanding entry requirements. As a result, TKT provides many unqualified practising teachers throughout the country who are working in private schools, private language institutes or on an individual basis with a test that will help them to develop as professional teachers. Thirdly, given the fact that TKT courses are being offered nationwide in face-to-face, blended learning and online modes, accessibility to teacher training has increased, often in parts of the country where professional development opportunities had been very limited or virtually non-existent in the past. A further positive impact of TKT in Uruguay seems to be the fact that it has motivated some teachers to start working as teacher trainers, thus contributing to their development as professional practitioners. In addition, it would seem that TKT is regarded very positively by experienced teacher trainers who believe that preparing candidates for TKT has had a positive impact on both their teaching and teacher training skills. Finally, it should be noted that decision-makers in organisations running TKT courses have also highlighted the positive impact of TKT upon candidates as well as upon their institutions. Offering TKT courses has increased the local reputation of some of these TKT preparation centres, which are now perceived as teacher training institutions in addition to language schools.

In conclusion, in the light of the findings of the present study it seems that the different stakeholders' perceptions of the impact of TKT at different levels within the ELT and mainstream private education sectors in Uruguay are generally positive. The challenge to be faced in the future is to find ways of extending such a positive impact not only within the private sector but also within the national state education system where there is an evident lack of qualified English language teachers and very ambitious goals have been set with regard to the learning of English in the next 15 years.

Note

* IPA stands for 'Instituto Profesores Artigas' and is the official teacher training institution in Uruguay which runs pre-service courses for teachers of English in the Secondary School sector in the National Education System.

References

Ashton, M. and Khalifa, H. (2005) Opening a new door for teachers of English: Cambridge ESOL Teaching Knowledge Test, *Research Notes* 19, 5–7.

Cambridge English (2013) *Principles of Good Practice: Quality Management and Validation in Language Assessment*. Cambridge: Cambridge English Language Assessment.

Cohen, L., Manion, L. and Morrison, K. (2000) *Research Methods in Education*. London: Routledge Falmer.

Freeman, D. (1996) The unstudied problem: Research on teacher learning in language teaching, in Freeman, D. and Richards, J. (Eds) *Teacher Learning in Language Teaching*. Cambridge: Cambridge University Press, 351–378.

Grossman, P. (1990) *The Making of a Teacher*. New York: Teachers College Press.

Harrison, C. (2007) Teaching Knowledge Test update — adoptions and courses, *Research Notes* 29, 30–32.

Milanovic, M. and Saville, N. (1996) Considering the impact of Cambridge EFL examinations, Cambridge ESOL internal report.

Randall, S. (2010) Cambridge ESOL's growing impact on English language teaching and learning in national education projects, *Research Notes* 40, 2–3.

Saville, N. (2012) Applying a model for investigating the impact of language assessment within educational contexts: The Cambridge ESOL approach, *Research Notes* 50, 4–8.

Spratt, M., Pulverness, A. and Williams, M. (2011) *The TKT Course Modules 1, 2 and 3*. Cambridge: Cambridge University Press.

Valazza, G. (2008) Impact of TKT on language teachers and schools in Uruguay, *Research Notes* 34, 21–26.

Woodward, T. (2013) The professional life cycles of teachers, Cambridge English Webinar, available online: www.cambridgeenglishteacher.org/resources

13 Testing knowledge about content teaching in English

Kay Bentley
Freelance teacher trainer, author and
CLIL/bilingual education consultant

This chapter discusses the development of a Teaching Knowledge Test (TKT) module that focuses on an area of increasing importance to education in the 21st century: Content and Language Integrated Learning (CLIL). The module was introduced by Cambridge ESOL in 2008 and is aimed at both practising teachers and those new to CLIL. CLIL teachers in primary, secondary and tertiary contexts teach curricular subjects such as art, science, geography and physical education, or parts of these subjects, through the medium of a language, often English, that is neither the learners' first language nor the official language in the country. The concept of CLIL is not new, yet despite reports written in the late 1990s that recommended specific training for CLIL teachers, assessment of teachers participating in CLIL programmes is a relatively recent development. To present the case for developing a TKT module related to CLIL, this chapter first provides a rationale for testing knowledge of CLIL. It then presents the main challenges related to assessing CLIL as an objective format intended for international cohorts of teachers. The similarities and differences between assessing a CLIL approach and assessing that of a general English language approach are also discussed. The second section of the chapter discusses samples of tasks taken from the two parts of TKT: CLIL:

Part 1: Knowledge of CLIL and principles of CLIL

Part 2: Lesson preparation, Lesson delivery and Assessment

Rationale for testing CLIL

In 1994, the term 'CLIL' was first used to describe one form of 'good practice' in European primary and secondary schools where teaching and learning in an additional language were taking place (Marsh, Maljers and Hartiala 2001 in Coyle, Hood and Marsh 2010: 3). Content is placed first in the acronym as it is subject content which determines language input, and which has then to be understood and communicated by pupils. In a survey by the European Commission in their 2004–2006 Action Plan for promoting language learning and linguistic diversity in Europe, it was noted that CLIL was 'of unusual interest' (Eurydice 2006: 3). Furthermore, it was considered that by offering pupils subjects and languages combined, i.e. the integration of content and language, CLIL would offer pupils a better preparation for life and opportunities for mobility in Europe. What differentiates CLIL from approaches such as content-based instruction is 'the planned pedagogic integration of contextualised content, cognition, communication and culture into teaching and learning practice' (Coyle *et al.* 2010: 6).

Once CLIL had been defined and implemented, educators and researchers in the field began exploring CLIL contexts to examine what effective CLIL practice was, and to analyse how knowledge of effective classroom practice could be used to create a planning framework for teacher education. Although CLIL models across the globe are diverse and implemented in different ways, CLIL methodology has common practices. As Coyle (2006: 3) notes, 'since effective CLIL depends on a range of situational and contextual variables, the need for a shared understanding about CLIL pedagogies became a priority'. One framework devised by Coyle in 1999 to help CLIL teachers and teacher educators, 'to focus, examine and evaluate their planning and lesson delivery' (Wiesemes 2009: 53) was the 4Cs Framework which identifies four key components: content, communication, cognition and culture. These 4Cs thus provided the first theoretical and practical framework to conceptualise CLIL and subsequently, to map a way forward for the design of TKT: CLIL.

The decision to use a multiple-choice question format for TKT: CLIL followed from its parent, TKT. The TKT framework is based on a closed, multiple-choice, fixed response format. For TKT: CLIL this could have been limiting. TKT: CLIL items, possible responses and distractors had to accommodate the different teaching contexts of CLIL candidates; address

CLIL teaching of both young and older secondary school learners; represent a range of curricular subjects. It was vital that task items should reflect authentic CLIL contexts yet accept that tasks 'can be relatively realistic but they can never be *real*' (McNamara 2000: 8). The complexities of testing an approach such as CLIL with its range of variables: subject versus language teachers; primary versus secondary contexts; range of curricular subjects taught, were considerable. In short, TKT: CLIL needed to be accessible to diverse groups of CLIL teachers, many of whom knew little about CLIL so test developers and item writers had to take all variables into consideration. Ultimately, it was considered that a multiple-choice format was suitable as a first step in testing teachers' knowledge of CLIL.

TKT: CLIL was designed in two parts with 80 items in total. The four areas addressed in TKT: CLIL are, firstly, knowledge of CLIL and the principles of CLIL. Secondly, candidates are tested on their knowledge about preparing for teaching CLIL lessons. Thirdly, knowledge of lesson delivery for CLIL is tested. This 'requires teachers to "transform" their subject matter knowledge for the purpose of teaching' (Shulman cited in Cochran 1997: 2) so that it is comprehensible to learners. Lastly, in the final section of Part 2, candidates are tested on their knowledge of assessment for CLIL. What is not assessed in TKT: CLIL is teachers' knowledge of specific curricular subjects in science (physics, biology and chemistry) social science (history, geography and economics) and arts (art and music). This is because, unlike primary generalists, secondary and primary subject teachers as well as language teachers cannot be expected to have detailed knowledge of curricular concepts beyond the scope of their own subject specialism. Nor is there assessment of candidates' 'proficiency in the English language or their performance in classroom situations' (Cambridge ESOL 2010: 4). What TKT: CLIL does do is provide teachers with the opportunity to engage with CLIL concepts and raise their awareness of the complexity of the approach. TKT: CLIL also reflects how CLIL is understood and practised in effective contexts. Table 1 shows the syllabus areas of the test in the first column with the specific testing focus in both parts of TKT: CLIL in the second column.

After consideration of Ashton's (2006, 2007) two internal reports to Cambridge ESOL, TKT: CLIL was deemed to have construct validity. In other words, it was considered that 'the items in the test reflect the essential aspects of the theory on which the test is based' (Richards, Platt and Platt 1992: 80).

Table 1 Syllabus areas for TKT: CLIL

TKT: CLIL syllabus area	Testing focus
Part 1 **Knowledge of CLIL and** **principles of CLIL**	The aims and rationale for CLIL (including the 4Cs Framework of CLIL: content, communication, cognition and culture) Language used across the curriculum Communication skills across the curriculum (Coyle's second 'C') Cognitive skills across the curriculum (Coyle's third 'C') Learning skills across the curriculum
Part 2 **Knowledge of CLIL lesson** **preparation**	Planning a lesson or a series of lessons Language demands of subject content and accompanying tasks Resources including multi-media and visual organisers Materials selection and adaptation Activity types and their purpose
Knowledge of CLIL lesson **delivery**	Classroom language and its purposes for CLIL Scaffolding content and language learning Methods to help learners develop learning strategies Consolidating learning and differentiation
Knowledge of CLIL **assessment**	Focus of assessment Types of assessment Support strategies for assessment

Assessment challenges arising from a CLIL approach

There were four main assessment challenges which had to be addressed in the construct of the TKT: CLIL module. These were described as 'challenges' because they involved issues which would not be relevant to general language teaching assessment. The first key assessment challenge for TKT: CLIL related to designing the test so that it was applicable to both subject teachers and language teachers working in diverse CLIL contexts. As was noted before CLIL became an innovative approach, '[i]n subject matter learning we overlook the role of language as a medium of learning. In language learning we overlook the fact that content is being communicated' (Mohan cited in Snow, Met and Genesee 1989: 202). So, the test design had not only to take account of the complexities of a CLIL approach, some of which are addressed in Part 1 of TKT: CLIL, it had also to be relevant to the needs of a variety of CLIL practitioners who might take the test. These candidates could be: secondary subject or language teachers, primary classroom teachers, primary language or primary subject-specialist teachers. In other words, the design of each test had to accommodate CLIL candidates who worked in contexts from pre-school to tertiary education contexts. In addition, the test had to be suitable for subject teachers new to teaching their subjects through a CLIL approach as well as to English language teachers new to teaching curricular subjects through the medium of English. The former group tend to be secondary teachers, the latter, teachers in primary or junior sectors of education.

In order to support subject teachers new to CLIL, it was recommended that candidates taking TKT: CLIL should be 'familiar with the language of teaching as represented in the separate TKT Glossary' (Cambridge ESOL 2015: 4). This was suggested because it was felt that CLIL practitioners should understand key principles of language teaching in general as well as the principles of a CLIL approach. TKT: CLIL candidates are also expected to have knowledge of grammatical forms and functions commonly used in all subjects. The reason is that although in many CLIL contexts, primary and secondary subject teachers tend not to teach grammar or pronunciation explicitly, they are encouraged to help learners notice grammatical forms which are required to understand and communicate subject content. For instance, candidates should have knowledge of past, present and future forms and their meanings such as the use of *fought, conquered, negotiated* to indicate finished past events in history; the use of *flows, meanders, floods* to show general states of a river in geography; the use of *is expanding, is producing, isn't employing*, to convey current temporary situations in economics. Candidates are not expected, however, to have knowledge of infrequently used grammatical forms such as past perfect continuous. For all candidates, concepts specific to teaching subjects through English are explained in a separate TKT: CLIL Glossary available online.

In addition, because TKT: CLIL was designed to be relevant to teachers from diverse CLIL contexts, whole tasks and individual test items use subject-specific vocabulary but do not expect candidates to have knowledge of subject-specific concepts. In order that TKT: CLIL was meaningful, subject-specific wordlists were compiled with vocabulary commonly used in key subjects in the first seven to eight years of mainstream education. Some words included are also found in academic wordlists (Coxhead 2000) such as *estimate, formula* and *environment*. Subject vocabulary wordlists are included in the TKT: CLIL *Handbook* because this additional subject-specific vocabulary enables item writers to construct tasks with authentic items without testing knowledge of subject-specific concepts. For example, an item such as, 'Which stages in the life cycle of a frog are similar to those in the life cycle of a butterfly?' would be rejected at the pre-editing stage of test production as this item tests scientific knowledge rather than knowledge of CLIL pedagogy. However, an item such as 'Which diagram can a teacher use to show the similarities and differences between the life cycle of a frog and the life cycle of a butterfly?' would be accepted in a matching task to test candidates' knowledge of use of specific visual organisers, or diagrams which 'help students generate non-linguistic representations' (Marzano, Pickering and Pollock 2001: 75), in this example, a Venn diagram. In other words, the second item tests knowledge of types of organisers and their purposes in CLIL contexts, without candidates requiring knowledge of specific stages in life cycles.

Secondly, the frequently asked question, 'What is CLIL?' is a challenge for CLIL assessment because of different interpretations of the approach. Despite CLIL courses containing the CLIL acronym in their titles, teachers may be unaware or uncertain of what CLIL is. Although research from Europe reported that 'a significant number of respondents (88%) claim that they know what CLIL refers to … almost all of them (98%) would like to know more about it' (Savic 2010: 2). In the same research it was noted that in CLIL teacher training, EFL teachers, 'generally have a very vague idea of what CLIL refers to' (Savic 2010: 2). In addition, an Italian researcher stated it was apparent that CLIL teachers 'had been given no CLIL pedagogical/ methodological guidelines other than 'do what you've always done, only change the language' (Lucietto 2012: 18). What is important is that teachers understand that CLIL is not simply translating the content of school subjects, such as history and mathematics into the medium of English or another non-native language. A CLIL approach is complex. It aims to develop pupils' knowledge of both subject content and language, to promote the conscious development of pupils' cognitive processes, as well as encourage experiential learning and build pupils' confidence in learning how to learn subject concepts in a non-native language. Prior to the publication of the European research findings above in 2010 and 2012, it had become clear that one of the main aims underpinning TKT: CLIL was, 'to test candidates' knowledge of concepts related to a CLIL approach' (Cambridge ESOL 2010: 4). Establishing what CLIL is and the key concepts surrounding CLIL is paramount in CLIL assessment.

Key concepts are: identifying the components of the 4Cs Framework i.e. content, communication, cognition and culture in CLIL lesson plans or materials; recognising the difference between examples of everyday, social language of routine classroom discourse, for instance the interpersonal language used during pair or group work, and the oral and written language required for communicating ideas about specific curricular subjects. Cummins (2001: 64) explained the distinction between these two types of language as basic interpersonal communicative skills (BICS) and cognitive academic language proficiency (CALP). An example of the former is, 'Let's look at the worksheet', an example of the latter, 'In my opinion, we should consider converting the mixed number into an improper fraction.' It has been stated that, 'CLIL must take account, and early account, of the need for students to acquire as quickly as possible a firm knowledge of the most frequent words in the English lexicon, as well as basic content and transactional lexis' (Eldridge, Neufeld and Hancioğlu 2010: 82). The linguistic distinction between BICS and CALP also relates to Coyle's second 'C', communication, and her third 'C', cognition because, 'CLIL offers a means by which learners can continue their academic or cognitive development while they are also acquiring academic language proficiency' (Navés 2009: 26). Despite recent research which highlighted that in some CLIL contexts, students have limited opportunities 'to develop their BICS' (Llinares, Morton and Whittaker 2012: 220), research in Spain concluded, 'a CLIL class needs to give space to both academic and social language practices' (Llinares *et al.* 2012: 239). CLIL assessment should therefore test understanding of BICS and CALP.

As the development of learners' communicative competence and cognitive processes is fundamental in a CLIL approach, these two 'Cs' need prominent focus in CLIL assessment. Communication involves the ability of teachers and learners to produce meaningful oral and written language related to specific curricular subjects, and it has been noted that, 'CLIL practitioners generally agree that the focus on communication is essential for their students' success' (Llinares *et al.* 2012: 189). What CLIL teachers should do is 'draw learners' attention to language forms while retaining a communicative approach' (Llinares *et al.* 2012: 188). CLIL teachers also need to be aware of a range of communicative functions that they could use and model during lessons while describing data, giving reasons, explaining cause and effect. CLIL teachers should then be able to provide opportunities for students to use the language in their particular subject specialism. As a result of the importance of communication in CLIL lessons, and because subject teachers new to CLIL tend not to take time to develop learners' oral skills in English, CLIL assessment needs to test knowledge of exponents of communicative functions and their meanings.

Developing students' cognitive processes is also considered an intrinsic part of CLIL. Researchers Cummins (2001), Hall (1995) and Gibbons (2008) have each produced diagrams in the form of quadrants in order to support teachers' understanding of the cognitive demands of CLIL materials and tasks. Moreover, an adapted version of Anderson and Krathwohl's reconceptualisation of Bloom's taxonomy (Coyle *et al.* 2010: 31) provides teachers with a guide for planning how to develop students' cognitive processes from lower to higher order thinking. By matching examples of CLIL tasks with the six key progressively demanding cognitive processes — remembering, understanding, applying, analysing, evaluating and creating — cognitive challenge can be tested. Although Cummins was first to map demands of particular curricular language tasks into a quadrant, subsequent researchers interpreted Cummins' quadrant to meet more practical classroom contexts. In a keynote presentation, Gibbons (2008) relabelled Cummins' x-axis with 'high' and 'low' support, and his y-axis with 'low' and 'high' challenge. This quadrant (Figure 1) helps CLIL teachers to assist in analysing CLIL tasks to decide how cognitively challenging they are. Should tasks fall into the top left box, students are likely to need considerable, though temporary language support, or scaffolding. Mapping tasks into the quadrant also alerts teachers to any tasks that may lack cognitive challenge. Gibbons advises teachers to avoid 'low challenge', 'high support' tasks.

Gibbons also claims that in order for subject learning to take place, students need to be engaged in classroom work that presents high challenge, and because the work is undertaken in a non-native language, students need to be given an abundance of support. So, assessment of particular cognitive processes required for different task types needs to form part of CLIL assessment.

high challenge

high support ◄—————————————————► low support

low challenge

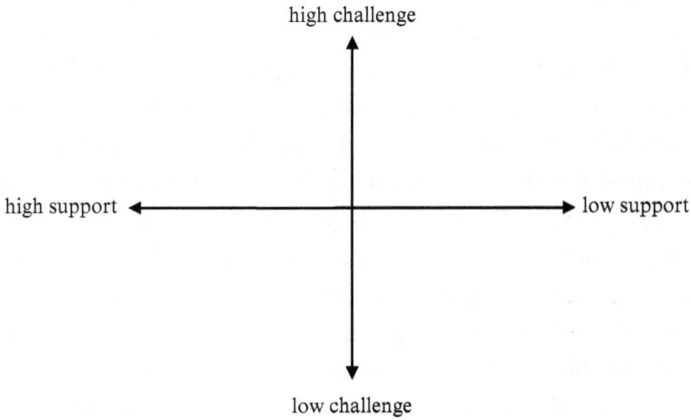

Figure 1 Quadrant of curricular language tasks (adapted from Gibbons 2008)

The third main assessment challenge for the design of TKT: CLIL was the contentious issues of teachers' language level for working in CLIL contexts, and use of the learners' first language (L1) in the classroom. Despite the fact that there are teachers who embark on teaching through a CLIL approach with language levels described as B1 in the Council of Europe's Common European Framework of Reference (CEFR), increasingly, European CLIL programmes, in particular, expect teachers to have a minimum level of B2, C1 or C2 depending on the country, region or school policy. So, although TKT: CLIL is aimed at teachers with B1 levels and above, and although much of the language used in the test is limited to the vocabulary listed in the Cambridge English: Preliminary (PET), knowledge of many CLIL concepts in the TKT: CLIL Glossary entails a language level of B2 and above. The challenge was therefore to make the test accessible to teachers with CEFR English levels of B1 and above. However, to reflect the change in European CLIL teachers' expected minimum language levels, the latest version of the TKT: CLIL Handbook states, 'in CLIL, teachers are advised to have at least an upper intermediate level of English — B2, FCE or IELTS band score 5.5' (Cambridge ESOL 2010: 4).

The use of L1 in CLIL lessons cannot be ignored. Although there is a strong argument for linguistic interdependence, when 'knowledge of one language bolsters knowledge of the other' (Navés 2009: 28), in some CLIL programmes, use of the L1 is discouraged. In others, teachers acknowledge that they do use some L1, for example to check understanding or to clarify meanings of subject concepts. Teachers may also draw learners' attention to similarities in sound or spelling between subject-specific vocabulary in the L1 and in English in order to help learning of key new words. Many teachers report that their students use some L1 in the early stages of CLIL and when participating in pair or group work. This 'code-mixing' 'refers to combining elements from each language' (García 2009: 50) when speakers don't know the target language needed to communicate their ideas. It has been acknowledged that 'allowing learners to use their L1 at early stages and also providing some academic instruction in the learners' L1' (Navés in Ruiz de Zarobe and 2009: 28) empowers learners. Once students become more fluent and confident, they regularly code switch, i.e. they use two languages in the same interaction and, '[i]t has been shown that code switching is a sophisticated linguistic skill and a characteristic of the speech of fluent bilinguals' (Navés 2009: 28). Rather than viewing use of L1 as interference, in CLIL code switching is considered to be a positive, bilingual strategy. So, when and why some L1 may be used in some CLIL classrooms should form part of CLIL assessment.

The fourth and final assessment challenge in the design of TKT: CLIL was to produce a test which was different from a general language teaching approach such as found in TKT. The main differences between designing a test for a CLIL approach and one for ELT therefore had to be considered. Before identifying differences, it was useful to note similarities.

What are the similarities and differences between a test applicable to a CLIL approach and a test for a general language teaching approach?

The following are key areas of knowledge that both language teachers and CLIL teachers require and which are tested in Part 2 of TKT: CLIL:

- knowledge of lesson planning
- knowledge of selection, adaptation and use of appropriate resources, materials and activity types
- knowledge of classroom language and its purposes
- knowledge of support or scaffolding strategies, and learning strategies
- knowledge of types of summative and formative assessment.

Although all teachers, including L1 subject teachers, need knowledge of the five areas above, because CLIL is more complex, teachers need knowledge of how to plan learning outcomes which reflect both how subject content will be taught and how language learning will be integrated. Teachers have to consider how to analyse the cognitive demands of CLIL tasks, how to prepare materials which take into account the L1 subject curriculum, and which also consider student language levels. In order to plan effective CLIL lessons that incorporate sound pedagogical practice, CLIL teachers need an understanding of how to write short and medium-term plans. This places higher demands on lesson preparation so CLIL assessment needs to include a focus on knowledge of planning lessons.

Teachers also need to be able to select and adapt materials for CLIL lessons from a broader range of resources than those available to teachers of general English. CLIL materials may be found in ELT sections of coursebooks, in subject coursebooks produced for specific country markets or in materials designed for first language speakers, all three sources in either digital or hard copy. Teachers who have neither access to CLIL materials appropriate for their subject and language learning outcomes, nor materials relevant to the stage and age of their students, typically spend time locating first-language subject materials and then adapting them. If these resources are inappropriate, many CLIL teachers find themselves creating their own materials. Teachers therefore need to gain confidence in their ability to adapt or to plan and produce materials for effective CLIL lessons, as it has been found that 'there is a clear link between appropriate materials and curriculum and student academic outcome' (Navés 2009: 33). So a test of knowledge about CLIL needs to incorporate assessment of candidates' knowledge of how to select and how to adapt materials for CLIL lessons.

Moreover, 'it is important to plan how teaching aids are employed to ensure student activity and understanding of the content' (Gefäll 2009: 83). Teaching aids and support strategies are forms of scaffolding and because of the dual nature of CLIL, effective teachers need to provide 'an abundance of scaffolding ... (and many strategies including) ... activating students' prior knowledge of subject content, providing a rich contextual background, providing comprehensible input, supporting comprehensible output, making language explicit, supporting learners to become independent' (Gibbons

2008). CLIL assessment therefore needs to test teachers' knowledge of activity types and their purposes, their knowledge of scaffolding techniques for content and language learning, and their knowledge of resources such as multi-media and visual organisers. According to Marzano, Pickering and Pollock (2001: 83), 'organisers are one of the most underused instructional tools in education ... (yet they) ... help students understand content in a whole new way'. Organisers are used in most CLIL subjects for the purpose of note-taking, organising ideas, and are also used as prompts or scaffolds for oral and written communication. Assessment of the names and purposes of visual organisers in CLIL contexts is therefore useful.

Although both English language teachers and CLIL teachers need knowledge of types and purposes of assessment, in CLIL the question often arises as to whether assessment should focus on content and language or simply content. The answer is more complex. As CLIL promotes the development of communicative, cognitive and learning strategies, all these need consideration in assessment. For example, can students define, describe and explain subject concepts? Can they recall facts, understand new ideas and demonstrate creative thinking during CLIL lessons? Can they locate data and take accurate notes? A further difference between general ELT assessment and CLIL assessment is that in some schools, teachers may use a range of support strategies during informal or formative assessment. These include reading rubrics aloud; writing instructions in the L1; allowing use of glossaries, adding on extra time to the test. CLIL assessment therefore needs to address how teachers can assess the progress and achievement of learners on CLIL courses using both summative and formative assessment and which, if any, support strategies can be used.

Major differences in the design of CLIL assessment, which differentiate it from general English teaching assessment, necessitate CLIL teachers having additional knowledge of the following:

1. Knowledge of the 4Cs Framework of CLIL, in particular the testing of cognitive processes; the difference between BICS and CALP (tested in TKT: CLIL Part 1).
2. Knowledge of different genres used in CLIL and the language demands of subject content and accompanying tasks (tested in TKT: CLIL Part 2).
3. Knowledge of scaffolding strategies for integrating content and language including possible use of some L1, and differentiation of input

and output for less as well as more-able learners (tested in TKT: CLIL Part 2).

4. Knowledge of support strategies or 'accommodations ... to give test-takers an opportunity to perform to their best ability' (McKay 2006: 94) (tested in TKT: CLIL Part 2).

At test construction, it was decided that the two parts of TKT: CLIL should be subdivided so that each subdivision represented a key area of CLIL knowledge which candidates should understand and then apply during their own teaching. The two parts also reflect the challenges which CLIL practitioners and researchers highlight, and which have been discussed above.

Testing knowledge of a CLIL approach

The main challenge of understanding a CLIL approach was addressed in the design of Part 1 of TKT: CLIL — knowledge of CLIL and principles of CLIL. In this part, the five areas of knowledge tested are listed in Table 2. The aims of and rationale for CLIL includes knowledge of the 4Cs Framework; knowledge of the difference between BICS and CALP; knowledge of lower- and higher-order thinking processes. To ensure candidates understand the interrelatedness of the 4Cs, many TKT: CLIL items include more than one of the 4Cs. Moreover, in Part 1, tasks and items are written so they are applicable to CLIL teachers who are specialists in subjects from across the curriculum in addition to language teachers who may work in CLIL contexts. In Part 1, TKT: CLIL candidates are expected to identify key aims of a CLIL approach. These include introducing learners to new ideas and concepts in curricular subjects in a non-native language, improving learners' performance in both curricular subjects and the target language, providing cognitively demanding materials from the start of CLIL, including a focus on culture and providing an abundance of scaffolding. Further key aims are listed in the TKT: CLIL Handbook.

Table 2 Five areas of knowledge tested by TKT: CLIL

Part	Title	Area of teaching knowledge
1	**Knowledge of CLIL and principles of CLIL**	Aims of and rationale for CLIL Language across the curriculum Communication skills across the curriculum Cognitive skills across the curriculum Learning skills across the curriculum

The following example is from Part 1 of TKT: CLIL and tests candidates' knowledge of the aims and rationale for CLIL.

For questions **1–6**, choose the best option (**A, B or C**) to complete each statement about CLIL.

Mark the correct letter (**A, B or C**) on your answer sheet.

1. Learning school subjects in a CLIL approach involves learners in
   A   developing similar cognitive skills across the curriculum.
   B   learning similar vocabulary across the curriculum.
   C   reading similar texts across the curriculum.
2. The 4Cs of CLIL provides a guide for developing learners'
   A   content knowledge and creative skills.
   B   comparing and contrasting skills.
   C   communicative and cognitive skills.
3. In CLIL, developing CALP helps learners to
   A   communicate using basic vocabulary and grammatical forms.
   B   interpret and produce increasingly complex language.
   C   focus on improving their listening and speaking skills.
4. One of CLIL's main aims is to
   A   reduce student talking time in the classroom.
   B   develop learners' ability to write essays in all subjects.
   C   increase learners' cultural and intercultural awareness.
5. Examples of higher-order thinking skills are
   A   identifying and classifying.
   B   evaluating and creative thinking.
   C   predicting and sequencing.
6. Communication in CLIL aims to
   A   develop skills of expressing ideas across the curriculum.
   B   increase the use of ICT across the curriculum.
   C   improve skills of self-assessment across the curriculum.

Key: 1 A, 2 C, 3 B, 4 C, 5 B, 6 A

The task consists of six multiple-choice items which test understanding of a CLIL approach, its aims and key concepts associated with learning subject content and language in a non-native language. The task does not test teaching skills; instead, it tests knowledge of the application of the 4Cs in the CLIL classroom. To understand why item 4B is incorrect, it is important that teachers understand that CLIL is about subjects across the curriculum; 'it is content-driven' (Coyle *et al.* 2010: 12). However, learners' ability to write essays in subjects such as Physical Education (PE) and Art is not a main aim in these particular subjects.

Testing language for CLIL

As 'language and communication are crucial elements in CLIL' (Wiesemes 2009: 57) it was decided that in TKT: CLIL, testing teachers' knowledge of language would therefore appear in both Part 1 and Part 2 of the test. Each part, however, would have a different focus; in Part 1, firstly, in 'language across the curriculum', where the focus is on testing knowledge of grammar and lexis common to all subject areas, such as knowledge of tenses, modal forms, connectors and synonyms and secondly in 'communication skills across the curriculum', where the focus is on the purpose of functional exponents such as describing cyclical processes and hypothesising. In Part 2 of TKT: CLIL, knowledge of the purposes of classroom language in CLIL contexts is tested as well as knowledge of ways to encourage student talking time. Examples of the former include the purpose of teacher questions and learner communication, while examples of the latter include task-based learning, role-play and peer feedback. The concept of code switching is also tested. In Part 2, knowledge of the language demands of subject content and accompanying materials at word, sentence and text levels are tested. Here examples include language used in common CLIL genres, or 'the different text types which learners of all subjects have to understand and produce' (Llinares *et al.* 2012: 14). Examples include imperative forms and sequencing connectors found in procedures. The following example, also from Part 1, tests candidates' knowledge of language across the curriculum.

For questions **1–6**, match the CLIL teachers' comments with the grammatical features needed for the communicative tasks listed **A–G**.

Mark the correct letter (**A–G**) on your answer sheet.

There is one extra option which you do not need to use.

Grammatical features needed for communicative tasks

A passive verbs
B prepositions of place
C reporting verbs
D past tenses
E modal verbs
F superlative forms
G adverbs

CLIL Teachers' comments

1. I'd like my learners to use the language of predicting and possibility so they can share their ideas before they do the experiments.
2. My learners need to practise how to describe the location of natural and human features on a map.
3. In maths, I'd like my learners to label their graphs with words to describe how often they use calculators to solve problems.
4. I'd like my learners to describe where rocks are found, how they were formed and what they are used for.
5. All of my learners need to recount events leading up to important historical events.
6. My learners need to practise telling the class what other groups think and say about their art work.

Key: 1 E, 2 B, 3 G, 4 A, 5 D, 6 C

This is a one-to-one matching task with seven options and six items. It focuses on testing language terminology such as grammatical forms. However, as previously noted, candidates are not expected to know advanced points of grammar, or to teach grammar explicitly. In the example above, the language forms listed in the options are used in all curricular subjects and teachers should know how to help their learners 'become aware of how language features create meaning in their subjects, and so improve both their comprehension and their spoken and written production' (Llinares *et al.* 2012: 154). This is a task which language teachers involved in CLIL are competent and confident at answering. Subject teachers, however, find a TKT: CLIL task such as this more challenging.

Testing knowledge about CLIL methodology

In order to address the many facets of methodology as well as planning and assessment evident in a CLIL approach, it was agreed that TKT: CLIL would test the most common issues teachers raise. In Part 2, therefore, candidates' knowledge of lesson preparation, lesson delivery and CLIL assessment are tested. The syllabus for lesson preparation and lesson delivery is shown in Table 3.

Table 3 TKT: CLIL syllabus for lesson preparation and lesson delivery

Part	Title	Area of teaching knowledge
2	**Planning, teaching and assessing**	Planning a lesson and a series of lessons Language demands of subject content and accompanying tasks
	Lesson preparation	Resources, including multimedia and visual organisers Materials selection and adaptation Activity types and their purpose
	Lesson delivery	Classroom language for CLIL Scaffolding content and language learning Methods to help learners develop learning strategies Consolidating learning and differentiation of learning

In the following example from Part 2, Lesson Preparation, teachers' knowledge of lesson planning is tested in an odd-one-out task type. This task format is also closed. Although CLIL lesson planning is complex, the purpose here is simply to test teachers' knowledge of what can and can't be included within each component of a sample CLIL lesson plan. The lesson headings, 'Communication' and 'Language support' are rarely found in an ELT lesson plan.

For questions **1–5**, look at the CLIL lesson plan headings and the three examples listed **A, B** and **C**.

Two of the examples are appropriate for the lesson plan heading. One is **NOT**.

Mark the letter (**A, B** or **C**) which is **NOT** an appropriate example for the lesson plan heading on your answer sheet.

1. Learning outcomes
    A to be able to identify different musical rhythms
    B to check answers on a text about musical rhythms
    C to know that musical rhythms can be played at different volumes and speeds

2. Procedure (activating prior knowledge)

   A Learners brainstorm 6–8 words they want to learn after watching a video of how a musician plays different musical instruments.

   B Learners tell each other 6–8 words or phrases they can use to describe different musical rhythms.

   C Learners word process 6–8 words or phrases they remember from the first lesson about playing rhythms on different musical instruments.

3. Communication

   A describe the rhythms heard in the three short pieces of music

   B play one of the rhythms loudly, softly, slowly then quickly

   C think how the rhythm could be played on a different instrument

4. Language support

   A drawings of musical notes

   B sentence starters for describing rhythms

   C word banks with groups of instruments

5. Procedure (final plenary)

   A learners listen to a musical rhythm and predict what the lesson will be about

   B learners think about how they played the rhythms and say what could be improved

   C learners say what they learned about musical rhythms

   Key: 1 B, 2 A, 3 C, 4 A, 5 A

The task has five items, all of which are related to one subject area: music. In Part 2, candidates may have to answer items in one task which focuses on one CLIL subject. As previously stated, candidates are not tested on subject knowledge. Rather, they are tested on their knowledge of, for example, planning or use of resources in a CLIL lesson. In the above task, items focus on knowledge of CLIL learning outcomes, activating prior knowledge, communicative tasks, language support and ways to conclude a CLIL lesson. Each of these lesson plan components can be applied to different subject lessons. CLIL learning outcomes relate to content and language and to the 'acquisition of new knowledge, skills and understanding' (Coyle *et al.* 2010: 53), which learners will work towards achieving during a lesson or a series of lessons. Activating prior knowledge of subject content is a stage in a lesson when in some CLIL contexts, some use of the L1 may be acceptable. The importance of including communicative tasks and language support cannot be overstated. CLIL teachers need to ensure learners have opportunities to produce the language of subject concepts during lessons and, when this occurs, planning language support so learners can communicate their ideas is vital. The final plenary is a stage which teachers may omit but it is one which is particularly effective in CLIL because learners need time to process and reflect upon new subject content and new language learning.

In Part 2 'Assessment', candidates are tested on their knowledge of three areas of assessment. This final part of TKT: CLIL has only 10 items and is the shortest part because of the considerable differences in how CLIL is assessed in different countries and regions. The areas of testing are in Table 4.

Table 4 Areas of testing in Part 2 of TKT: CLIL

Part	Title	Area of teaching knowledge
2	*Assessment*	Focus of assessment Types of assessment Support strategies

Here is a task from Part 2, Focus of Assessment.

For questions **1–5**, match the test instructions with the focuses of CLIL assessment to be tested listed **A–F**.

Mark the correct letter (**A–F**) on your answer sheet.

There is one extra option which you do not need to use.

Focuses of CLIL assessment

A	content and language
B	noticing language forms
C	learning strategies
D	subject knowledge only
E	creative thinking
F	practical skills

Test instructions

1. Quickly write down three differences between the data on the line graph and the bar chart.
2. Listen to the four pieces of music then write down the number of beats you hear.
3. Use these tools to show how you can make different patterns on the mosaic.
4. Circle all the verbs you heard the basketball player say when he was giving instructions.
5. With a partner write down ways you helped your group remember all the new words to describe 2d and 3d shapes.

Key: 1 A, 2 D, 3 F, 4 B, 5 C

This task consists of options which are all possible testing areas in CLIL, and most can be used as a means of both summative and formative assessment. It could be argued that content and language is required in each of the items as learners need to understand instructional language. However, here the focus of assessment is on what learners produce, not on what they read and understand from the rubrics. It is acknowledged that 'the problem of assessment on the language side of the equation is an important area for implementers of CLIL programs' (García 2009: 214). As one teacher admitted, 'We tried testing students who had gone through a lot of CLIL, and found big problems, not with the youngsters but with the tests' (García 2009: 214). It is important therefore that TKT: CLIL candidates understand key principles of testing in a CLIL approach and that testing should involve language competence as well as content knowledge and skills, especially at later stages of CLIL.

Testing knowledge of resources

TKT: CLIL tests teachers' knowledge of resources in Part 2, 'Lesson Preparation' where resources include multi-media and visual organisers. The following example is from Part 2, 'Lesson Preparation'.

For questions 1–6, match the teachers' comments with the visual organisers which would support the learners, listed **A–G**.

Mark the correct letter (**A–G**) on your answer sheet.

There is one extra option which you do not need to use.

Teachers' comments	Visual organiser
1. Before they design a shoe, I'd like my learners to write down the names of types of shoes.	A 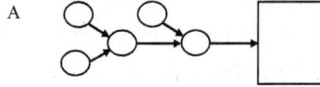
2. To help them learn some subject-specific vocabulary, I want my learners to identify the leaves by answering some questions.	B 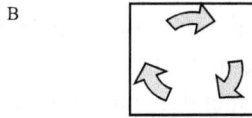
3. Learners need support to visualise several actions and events that might lead to a world water shortage.	C 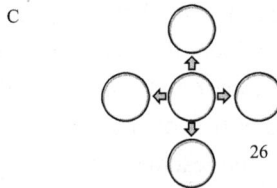
4. I'll ask my learners to categorise types of factories that started producing goods 150 years ago and to give examples of the goods they made.	D 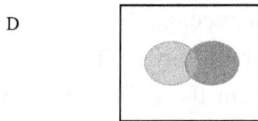
5. I'll ask my learners to show which numbers are square numbers under 100, which numbers under 100 can be divided by 5, and which numbers belong to both sets.	E 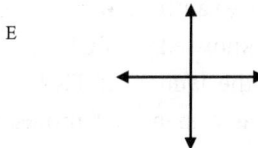
	F 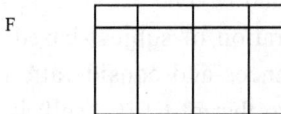
6. Some learners had difficulty understanding the text about the carbon cycle so I'll give them a diagram to show what happens.	G 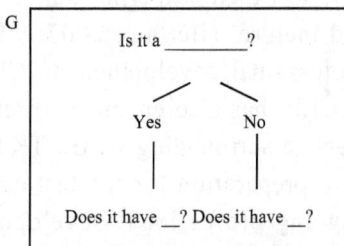

Key: 1 C, 2 G, 3 A, 4 F, 5 D, 6 B
(Adapted from Bentley 2010: 105–106)

Visual organisers are considered to be a useful way for learners to use and create diagrams to organise information. In CLIL, visual organisers are particularly helpful as 'they use words and phrases and ... symbols, arrows and lines to represent relationships' (Marzano, Pickering and Pollock 2001: 75). They therefore avoid the use of semantically dense text about subject-related concepts. It is important that CLIL teachers know a range of organisers, the purpose of each organiser, and how they and their learners can use them. In TKT: CLIL knowledge of visual organisers and their purposes is therefore an important test area.

It can be seen from the sample tasks that TKT: CLIL is indeed different from a test designed for a general English language approach to teaching. It is also evident that the test construct addresses knowledge of content and language integrated learning rather than avoiding Mohan's criticism that we overlook the role of language in the teaching of subjects, and the role of content in the teaching of language. However, there is only one TKT: CLIL test and although it tests knowledge of CLIL as an approach, it cannot test for example, pedagogy used in different subject disciplines. Future tests may be able to build upon TKT: CLIL and indeed, cater for the needs of CLIL teachers from the different disciplines of Sciences, Arts and Humanities. An examination such as is currently available for candidates who require a Business examination may be a way forward in expanding upon and deepening knowledge of CLIL.

Since the launch of TKT: CLIL in 2008, the test has evolved and is now used as a means of professional development in training contexts in Europe and beyond. Coyle's 4Cs Framework has also expanded to include consideration of subject-based methodology, subject literacy, European competences and consideration of local practices. TKT: CLIL today is similar to that of CLIL itself: it is now certain that CLIL and TKT: CLIL have lost their 'experimental character ... (and they) ... will both expand and mature' (Bertaux 2007: 92). What started as a means of offering professional development to CLIL teachers by testing their knowledge of CLIL has also encouraged reflection and debate on the principles and practice surrounding CLIL. TKT: CLIL is therefore not simply a testing tool; preparation for the test can support teachers in pre-service and in ongoing professional development courses as it stimulates important discussion of key challenges surrounding content and language learning and teaching. As Marsh (2009) stated in an interview recorded in *IH Journal*, 'CLIL is no longer an idea, a fashion, it is a reality.'

References

Ashton, M. (2006, 2007) TKT: Content and language integrated learning, Cambridge ESOL internal report.

Bentley, K. (2010) *The TKT Course CLIL Module*. Cambridge: Cambridge University Press.

Bertaux, P. (2007) France, in Maljers, A., Marsh, D. and Wolff, D. (Eds) *Windows on CLIL: Content and Language Integrated Learning in the European Spotlight*. The Hague: Platform for Dutch Education, available online: ebookbrowse.com/windows-on-clil-france-pdf-d118853357

Cambridge ESOL (2015) *TKT: CLIL Glossary*, available online: www.cambridgeenglish.org/images/22194-tkt-clil-glossary.pdf

Cambridge ESOL (2010) *TKT: CLIL Handbook for Teachers*, available online: www.cambridgeenglish.org/images/22191-tkt-clil-handbook.pdf

Cochran, K. (1997) Pedagogical content knowledge: Teachers' integration of subject matter, pedagogy, students and learning environments, *Research Matters — to the Science Teacher*, available online: www.narst org/publications/research/pck.cfm

Coxhead, A. (2000) A new Academic Word list, *TESOL Quarterly* 34 (2), 213–238.

Coyle, D. (2006) Content and language integrated learning: Motivating learners and teachers, *Scottish Languages Review* 13, available online: blocs.xtec.cat/clilpractiques1/files/2008/11/slrcoyle.pdf

Coyle, D., Hood, P. and Marsh, D. (2010) *Content and Language Intergrated Learning*. Cambridge: Cambridge University Press.

Cummins, J. (2001) *Negotiating Identities*. Los Angeles: Californian Association for Bilingual Education.

Eldridge, J., Neufeld, S. and Hancioğlu, N. (2010) Towards a lexical framework for CLIL, *International CLIL Research Journal* 1 (3), 79–95, available online: www.icrj.eu/13/article8.html

Eurydice (2006) *Content and Language Integrated Learning at School in Europe*. Strasbourg: European Commission.

García, O. (2009) *Bilingual Education in the 21st Century*. Chichester: Wiley-Blackwell.

Gefäll, C. (2009) *Empirical and Theoretical Perspectives on Language Learning in CLIL: Delineating Opportunities and Limitations*, MA thesis. Vienna: University of Vienna.

Gibbons, P. (2008) Challenging pedagogies: More than just good practice, paper presented at NALDIC Conference Institute of Education, London, available online: www.naldic.org.uk/eal-professional-development/conference-reports/conference18

Hall, D. (1995) *Assessing the Needs of Bilingual Pupils*. London: David Fulton Publishers.

Llinares, A., Morton, T. and Whittaker, R. (2012) *The Roles of Language in CLIL*. Cambridge: Cambridge University Press.

Lucietto, S. (2012) In-service CLIL teachers' continuous professional development: Reflections from the field of evaluative research study, *ELT Research Issue* 26, 17.

Marsh, D. (2009) CLIL: An interview with Professor David Marsh, *International House Journal of Education and Development* 26, available online: ihjournal.com/content-and-language-integrated-learning

Navés, T. (2009) Effective content and language integrated learning (CLIL) programmes, in Ruiz de Zarobe, Y. and Jiménez Catalán, R. M. (Eds) (2009) *Content and Language Integrated Learning: Evidence from Research in Europe*. Clevedon: Multilingual Matters.

Marzano, R., Pickering, D. and Pollock, J. (2001) *Classroom Instruction That Works*. Alexandria: ASCD.

McKay, P. (2006) *Assessing Young Language Learners*. Cambridge: Cambridge University Press.

McNamara, T. (2000) *Language Testing*. Oxford: Oxford University Press.

Richards, J., Platt J. and Platt, H. (1992) *Dictionary of Language Teaching and Applied Linguistics*. Harlow: Longman.

Savic, V. (2010) Are we ready for implementing CLIL in primary language classrooms? *ELTA Newsletter* May 2010, available online: www.britishcouncil.org/cy/serbia-elta-newsletter-2010-may.htm

Snow, M.A., Met, M. and Genesee, F. (1989) A conceptual framework for the integration of language and content in second/foreign language instruction, *TESOL Quarterly* 23 (2), 201–217.

Wiesemes, R. (2009) Developing theories of practices in CLIL: CLIL as post-method pedagogies? in Ruiz de Zarobe, Y. and Jiménez Catalán, R. M. (Eds) (2009) *Content and Language Integrated Learning: Evidence from Research in Europe*. Clevedon: Multilingual Matters.

14 Using international teacher education programmes in local contexts

Peter Watkins
University of Portsmouth
with
Bill Harris
Freelance teacher and trainer
Alan Pulverness
Norwich Institute for Language Education
(NILE)

Introduction

Evidence suggests that there is continuing demand for internationally recognised pre-service and in-service teacher education programmes, as well as those that serve local areas. An indication of this demand is that the Cambridge English Teaching Qualifications are offered in over 340 centres around the world. This demand for courses may be partly as a result of a higher degree of professionalism, or at least perception of professionalism, within English language teaching (ELT) than was the case in the past (Burns and Richards 2009: 2), and this shift is itself part of a wider trend, including within education, towards 'measurable accountability in public service' (Leung 2009: 52). The combination of the spread of English (Graddol 2006) and a desire for accountability explains the increased demand for English language teacher training programmes that are well established and thoroughly validated. Given their popularity, these courses clearly have a direct impact on many lives and an indirect impact on many, many more and so research to gain a richer understanding of the challenges they present and the effects they have is beneficial. In this chapter we use three case studies from different contexts to consider briefly the diversity of participants' experience of teacher education programmes and how such programmes can be adapted and implemented to suit the local context. We use qualitative data to move towards gauging the impacts of such courses.

The potential benefits of internationally recognised courses are easy to see, including the opportunity to share best practice and establish international standards in teacher education. However, a note of caution is immediately required. There have long been concerns about the appropriateness, or otherwise, of exporting language teaching methodologies developed in the inner circle (Kachru 1985) of the UK, USA and Australasia to contexts with markedly different learning and teaching traditions and constraints (for example, Bax 2003; Holliday 1994, 2008; Phillipson 1992). The acceptance that methodologies cannot be developed in one context and simply applied to another leads to the realisation that there cannot be one 'best' approach to teaching (Prabhu 1990). This means that the 'sharing of best practice' becomes a potentially problematic concept outside of specific contexts and there is resultant challenge for the assessment of teaching and attempts to set standards.

The adoption of communicative language teaching

Despite the need to be alert to the possible need to adapt practice to context (as outlined above), Richards and Rodgers (2001: 151) point out that 'the general principles of communicative language teaching (CLT) are today widely accepted around the world'. The apparent contradiction between 'no best method' (Prabhu 1990) and the dominance of one approach can be explained by CLT being something of an umbrella term, understood and applied in a variety of ways. Hall (2011: 93) elaborates: 'Discussing CLT is in some ways problematic as the term means different things to different people and everyday classroom practices can appear to be quite different when CLT principles are applied in different social and educational contexts.' In other words, while CLT may have been adopted in some guise or other in various contexts, in reality it is a rather fragmented notion, impacted by the context in which it is applied every bit as much as it impacts on that context. Therefore, as well as 'technical competence in teaching' (Richards 2002: 25), training courses need to equip prospective teachers with a knowledge and understanding of the contexts in which they (will) operate (Richards 1998; Roberts 1998), or at the very least an appreciation of the importance of context, so that sensitive decisions can be made as teachers adopt, amend or reject practices based on their own 'sense of plausibility' (Prabhu 1990). Part of any context is the prevailing educational culture that exists, which includes, but is not limited to, such issues as the hierarchical distance between learners and teachers, whether knowledge is viewed as transmitted or constructed, and the common roles adopted by learners and teachers. These are all issues to which we will return in the case studies.

It follows that the assessment criteria used in international teacher education programmes need to reflect the importance of context and educational culture in particular. Here are some examples of how such criteria can be framed, taken from the Cambridge English Certificate in Teaching English to Speakers of Other Languages (CELTA) programme:

1a teaching a class with an awareness of the needs and interests of the learner group
1b teaching a class with an awareness of learning styles and cultural factors that may affect learning
1c acknowledging, when necessary, learners' backgrounds and previous learning experiences (Cambridge ESOL 2010).

These criteria implicitly acknowledge that no best method can exist because, for example, each context will have different 'cultural factors that may affect learning' and therefore for assessment purposes there is a need to frame descriptions of teaching within a model of appropriate (rather than prescribed) action. Here are some examples taken from the same document:

4c selecting, adapting or designing materials, activities, resources and technical aids appropriate for the lesson
4f including interaction patterns appropriate for the materials and activities used in the lesson
5b setting up whole class and/or group or individual activities appropriate to the lesson type
5c selecting appropriate teaching techniques in relation to the content of the lesson

Such an approach, which clearly promotes appropriacy, is commendable in that, in theory, it allows for flexibility and diversity of practice. However, there are implicit assumptions that should also be questioned. It assumes that the trainee teachers will sufficiently understand the local context to be able to understand learning backgrounds and traditions, for example. However, in some cases course participants may travel to an area specifically to follow the course, arriving only a day or two before it begins and with little or no knowledge of the context. Moreover, there is an assumption that those assessing the teaching will be sufficiently familiar with a teaching context to be able to make informed, sensitive judgements as to what constitutes 'appropriacy'. Where trainers themselves have substantial experience of a particular context, this is likely to be the case but where outside 'experts' are used who are not familiar with the context, such judgements may be harder to make (see Palfreyman, Chapter 16). Further, the very notion of an international qualification suggests that the skills learned are portable and can be transferred from the context in which a teacher is trained to other contexts. This suggests that intercultural competence needs to be included in any course, so that teachers can successfully adapt to the contexts in which they eventually work.

Prior experience

We saw in criterion 1c (above) the need to take into account learners' previous learning experience. This can equally be applied to teacher education as even trainees who have never themselves taught will bring with them beliefs about teaching, rooted in their previous experience of classrooms (Lortie 1975) and what teachers think, know and believe is vital to their interpretation of new input (Borg 2006; Pennington 1996). Borg (2009: 164) highlights that failure to take these cognitions into account will hinder development, particularly where prior understandings are 'inappropriate, unrealistic, or naive'. This suggests that courses need to be prepared to investigate, and even challenge, the cognitions that trainees bring with them to courses.

Course tutors may find that there are difficult balances to be found between accommodating what teachers already believe, and in practice do, within their teaching context, and making interventions which may challenge unfounded assumptions about learning and teaching. We will now move on to consider how such challenges have been met in three specific contexts and the impacts on the participants.

Case study 1 — CELTA in Sudan

The course took place at the British Council, Khartoum, in June 2012. It was the fourth in a series to provide training for local teachers. The course attracted a combination of those who were already working in the state secondary system and also those who were either working, or hoped to work, in private language schools.

There were 12 participants, four women and eight men, and all were native Arabic speakers. Most of the participants had already gained some teaching experience, with two of the older men having taught English in secondary schools for well over 20 years. Trainers on the course observed that there were a range of English language abilities within the group and also that the participants were supportive of each other in this regard. For example, it was not unusual for a stronger participant to give a brief summary in Arabic of the salient points from input for those that were struggling to follow. This use of their first language (L1) in the training room could be seen as not just a sensible strategy for supporting the participants in this particular case, but also more generally as a good model of a positive use of L1 in classes (Cook 2008, 2010) that could perhaps be adopted by the participants in their own teaching.

The training team consisted of two UK-based male trainers with a wide experience of teaching and training in many contexts but who were less experienced in working in Sudan. This was counteracted to some extent by a third member of the team, a tutor-in-training, who had worked in Sudan for several years and had in-depth knowledge of the learning and teaching context.

Making it local

The students used for the teaching practice element of the course were largely young adults and they responded enthusiastically to communicative sections of the lessons. When teaching, the participants generally made good use of their shared understanding of the culture to generate humour, which in turn could promote and sustain motivation (Dörnyei 2001). Moreover, the trainees made use of their shared understandings and interests to contextualise language input. For example, one teacher presented 'used to + infinitive' by telling a story about his childhood in Khartoum. Another participant adapted the coursebook provided by rejecting a text focusing on a European city and instead created a text describing Khartoum.

When required to exploit authentic material (in the sense of that not originally designed for language teaching purposes) one trainee selected a reading text about refugee camps in Darfur and another exploited a song calling for African peace. Observation of the lessons suggested that the Sudanese learners engaged enthusiastically with these topics, which no doubt had great relevance for them. That the participants developed the confidence to trust their own instincts and abilities in this process of selecting and adapting material was an important element of the course because many coursebooks aimed at the international market might fail to address the needs and interests of Sudanese learners.

Roles of teachers

Traditional understandings of education see teachers as 'knowledge providers and sole controllers of the class' (Farrell and Jacobs 2010: 2) and this view has been very influential in Sudan. The older trainees, with more experience of teaching, seemed more at ease in the teacher-centred plenary phases of lessons and when explaining new language to the learners in a deductive manner. It should be noted that the learners eagerly took notes during these phases and in some ways this approach seemed to fit with their expectations of lessons. In trying to wrestle with what constitutes an 'appropriate methodology' these expectations need to be included along with other pedagogical considerations. Larsen-Freeman (2011: 162) points out that '[t]hese days it is common to be critical of a knowledge transmission view of teaching for the passive role it ascribes to learners ... However, knowledge transmission remains a common practice in many parts of the world. A skilled teacher's organisation of knowledge can help students understand and remember what has been transmitted'. This suggests that knowledge transmission models of teaching need not be automatically rejected.

In the Sudanese context it was clear from observation that the students valued communicative phases of lessons *and* a more traditional transmission model of learning. It may be that appropriate methodology here depends on combining both, helping new teachers to make transmission moments organised and memorable, as well as providing opportunities for genuine communication. This would seem preferable to encouraging a teacher to completely abandon what they already do confidently and what forms part of their existing identity as a teacher.

Impact of the course

It is always hard to assess the long-term impacts of a training course (Almarza 1996). However, it seems that there is some evidence that allows us to be optimistic about this programme. Feedback was overwhelmingly positive from the participants with one candidate saying: 'I can see that I am not the same teacher of English language I used to be before the CELTA.' Another trainee worked very happily after the course in a language school, editing the local TESOL magazine and looking forward to taking the Delta. When asked if the CELTA had met her expectations, she replied: 'Yes, indeed. It was what I had expected it to be; intensive, informative, practical, developing, aspiring, applicable, and clearly guiding.'

One of the most experienced teachers, who had a senior advisory role in his region, made what his tutors judged to be 'very impressive' changes and adaptations to his teaching approach so that by the end of the course he had gone from producing lessons with little student participation to promoting a lot of student-centred oral practice. Given his advisory role in ELT, this may potentially create the conditions for a trickle-down benefit from the course, with new ideas being passed on to others.

Unfortunately, two of the more experienced state school teachers did not complete the feedback questionnaire and it might be that the state school context provides greater challenges for teachers when trying to implement a more communicative methodology than is the case for their private sector counterparts. The practical nature of teaching means that trainees typically value the practical teaching component of their courses above all else (Watkins 2011). However, the value of these phases is weakened if the context found on courses does not closely mirror the contexts in which new teachers find themselves working (Borg 2008).

Case study 2 — CELTA in Perm

The education ministry in Perm Krai, Russia, saw the CELTA scheme as a way of providing teacher development for selected secondary school teachers and as a result ran a series of 10 courses over 18 months in conjunction with the Norwich Institute for Language Education (NILE) between 2011 and 2013.

The participants

One of the unusual features of these CELTA courses was that the participants were all practising English teachers (as opposed to the preservice profile of the majority of CELTA trainees). However, up until this point, many of them had had very few opportunities for Continuous Professional Development (CPD) and few colleagues, if any, with whom to share ideas and discuss teaching. The participants appeared eager to use this opportunity to update their knowledge and get a recognised qualification, as well as develop their own use of English.

The background of the participants and their relatively extensive experience impacted on the course in several ways. For example, the traditional language awareness sessions (for example, Thornbury and Watkins 2007) were virtually redundant because the participants had already developed a strong declarative knowledge of English. This gave the opportunity to move away from the more usual emphasis on how written and phonological forms map to functions and meanings, and instead move towards how those forms could be introduced and consolidated in communicative ways. Tutors also found that the group was particularly appreciative of the opportunities to observe practising teachers and they ascribed this to participants being able to compare the classes they saw with their own teaching situations. They also found that in feedback discussions on teaching practice the participants made good use of their substantial bank of prior experience to discuss features of lessons.

Teaching paradigms

It was clear that grammar-translation, substitution drills and tables and learning by heart played a major role in how these participants saw the learning and teaching process. The desire to produce and deliver grammar presentations was dominant, with much use of decontextualised examples, teacher explanation of rules and controlled practice exercises.

In line with this, the participants favoured a teacher-centred approach and tended to exercise a high degree of control over lessons, often inviting contributions individually around the class. The teaching practice (TP) classes provided on the course usefully mirrored the participants' 'real-life' teaching contexts, with the TP students being secondary school teenagers, still wearing their uniforms. Much of the teachers' desire to control was connected with discipline, and discipline was indeed a problem at times in the TP classes. However, many trainees did experiment with handing over more to the students, sitting down, and even accepting a certain level of boisterousness without feeling the need to step in immediately. While this was effective in encouraging more interaction and communication, it also led, at times, to a great deal of noise and distraction and so demonstrated the difficulties of implementing more learner-centred approaches in this context.

The participants were also used to using L1 as a means of managing classes, and found it quite difficult to grade their language to make instructions comprehensible in English. However, they saw an advantage in providing more exposure to English for their learners by managing much of the class in their second language (L2) and so were prepared to persevere with this. They were also keen to experiment with other techniques introduced and some were particularly enthusiastic about guided discovery activities (Thornbury 2006: 102). This may have been because the nature of guided discovery allows for a more learner-centred treatment of language, while offering enough teacher control to prevent learners going off task or becoming disruptive. Also, if students use L1 for this sort of pedagogic task, there will still be a benefit because they are studying a system of English, whereas excessive L1 use in a task designed to develop oral fluency would render the task pointless (Harmer 2001: 132).

Building relationships

One assumption in CLT is the value of affective engagement in the teaching-learning process (for example, Arnold 1999; Benesch 2012; Tomlinson 2008). The desirability of personalisation, encouraging learners to express their thoughts and feelings and promoting emotional involvement with materials and activities, while acknowledged by the participants in principle, was often hampered in practice by the hierarchical distance between teachers and students and the teacher roles that the participants felt comfortable adopting, as referred to above. Many of the participants had had experience of dealing with discipline problems in their own teaching contexts and felt that smiling or giving praise in the classroom might be construed by students as signs of weakness or favouritism. This was particularly noticeable with lower level (and younger) TP students, where many of the participants wanted to preserve a 'traditional' distance between themselves and the learners, and attempts at personalising activities often had very limited success because there appeared to be a lack of conviction in their implementation. For new ideas to have an impact, they must appeal to a teacher's 'sense of plausibility' (Prabhu 1990) and perhaps that was simply not the case in this instance.

Impact of the course

As noted above, there are difficulties in measuring the sustained impact of a course and where teachers return to their schools after a course there is the added pull to revert to the existing norm of the context they are in. However, it seems that this series of courses did have some impact on the participants. For example, during an end-of-course party an older trainee took one of the tutors aside and somewhat timidly explained that he had 'changed her life', and that she really didn't know how she could go back into her classroom on Monday morning knowing what she knew now. She said with obvious emotion that she couldn't just do the same as she had been doing for many years as she now felt this was a flawed approach. Unsurprisingly, she expressed both excitement and fear at the prospect of this new beginning. It can only be hoped that her new beliefs supported successful learning and teaching outcomes, rather than led to disenchantment. However, there is no doubt that the course had had a very significant impact on her concept of teaching.

Fortunately, the course provider has had the opportunity for subsequent contact with some of the participants of these courses and so could gather data on their impact. Admittedly, the nature of that contact (through participant choice) may mean that the feedback is not representative of the entire group but there is some indication that the courses brought about change in the classroom. One former participant commented that after the classroom was configured in a horseshoe format a class joke had developed that there was now 'no hiding place for the lazy guys'. This might be indicative of broader learner participation, and another teacher also referred to her new classroom layout and the interest it had generated in her colleagues.

Another teacher commented: 'I am trying to use all your methodological tips with my learners. Today we had a lesson for 60 minutes and they didn't notice it at all!' This might suggest that the introduction of more communicative phases of lessons had made learning more enjoyable and less of a chore. Another commented: 'I'm so pleased you've taught us modern teaching styles and methods that are of great help now.' However, it was unclear which particular styles and methods were being referred to.

Another significant impact is that a small group of former participants, who live outside Perm, have set up a teachers' group which meets once a month to help each other with lesson planning and simply to exchange experiences. In addition, these teachers have set up a Facebook page where they communicate with one another on matters relating to their post-CELTA experiences. This stands in some contrast to the isolation that some participants felt at the start of their courses and suggests the beginning of a building of a community of teachers (Lave and Wenger 1991) with opportunities to continue learning from each other. This was brought about by the sense of togetherness, developed during the course.

So it seems that the courses in Perm had a real impact on at least some of the participants. Of course, change requires support to flourish, often at institutional and government levels and whether sufficient support will be available for these teachers to continue to grow remains to be seen.

Case study 3 — the use of ICELT by a teacher association in Pakistan

We are indebted to Zakia Sarwar, one of the founder members of the Society of Pakistan English Language Teachers (SPELT), for her invaluable insights and contribution to this section.

Background

Teacher associations have become widespread in recent years and can no doubt work towards the improvement of ELT, fostering high professional standards, disseminating information and taking a lead in in-service training opportunities (Falcao and Szesztay 2006). One of the earlier examples of such an association is the SPELT. This was born in 1984, as an informal teachers' network, where eight founder members wanted to share ideas and improve their own teaching practices. To some extent the association developed out of a growing frustration with a lack of support for teachers of English at state level and also a desire to get out of the 'foreign experts syndrome' (Beaumont 1997: 72). Local teachers both wanted, and needed, to take control of their own professional development.

From these beginnings, SPELT soon grew and the following objectives emerged:

- to provide a professional forum for English language teachers in Pakistan
- to serve as a centre for dissemination of current ideas and development in ELT
- to organise in-service courses, conferences and workshops for teacher development
- to develop a resource centre complete with up-to-date ELT materials and audio-visual aids with loan facilities for members.

In order to serve these objectives, particularly the third, the possibility of a substantial intervention through the provision of a formal course seemed a very exciting opportunity. In January 1986 this idea led to a 3-day pilot course, and, encouraged by the response of the participants, a fully fledged one-year, part-time 'Practical Teacher Training Course' (PTTC) was launched in June 1986. The course was taught by a combination of both local tutors and those supplied by the British Council (BC), Asia Foundation, and the US Information Service. The programme seemed to address an obvious need for CPD and the participant response was exceptionally positive. On completion the participants hoped for government recognition of the course and possible salary increases. However, the Pakistan government of the time did not respond to SPELT's application for recognition and to fill this vacuum the BC suggested future courses be run as iterations of the RSA — Cambridge Certificate for Overseas Teachers of English (COTE). This suggestion was followed up and has continued as COTE developed into the In-Service Certificate in English Language Teaching (ICELT).

From 12 participants on the first COTE course in 1989, between 25 and 30 now enrol each year. Teachers choose to follow the course, with no discernible pressure from their employers to do so. Attendance at taught sessions is around 95%, despite the demands of their busy lives outside teaching, an indicator that participants are motivated and value the input they receive.

Filling the professional development void

Coleman (2010), analysing the ELT situation in Pakistan, points out the gap between plans and intentions and actual outcomes. He concludes that '[s]ince independence in 1947 ... implementation has generally failed to develop in line with the policy'. For example, a new curriculum for Bachelor of Education (B. Ed) and Master of Education (M. Ed) programmes was approved by the Federal Ministry of Education, Islamabad (2006) and plans included strengthening the infrastructure and developing training facilities. It was hoped that the BEd programme could be launched by 2008. However, no obvious steps seem to have been taken to implement the programme. To some extent, SPELT, through running the professional development courses it does, begins to fill the void in leadership in two distinct ways. First, it builds a community of teachers who can learn from, and with, each other and secondly it provides an internationally recognised qualification.

Adapting the ICELT course

When SPELT delivers ICELT programmes in Pakistan there are some additions to the standard model. ICELT is designed for already practising teachers and pre-supposes some knowledge of the four skills and how to develop them. However, SPELT feels that their participants need much greater support in teaching language skills and therefore, besides the seven standard units, one specifically on the four skills is added. The evaluation and adaptation of materials is also given special focus because there is a perception that textbooks commonly prescribed in Pakistan are outdated and contribute little to the motivation of learners. In such ways the course is adapted to better suit local needs in these specific areas.

Another important feature that helps to explain the success of the programme is that by being an in-service, part-time course it maximises the opportunities for participants to test out new ideas by applying them in their own classrooms. This ensures that ideas introduced on the course remain applicable to the local context.

Impact of the course

The course includes participant evaluation, which remains extremely positive. In addition, as the course is run by a teachers' association, there is a greater opportunity to track the effects on those who follow it because contact with them is often maintained. One teacher described the transformative experience of the course, as he was introduced to more learning-centred practices:

> I started off my career as a primary school teacher in one of the most low-income, marginalised areas in Karachi. It was all about ME, talking, providing instructions and being the so called teacher. As I reflect back I feel embarrassed about what I was doing in the name of teaching and learning ... When I joined [the course], I felt I was re-born and regained the passion for my profession. The teaching principles and strategies being imparted were practical and applicable to my classroom immediately and converted my class to an interactive learner-centred, fun place.

This embracing of more learner-centred practices is far from unique. Another commented that her 'focus changed to making learners independent' and also how rewarding she found it when the learners responded positively, which further enhanced her belief in these practices. However, making a substantial shift in perspective is not easy and not surprisingly some teachers found it difficult to relinquish their traditional roles. One participant charts the gradual change in her outlook:

> My beliefs did begin to change, yet there was a conflict, a dilemma and above all a mental dissonance ... I felt inwardly awkward and threatened to give up my total control and authority and above all power, that I enjoyed in doing things as I liked ... However, I also loved what was being taught through the [Practical Teacher Training Course] PTTC/COTE, because it reawakened my dormant belief that learners should have the freedom to do things in the manner they liked and which was compatible to their natural developmental process ... Within 6 months, I started devising interactive materials, using group/pair work and discussions, allowing learners to talk. I began to believe in the importance of talk in children's language development.

It is worth noting how the part-time nature of the course gave the teacher time to gradually shift her practice towards those promoted on the course. Another teacher also explains how her initial reservations were overcome through seeing the effect the more learner-centred work had on the students:

> At first I was rather sceptical about the learner-centred, activity-based teaching but when I applied these in the classroom, I saw the difference. Their [the learners'] attitudes and responses were so heartening and encouraging, that it was difficult to believe! They were more active, more motivated, therefore, better able to learn. Their responses led to a gradual change in my beliefs ... The change in me was a conscious one, brought about by the realisation that the

learner-centred approach was much more effective than the traditional method I had been using all along.

We can see that the opportunity to test out ideas and gauge the effects of new practices led to a 'gradual change' of beliefs and a reconstruction of the teacher's understandings, based on the evidence that she saw in her own classroom. We may question whether all learners in this context would respond so positively but the feedback received by SPELT suggests that learners have generally welcomed the changes their teachers introduce, particularly enjoying more interactive, communicative, activities, with resultant benefits in fluency.

Another teacher reported the course having a very different impact on them as a teacher. Rather than being sceptical about more learner-centred approaches, they had always believed in such approaches but this had brought a certain amount of conflict:

> I always believed learners should be allowed to find their way, and be allowed to ask questions. This got me off the track from the syllabus sometimes. It brought friction between me, and the management, and sometimes even parents because my written work copies were not filled with rote learning work. Also as I allowed questions, my students would put questions to other teachers as well, which got me in trouble with them. Through learner-centred approach — it was like I got a 'home ground' — and I was able to justify myself. And now I am in a position to introduce the concept of learner autonomy to my colleagues and answer their queries with confidence. My beliefs did not change. They were clarified, modified, polished and endorsed. It was as if I found the missing parts of the jigsaw puzzle I had been struggling with. ICELT helped me to question and reflect on all that I was doing and to consolidate my theoretical learning to classroom practice. I also learnt that it is only through trial, error and reflection that I can bring out the effective teacher in me.

It is noticeable how the course, and no doubt the status brought about through certification and international recognition of that course, had the impact of giving the teacher added confidence in promoting their own beliefs and challenging the traditional teaching status quo. It seems that this course can be a genuinely transformative experience for many of those who follow it.

Comparing the cases

It is easy to see some similarities between these cases. Unusually in the case of CELTA courses, the participants in Perm and many in the Sudan had already gained significant classroom teaching experience. This meant that new ideas and methods could be judged against a very real classroom context which was already fully understood by the participants. In the case of ICELT in Pakistan the part-time structure of the course allowed this to be taken a step further and ideas could be taken away, experimented with and discussed again. The participants' strong knowledge of the local teaching context in these cases helps to ensure that new ideas will be adopted with sensitivity, rather than being foisted inappropriately onto the context.

In all three contexts the participants were generally more familiar with knowledge transmission approaches to teaching and were challenged to evaluate the extent to which more learner-centred, constructivist views of learning could operate effectively in their situations. This often involved relinquishing some traditional teacher roles relating to authority and also aiming to set up more opportunities for communication in lessons. This required the participants to consider seeking a new balance between explicit instruction and more communicative phases of lessons (Ortega 2009: 179). One of the key considerations in designing courses to be used internationally is to create the flexibility necessary for teachers to find the balance that is right for them and their context.

Another feature common to these courses, particularly those in Perm and Pakistan, is how the course helped to build a community of teachers, who were prepared to support each other. In the case of Pakistan, the desire to build this community preceded the decision to run formal courses. In the case of Perm, it was a very beneficial by-product, with the intensive nature of the CELTA course helping to form a camaraderie between participants (Senior 2006: 40).

It is also interesting to note that these courses have been adapted to suit local needs. For example, in Perm the traditional language awareness sessions were replaced and in Pakistan ICELT course content has been added to ensure it meets the needs of the participants. Ensuring this flexibility is hugely important when courses are used internationally.

Conclusion

Any move towards the professionalisation of ELT must be welcomed and courses with a strong reputation and a validation history can play an important part in this. Evidence suggests that even short courses, such as CELTA, can have a significant impact on teachers and their beliefs, most probably through their highly practical and intensive nature (Borg 2006: 64). However, there is also a very clear need to avoid imposing a teaching methodology developed in one context on another. In addition, while it seems that the training experience can be transformative, more tracking studies are required to investigate whether the gains from initial teacher education courses survive in the longer term, when other factors impact on teachers. There is some evidence, for example, that new teachers are particularly influenced by the existing teachers and prevailing practices in the schools in which they work (Shin 2012) and that these factors can potentially diminish the impact of initial training. Further research that takes a longitudinal case study perspective, following teachers from their short course training experience through their formative teaching years would be a very welcome addition to the existing literature on teacher education.

We should also remember that even courses that are aimed at an international market are locally situated at the point at which they are delivered. For example, courses that are delivered in UK private language schools are likely to draw TP students from the mix available at such a school. This will usually result in multi-lingual classes of young adults. On the other, a course delivered, albeit with the same title, in a completely different context, such as those described above, will result in a potentially quite different TP experience. Borg's (2008) findings suggest that that teachers moving into the workforce after initial training found it harder to make the transition if they entered unfamiliar teaching contexts. The inevitable conclusion would seem to be that the closer the training context is to the eventual working context, the smoother preparation for entry to the profession it is likely to provide. However, ELT is known for its diversity (Brandt 2006: 14) and the tendency for teachers to move between contexts means that they will sometimes find themselves in unfamiliar situations. As preparation for this, Borg calls for trainees to be supported in analysing teaching techniques as part of 'culturally-situated practice' (2008: 116) — in other words seeing the appropriacy of teaching procedures as being culturally dependent.

It is therefore important that the specification of international courses emphasises the need for appropriacy of methods, as opposed to prescribing practices, and that they encourage participants to constantly consider how changes in context would affect their practice. However, it is equally important that local centres providing international courses seek to take ownership of them. This can include adapting the focus so that local concerns and needs are catered for and, when presented with practices that may be taken for granted in some ELT contexts, analysing those practices in the fresh light of knowledge of the local context.

It may well be that the international organisations providing teaching awards need to go beyond designing assessment criteria that allow for context-appropriate decisions on practice at a local level, but also actively encourage local centres to discuss these issues through, for example, organising workshops, seminars and creating other platforms that encourage such discussion. This would support local 'ownership' and would help to ensure that courses that are designed in potentially flexible ways become flexible in reality.

References

Almarza, G. (1996) Student foreign language teachers' knowledge growth, in Freeman, D. and Richards, J. C. (Eds) *Teacher Learning in Language Teaching*. New York: Cambridge University Press, 50–78.

Arnold, J. (Ed) (1999) *Affect in Language Learning*. Cambridge: Cambridge University Press.

Bax, S. (2003) The end of CLT: A context approach to language teaching, *ELT Journal* 57 (3), 278–287.

Beaumont, M. (1997) Teacher training, in Abbott, G. and Beaumont, M. (Eds) *The Development of ELT: The Dunford Seminars 1978–1993*. Hemel Hempstead: Prentice Hall.

Benesch, S. (2012) *Considering Emotions in Critical Language Teaching*. Abingdon: Routledge.

Borg, M. (2008) Teaching post-CELTA: The interplay of novice teacher, course and context, in Farrell, M. (Ed) *Novice Language Teachers: Insights and Perspectives for the First Year*. London: Equinox, 104–117.

Borg, S. (2006) *Teacher Cognition and Language Education: Research and Practice*. London: Continuum.

Borg, S. (2009) Language teacher cognition, in Burns, A. and Richards, J. C. (Eds) *The Cambridge Guide to Second Language Teacher Education*. New York: Cambridge University Press, 163–171.

Brandt, C. (2006) *Success on Your Certificate Course in English Language Teaching*. London: Sage.

Burns, A. and Richards, J. C. (2009) Introduction: Second language teacher education, in Burns, A. and Richards, J. C. (Eds) *The Cambridge Guide to Second Language Teacher Education*. New York: Cambridge University Press, 1–8.

Cambridge ESOL. (2010) *CELTA Syllabus and Assessment Guidelines*. Cambridge: Cambridge ESOL.

Coleman, H. (2010) *Supporting English Language Teaching and Learning in Pakistan: Context and Strategy*. Islamabad: British Council.

Cook, G. (2008) An unmarked improvement: Using translation in ELT, in Beaven, B. (Ed) *IATEFL 2007 Aberdeen Conference Selections*. Canterbury: IATEFL Publications, 76–85.

Cook, G. (2010) *Translation in Language Teaching: An Argument for Reassessment*. Oxford: Oxford University Press.

Dörnyei, Z. (2001) *Motivation Strategies in the Language Classroom*. Cambridge: Cambridge University Press.

Falcao, A. and Szesztay, M. (2006) *Developing an Association for Language Teachers*. Canterbury: IATEFL Publications.

Farrell, T. and Jacobs, G. (2010) *Essentials for Successful Language Teaching*. London: Continuum.

Federal Curriculum Wing. (2006) *National Curriculum for English Language Grades 1–12*. Islamabad: Federal Ministry of Education.

Graddol, D. (2006) *English Next*. London: The British Council.

Hall, G. (2011) *Exploring English Language Teaching: Language in Action*. Abingdon: Routledge.

Harmer, J. (2001) *The Practice of English Language Teaching* (3rd edition). Harlow: Longman.

Holliday, A. (1994) *Appropriate Methodology and Social Context*. Cambridge: Cambridge University Press.

Holliday, A. (2008) Standards of English and politics of inclusion, *Language Teaching* 41 (1), 115–126.

Kachru, B. (1985) Standards, codification and sociolinguistic realism: The English language in the outer circle, in Quirk, R. and Widdowson, H. (Eds) *English in the World: Teaching and Learning the Language and Literatures*. Cambridge: Cambridge University Press, 11–36.

Larsen-Freeman, D. (2011) Key concepts in language learning and language education, in Simpson, J. (Ed) *The Routledge Handbook of Applied Linguistics*. Abingdon: Routledge.

Lave, J. and Wenger, E. (1991) *Situated Learning: Legitimate Peripheral Participation*. Cambridge: Cambridge University Press.

Leung, C. (2009) Second language teacher professionalism, in Burns, A. and Richards, J. C. (Eds) *The Cambridge Guide to Second Language Teacher Education*. New York: Cambridge University Press, 49–58.

Lortie, D. (1975) *Schoolteacher: A Sociological Study*. London: University of Chicago Press.

Ortega, L. (2009) *Understanding Second Language Acquisition*. London: Hodder.

Pennington, M. C. (1996) When input becomes intake: Tracing the sources of teachers attitude change, in Freeman, D. and Richards, J. C. (Eds) *Teacher Learning in Language Teaching*. New York: Cambridge University Press, 320–348.

Phillipson, R. (1992) *Linguistic Imperialism*. Oxford: Oxford University Press.

Prabhu, N. S. (1990) There is no best method — Why? *TESOL Quarterly* 24 (2), 161–176.

Richards, J. C. (1998) *Beyond Training*. Cambridge: Cambridge University Press.

Richards, J. C. (2002) Theories of teaching in language teaching, in Richards, J. C. and Renandya, W. (Eds) *Methodology in Language Teaching*. New York: Cambridge University Press, 19–25.

Richards, J. C. and Rodgers, T. (2001) *Approaches and Methods in Language Teaching* (2nd edn). Cambridge: Cambridge University Press.

Roberts, J. (1998) *Language Teacher Education*. London: Arnold.

Senior, R. (2006) *The Experience of Language Teaching*. Cambridge: Cambridge University Press.

Shin, S. K. (2012) It cannot be done alone: The socialization of novice teachers in South Korea, *TESOL Quarterly* 46 (3), 542–567.

Thornbury, S. (2006) *An A–Z of ELT*. Oxford: Macmillan.

Thornbury, S. and Watkins, P. (2007) *The CELTA Course Trainee Book*. Cambridge: Cambridge University Press.

Tomlinson, B. (2008) *English Language Learning Materials: A Critical Review*. London: Continuum.

Watkins, P. (2011) A bottom-up view of the needs of prospective teachers, *ELT World Online* 3, available online: http://files.campus.edublogs.org/blog.nus.edu.sg/dist/7/112/files/2012/06/A-Bottom-Up-View-of-the-Needs-of-Prospective-Teachers_editforpdf-1d8hpqy.pdf

15 Integrating theory and practice: The case of Delta at Bilkent University

Simon Phipps
Freelance teacher trainer and ELT consultant

Introduction

For many decades the field of teacher education has debated the nature of teaching in an attempt to define the knowledge and skills required to be an effective teacher, and how such knowledge and skills can be best imparted through teacher education programmes. The increasing move towards professionalism in English language teaching, in both English as a Foreign Language (EFL) and English as a Second Language (ESL), during the past 20 years has also created a drive to identify clear standards by which to measure teacher knowledge and skills, whether to make decisions about *pre-service* teachers' potential to enter the teaching profession, or to make judgements about *in-service* teachers' performance for the purposes of higher professional qualifications.

Teacher education programmes usually aim to help teachers improve their professional knowledge and skills, and part of this process inevitably involves some form of assessment. Any decisions regarding how best to assess teachers' knowledge and skills are, therefore, inextricably linked, either explicitly or implicitly, to:

- the aims and content of teacher education programmes
- what effective teachers need to know and do, both at the start of their teaching careers and after some years of experience
- how teachers learn, and progress from 'novice' to 'expert'
- what processes of teacher education programmes best facilitate

teacher learning
- how assessment contributes to teacher learning
- how best to assess what teachers need to know and do
- how best to integrate theory and practice in the content, delivery and assessment of teacher education programmes.

This chapter explores the above issues, and presents the case of an in-service teacher education programme at Bilkent University, Turkey, which integrates the Diploma in Teaching English to Speakers of Other Languages (Delta) into an MA.

Language teacher education, teacher learning and assessment

In order to discuss how best to assess language teachers' professional knowledge and skills, it is first necessary, then, to explore teacher education and teacher learning.

Teacher education and teacher learning

Types of teacher education programmes

Language teacher education programmes can be categorised in terms of their aims, context and participants, content, structure, pedagogical approach and assessment: all of which are inter-related (see Figure 1). Historically, the main aims of teacher education programmes were to deliver subject knowledge and skills training, although the past 25–30 years have seen a shift from transmission-based, product-oriented theories to constructivist, process-oriented theories of learning, teaching and teacher learning, as Crandall (2000) noted.

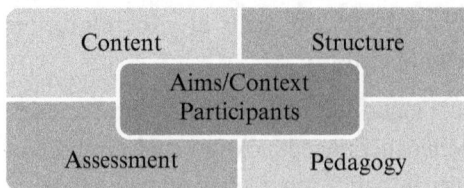

Figure 1 Components of teacher education programmes

Different writers (e.g. Calderhead and Shorrock 1997; Feiman-Nemser 1990; Korthagen 2001; Korthagen, Loughran and Lunenberg 2005; Richards 1998; Zeichner and Liston 1990) have attempted to categorise different possible orientations to teacher education:

- *Academic*: This involves transmitting knowledge about language and teaching, often by means of separate, often unrelated, courses on an MA — here without explicit links to practice.
- *Applied science*: This involves imparting 'expert knowledge', principles of effective teaching, based on empirical research and science, often by means of methodology courses on an MA — here theory informs practice.
- *Craft*: This involves apprenticeship and imitation of 'good practice' handed down from generations of masters or experienced practitioners, often by means of an MA practicum or some form of mentoring, as well as by many teacher training courses — here theory is derived from 'good practice'.
- *Reflective*: This model gives equal weight to 'received knowledge', which is based on science and research, and 'experiential knowledge' (Wallace 1991), which teachers gain by reflecting on their classroom experience, and involves developing teachers' capacity to reflect — here theory and practice inform each other.

The reflective approach follows constructivist learning theory, and is increasingly becoming the dominant paradigm in both mainstream teacher education (Cochran-Smith and Zeichner 2005; Cochran-Smith, Feiman-Nemser, McIntyre and Demers 2008; Darling-Hammond 2006; Korthagen *et al.* 2005) and language teacher education (Barkhuizen and Borg 2010; Barnard and Burns 2012; Borg 2011a; Burns and Richards 2009; Farrell 2007; Johnson and Golombek 2011), and is commonly followed on teacher training courses such as Delta. Table 1 compares the four models: the potential contradiction between MA and teacher training courses is of particular relevance to the case of Delta integrated into an MA programme which is discussed later in this chapter. It is, of course, worth noting that there are some teacher training courses which focus first on theory before teaching practice, and also that there are some MA courses which have a more practical focus.

Table 1 Models of teacher education

Model	Type of knowledge	Practice and theory	Mode of teacher education
Academic	Expert	Theory	MA courses
Applied science	Expert	Theory into Practice	MA courses
Craft	Master	Practice into Theory	MA practicum, Mentoring, Teacher training courses
Reflective	Received and experiential	Practice ⟷ Theory	Teacher training courses

Teacher learning

Clearly each of the above models is likely to differ in terms of content, structure, pedagogy and assessment. The content of language teacher education programmes has traditionally been informed by a common knowledge-base from linguistics, second language acquisition (SLA), psychology and teaching methodology (Ellis 2009). However, there is now a greater understanding of 'how language teachers conceive of what they do: what they know about language teaching, how they think about their classroom practice, and how that knowledge and those thinking processes are learned through formal teacher education and informal experience on the job' (Freeman and Richards 1996: 1). Language teacher education programmes no longer 'view L2 teaching as a matter of simply translating theories of second language acquisition into effective instructional practices, but as a dialogic process of co-constructing knowledge that is situated in and emerges out of participation in particular ... contexts' (Johnson 2009: 21). This has stimulated a growing interest in teacher cognition and contributed to a gradual re-conceptualisation of this knowledge-base (Graves 2009), as previously called for by Freeman and Johnson (1998).

A central point to emerge from research on teacher cognition in both mainstream and language education is that teachers' thinking and behaviour are guided by a set of beliefs which are personal, practical, systematic, dynamic and often unconscious (Borg 2006). Teacher learning is increasingly seen as a complex process whereby teachers' prior beliefs about teaching and learning are mediated by their experience of teaching, input from teacher education and their own reflection (see Figure 2). Beliefs are informed initially by teachers' schooling and L2 learning experience. Input from teacher education and reflection on classroom experience is filtered by these beliefs before becoming 'intake', which in turn is filtered before teachers incorporate this into their daily teaching and it becomes 'uptake' (Pennington 1996).

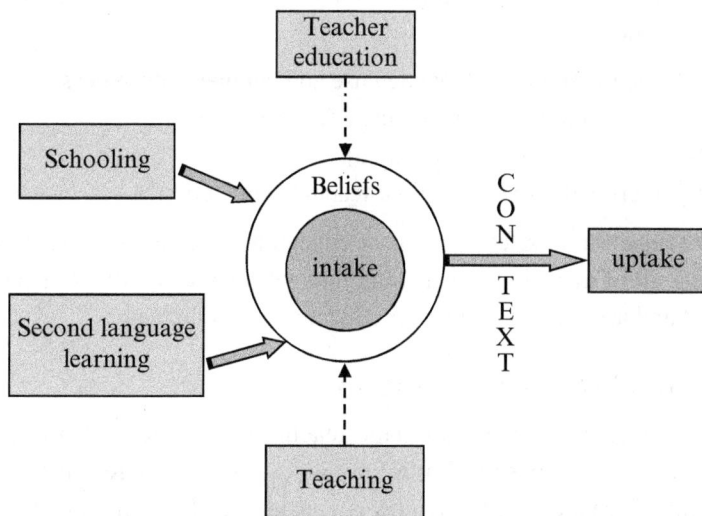

Figure 2 Language teacher beliefs, input, intake and uptake (Phipps 2010: 20)

Studies of 'novice' and 'expert' teachers suggest that the concept of expertise involves the development of schemata or routines based on extensive experience of classrooms and learners, which 'expert' teachers rely on unconsciously for much of their instructional decisions (Tsui 2003). This suggests that 'the process of learning to teach is not a linear accrual of various aspects of teaching, but rather a gradual process of proceduralising aspects of formal and experiential knowledge gained from teacher education and classroom experience mediated by beliefs and contextual constraints' (Phipps 2010: 23). Research into 'teacher expertise' suggests three main characteristics of expert teachers (Tsui 2009):

- a rich, organised and integrated knowledge-base
- availability of routines which enable teachers to devote energy to higher level tasks
- ability to integrate information quickly to solve problems.

Research has also identified the need for teachers to be confronted with 'challenges' which extend their expertise and develop their abilities beyond their current levels of competence (Bereiter and Scardamalia 1993; Tsui 2003).

Summary

The discussion of teacher learning so far indicates that the professional skills and knowledge that effective language teachers need to develop include the following:

- knowledge of language (language use and language awareness)
- knowledge of how to teach language (methodology)
- skills of teaching (teaching practice)
- ability to critically reflect on their teaching (reflection).

This suggests that effective teacher education needs to consider ways of developing all of these in teachers, and this will inevitably affect the choice of content and assessment on teacher education programmes.

Assessment in teacher education

The change in the way language teaching and teacher learning are conceptualised, discussed above, has also led to changes in the way assessment of teachers and teaching is considered (Barduhn and Johnson 2009). Any teacher education programme, having decided its aims, content, structure and pedagogical approach, needs to consider two fundamental questions: *what* to assess, and *how* to assess it. This means deciding how to assess what teachers need to know according to the aims of the programme and its inherent assumptions about effective teaching and teacher learning.

Assessing teachers' professional skills and knowledge

Assessment is 'a process of inquiry that interprets multiple sources of evidence ... to support an interpretation, decision or action' (Moss, Girard and Haniford 2006: 152). Possible reasons for wanting to assess language teachers' professional skills and knowledge include:

- gate-keeping function for entry into the profession (pre-service teacher education)
- provision of higher level teaching qualifications (in-service teacher education)
- award of academic qualifications (such as MA courses).

Each of the above will inevitably lead to differences in the *focus* and *mode* of assessment (Freeman, Orzulak and Morrissey 2009). Assessment may also be used in teacher education programmes as a tool for professional learning, as will be discussed later in this section.

The question of *what* to measure is arguably more complex, and requires detailed understanding of the processes of teaching and teacher learning. Any assessment of teachers and teaching is based on an assumption that teacher knowledge and teaching skills can be quantified and broken down into clearly measurable objectives, but this raises many issues. In pre-service teacher education, such as teacher preparation programmes, it is likely that teachers' *potential* to become effective teachers in the future is at least as important as their *performance* against certain criteria, whereas many in-service teacher training programmes are concerned with whether teachers meet certain criteria at a recognised standard across a wide range of teaching and learning contexts. Many MA courses may seek demonstration of understanding of different subject areas through an ability to analyse, synthesise and write academically. In-service teacher education programmes which follow a reflective model are also likely to want to find ways to assess reflective ability.

In the field of language teaching there is a further complication in that it is hard to define what represents content knowledge: whether it is knowledge of the language (fluency in English), or knowledge about the language (language awareness), or both. Freeman *et al.* (2009) also suggest that it is hard to separate assessment of content and methodology, and propose that the focus of assessment should be on: knowing the language, knowing about the language and knowing how to teach the language (see Figure 3).

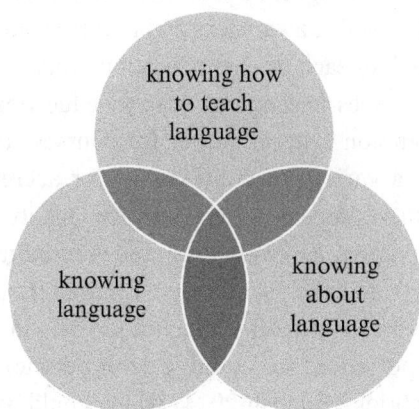

Figure 3 Language knowledge for and in teaching (adapted from Freeman *et al.* 2009: 86)

In-service teacher education needs to consider the core components of teacher expertise (rich knowledge-base, well-developed routines, problem-solving ability), as well as the key role played in teacher learning by teacher beliefs and critical reflection in order to establish the focus of any assessment. This suggests that effective assessment of teachers and teaching will not only focus on the outcome of learning, but also on the learning process itself. This requires a balance between formative and summative assessment, as well as between the product and process of teacher learning. Such a balance inevitably leads to a complex assessment matrix with a variety of different modes of assessment in order to capture the complexities of the processes of teaching and teacher learning.

Modes of assessment are chosen not only to ensure validity and reliability, but also due to concerns of practicality, and are again related to the aims of the assessment as well as underlying assumptions about the nature of teaching and teacher learning. So, for example, if the main aim is to measure teachers' skills and knowledge against a common standard, as is the case in such externally validated qualifications as CELTA and Delta, then validity of the assessment instruments and reliability of the assessment procedures become crucial concerns; hence the use of trialling, common instruments and standardisation. If the aim, however, is to reward effort or progress, then there may be less concern with meeting specific criteria and 'success' in assessment is likely to be a more relative concept. Ultimately the decision as to the focus, mode and weighting of assessment of aspects of teacher knowledge, skills, awareness and reflective ability will depend on the aims and approach of each teacher education programme.

One of the key issues in language teacher education assessment is the development of common criteria, either for courses such as Delta which are delivered over a variety of contexts, or for accreditation purposes. Initiatives such as the European Association for Quality Language Services (EAQUALS; now known as Evaluation and Accreditation of Quality in Language Services) and the Cambridge English Teaching Framework (2014) have endeavoured to outline teacher profiles in terms of language, qualifications, experience, knowledge, competencies and skills (see Rossner 2009; Cambridge English 2014) which could in future be used for assessment and accreditation purposes for teacher education programmes or training courses.

Assessment as a tool for teacher learning and professional development

In general education it has long been recognised that assessment of teacher knowledge and skills also has 'the potential to promote teacher learning and reflective teaching' (Chung 2008: 7). This idea is grounded in the 'reflective practitioner' tradition (Schön 1983; Schulman 1987), which suggests that teachers learn through 'pedagogical reasoning and action' when investigating, analysing and solving problems. As Darling-Hammond (2006) explains, 'performance assessment' can help teachers understand more deeply, and plays an important role in developing competence. Thus, assessment is not just a means of measuring learning outcomes, but an integral part of the process of teacher learning (Kennedy 2010).

Research in language teacher education also highlights the complex ways in which the development of teachers' professional knowledge and skills is enhanced by means of formal assessment tools. Borg (2011b, 2011c), in a study of six teachers taking the Delta in the UK, found clear evidence of a range of ways in which written assignments, assessed observations, and professional development assignments helped teachers learn during and after the course. Phipps, in a study of one teacher taking the Delta (2007) and three teachers taking the Delta as part of an MA (2010) in Turkey, also found that formal assessment tasks, such as classroom observations, written assignments and reflective tasks, contributed greatly to the development of teachers' knowledge, skills, confidence and awareness. Similarly, Richards, Ho and Giblin (1996) found that assessed teaching practice led to much learning on a CELTA course, while Wallace (1996) found that an assessed action research project stimulated learning on an MA course. Gebhard (2009) and Farrell (2007) have also highlighted the important role of the assessed practicum in pre-service language teacher education, although both Johnson (1996) and Ong'ondo and Borg (2011) suggest it may not always be effective.

Developing assessment literacy in teachers

Another important role of assessment tools in language teacher education is that of developing the concept of 'assessment literacy' in teachers (Stiggins 1995). This implies both a conscious understanding of principles of assessment, as well as the necessary skills to design, mark and give feedback on effective tests. Both EAQUALS and the Cambridge English Teaching Framework (Cambridge English 2014) have identified an understanding of assessment as key teacher competencies, and this is clearly something valued greatly by many employers too. Coombe, Al-Hamly and Troudi (2009) suggest that this should be a key component of in-service language teacher education.

Delta integrated into an MA programme

Background

Bilkent University School of English Language (BUSEL) provides a tertiary-level preparatory programme within a private English-medium university in Turkey. It aims to bring students' level of English up to B2 level, approximately equivalent to *Cambridge English: First*, and provides English for academic purposes (EAP) instruction to prepare students for academic study in the departments within the university. BUSEL employs over 250 full-time EFL teachers, approximately 70 of whom are native speakers. It actively promotes teachers' professional development by offering the following Cambridge English training courses to its teaching staff: ICELT (In-service Certificate in English Language Teaching) and/or CELTA for newly recruited teachers, and Delta for teachers with at least three years' experience. These courses are offered to teachers working in the institution as part of their contractual professional development, and a reduction is usually given from teachers' normal teaching hours to enable them to take the courses.

In 2003 BUSEL made a strategic decision to start a three-year, part-time, in-house MA programme which was integrated with the Delta course. Previously many local teachers tended to choose to do an MA instead of Delta as it was felt to be more valuable for their careers, yet traditionally MA courses are not teacher training-oriented and often do not contain a practical teaching component. However, practical teaching qualifications such as the Delta, which focus on improving classroom teaching, are crucial in helping to improve the overall quality of teaching. The MA programme, integrated with the Delta course, was seen as a way of attracting both local and foreign staff, and of enabling teachers to improve their classroom teaching while also working towards an academic qualification.

Conscious choices were made concerning the content, structure, pedagogy and assessment of the MA based on institutional beliefs about teaching, teacher education and teacher learning. Overall aims were defined (see Figure 4), and it was decided that the individual courses on the MA

GOAL

To develop students' knowledge and ability to integrate best practice in the management of the classroom, the curriculum, and the organization in order to achieve successful learning outcomes

CLASSROOM

- by developing an active and systematic understanding of theories of learning and pedagogical principles

- by demonstrating the ability to apply appropriate methodology to achieve learning objectives

- by developing an awareness of how effective teaching contributes to successful learning

CURRICULUM

- by developing an active and systematic understanding of the development, management and assessment of the curriculum

- by demonstrating the ability to define and assess learning objectives

- by developing an awareness of how effective curriculum management contributes to successful learning

MANAGEMENT

- by developing an active and systematic understanding of strategic management, in particular related to education

- by demonstrating the ability to manage the operations of departments/schools

- by developing an awareness of how effective management contributes to successful learning

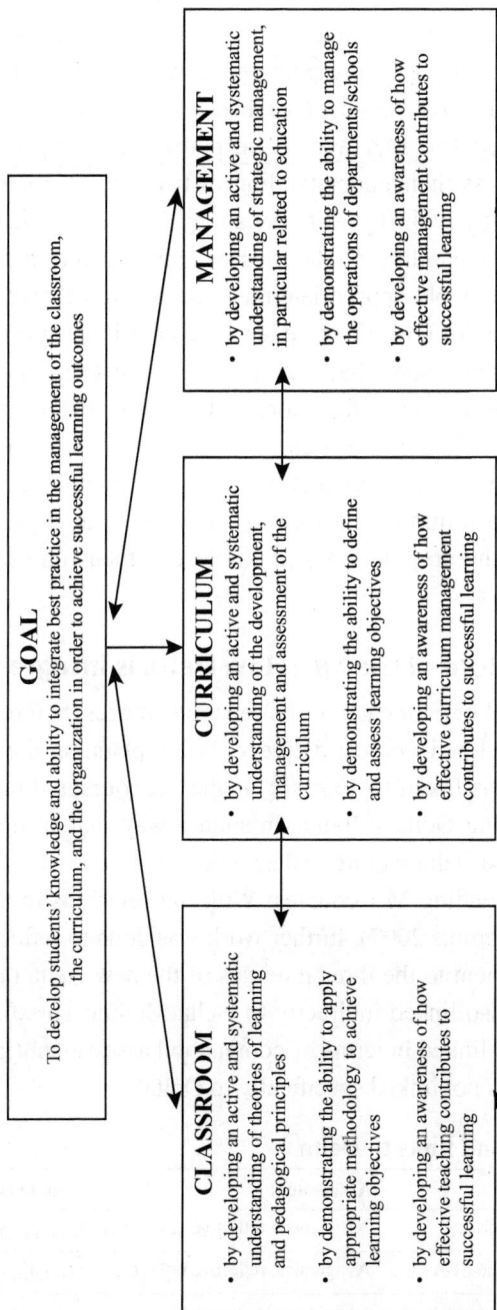

Figure 4 Aims of the MA (BUSEL MA Handbook 2012: 1)

should be logically sequenced to ensure the most effective development of teachers' knowledge, awareness and skills. In this sense the programme differs from more traditional MA programmes in which individual courses do not necessarily build on one another (see discussion above).

The main aims of the MA are to help teachers improve their teaching skills as well as their understanding of teaching, curriculum and management. Specifically with regard to pedagogy it aims to help teachers develop their: (1) understanding of theories of learning and pedagogical principles; (2) ability to apply appropriate methodology to achieve learning objectives; (3) awareness of how effective teaching contributes to successful learning. It is expected, then, that teachers develop their theoretical knowledge, understanding of learning theory and teaching methodology, but also that they reflect on and improve their actual classroom practice. To this end, teaching practice is assessed as part of the MA. An entry requirement is that teachers have a minimum of three years' full-time experience of teaching EFL so that the programme as a whole can focus on developing 'teacher expertise'.

Content and structure of the MA: How Delta is integrated

Aims were then defined for each of the separate courses, before detailed planning of content and pedagogical delivery. When planning the separate courses, a decision was taken to link six of the 15 courses directly and indirectly to the existing Delta syllabus in such a way that would enable teachers to complete the Delta requirements while at the same time receiving credits for the corresponding MA courses. With the revisions to the Delta courses in 2008 (see Zeronis 2007), further work was done to refine the MA courses to better link them to the three modules of the new Delta (a seventh MA course was then also linked indirectly to Delta Module Three). Table 2 shows how the two are linked in terms of content and assessment (italics are used to indicate courses not linked specifically to Delta).

Table 2 MA courses and links to Delta

yr/semester	MA course*	Assessment	Link to Delta
1 1	Learning theories	Assignment, reflective tasks, quiz	Module One
	Linguistics and SLA	Assignment, reflective tasks, quiz	Modules One, Two

(To be continued)

(Continued)

yr/semester		MA course*	Assessment	Link to Delta
2		Methods 1: Language systems	LSA 1 assignment, peer observation, quiz, reflective tasks	Module Two LSA 1
		Methods 2: Language skills	LSA 2 assignment, peer observation, quiz, reflective tasks	Module Two LSA 2
	Summer	Curriculum	Simulation, needs analysis, course plan, testing plan	Module Three EA
2	1	Developing Practice 1	LSA 3 assignment, peer observation, quiz, reflective tasks	Module Two LSA 3
		Reflection on practice	PDA (stages 1–4 as one assignment), experimental practice, quiz, reflective tasks	Module Two PDA/ EP
	2	Classroom practice	3 × TP/lesson plan/commentary/ post-lesson evaluation *1 TP/lesson plan/commentary/ post-lesson evaluation*	Module Two TP1–3
		Developing Practice 2	Reflective tasks, mock exam Qs, quiz, language analysis	Module One, Two
	Summer	*Assessment*	*Assignment, tasks, presentation*	n/a
		Research methods	*Proposal for research project*	
3	1	*Introduction to educational management*	*Assignment, reflective tasks, quiz*	n/a
		Human resource management	*Assignment, reflective tasks, quiz*	
	2	*Budgeting and finance*	*Assignment, reflective tasks, quiz*	
		Research project	*8–10,000-word research project (minithesis)*	

*LSA = Language Skills/Systems Assignment, TP = Teaching Practice, PDA = Professional Development Assignment, EP = Experimental Practice, EA= Extended Assignment

As mentioned above there is often a tension between academic and professional qualifications, so an important aspect of this integration was felt to be the linking of theory and practice, and it was decided that all courses on the MA should be designed in such a way that teachers' professional knowledge, awareness and skills are developed. The logic behind this sequencing of individual courses is that teachers on the MA/Delta first get a grounding in general learning theories (in the 'Learning Theories' course), theories of SLA and cognitive theories of language learning (in the 'Linguistics/

SLA' course) in the first semester before starting the Delta course in the second semester of the first year. During the following three semesters (approximately 16 months) teachers complete the requirements of the three modules of Delta which count directly towards six of the MA courses, and indirectly to one other. Teachers wishing to take the Delta only usually already have an MA and are therefore not required to take the additional MA courses or to do additional assessments beyond the Delta requirements, and complete the three Delta modules over a period of 16 months: thus any Delta group will consist of some teachers taking Delta/MA and others just taking Delta.

All internally assessed written assignments and observed lessons for Delta (including background essays, lesson plans, commentaries and post-lesson evaluations) are also marked by the Delta tutors and contribute to course grades for the MA (see the discussion below for more details). The following externally assessed components of Delta are not, however, graded for MA purposes: the written examination (Module One), externally assessed lesson and assignment (Module Two), and extended assignment (Module Three). This is because the university Master's award rules require all assignments to be internally validated. Table 3 shows how the various assessments are linked and spread out over three semesters.

In terms of the assessment for the MA courses linked to Delta, approximately 50–60% of the assessment for each course is covered by Delta-required tasks (LSA, teaching practice, PDA, etc.); the remainder being a mixture of reflective tasks, terminology quizzes, response tasks on Moodle, active participation in input sessions, etc. (see Figure 5).

When designing the content of the MA courses, much consideration was given to the revised Delta syllabus (Cambridge ESOL 2008b) and Delta Handbook (Cambridge ESOL 2008a). Table 4 shows how the main syllabus areas in the three Delta modules are covered through the different MA courses.

Table 3 Assessments for MA/Delta: Timeline and links

Year/Semester	Delta assessment		MA assessment
Year 1	LSA 1		Methods 1
Semester 2	TP 1		Classroom Practice
		peer observation	Methods 1
		PDA 1–2	Reflect/Practice
	LSA 2		Methods 2
	TP 2		Classroom Practice
		peer observation	Methods 2
Year 1		PDA 3	Reflect/Practice
Summer		EA plan	Curriculum
Year 2		EA plan	Curriculum
Semester 1		EP	Reflect/Practice Dev
		peer observation	Practice 1
	LSA 3		Dev Practice 1 Classroom
	TP 3		Prac
		peer observation	Dev Practice 1
		PDA 4	Reflect/Practice
Year 2	Exam tasks		Dev Practice 2
Semester 2	Mock exam		Dev Practice 2

LSA = Language Skills/Systems Assignment, TP = Teaching Practice, PDA = Professional Development Assignment, EP = Experimental Practice, EA = Extended Assignment

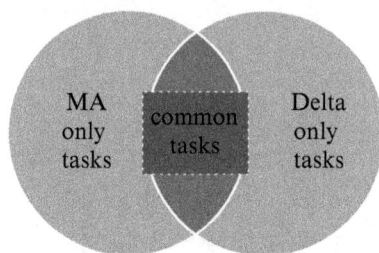

Figure 5 Overlap of Delta and MA

Table 4 Delta syllabus and links to the MA

Delta syllabus	Delta assessment	MA course*
Module One: Understanding Language, Methodology and Resources for Teaching		
Theories of SLA	Exam	Linguistics/SLA
Awareness of ELT approaches/methods		Developing Practice 2
Language skills and learner problems		Developing Practice 1, 2
Language systems and learner problems		Methods 1, 2 Developing Practice 2
Knowledge of materials/resources		Developing Practice 2
Assessment terms/concepts		Developing Practice 2 Curriculum
Module Two: Developing Professional Practice		
Language learner and learning context	– LSA background essay	Methods 1, 2 Developing Practice 1, 2
Preparation for teaching	– LSA lesson plan	Methods 1, 2 Developing Practice 1, 2
Materials evaluation/selection/use	– LSA lesson plan + commentary	Methods 1, 2 Developing Practice 1, 2
Manage and support learning	– assessed teaching practice	Classroom practice
Evaluation of lesson preparation and teaching	– post-lesson evaluation	Classroom practice
Observation/evaluation of other teachers	– peer observation	Methods 1, 2 Developing Practice 1
Professional development	– PDA	Reflection on practice
Module Three: Extending Practice and ELT Specialism		
Research into specialist areas	Extended assignment	Curriculum
Syllabus design principles		
Types of syllabus and needs analysis		
Needs analysis and course design		
Assessment principles and practice		

see Table 2 on Page 375 for the complete list of MA courses

Pedagogical approach on the Delta/MA

Considering the four models of teacher education as outlined in Table 1, the pedagogical approach followed on the MA is principally reflective, although it also contains elements of the academic, applied science and craft models. Some courses are more theoretical in nature (such as 'Learning Theories' and 'Linguistics/SLA'), while others are more practical (e.g. 'Classroom Practice' and 'Reflection on Practice'). Theory and practice, however, are not viewed as separate: rather they both inform each other, and participants are encouraged to make links between the two. It is also emphasised to participants at the start of the Delta/MA programme that critical reflection on their beliefs, teaching, input and reading is an essential element of their learning:

> The purpose of input sessions is to improve participants' subject knowledge, enable them to reflect critically on their own practice in the light of this knowledge, and ultimately to improve their professional practice. Course tutors will employ a mixture of lecture style, group work, individual work, discussion and questioning techniques to promote critical thinking and encourage participants to critically reflect on the reading and content of the session (BUSEL MA Handbook 2012: 2).

For example, on the 'Linguistics/SLA' course participants are given an initial questionnaire (adapted from Lightbown and Spada 2006) to elicit their existing beliefs about teaching and learning, and are encouraged to discuss their answers with their peers, considering the reasons for their answers and how these beliefs are reflected in their teaching. The first assessment task on the course then consists of a guided reflection task which is completed regularly throughout the course, whereby participants choose three of the statements from the questionnaire which they wish to further explore, using the following prompts:

- What is your belief (about the statement) now (at the start of the course)?
- How is this manifested in your teaching now (at the start of the course)?
- Evidence in support of your belief (during the course from input, readings, discussions, observations from own teaching, peer observations, etc.)?
- Evidence against your belief (as above)?

- What is your belief at the end of the course (whether it has strengthened or changed)?
- How might you adapt your teaching in the future?

The questionnaire, revised at the end of the course, then feeds into the PDA assignment which participants do as part of Delta Module Two, as it helps provide a focus for aspects of teaching that they wish to explore in further depth during Delta. The completed PDA (stages 1–4) is submitted as a single assignment at the end of Delta Module Two and is graded as an MA assignment on the 'Reflection on Practice' course in addition to the Delta Experimental Practice assignment, and various other reflective tasks. Such reflective assignments can be useful tools for assessing teachers' personal practical knowledge, although there is always a risk that teachers may simply complete the assignments to pass the assessment. (See Borg and Albery, Chapter 3 and Anderson, Chapter 4.)

Criteria for assessing teachers' professional skills and knowledge

The discussion earlier highlighted the importance of assessing the extent to which teachers know *the* language, know *about* the language and know *how to teach* the language. The EAQUALS profiling grid for language teachers, now the European Profiling Grid (Evaluation and Accreditation of Quality in Language Services 2013), also emphasises the need to assess and encourage self-assessment of (among other competences) teachers':

- language proficiency and language awareness:
- knowledge of methodology, learning theory, learning styles/strategies, etc.
- skills in teaching practice, lesson/course planning and classroom management
- assessment literacy.

The Delta/MA programme uses a variety of modes of assessment to assess key professional skills and knowledge in line with the aims of the programme and current thinking in language teacher education. Written evidence plays a vital role in assessing teaching competence. Table 5 shows how the above competences are assessed using different assessment tools, and how theory and practice are given equal importance.

Table 5 Assessment tools used on the Delta/MA

Key competencies	Assessment tools	
Language proficiency	Written assignments (*all courses**)	Observed lessons (*Classroom Practice*)
Language awareness	Written tasks (*Developing Practice 2*)	
Knowledge of methodology	Written assignments, terminology quiz (*Methods 1, 2, Developing Practice 1, 2*)	Lesson plans (*Classroom Practice*)
Teaching skills		Observed lessons (*Classroom Practice*)
Classroom management		Observed lessons (*Classroom Practice*)
Lesson planning		Lesson plans (*Classroom Practice*)
Course planning	Extended assignment (*Curriculum*)	
Assessment literacy	Written tasks (*Developing Practice 2*) Extended assignment (*Curriculum*)	

*MA courses specified (in italics)

As discussed above, the assessment tools also play a key role in teacher learning on the Delta/MA programme:

> Assessment is an integral part of the learning process and provides participants with the opportunity to read further, conduct research, reflect critically, analyse and synthesise information and knowledge, and to further develop their academic writing skills (BUSEL MA Handbook 2012: 3).

Thus, modes of assessment are not only chosen for validity and reliability in assessing teachers' knowledge and skills, but also for their potential to promote professional learning.

A mixture of holistic and analytic criteria are used for Delta/MA written assignments in order to arrive at a final grade. Delta assessors use both a set of analytic criteria to identify strengths and weaknesses, and a holistic band system to allocate a specific grade. For the MA courses a similar approach is used, and there is a common set of marking criteria used for all written assignments, except for those which are also marked for Delta purposes, as will now be explained. One potential tension identified when initially planning the Delta/MA programme was that of parallel or overlapping assessment criteria. Following the principle of not assessing the same piece of work twice using different criteria, written assignments which require grading for both Delta and MA (such as LSA) are marked first using Delta criteria and then converted to an MA grade using a simple conversion chart, whereby Delta bands such as Distinction, Merit, Pass, Fail correspond to letter grades on the MA. In this way participants are not expected to write one assignment according to multiple criteria.

Assessment of teachers' professional skills is carried out through the MA course 'Classroom Practice' using the existing Delta criteria which focus on:

- planning and preparation (assessed through lesson plan and commentary documents)
- creating and maintaining an atmosphere conducive to learning
- understanding, knowledge and explanation of language and language skills
- classroom procedures and techniques
- classroom management
- reflection and evaluation (assessed through post-lesson evaluation documents).

As mentioned in the previous paragraph, assessors use a mixture of holistic and analytic criteria to reach a final grade for each assessed lesson. This grade is then converted into an MA letter grade for each assessed lesson (four in total, three of which count towards Delta). For each lesson a separate grade is given for the lesson plan, commentary, and post-lesson evaluation using specially designed holistic bands derived from the analytic Delta criteria.

Tensions between Delta and MA assessment requirements/ expectations

Delta has been accredited at Level 7 on the Qualifications and Credit Framework in England which is equivalent to MA level, so it is recognised that both require similar knowledge and skills. Yet, as discussed earlier, MAs are often seen as academic qualifications, while teacher training courses such as Delta are often considered to be professional qualifications. This creates a possible tension in terms of the expectations of academic writing from MA and Delta. When initially planning the Bilkent Delta/MA, it was agreed that participants would be expected to write a range of different assignments, each with emphasis on slightly different types of academic writing. Figure 6 shows these on a continuum from traditional discursive/academic writing conventions to more reflective types of writing.

discursive/academic				reflective	
MA course assignments	EA	LSA 1–3	PDA	peer observation	MA reflective papers

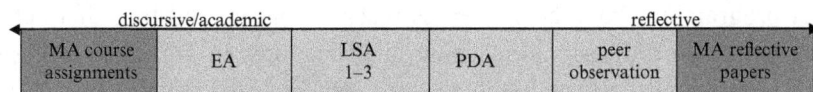

EA = Extended Assignment, LSA = Language Skills/Systems Assignment, PDA = Professional Development Assignment

Figure 6 Types of academic writing criteria used*

Most of the MA courses (for 'Learning Theories', 'Linguistics/SLA', etc.) require a 3,000-word discursive assignment based on background research/reading, analysis and separation of ideas into a coherent argument following academic conventions, such as American Psychological Association (APA) format (see www.apa.org), which is then assessed according to the following equally weighted criteria:

- academic writing (language, presentation, organisation, use of references)
- subject knowledge (familiarity with theory, evidence of reading, use of terminology)
- analysis/synthesis (clarity of argument, quality of ideas, use of supporting evidence).

The 4,500-word EA on Delta is very similar in terms of expectations, but less weighting is given to academic writing, clarity of argument and clarity of ideas. The 2,500-word LSA assignments on Delta follow a more rigid format, place less emphasis on academic conventions, and require fewer references. In the PDA there is also an expected format to be followed, but participants focus mainly on reflecting on their own learning. Peer observation reports are submitted as MA assignments and again the focus is more on what participants have learned about their own teaching. There are other reflective tasks on some of the MA courses which do not require references and focus more on participants' ability to critically reflect than on following academic conventions or developing a coherent argument. Although some members of academia may contest that reflective writing has less 'academic rigour' than traditional discursive writing, contemporary thinking on teacher education (e.g. Burns and Richards 2009; Cochran-Smith *et al.* 2008; Darling-Hammond 2006) suggests that both have a valuable role to play in promoting teacher learning.

Another tension relates to the conception of research and its place within teacher education programmes such as MAs. Traditionally many

MA programmes have been seen as research-based, and thus distinctly different from professional teaching qualifications. In Turkey non-thesis MA programmes tend to be considered 'professional developmental' as opposed to MA-with-thesis programmes which are seen as 'research-based'. However, today mainstream teacher education recognises the vital role played by various forms of practitioner or teacher research, while language teacher education similarly places great emphasis on exploratory practice, reflective practice and action research (Allwright and Hanks 2009; Burns 2009; Burton 2009). On the Delta/MA programme at Bilkent, teachers are assessed on the following types of research:

- action research (assessed through the Delta PDA)
- exploratory/reflective practice (assessed through reflective assignments/ tasks)
- classroom research (assessed through an 8–10,000-word research project).

Impact on teacher learning

An important aspect of any teacher education programme is its impact on teacher learning. Of particular concern in this chapter is the extent to which the assessment focus and modes used in the Delta/MA contribute to teacher learning, and also the extent to which the integration of MA and Delta has encouraged a more reflective approach to teacher learning. To date, two separate studies by this author have shed light on this.

Phipps (2010), in a study of three teachers doing the Bilkent Delta/MA, identified a number of ways in which it positively impacts on teacher learning. Firstly, the reflective approach employed in the pedagogical approach and assessment tools plays an important role in enabling participants to become aware of their initial beliefs and to question them critically, as feedback from participants shows:

> I started to see what I had in my mind. The MA created circumstances to question more, and supporting these questions through readings and input helped reshape my beliefs, and feel more confident about those beliefs and teaching ... Reflection on my practice helped me a lot ... having to prepare observed lessons in such a staged way, because it was such a meticulous way of thinking ... The input is so linked with the practical input ... it's logically sequenced ... so it really made my learning more meaningful. I could relate things and understand why I believed such things. (T1)

> The experimental practice assignment, portfolio tasks, and peer observations are quite useful ... not only are you reading it, but you're really forced to put it into practice, and also you have that stage in-between where you're questioning, but instead of just questioning ... actually applying it ... and then you have a chance to reflect on it as well. (T2)

Such questioning of initial beliefs seems to provide a springboard for subsequent learning, as it encourages participants to explore 'tensions' (Phipps and Borg 2009; see also Basturkmen 2012), which they themselves wished to work on.

Secondly, the assessment tools used on the Delta/MA seemed to have a very positive impact on teacher learning, in particular the links between theory and practice, between the 'MA Linguistics/SLA' course and Delta, and between reflective assignments/tasks on the MA and assessed teaching practice:

> Learning about different approaches ... having to plan assessed lessons justifying my choice of approach helped me question my beliefs and deepen my understanding ... Now I'm very clear about my beliefs, before planning a lesson I can see learners' needs better and find answers to my classroom management questions ... so I feel much more confident ... when planning and in class ... as I can see why I should pre-plan in a particular way. I have my justifications now because of the readings and all we did in the MA. (T3)
>
> The TP cycles were a complete link between theory and practice ... I learnt particular points about lesson preparation, classroom management ... thinking in a more detailed way ... the observation cycle, discussing issues was good to reflect on ... getting answers to my questions and reacting to them quickly makes learning more effective. The background essays linked to the TP cycle, seeing language learning theory, and being able to practise this in detail, and having this formality in the assignment ... detailed research about the language point, then linking this theoretical input to teaching was good. (T1)

The findings of the study also suggest that the following characteristics of the Delta/MA exert a powerful influence on the development of teachers' beliefs and practices:

- *explicit focus on beliefs:* enabling teachers to become aware of their beliefs and to critically question them in the light of input and their practices
- *reflective practice:* encouraging teachers to critically reflect on their beliefs, practices and input

- *link between theory and practice:* helping teachers put ideas into practice, and theorise their practices
- *language awareness:* enabling teachers to improve their awareness of the complexities of grammar and reasons for learners' difficulties
- *practical examples:* helping teachers see the 'plausibility' of alternative practices especially if modelled by teacher educators
- *experimentation:* enabling teachers to personally experience the benefits of alternative practices
- *practical assignments/tasks:* encouraging teachers to plan assessed lessons in detail considering different options and justifying their choices (Phipps 2010: 182).

Thus, the combination of more theoretical MA courses with more practical courses delivered through Delta impacts positively on teacher learning.

Phipps (2012), in a study of nine teachers doing the Delta/MA, found further support for the integration of MA and Delta, as shown by participants' comments:

> I think the MA and Delta link well. For example most of us used the things that we learnt in your course [Linguistics/SLA] and throughout the Delta. It was all nicely interrelated. If I had done Delta without the MA … I wouldn't be able to make sense of the process that the students go through. For example even though we're in the last stage of MA, even when I'm doing my research project I used the things I learnt in your course so I can make sense of the things the students are saying. I can't separate what I learnt from MA and Delta I think. (T2)

> MA and Delta help each other because for example with 'Learning Theories' we focused on our interaction with the students and the things that shaped the learning environment and it affected my whole teaching actually. I started to feel like a better teacher, better person actually. This is very important and in your course [Linguistics/SLA] for example you see how the teacher should be because you feel safe with the teacher and you say that if I act like this my students are going to be more motivated … and the linguistics course helped us a lot in our assignments and TPs and we always referred to the terminology and ideas. (T9)

Thus, the links in particular between the 'Learning Theories' and 'Linguistics/SLA' courses and the Delta are seen as very useful. Another factor which was identified as being attractive to participants was that integrating the Delta into the MA saved time and enabled some of the teachers' work to contribute to both qualifications simultaneously:

> MA is like the theoretical side, Delta is the practical one. The MA courses are really vital because before the course I had no idea about Piaget or Vygotsky, so those are really helpful and I'm happy that Delta is accepted as part of the MA without doubling what we have to do. (T5)
>
> Actually that is why I'm here, because while applying for this job I looked at the courses you give … I really liked the idea because at that time I was accepted to [another university] for another MA and then I changed my mind because doing MA with Delta is a really good idea and you don't lose time. It saves your time because they are all related … for example linguistics definitely helped me while doing the LSA 2 assignment and 'Curriculum' helps while designing lessons and the tasks in the lesson and in that course we learnt how to reflect on what we are doing in class, it was really helpful and they are all related to Delta. (T6)

The main negative points to emerge from the study were the difficulty of maintaining a pace of study over three years while also doing a demanding full-time job, and the challenge of keeping track of all the various assessment tasks and how they contribute to both the MA and Delta.

The integration of the Delta/MA over the past 10 years has been highly successful in achieving the aims of the programme (see Figure 4 above), meeting institutional needs and contributing to a considerable increase in teachers' professional skills and knowledge, as well as to their confidence and awareness. It has not only helped increase the importance of Delta as a practical teaching qualification in Turkey (where more non-native than native-speaker teachers now take and pass Delta), but also shown that it is both feasible and desirable to integrate it into an academic degree programme. Future challenges for the programme will be to continue to adapt to find innovative ways of maximising the impact of the content, structure, pedagogical approach and assessment tools on the development of teachers' professional skills and knowledge.

Conclusion

This chapter has highlighted some of the key issues in language teacher education and teacher learning, and addressed some of the main concerns related to the focus and mode of assessment of teachers' professional skills and knowledge. A central feature of the above discussion is that decisions regarding the content, structure, pedagogical approach and assessment of any teacher education programme should be conscious and explicit, and should be informed by the aims of the programme, its context and participants.

The case of Delta integrated into an MA at Bilkent has demonstrated how such decisions can be taken in in-service teacher education, and has provided an example of how language teachers' competence can be assessed in terms of language, knowledge and practical teaching skills. It has shown that academic and professional qualifications need not be mutually exclusive, that theory and practice can be thoughtfully integrated, and that a reflective approach to teacher education need not mean sacrificing academic rigour. The case study also suggests that experienced teachers' knowledge, skills, confidence and awareness can be greatly enhanced by integrating practical teaching into an MA programme, and that this can appeal to many teachers' career aspirations. It also provides evidence that a variety of modes of assessment can be used in imaginative and complex ways to assess a range of teacher competences, and that such modes of assessment also play an important role in teacher learning. A final point is that different types of academic writing and different research orientations can be assessed within one programme.

Challenges for language teacher education in the future include finding better ways to measure the impact of such programmes on teachers, institutions and ultimately learners, as well as further defining the essential characteristics of 'expert teachers' and devising more effective ways of assessing teachers' professional skills and knowledge.

References

Allwright, D. and Hanks, J. (2009) *The Developing Language Learner: An Introduction to Exploratory Practice*. London: Palgrave MacMillan.

Barduhn, S. and Johnson, J. (2009) Certification and professional qualifications, in Burns, A. and Richards, J. (Eds) *The Cambridge Guide to Second Language Teacher Education*. New York: Cambridge University Press, 59–65.

Barkhuizen, G. and Borg, S. (2010) Researching language teacher education, *Language Teaching Research* 14 (3), 237–240.

Barnard, R. and Burns, A. (Eds) (2012) *Researching Language Teacher Cognition and Practice*. Bristol: Multilingual Matters.

Basturkmen, H. (2012) Review of research into the correspondence between language teachers' stated beliefs and practices, *System* 40, 282–295.

Bereiter, C. and Scardamalia, M. (1993) *Surpassing Ourselves*. Peru: Open Court.

Borg, S. (2006) *Teacher Cognition and Language Education: Research and Practice.* London: Continuum.

Borg, S. (2011a) Language teacher education, in Simpson, J. (Ed) *The Routledge Handbook of Applied Linguistics.* London: Routledge, 215–228.

Borg, S. (2011b) The impact of in-service teacher education on language teachers' beliefs, *System* 39 (3), 370–380.

Borg, S. (2011c) Teacher learning on the Delta, *Research Notes* 45, 19–25.

Burns, A. (2009) Action research and second language teacher education, in Burns, A. and Richards, J. (Eds) *The Cambridge Guide to Second Language Teacher Education.* New York: Cambridge University Press, 289–297.

Burns, A. and Richards, J. (Eds) (2009) *The Cambridge Guide to Second Language Teacher Education.* New York: Cambridge University Press.

Burton, J. (2009) Reflective practice, in Burns, A. and Richards, J. (Eds), *The Cambridge Guide to Second Language Teacher Education.* New York: Cambridge University Press, 298–308.

Calderhead, J. and Shorrock, S. (1997) *Understanding Teacher Education.* London: Falmer Press.

Cambridge English (2014) *Cambridge English Teaching Framework*, available online: www.cambridgeenglish.org/images/172992-full-level-descriptors-cambridge-english-teaching-framework.pdf

Cambridge ESOL (2008a) *Delta Module 1, Module 2, Module 3: Handbook for Tutors and Candidates.* Cambridge: Cambridge ESOL.

Cambridge ESOL (2008b) *Delta Syllabus Specifications.* Cambridge: Cambridge ESOL.

Chung, R. (2008) Beyond assessment: Performance assessments in teacher education, *Teacher Education Quarterly (Winter)*, 7–28.

Cochran-Smith, M. and Zeichner, K. (Eds) (2005) *Studying Teacher Education: The Report of the AERA Panel on Research and Teacher Education.* Mahwah: Lawrence Erlbaum. Associates

Cochran-Smith, M., Feiman-Nemser, S., McIntyre, D. and Demers, K. (Eds) (2008) *Handbook of Research on Teacher Education*, (3rd edition). New York: Routledge.

Coombe, C., Al-Hamly, M. and Troudi, S. (2009) Foreign and second language teacher assessment literacy: Issues, challenges and recommendations, *Research Notes* 38, 14–17.

Crandall, J. (2000) Language teacher education, *Applied Linguistics* 20, 34–55.

Darling-Hammond, L. (2006) *Powerful Teacher Education.* San Francisco: Jossey-Bass.

Ellis, R. (2009) SLA and teacher education, in Burns, A. and Richards, J. (Eds) *The Cambridge Guide to Second Language Teacher Education.* New York: Cambridge University Press, 135–143.

Evaluation and Accreditation of Quality in Language Services (2013) *Teacher Profiling Grid*, available online: egrid.epg-project.en

Farrell, T. (2007) *Reflective Language Teaching.* London: Continuum.

Feiman-Nemser, S. (1990) *Conceptual Orientations in Teacher Education*, available online: ncrtl.msu.edu/http/ipapers/html/pdf/ip902.pdf

Freeman, D. and Johnson, K. (1998) Reconceptualising the knowledge base of language teacher education, *TESOL Quarterly* 32 (3), 397–417.

Freeman, D. and Richards, J. (1996) A look at uncritical stories, in Freeman, D. and Richards, J. (Eds) *Teacher Learning in Language Teaching.* Cambridge: Cambridge University Press, 1–6.

Freeman, D., Orzulak, M. and Morrissey, G. (2009) Assessment in second language teacher education, in Burns, A. and Richards, J. (Eds) *The Cambridge Guide to Second Language Teacher Education.* New York: Cambridge University Press, 77–90.

Galaczi, E. and Benjamin, T. (2014) Cambridge English teaching framework: Validation trial, Cambridge English Language Assessment internal report.

Gebhard, J. (2009) The practicum, in Burns, A. and Richards, J. (Eds) *The Cambridge Guide to Second Language Teacher Education*. New York: Cambridge University Press, 250–258.

Graves, K. (2009) The curriculum of second language teacher education, in Burns, A. and Richards, J. (Eds) *The Cambridge Guide to Second Language Teacher Education*. New York: Cambridge University Press, 115–124.

Johnson, K. E. (1996) The vision versus the reality: The tensions of the TESOL practicum, in Freeman, D. and Richards, J. (Eds) *Teacher Learning in Language Teaching*. Cambridge: Cambridge University Press, 30–49.

Johnson, K. E. (2009) Trends in second language teacher education, in Burns, A. and Richards, J. (Eds) *The Cambridge Guide to Second Language Teacher Education*. New York: Cambridge University Press, 20–29.

Johnson, K. E. and Golombek, P. (2011) *Research on Second Language Teacher Education*. London: Routledge.

Kennedy, M. M. (2010) *Teacher Assessment and the Quest for Teacher Quality*. San Francisco: Jossey Bass.

Korthagen, F. (2001) A reflection on reflection, in *Linking Practice and Theory: The Pedagogy of Realistic Teacher Education*. Mahwah: Lawrence Erlbaum Associates, 51–68.

Korthagen, F., Loughran, J. and Lunenberg, M. (2005) Teaching teachers: Studies into the expertise of teacher educators, *Teaching and Teacher Education* 21 (2), 107–115.

Lightbown, P. and Spada, N. (2006) *How Languages Are Learned* (3rd edition). Oxford: Oxford University Press.

Moss, P., Girard, B. and Haniford, L. (2006) Validity in educational assessment, *Review of Research in Education* 30, 109–162.

Ong'ondo, C. and Borg, S. (2011) We teach plastic lessons to please them: The influence of supervision on the practice of English language student teachers in Kenya, *Language Teaching Research* 15 (4), 509–528.

Pennington, M. (1996) The cognitive-affective filter in teacher development: Transmission-based and interpretation-based schemas for change, *System* 24 (3), 337–350

Phipps, S. (2007) What difference does Delta make? *Research Notes* 29, 12–15.

Phipps, S. (2010) *Language Teacher Education, Beliefs and Classroom Practices*. Saarbrucken: Lambert Academic Publishing.

Phipps, S. (2012) BUSEL internal report on the impact of MA/Delta, Bilkent University.

Phipps, S. (2013) Report on the draft Cambridge English Language Assessment CPD framework, Cambridge English Language Assessment internal report.

Phipps, S. (2014) Cambridge English Language Assessment CPD framework descriptions (version 4), Cambridge English Language Assessment internal report.

Phipps, S. and Borg, S. (2009) Exploring tensions between teachers' grammar teaching beliefs and practices, *System* 37 (3) 380–390.

Richards, J. (1998) *Beyond Training*. Cambridge: Cambridge University Press.

Richards, J., Ho, B. and Giblin, K. (1996) Learning how to teach in the RSA Cert, in Freeman, D. and Richards, J. (Eds) *Teacher Learning in Language Teaching*. Cambridge: Cambridge University Press, 242–259.

Rossner, R. (2009) Developing common criteria for comparison and assessment in language teacher education, *Research Notes* 38. Cambridge: University of Cambridge Local Examinations Syndicate, 4–14.

Schön, D. (1983) *The Reflective Practitioner: How Professionals Think in Action.* London: Basic Books.

Schulman, L. (1987) Knowledge and teaching: Foundations of the new reform, *Harvard Educational Review* 57 (1), 1–22.

Stiggins, R. (1995) Assessment literacy for the 21st century, *Phi Delta Kaan* 77 (3), 238–245.

Tsui, A. (2003) *Understanding Expertise in Teaching.* Cambridge: Cambridge University Press.

Tsui, A. (2009) Teaching expertise: Approaches, perspectives and characterizations, in Burns, A. and Richards, J. (Eds) *The Cambridge Guide to Second Language Teacher Education.* New York: Cambridge University Press, 190–198.

Wallace, M. (1991) *Training Foreign Language Teachers: A Reflective Approach.* Cambridge: Cambridge University Press.

Wallace, M. (1996) Structured reflection: The role of the professional project in training ESL teachers, in Freeman, D. and Richards, J. (Eds) *Teacher Learning in Language Teaching.* Cambridge: Cambridge University Press, 281–294.

Zeichner, K. and Liston, D. (1990) Traditions of reform in US teacher education, available online: ncrtl.msu.edu/http/ipapers/html/pdf/ip901.pdf

Zeronis, R. (2007) The DELTA revision project, *Research Notes* 29, 4–8.

16 Culture and context in the external assessment of teaching

David M. Palfreyman
Zayed University, Dubai

Introduction

Cambridge English Teaching Qualifications are an international system of qualifications coordinated and moderated with the aim of ensuring that candidates awarded the qualifications have shown a certain level of particular kinds of awareness and skills deemed relevant to (their) teaching. On the other hand, the teaching itself takes place in a wide range of locations and contexts and with a wide variety of students, from middle-aged asylum seekers in the UK to early teenagers in Sri Lanka, to university students in Romania.

This interface between an assessment system based in the UK English language teaching (ELT) profession and teachers and students in a wide variety of other contexts requires a certain amount of accommodation on both sides. The purpose of this paper is to explore how cultural issues and cultural awareness are involved in the assessment of teaching, and specifically how they are perceived by assessors in external observation of lessons for the Cambridge Delta (Diploma in Teaching English to Speakers of Other Languages). I will consider how culture and context are important in teaching, teacher education and the assessment of teaching, analyse comments made by external assessors which explicitly or implicitly reference cultural elements of classroom teaching, and draw conclusions about how an awareness of cultural factors can be enhanced in the community of practice of assessors and tutors.

Key concepts

Culture and context

'Culture' and 'context' are often invoked as important influences in discussions of education and learning: arrangements or difficulties are explained by reference to 'the learners' culture' or 'the local context'. I will use the term 'culture' to mean 'the shared patterns of behavior *and associated meanings* that people learn and participate in within the groups to which they belong' (Whitten and Hunter 1992: 3, emphasis added). These 'shared patterns' are often interpreted as linked to nationality or ethnic background (e.g. 'Japanese culture' or 'Western culture'); culture may be viewed as more or less monolithic and constant: a body of knowledge or a set of regular habits which can be reliably mapped by, for example, surveying large numbers of people from the 'same' culture (e.g. Hofstede 1997). However, work from a more qualitative, critical perspective (e.g. Pavlenko and Norton 2007) presents culture as more fluid than this. While there certainly are some large-scale patterns in interpretation and behaviour, the idea of a monolithic national/ethnic culture is more a theoretical construct or simplification than a straightforward representation of reality. For example, teaching in the tertiary education sector may work according to a 'culture' which differs considerably from that of the secondary sector within the same country, with further differences between the private and state sectors; and a state university in China may have significant features in common with a state university in Egypt (Holliday 1994). Furthermore, each institution or organisation has a more or less distinctive 'organisational culture'; even a particular class can have its own 'culture', tacitly understood by all or most of the participants but perhaps not by 'outsiders'.

These intersecting cultures may be seen as differences in 'context', and indeed 'the local context' is often used as shorthand for a range of cultural and material conditions. Pasassung (2003: ii), for example, summarises how contextual factors combine in rural Indonesia:

> [T]he failure of EFL teaching and learning in rural Indonesia is due to the complex interplay of a number of issues, including the following: 1. cultural values, i.e. the value of harmonious relationships in a feudal community, 2. sociolinguistic situation, i.e. the status and function of English, 3. material conditions, and 4. methodology, i.e. teachers' teaching practices.

393

The four contextual factors mentioned by Pasassung can be conveniently distinguished; but they can also all be related to culture in a broad sense: 'cultural values' is interpreted here as referring to widely shared norms of interaction in (rural) Indonesia, but the 'status and function of English' is also a subsystem of values in that particular context, and 'teachers' teaching practices', too (unless this refers to purely idiosyncratic variation) are to some extent shared by the teachers of this school, of this region, or perhaps more widely. The third factor, 'material conditions' clearly has a physical reality, but people's responses to similar material conditions also vary according to their shared cultural understandings of the circumstances they find themselves in. Lave (1988) distinguishes between the objective economic/physical context, which she calls the 'arena' for activity, and the subjective context (the 'setting') as created by individuals or groups through their interpretation of, selection from, and interaction with that arena.

The context for education and learning may be analysed in terms of scope; Bronfenbrenner (1979) considers the influences from 'microsystems' such as the school or peer group, up to 'macrosystems', which form the society or global context. On similar lines, McWilliam, Kruif and Zulli (2002) identify four 'contexts' within which a lesson or activity takes place, from more macro to more micro, but also linked to location in time:

> *environmental* context [e.g. state guidelines, size of classrooms, teacher's beliefs, parents' involvement ...], *planning* context [e.g. selection of materials, room arrangement, role of teacher, purpose of activities, ...], *approach* [to the interaction with the learners, e.g. observing, [framing] goals of the interaction, seizing teachable moments, responding to learner initiations, ...] and *interaction* [e.g. expanding, recasting and rephrasing learner behaviors, eliciting, questioning, use of verbal, material and physical prompts, ...] (McWilliam *et al.* 2002: 153).

A given learning activity therefore unfolds within these nested contexts, and is influenced by them in different ways.

As mentioned above, these contexts have more and less tangible aspects. Palfreyman (2006) looks at learning in terms of different types of 'resource': material resources (e.g. seating, computers, worksheets), social resources (e.g. the teacher, the students, visitors or recorded speakers) and discursive (cultural) resources (e.g. ideas about teacher and learner roles and appropriate behaviour/language use). These resources offer certain 'affordances' (potential uses), but teachers and learners will draw on them in varying ways. Furthermore, the interplay between these resources means that they are all, to some extent, 'cultural'; for example, the same materials may be engaging and useful for learners (or made so by the teacher) in one context, but inaccessible or meaningless in another context.

Finally, it should be noted that the 'shared patterns of behavior and associated meanings' referred to by Whitten and Hunter are not fixed from birth in all members of a group: they *become* shared to a greater or lesser extent over time, they are reaffirmed and evolve with time, and on particular occasions may be invoked or flouted by individuals for purposes of their own.

Culture and teaching

Culture is important in language teaching in various ways. Firstly, teaching a language usually involves (overtly or covertly) teaching a 'target culture'. This is visible in pragmatic aspects of language comprehension or production (e.g. LoCastro 2012), such as how to apologise appropriately (using language forms suitable to a particular context as understood with reference to a particular culture) as well as *when* to apologise (cultures differ as to when an apology is necessary at all). Efforts to teach these aspects of language (e.g. through a functional syllabus) assume some cultural frame of reference. Cultural meanings may be infused in texts and materials and, more subtly, in the way readers approach those texts and materials (e.g. Sellami 2006); such processes are one facet of intercultural (communicative) competence (Byram 1997): *the ability to communicate and operate effectively with people from another culture*. In all these cases, culture is part of the *content* of language teaching.

More broadly, effective teaching in any field is likely to draw on the teacher's awareness of culture and context, in that it involves mediating between the learners' own (culturally formed) understandings and the knowledge/skills to be learned. Awareness of learners' cultural background enables teachers to:

> select materials that are relevant to the students' experiences, to use pertinent examples or analogies drawn from the students' daily lives to introduce or clarify new concepts, to manage the classroom in ways that take into account cultural differences in interaction styles, and to use evaluation strategies that

maximize students' opportunities to display what they actually know in ways that are familiar to them (Villegas and Lucas 2002: 18).

Learning and teaching are conducted with reference to local (or sometimes imported) cultures of learning (Cortazzi and Jin 2013) or 'pedagogic cultures' (Palfreyman 2007). Considerable effort has been made to research these cultures from two main perspectives: a quantitative survey approach (e.g. Hofstede 1997; Joy and Kolb 2009) and an ethnographic approach (e.g. Coleman 1996; Holliday 1994). Both approaches have highlighted the existence of different types of culture (e.g. institutional culture, academic culture, peer group culture, as well as national culture) and have led to quests for 'cultural synergy' (Jin 1992), 'appropriate methodology' (Holliday 1994), or 'culturally responsive teaching' (Villegas and Lucas 2002).

Culture and teacher education

In recent years, with impetus from the 'sociocultural turn' in applied linguistics and language teaching, there has been a move to build on teachers' practical knowledge and to locate second language teacher education with reference both to local knowledge and to the broader context of education (Johnson 2006). If, as outlined above, teaching works via cultural mediation between the learners and what is to be taught, this role should be acquired by the teacher in the process of teacher education/development. Stanley and Murray (2013) discuss what kinds of knowledge or skill 'qualify' someone to teach English as a Foreign Language (EFL) in the modern world, and highlight the importance of teachers' intercultural competence in addition to knowledge of language and methodology. They point out that the intercultural element is often not directly addressed in teacher preparation courses, but that it may easily fit into existing frameworks; they cite, for example the following criteria used in the Cambridge Certificate in Teaching English to Speakers of Other Languages (CELTA):

1b) Teaching a class with an awareness of learning styles and cultural factors that may affect learning

1c) Acknowledging, when necessary, learners' backgrounds and previous learning experiences

1d) Establishing good rapport with learners and ensuring they are fully involved in learning activities

2c) Providing clear contexts and a communicative focus for language

2f) Showing awareness of differences in register (Cambridge ESOL 2010: 15–16).

Criteria 1b, 1c and 1d involve an awareness of learners' backgrounds and how to engage with these, although only the first explicitly mentions culture; criteria 2c and 2f implicitly invoke some cultural context with respect to which language can be communicatively appropriate or meaningful. While emphasising that cultural awareness fits naturally into these areas of teacher education, Stanley and Murray point out that 'there is little backwash pressure from assessment to make it integral' (2013: 112), resulting in its absence from many such courses. On the contrary, teacher socialisation through teacher training programmes in general tends to promote cultural 'invisibility' (Mahon 2006), whereby people are seen as 'learners' in the abstract, rather than as heterogeneous individuals in a particular context. Stanley and Murray further note that the increase in teachers (both 'native speakers' and 'non-native speakers') working outside their 'own' culture makes it all the more important not to take teachers' cultural awareness for granted: to some extent they need to be able to set aside cultural baggage (including that inculcated in training courses) and use their intercultural competence to adapt to new teaching contexts.

Culture and assessment

If teachers need to be aware of their teaching context and to be competent with respect to their context, how are these areas to be assessed? This leads us to broader cultural issues in the reliability and validity of assessment. The 'appropriate methodology' and 'culturally responsive teaching' movements mentioned above (Holliday 1994; Villegas and Lucas 2002) have prompted calls for greater understanding of how learning is assessed across different cultural contexts and ways to design, apply or adapt assessment in a context-sensitive way (Baumgart and Halse 1999; Johnston 2010; Slee 2010). This involves not only the ability to 'maximize [...] opportunities to display what [learners or teachers] actually know in ways that are familiar to them' (Villegas and Lucas 2002), but also an understanding of assessment as a socio-cultural context in itself (Filer 2000). Any assessment is a social encounter between an assessor, who brings various frameworks and assumptions with her, and an assessment candidate, who has to relate to his context in a way that makes sense both to himself and to the assessor.

Cambridge ESOL's *Broadening the Cultural Context* initiative (Murray 2007) was one effort to ensure that widely dispersed assessment materials are accessible, meaningful and fair (and so more likely to be reliable in a range of contexts). Key points from this initiative included:

1. It should not be assumed that candidates are knowledgeable about, or interested in, British culture.
2. Texts and other task input material should not assume that candidates enjoy the lifestyles of particular income groups or nationalities.
3. Exam materials should be drawn from as wide a range of sources as possible, including examples of non-British English.
4. Good exam materials are often drawn from sources that have the widest possible original target audience. Where cultural assumptions might impede understanding, materials should be edited to gloss or, if necessary, remove cultural allusions or references.
5. Assumptions should not be made about a candidate's location, cultural background and/or lifestyle (Murray 2007: 20–21, numbering added).

The above points focus on cultural *assumptions* in materials (in either texts or tasks), which could affect the assessment of candidates' language skills such as inference in reading, or the quality/quantity of response to a picture in a speaking task. Point 3 refers directly to *language*, and point 2 to *economic* inequalities. There is a concern overall for *generality* (particularly to avoid being restricted to the specifically British provenance of the Cambridge English exams) and to provide a wide *range* of input material (points 3 and 4). Note that these latter two points illustrate a balance to be struck between including a range of specific language varieties (3) and editing out culturally specific assumptions/references (4). Indeed, 'widest possible [...] target audience' these days might allow, for example, superficial knowledge of Manchester United football team, Superman or Harry Potter: icons with a Western provenance which have become widespread in global media and discourse. Note that the points above do not focus on the *criteria* for assessment, which may also need to take account of cultural norms in order to be seen as valid (Young 2002).

In teaching and teacher education, a distinction should be made between appropriate purposes for education and appropriate means for achieving those purposes:

> Policy makers and practitioners, under pressure to reform, too often concentrate on identifying 'surface similarities' and assume that what has been done successfully over there would produce similar outcomes here [...] Adopting policies, theories and practices across cultures without recognizing their distinctive historical and cultural dimensions risks 'false universalism' (Nguyen, Terlouw and Pilot 2006: 3–4).

This 'false universalism' consists in treating particular teaching techniques or approaches as universal without questioning the assumptions embedded in them. A more culturally responsive approach is to identify overall goals which may be considered widely relevant (such as to engage learners in the learning process or to prepare them for their likely future life), and to look to the local context for resources to build locally relevant ways of (a) making these goals more specific and (b) achieving them (Holliday 1994). The challenge for the teacher is therefore to draw on locally available and locally appropriate means to achieve these goals, while not being limited by the arena in which she finds herself: 'respond[ing] to features of local context in a critical, rather than a routine and passive fashion' (Hunter 2013: 480). This may involve using locally established ways of teaching and learning, or selective use of 'new' methods; it may also involve reframing the learning situation in a locally meaningful but innovative way. One example of this last possibility is Coleman's (1987) experiment in reframing language lessons in Indonesia from the locally established 'teaching spectacle' (where learners sit and listen) to a 'learning festival' (where learners participate and interact with each other): this adapts the locally established idea of a 'festival' to an educational purpose, reconfiguring teacher and learner roles using available cultural resources.

The assessment of teaching aims in the Cambridge English Diploma in Teaching English to Speakers of Other Languages (Delta) focuses on underlying, relatively 'context-neutral' purposes of teaching, with the teacher choosing means and techniques to address these which are appropriate to the local context:

> The teaching will take place within a wide variety of contexts across the range of approved Delta Module Two providers and so uniformity in delivery is not

expected. There will be variation in teaching style relative to individuals and the teaching contexts in which they are operating (Cambridge English 2014: 65).

The Delta criteria are expressed in keeping with this principle, e.g.:

> (6a) teach the class as a group and individuals within the group, with sensitivity to the learners' needs and backgrounds, level and context, providing equal opportunities for participation.
> (7a) use language which is accurate and appropriate for the teaching and learning context.

These two criteria refer explicitly to the local cultural and social context, while criterion 9b ('manage the classroom space, furniture, equipment, materials and resources'), for example, refers to the physical context. Other criteria use the word 'appropriately' (e.g. '(6d) listen and respond appropriately to learner contributions') or 'suitably' ('(8c) deliver a coherent and suitably varied lesson'), which suggest a link to context. For each criterion the Delta Handbook suggests a range of means (not exhaustive) which might be used for achieving it.

Note, however, that criteria using words such as 'appropriate' may not specify the terms of reference of this word: in the 'appropriate methodology' framework this would mean 'appropriate to the usual learning and teaching context of this class', but it could also be interpreted as 'appropriate to the *assessor's* frame of reference'. Similarly, in relation to the criterion for post-lesson reflection 'identify key strengths and weaknesses in planning and execution (10b)', one might ask 'key for whom, in terms of what?'. This leads us to the issue of the assessment itself as a social context.

Activity Theory (Engeström, Miettinen and Punamäki 1999) views any participation by a person in an activity as involving a *subject* (the person participating in the activity), an *object* (or 'goal') and *mediational means* (such as words, documents or physical props) which the person uses or engages with to try and achieve the goal. This takes place within the context of a *community* with associated *rules* of participation and engagement, as well as expectations about roles: the *division of labour* for example between a teacher and students. This framework is particularly helpful in cases where participants with different frames of reference are *co-constructing* an activity. For example, an externally assessed lesson observation can be seen as co-constructed by a teacher, a group of students (who may be more or less heterogeneous) and an assessor; each of these participants may be seen as a subject, and is likely to have a different goal and make use of different mediational means, with reference to different communities, rules and divisions of labour. Thus teachers have one goal with reference to the students and the classroom community (for them to learn) and another with respect to the assessor: to show themselves as competent teachers, in line with the *teachers'* understanding of the assessor's criteria. In addition, of course, teachers and learners (and sometimes the assessor) also orient to norms of the broader local community (e.g. to maintain respect from peers/ others). Ideally, all these goals will coincide, and will further match the criteria and indicators that the assessor is *actually* using to judge the lesson; however, there is ample potential for (perceived) mismatch, hence 'it is understood and understandable that teaching under assessment conditions can be potentially stressful for both candidates and learners alike' (Cambridge English 2014: 65).

Context and focus of this study

In this study I will focus on data from externally assessed lesson observations for the Cambridge Delta. These observations are relatively self-contained events which aim to assess teachers' procedural knowledge (as opposed to written coursework, including the 'background essay' which accompanies the Delta observed lessons and elicits teachers' declarative knowledge on the topic area). The external assessment is a single lesson observation by a trained assessor (in all cases included here a British native speaker) who must not be acquainted with the teachers and their work: it is a summative assessment, which aims to apply standards objectively; it supplements the internal observations by teachers' regular Delta tutors, which combine standards with formative assessment of teaching.

The data analysed here consists of a sample of external assessors' reports, written by a number of different assessors, mainly on lessons in the United Kingdom (UK) and the United Arab Emirates (UAE), a small oil state in the Persian/Arabian Gulf. 80% of the UAE's population are expatriates: lessons in the UAE may involve teachers and (in private institutions) various mixes of students from the UAE itself, from other Arab countries, from the West and from the Indian Subcontinent, as well as other backgrounds. Classes in state institutions are usually single-gender and include only local students.

The sample analysed here comprises:

- all reports from external assessments in the United Arab Emirates in 2010–2012 (N=62, of which 31 were by male teachers)
- a sample from assessments in the UK during the same period (N=44, of which 20 were male), taken in equal proportions from a private language school, a college of further education and a university context.
- a smaller number of reports from the UK and other countries in the Gulf/Subcontinent, flagged by Cambridge English as referring to cultural factors (N=9).

Each report consists of a form which is completed by the assessor with information about the candidate and the lesson (e.g. name, Delta centre, the topic chosen, the level of the class and number of students) and comments about the lesson and associated documentation provided by the candidate. These associated documents comprise:

- a pre-lesson plan: this includes information about the students, an outline of the planned lesson and its aims, and a commentary which gives a rationale for the lesson
- a post-lesson reflection: in this the candidate reflects on the strengths and weaknesses of the lesson as it was taught, and how the learning in this lesson could be followed up in the future.

The candidate also provides a Background Essay which analyses a broader area of language, learning and teaching within which the lesson fits (e.g. developing learners' knowledge of phrasal verbs). Since this study is focusing on the lesson itself, I will consider only the sections of the report dealing with the plan, the lesson and the reflection.

This data set was anonymised and analysed both quantitatively and qualitatively. Quantitative analysis involved counts of information about the lesson and the assessment, insofar as this could be read or inferred from the Delta 5a form and accompanying information: the location of the lesson, the grade awarded and the teachers' ethnicity and gender (inferred from their names: see below). Qualitative analysis involved detailed reading, coding and comparison of the assessors' comments on various aspects of the lessons, focusing on explicit reference to cultural issues (relatively rare, as explained below), and also on implicit references or assumptions suggested by the comments.

There are certain limitations imposed by the nature of the dataset. Firstly, we see only the assessor's perspective on the lessons, with no direct teacher (or student) perspective. However, we do see the assessor's comments on the teacher's plan and reflection, which provide a more rounded impression of the teacher's approach to the lesson. Secondly, demographic information is limited to that on the Delta 5a form. For example, the teacher's ethnicity and gender are not indicated, so I made an informed guess about these from the teacher's name; the most represented ethnic groups inferred in this way are referred to here as 'Anglo' (26 reports in the UAE, 23 in the UK), 'Arab' (20 UAE reports) and 'Eastern European' (8 UK reports). Contextual information on the form is limited to the centre with which the candidate is preparing for the Delta: information about the context of the lesson itself (e.g. the location, the type of institution, the age of students) can be gleaned only as mentioned by the assessor's comments. Although this restricts what we can know about the physical/cultural *arena* of the lesson, we do gain a picture of the *setting* as perceived by assessors and their views of the teacher's responses to the environment.

Findings and discussion

I will now analyse assessors' comments in the sample reports, according to the assessment criteria invoked by the assessor (see Appendix B, pages 435–438). None of the Delta criteria refer explicitly to culture, but categories 5 (lesson planning and preparation), 6 (classroom atmosphere) and 7 (language) refer to 'context', and assessors' comments on categories 5 and 6 included the majority of their comments focusing explicitly on culture. I will focus primarily on these three assessment categories; I will also consider how culture plays an implicit part in the assessment of these categories, and of other lesson assessment categories which do not explicitly refer to context.

Lesson planning and preparation

The assessment criteria in category 5 for the Delta practical assignments focus on the teacher's lesson plan, which includes lesson aims, an outline of lesson stages, a commentary giving a rationale for these stages and other information about the learners and the lesson. In contrast to the cross-cultural testing situation involved in the *Broadening the cultural context* initiative described above, the teacher is expected to tailor the lesson to learners in context, for example teaching British idioms with learners living in the UK. Comments for criterion 5 indicate how the teacher has taken contextual (including cultural) factors into account in *planning* the lesson, although it also inevitably links with aspects of the lesson itself which are assessed in other criteria.

As suggested by Stanley and Murray (2013), cultural awareness is not a focal area in EFL teaching courses, and overt comments on this aspect of observations are rare in this data, indicating that it is not a major issue for the assessors. However, the comments which do occur were almost all in reference to category 5 (lesson planning) or category 6 (classroom atmosphere — see next section). For example, one assessor points out the Eurocentric assumptions underlying the context planned for the use of adjectives:

> It's interesting that one of the topics in the freer speaking activity is 'seeing people eat with their hands': most of her learners come from cultures where this is normal practice, so I'm not sure which adjective she expect[s] the students to use. (UAE)

This comment highlights how cultural assumptions can shape lesson tasks and expected responses; it is reminiscent of the considerations in the Cambridge ESOL *Broadening the Cultural Context* initiative mentioned earlier. Note that although the comment focuses on the teacher's cultural awareness, it relies on the assessor's awareness (or perception) of the students' cultural expectations. Since the teacher in question appears to be of Arab background, the assessor's point relates presumably not to a lack of cultural knowledge per se, but to thinking through the implications of materials selected.

Although candidates do refer to culture in their assignments, their cultural awareness appears to be sometimes tenuous; assessors comment on confusion in this area of lesson planning. One assessor notes that:

> [The candidate] refers to authentic culturally appropriate material but lists a range of adapted source book materials. (UAE)

This appears to be an example of the candidate knowing (declaratively) that culturally appropriate material is supposed to be a good thing, but being unable to implement this in her plan or lesson. This disconnect between declarative and procedural knowledge is a common issue in various aspects of teacher learning. Regarding another candidate in the UK, an assessor points out that the assumptions stated in the lesson plan are:

> very questionable [...] and contradict his [background] essay. The candidate assumes that the learners, who are from different cultures, tell anecdotes in their L1 and respond in a similar way as native speakers. Yet in [his essay] he argues that the importance of shared knowledge when telling anecdotes is culturally specific. (UK)

Like the preceding comment, this highlights a lack of thinking through cultural issues thoroughly, with consequent lack of clarity in lesson planning. In this case, the comment homes in on the teacher's understanding of the pragmatics of how anecdotes are used in conversation.

One aspect of the context referred to in comments on lesson plans is the teacher's awareness of the learners' previous learning experience. This sometimes relates to learners' needs, if they are lacking or strong in some aspect of language or learning:

> ... good coverage of the learners' previous learning experience and hence weakness in grammar. (UAE)

The above comment would inform the aims of the lesson; in other cases, the teacher may demonstrate awareness of learners' expectations and preferences, and the likely consequences of these for the methodology to be used. For example, one plan discusses:

> ... relevant problems that learners could potentially have with the lesson (e.g. [...] resistance to using pen and paper. (UAE)

In some cases assessors commented on the *lack* of such information in the plan, for example:

> Much more information about the individual learners needed to be provided. Information about their learning styles would have been important: many of them are obviously not used to communicative language teaching and have particular learning styles and views about what they like to do in the classroom. (UAE)

In this comment, 'learning styles' (which could elsewhere be interpreted as an individual, cognitive concept) seems to refer to something more cultural: learned preferences, shared by many of the learners, as to what learning in a classroom involves. The use of the word 'obviously' here refers to evidence observed during the lesson which has made the observer aware of this lack of information in the plan; it reminds us that the report form is written after the lesson has been observed. Although the assessor does not say that 'communicative language teaching' is preferable to the 'particular learning styles' of the class, comments such as this resonate with a broader discourse of modernity (CLT) versus entrenched and unhelpful learner habits (Holliday 1994; Palfreyman 2005).

Almost all of the above examples come from reports on lessons in the UAE, where cultural and other aspects of students' background were more salient in assessors' comments. However, one report from the UK comments explicitly (although tentatively) on the teacher's cultural awareness regarding specific learners. The focus in this case is the lesson content: a topic which the assessor considers could be culturally inappropriate:

> the [lesson] scenario included a situation which could be sensitive to some of the learners and indication was needed in terms of whether this had been considered — an assumption was made that the example of footballers fighting over who they had slept with would not be problematic. Evidence was needed if this was the assumption, as it could potentially be an issue. (UK)

This comment expresses the assessor's concern about the topic as 'sensitive' for the learners, in terms of lesson planning and justification. The assessor feels that this topic could be problematic, but acknowledges that it may not be; this is reconciled by pointing out that the teacher should at least provide evidence. In the UK context it is perhaps more difficult than in the UAE to be sure what is culturally problematic, because this lesson is after all based on an authentic news text of general readership in the host society; furthermore the range of cultures in the class, as well as their acculturation to mainstream British media and discourse, is likely to be variable. Above all, the assessor has not met the class at the time of reading the plan, and may have limited opportunity even in the lesson to see how the learners respond to it. The following comment on the lesson as a whole reveals how the assessor's quandary on this point continues after the lesson:

> The lesson would have been a much stronger lesson if […] a less culturally risky context had been identified […]. However the context did seem to be accepted

by most if not all of the students. Nevertheless, in one case it was difficult to assess whether one of the more conservative learners was withdrawing because of lower proficiency, or through being unable to identify with the context. There were a lot of learners from the Middle East in this class.

Note that the final sentence here (as in the comment above about the plan) leaves the reader to infer that learners from the Middle East are likely to be offended or at least unwilling to engage with this topic — although the group as a whole seems to have 'accepted' the topic.

Overall it appears that cultural awareness per se is not typically an issue on which assessors comment in lesson plans (although those overt comments which are made tend to be in this area of the assessment). However, 'previous learning experience' or 'learning styles' may be mentioned and linked implicitly to the learners' cultural background. Judgements of this kind are particularly difficult in the case of external observations because the assessor has limited contact with the learners. Furthermore, especially in a pluralistic society like the UK, assessors may find it hard to pick apart considerations of different cultures interacting within and outside the classroom. One approach is to require that teachers justify their cultural assumptions and that they be consistent in how they discuss and apply cultural considerations in their discussion of teaching decisions.

Classroom atmosphere

The criteria in category 6 for the Delta practical assignments focus on 'creating and maintaining an atmosphere conducive to learning', and (like the other categories discussed below) apply to the lesson itself. Criterion 6a focuses on the teacher's 'sensitivity to the learners' needs and backgrounds, level and context, providing equal opportunities for participation', while the other criteria in this section relate to engagement with and motivation of learners in response to their needs in the lesson.

As mentioned earlier, most overt comments about cultural factors are made under either category 5 (lesson planning) or category 6 (classroom atmosphere). Comments about classroom atmosphere reflect how cultural knowledge or accommodation can contribute to affective aspects of lessons. In some cases, assessors mention the teacher's 'insider knowledge' as an asset in building rapport and engagement with the learners:

The candidate is a peer and colleague of the class members. He knows them well, their culture, motivations and levels. He had an encouraging manner and went out of his way to avoid loss of face. All learners were engaged and participated diligently. (UAE)

Learners were engaged and involved throughout; [the candidate] used his knowledge of L1 and of local culture (e.g. football teams and singers) [...] which led to a high level of motivation [...]. (UAE)

In both these cases the candidate is an Arab teaching in the UAE, and the assessor has identified a connection between the candidate's local cultural knowledge and engagement of learners through teaching style (in the first case) or content (in the second). In the first, the teacher appears to be a work colleague of the students in the class, and so has very specific contextual knowledge; in the second case the teacher was older than the students but shared cultural knowledge about the UAE and the Arab world, as well as being of the same gender as the all-male class.

In other cases, the assessor's comments highlight the candidate's role as a knowledgeable or sensitive *out*sider. The following two comments in the UAE context both relate to Western teachers working with Gulf Arab learners of the opposite gender, and refer to ways of balancing a positive teaching manner with a distance appropriate to the context:

[The female candidate ...] demonstrate[ed] an encouraging and businesslike manner appropriate to a class full of military males of this level in this context.

The teacher created a positive working atmosphere, brisk and focused but encouraging and responsive, with sensitivity to his role as a male teacher in this female Gulf Arab class, e.g. getting a successful student to share an 'air five' (high five without physical contact).

These comments illustrate how 'an atmosphere conducive to learning' can be created and maintained in various ways depending on the context: sometimes by reference to local topics (e.g. football teams and singers — see above — or even the staff of the local teaching centre) and sometimes with reference to globally promoted topics such as the UK royal wedding; sometimes through informality and sometimes by maintaining a polite distance, indicated in locally significant ways.

In addition to the overt references to culture above, the wording of assessors' comments reveals something of their expectations about classroom culture. Holliday (1994) notes how the term 'learner' (used in much academic discourse about education, and throughout the Delta criteria) references a cognitive perspective and tends to connote an abstract, decontextualised figure, whereas 'student' refers to a *social* role and tends to be used in a more specific, located sense by teachers or other practitioners. In line with this distinction, in this sample more of the assessments (53%) used the word 'students' in the 'classroom atmosphere' category than in any other, in contrast to the more predominant use of 'learner' in other sections of the reports, especially in comments addressed to the moderator.

The question of what assessors look for as evidence of this rather subjective assessment category casts light on some cultural considerations in lesson observation. For example, *rapport* was mentioned mainly as a positive feature of the lessons. Evidence of rapport included use of students' names, enthusiasm, praise and signs of relaxation in students and/ or teacher (all admittedly quite subjective indicators). Lack of rapport was less commonly commented on, but the few cases of this (including a mix of ethnicities) were mainly male teachers in the UAE, with one female teacher in the UK. Lack of rapport was evidenced by addressing the students in a general way such as 'ladies' (in a lesson in the UAE) or in a patronising way (in a UK lesson), or by failing to respond to questions or other action by students. However, consider the following comment by an assessor on a lesson by a female Anglo teacher in the UAE:

> Continually addressing the group as 'girls' created distance between herself and the group. They are not children. (UAE)

The first part of this comment could mean that addressing the group (as opposed to individuals) had a negative effect on rapport; but the final comment suggests that it is the word 'girls' that the assessor felt was inappropriate. This may well have been the case; however, as noted earlier 'appropriacy' assumes a norm for interaction, which may vary from culture to culture or person to person; it also assumes a stance with respect to those norms (i.e. often embracing them, but participants could also often reject norms or caricature them). The term 'girls' (and its Arabic equivalent, *banaat*) is widely used by teachers and students to address/refer to young/ unmarried female students in the Gulf, is treated as normal, or even expected, by students, and need not indicate a patronising attitude.

Another aspect of teaching style which interacts with rapport is signalled by comments about 'respect', 'authority', 'control' or 'direction'. For example:

> There was a feeling the learners were doing the tasks because they were expected to and respected the teacher rather than that they understood their purpose. (UAE)

This comment mentions respect for the teacher apparently as a positive factor, but one which can disempower learners. Note also how the phrase 'there was a feeling' is used here, removing the assessor him/herself from the picture and representing the classroom atmosphere as self-evident. The tension between control and freedom is reflected in various turns of phrase in assessors' comments, such as:

> She maintained control and authority without being authoritarian. (UAE)

Here 'authority' is clearly a positive point, while being 'authoritarian' suggests that the lesson is 'teacher directed' — a phrase used in various reports in a pejorative sense. The lack of authority is commented on in another assessment as a problem:

> In her attempt to maintain a friendly atmosphere with the students I think the candidate lost sight of the fact that she was teaching a lesson which required discipline, order and control. (UAE — female Anglo teacher)

Thus authority and control have two faces: in some cases the positive, structuring aspect is commented on positively by assessors, and in others the disempowering aspect is focused upon. Both faces, however, are associated with an archetypal teacher role, as illustrated in this contrasting pair of comments:

> Reasonable rapport, albeit a bit 'teachery' (UK; female teacher of Indian ancestry)
>
> [The candidate]'s manner was pleasant, efficient and 'teacherly'. (UAE; female Arab/Muslim teacher)

Interestingly, two different words are coined here to reflect two attitudes to the teacher's authority: 'teachery' is a little negative, distancing the assessor slightly from traditional connotations, while 'teacherly' is used to invoke the proper fulfilment of a social role. It may be significant that the former was written by an assessor in the UK context, while the latter was by an assessor in the UAE.

The points above illustrate how qualities of teaching, especially those in the affective area of 'classroom atmosphere' are culturally implicated: demonstrating success in this area involves a performance by the teacher which takes into account both the learners' and the assessor's ideas of what such an atmosphere is and how it is appropriately created and maintained. The following vignette (male Arab teacher in the UAE; assessor from abroad) combines some of these considerations, showing how the assessor constructs an impression of the pedagogical culture of the classroom and of the teacher's skills through observation of interaction between teacher, students and their environment:

> 6a/d) The teacher was obviously very, very nervous and this manifested itself in a fairly frantic (and possibly uncharacteristic) speaking style where [students] were continuously told to hurry up and finish as they were 'slow' or 'lazy, lazy, lazy', but in a fairly good humoured way. The [students] just smiled sweetly when he did this (though the assessor found it a little unnerving) and he did give praise here and there. [...]
>
> 6c) The class took place in a large lecture hall with tiered seats, presumably in order to use one of the few smart boards available in [the institution]. This meant that much of the time, the class was teacher fronted, as the [teacher] manipulated the computer. However he did put [students] in pairs/[groups] at different stages but the grouping meant that he had to run from one side of the lecture hall to the other to cater for the [groups] huddled there (see 9c below).

In terms of Activity Theory, this teacher sees himself as an assessment candidate facing an assessor, and feels nervous in this role. Special preparations to deal with this situation include using a special room to enable use of a smart board, but this also restricts regrouping. The teacher's nervousness as a candidate affects his role as a teacher, exaggerating a humorous 'scolding' style with the students, which on more comfortable occasions perhaps contributes to rapport but in these circumstances gives a bad impression to the assessor. The students address the goal of saving the teacher's 'face' by responding good-humouredly to his scolding (suggesting that maintaining a harmonious classroom atmosphere is important to them).

Language use and awareness

The criteria in category 7 focus on 'understanding, knowledge and explanation of language and language skills'. Criteria 7a and 7b deal with the teacher's own use of language, relating this to the local teaching context and to the level of the learners in the class; 7c and 7d address information about language provided by the teacher; and 7e, the teacher's ability to respond to learners' emergent language in the lesson.

A key issue in the development of EFL teacher professionalism has been the status and competences of native English-speaking teachers (NESTs) and of non-native English-speaking teachers (NNESTs). These terms themselves smack of discrimination against NNESTs, and several authors (e.g. Braine 1999; Llurda 2005; Reeves 2009) have emphasised the potential advantages which NNESTs may enjoy (e.g. familiarity with the process of language learning, analytical knowledge about the second language, often a knowledge of their students' first language), in counterbalance to the accuracy, appropriacy and range assumed to be inherent in native speaker language.

The Delta criteria use the term 'language' to mean accuracy in or about English — the learners' second language (L2) (or perhaps L3 or L4) — and the reports tend to go along with this assumption. Errors in the teacher's 'language' are noted on several occasions in reports on lessons by teachers with non-Anglo surnames (mainly Arab candidates in the UAE and Eastern Europeans in the UK), and included errors in speech and on the whiteboard, as well as in materials. However, Anglo teachers were not immune to this, especially in spelling on the whiteboard, where things are often written 'on the fly'.

Of course, 'language' is implicated with culture and context, and includes much more than accuracy, and much more than English. However, comments about appropriacy, for example, tended not to link this to any explicit frame of reference (e.g. a particular target register or a local variety) but to general 'awkwardness' of language. Just one comment, on the language of an Arab teacher in a Gulf country, highlights the issue of local norms and 'World Englishes' (Kachru, Kachru and Nelson 2009):

> The only weakness was her own English, which [was] a problem for me but apparently not for the learners.

It seems that in this case the teacher's language is 'appropriate for the teaching and learning context' in the sense that it is comprehensible to the teacher's addressees, although putting a strain on an outside listener. It is mentioned as a weakness because it is not culturally 'neutral' (see Murray 2007), although it is unmarked in the local context, and so presumably fulfils Delta criterion 7a.

One potential advantage for NNESTs is that they often share their learners' L1 and so could make use of this knowledge to anticipate problems or to clarify misunderstandings. However, linguistic benefits of this sort were not highlighted in the assessors' comments; in general, use of L1 was mentioned in the assessors' reports only as a sign of student disengagement (category 6) or confusion (categories 8 or 9). However, one example of positive use of L1 genre knowledge was cited when an Arab teacher in the UAE showed the cover and key pages of a popular Arabic language magazine in order to elicit expectations of the magazine interview genre, which were then applied to predicting organisation and content of an English magazine interview. The focus here was not on L1 itself, and students were not expected to read Arabic text; rather the magazine was shown from a distance to activate schemata with a familiar exemplar of layout, fonts and other overall features of the genre.

Overall, it seems that language tended to be cited as a shortcoming in lessons (in contrast with criteria in category 6 such as rapport, which tended rather to be commended). In the case of NNESTs, criticisms tended to focus on production errors and in the case of NESTs, on disfluent or ungraded use or explanation of language; but both kinds of problem could be observed in both groups of teachers. There are signs of potential for beneficial use of L1 for particular purposes, but these are rarely mentioned by assessors.

Classroom procedures and other criteria

The criteria in category 8 focus on 'Classroom procedures and techniques'. This includes the exploitation of techniques and materials to support learning and address emergent needs in a varied way.

In a number of cases culture was mentioned as a resource for contextualising language and skills and making them relevant to learners' experience and schemata. For example, in asking questions to check understanding of vocabulary:

check[ing] understanding of […] 'freedom': 'Do prisoners have freedom? (No) Do you have freedom to go out at night? (No)' — the latter being an appropriate answer for Bedouin girls. (UAE)

When the learners come from a variety of cultures, this can be exploited for information gaps, e.g.:

> An excellent open discussion at the end of the lesson, about how we treat our old people, in Saudi, UK, Japan. (UAE)

On the other hand affective gaps can become too big (see the 'sleeping around' example discussed in the section on classroom atmosphere) and cultural background information may not be supplied as needed:

> 'Service' was introduced for use in the collocation 'wedding service' (meaning the church event — possibly culturally unfamiliar to many of the students). (UAE)

In this case, the nature of a cultural event in the 'target culture' (if not the general concept of a wedding) is seen as needing clarification with learners for whom a wedding involves quite different places, activities and roles.

Another way in which culture is significant in relation to classroom techniques is in particular cultures of learning (Cortazzi and Jin 2013). Even different kinds of institution in the same country may have different cultures of learning, and these may impinge on each other, especially in a classroom where teachers are enacting their professional development. In the following comment, the assessor places the lesson (a single event and the assessor's single experience of this candidate's teaching) within an imagined process of cultural transformation:

> The candidate effectively encouraged self- and peer-editing — which are valuable for developing learner autonomy and probably quite new to these students [...]. The teacher consciously played a facilitator role during most of the lesson [...]. The students were engaged (though subdued) and proud to read out their best phrases from their postcards. This student-centred approach is to be applauded in a context where most teaching is highly didactic 'chalk and talk'. (UAE)

Although the UAE is a multicultural environment, based on personal experience of the local context as a teacher, teacher educator and observer, the assessor has identified a coherent local pedagogical culture (with a ready-made term, 'chalk and talk'), and sees this lesson not just on its own merits, but also as a valuable step in innovating in this context. In the UK context, on the other hand, comments like this tend to be phrased as about a particular class rather than about a cultural context.

One final example, concerning an Arab teacher in a Gulf country, illustrates the interaction in the classroom of learner, teacher and assessor expectations, technology and modernity:

Personally I would have preferred [the teacher] to deliver a more traditional lesson as this would suit her teaching style better. The students really respect [her] and expect her to deliver a conventional lesson. However she dealt very well with the IWB [interactive whiteboard], the strips of paper, the frequent ICQs [instruction check questions].

Here we see the assessor taking into account the expectations of students, as well as the teacher's change from addressing these expectations to addressing those perhaps promoted in her Delta course. Technological, physical and interactional resources ('the IWB, the strips of paper, the frequent ICQs') are listed together as cultural props of the teaching style which the teacher and the assessor seem to see as desirable. This shows how the culture of learning is visible not only in the procedures of the lesson (assessment category 8) but also the management of material and other aspects of the context (assessment category 9).

Teacher reflection, too (assessment category 10), may be viewed as a cultural practice, associated with a particular professional culture which influences practice in various countries around the world, as well as having links to 'Western' discourses (Boud and Walker 1998; Cameron 2000). It is beyond the scope of this chapter to analyse this in depth. However, it was noticeable that assessors' comments on this category, as perhaps is inevitable given the assessor's role as a one-time visitor, tended to focus on the extent to which the teacher commented on the weaknesses in the lesson perceived by the assessor, and made little reference to culture and context.

To conclude this section, it appears that cultural knowledge (both local and less local, shared or shareable) is an invaluable element of context, which is in turn a keystone of communicative teaching. The difference between effective and less effective teaching lies in the awareness with which this cultural knowledge is identified, invoked and mediated by the teacher. In addition, teaching approaches themselves are shaped by professional, educational and other cultures, and are often hybrids or sites of struggle or development.

Conclusion

The concern of this chapter is with the role of culture in the assessment of teaching. Culture seems to have roles at a variety of levels:

- Cultural awareness is an important component of a teacher's skill set. Although culture is often rendered 'invisible' in teacher education courses (Mahon 2006), it appears in assessment of teaching via the notions of 'previous learning experience', 'learner expectations and schemata' and so on. Greater awareness raising and rigour would help teachers and assessors to understand the cultural demands put upon students, as well as the cultural resources available for teaching.
- Assessors (and teachers) should bear in mind that an assessment is a performance as well as a learning event. Assessors who observe lessons in a variety of contexts may, through discussion with other assessors and tutors, become used to looking through the surface of teaching to the underlying aims and the local resources which add up to good teaching in a particular context.
- Language is inextricably linked with culture, and teaching involves mediating between the host culture of the learners and the culture/language of an L2 community to which learners (may) aspire — although this community is not necessarily a national one such as the UK. Into this mediation process both NESTs and NNESTs bring strengths and needs of which observers and assessors should be cognisant, and regarding which they should be ready to comment and (in formative contexts) give feedback.
- Assessors and tutors should consider the cultures of learning and teaching with reference to which teachers and learners make sense of lessons and activities. Development in teaching may consist in teaching in a different way, or in teaching in a similar way but with a richer awareness.

References

Baumgart, N. and Halse, C. (1999) Approaches to learning across cultures: The role of assessment, *Assessment in Education* 6 (3), 321–339.

Boud, D. and Walker, D. (1998) Promoting reflection in professional courses: The challenge of context, *Studies in Higher Education* 23 (2), 191–206.

Braine, G. (1999) *Non-native educators in English Language Teaching*. Mahwah: Lawrence Erlbaum Associates.

Bronfenbrenner, U. (1979) *The Ecology of Human Development: Experiments by Nature and Design*. Cambridge: Harvard University Press.

Byram, M. (1997) *Teaching and Assessing Intercultural Communicative Competence*. Clevedon: Multilingual Matters.

Cambridge English (2014) *Delta Module One, Module Two, Module Three: Handbook for Tutors and Candidates*. Cambridge: Cambridge English Language Assessment.

Cambridge ESOL (2010) *CELTA Syllabus and Assessment Guidelines*. Cambridge: Cambridge ESOL.

Cameron, D. (2000) *Good to Talk? Living and Working in a Communication Culture*. London: Sage.

Coleman, H. (1987) Teaching spectacles and learning festivals, *ELT Journal* 41 (2), 97–103.

Coleman, H. (Ed) (1996) *Society and the Language Classroom*. Cambridge: Cambridge University Press.

Cortazzi, M. and Jin, L. (Eds) (2013) *Researching Cultures of Learning: International Perspectives on Language Learning and Education*. Basingstoke: Palgrave Macmillan.

Engeström Y., Miettinen R. and Punamäki, R-L. (1999) *Perspectives on Activity Theory*. Cambridge: Cambridge University Press.

Filer, A. (2000) *Assessment: Social Practice and Social Product*. London: Routledge Falmer.

Hofstede, G. (1997) *Cultures and Organizations: Software of the Mind*. London: McGraw-Hill.

Holliday, A. (1994) *Appropriate Methodology and Social Context*. London: Longman.

Hunter, D. (2013) Context as solution: A step too far? *ELT Journal* 67 (4), 475–481.

Jin, L. (1992) Academic cultural expectations and second language use: Chinese postgraduate students in the UK: A cultural synergy model, unpublished PhD thesis, University of Leicester.

Johnson, K. E. (2006) The sociocultural turn and its challenges for second language teacher education, *TESOL Quarterly* 40 (1), 235–257.

Johnston, P. M. G. (2010) Towards culturally appropriate assessment? A contribution to the debates, *Higher Education Quarterly* 64 (3), 231–245.

Joy, S. and Kolb, D. A. (2009) Are there cultural differences in learning style? *International Journal of Intercultural Relations* 33 (1), 69–85.

Kachru, B., Kachru, Y. and Nelson, C. (2009) *The Handbook of World Englishes*. London: John Wiley and Sons.

Lave, J. (1988) *Cognition in Practice: Mind, Mathematics and Culture in Everyday Life*. Cambridge: Cambridge University Press.

Llurda, E. (Ed) (2005) *Non-native Language Teachers: Perceptions, Challenges and Contributions to the Profession*. New York: Springer.

LoCastro, V. (2012) *Pragmatics for Language Educators: A Sociolinguistic Perspective*. New York: Routledge.

Mahon, J. (2006) Under the invisibility cloak? Teacher understanding of cultural difference, *Intercultural Education* 17 (4), 391–405.

McWilliam, R. A., de Kruif, R. E. L. and Zulli, R.A. (2002) The observed construction of teaching: Four contexts, *Journal of Research in Childhood Education*, 16 (2), 148–161.

Murray, S. (2007) Broadening the cultural context of examination materials, *Research Notes* 27, 19–22.

Nguyen P., Terlouw, C. and Pilot, A. (2006) Culturally appropriate pedagogy: The case of group learning in a Confucian Heritage Culture context, *Intercultural Education* 17 (1), 1–19.

Palfreyman, D. M. (2005) Othering in an English language program, *TESOL Quarterly* 39 (2), 211–233.

Palfreyman, D. M. (2006) Social context and resources for language learning, *System* 34 (3), 352–370.

Palfreyman, D. M. (2007) Introduction: Learning and teaching across cultures in higher education, in Palfreyman, D. M. and McBride, D. L. (Eds) *Learning and Teaching Across Cultures in Higher Education*. Basingstoke: Palgrave Macmillan, 1–8.

Pasassung, N. (2003) Teaching English in an "acquisition-poor environment": An ethnographic example of a remote Indonesian EFL classroom, PhD thesis, University of Sydney, available online: www.languageonthemove.com/wp-content/uploads/2013/01/Pasassung_English-language-learning-in-Indonesia.pdf

Pavlenko, A. and Norton, B. (2007) Imagined communities, identity and English language learning, in Cummins, J. and Davison, C. (Eds) *International Handbook of English Language Teaching*. New York: Springer, 669–680.

Reeves, J. (2009) A sociocultural perspective on ESOL teachers' linguistic knowledge for teaching, *Linguistics and Education* 20 (2), 109–125.

Sellami, A. (2006) Slaves of sex, money and alcohol: (Re-)Locating the target culture of TESOL, in Edge, J. (Ed) *(Re-)Locating TESOL in an Age of Empire*. Basingstoke: Palgrave Macmillan, 1–23.

Slee, J. (2010) A systemic approach to culturally responsive assessment practices and evaluation, *Higher Education Quarterly* 64 (3), 246–260.

Stanley, P. and Murray, N. (2013) Qualified? A framework for comparing ELT teacher preparation courses, *Australian Review of Applied Linguistics* 36 (1), 102–115.

Villegas, A. M. and Lucas, T. (2002) *Educating Culturally Responsive Teachers: A Coherent Approach*. New York: State University of New York Press.

Whitten, P. and Hunter, D. E. K. (1992) *Anthropology: Contemporary Perspectives*. London: Longman.

Young, R. F. (2002) Discourse approaches to oral language assessment, *Annual Review of Applied Linguistics* 22, 243–262.

Appendix A
CELTA performance descriptors

Appendix A is taken from pages 21–22 of the *CELTA Administration Handbook 2014* (Cambridge English 2014).

The following performance descriptors are to be interpreted in the CELTA context, bearing in mind that candidates are pre-service and undertaking initial teacher training including 6 hours of teaching practice.

The performance descriptors are for use **at the end of the course** to determine final recommended grades.

By the end of the course, candidates' performance must match **all** of the descriptors at a particular passing grade in order to achieve that grade.

Pass A

Candidates' planning and teaching show excellent understanding of English language learning and teaching processes.

- Candidates can plan effectively with minimal guidance. They can analyse target language thoroughly and select highly appropriate resources and tasks for successful language and language skills development.
- Candidates can deliver effective language and skills lessons, using a variety of classroom teaching techniques successfully.
- Candidates show very good awareness of learners and can respond so that learners benefit from the lessons.
- Candidates can reflect on key strengths and weaknesses and can consistently use these reflections to develop their teaching skills.

All CELTA assessment criteria are achieved and most are well achieved. CELTA requirements for written work are met.

Pass B

Candidates' planning and teaching show good understanding of English language learning and teaching processes.

- Candidates can plan effectively with some guidance. They can analyse target language well and select appropriate resources and tasks for successful language and language skills development.
- Candidates can deliver effective language and skills lessons, using a variety of classroom teaching techniques successfully.
- Candidates show good awareness of learners and can respond so that learners benefit from the lessons.
- Candidates can reflect on key strengths and weaknesses and can generally use these reflections to develop their teaching skills.

All CELTA assessment criteria are achieved and some are well achieved. CELTA requirements for written work are met.

Pass C

Candidates' planning and teaching show satisfactory understanding of English language learning and teaching processes.

- Candidates can plan effectively with guidance. They can analyse target language adequately and generally select appropriate resources and tasks for successful language and language skills development.
- Candidates can deliver satisfactory language and skills lessons, using a variety of classroom teaching techniques with a degree of success.
- Candidates show some awareness of learners and some ability to respond so that learners benefit from the lessons.
- Candidates can reflect on some key strengths and weaknesses and generally use these reflections to develop their teaching skills.

All CELTA assessment criteria are achieved. Some may be less well achieved. CELTA requirements for written work are met.

Fail

Candidates' planning and teaching show minimal understanding of English language learning and teaching processes.

Candidates' performance does not match all of the Pass descriptors.

Some CELTA assessment criteria are not achieved and/or CELTA requirements for written work are not met.

Appendix B

Specifications for Delta Module Two assessment

Appendix B is taken from pages 53–54 and 56–60 of the *Delta Handbook* (Cambridge English 2014).

Professional Development Assignment (PDA) specifications

The focus of this assignment is development and extension of the candidate's teaching skills. It includes:

- Part A: Reflection and Action — 2,000–2,500 words.
  Reflection and Action includes a series of tasks and activities which candidates work on throughout the course.

  See page 57 (page 430 of the volume) for suggested timings and stages.

- Part B: Experimental Practice — 1,500–2,000 words plus lesson outline.
  Experimental practice involves exploration into a specific lesson approach/procedure/technique with which the candidate is unfamiliar.

Specifications for Part A: Reflection and Action

The focus of Reflection and Action is on personal and professional development.
It includes:

- reading and research related to procedures for reflection, methods and/ or documents for gathering data for reflection purposes
- reflection on the candidate's own beliefs and practices in the ELT classroom
- selection of approaches, methods, techniques and materials that might enhance their practices and justification of this selection
- use and evaluation of some of the approaches, methods, techniques and materials as a means of developing the candidate's teaching skills

- 10 hours' observation of other teachers and reflection on these observations. (Observations of other teachers can be filmed or 'live'.)

Part A: Reflection and Action: Outline and summary of stages

Stage 1 Diagnostic observation (There is no written submission for Stage 1.)

- At the beginning of the course the candidate plans and teaches a lesson or part of a lesson (minimum 40 and maximum 60 minutes).
- The lesson is observed by an approved Delta tutor.
- A post-lesson discussion is held between the candidate and the tutor (and, if appropriate/relevant, includes feedback from colleagues and/or peers).
- During the discussion full oral and written feedback is given by the tutor and included in the candidate's coursework portfolio as an appendix to the PDA.
- The lesson is not formally assessed or graded and does not contribute to the grade received by the candidate in this module.

Stage 2 (maximum 1,000 words)

After the diagnostic observation, candidates:

- reflect and comment on their beliefs and practices as a teacher, identify key strengths and weaknesses in their teaching and comment on the positive and negative effects of these on their learners
- identify the possible reasons for these key strengths and weaknesses
- produce an action plan for the development of their teaching in response to the significant weaknesses they have identified
- select approaches, procedures, techniques or materials that will allow them to develop their teaching skills and enhance their learners' learning experiences
- select and/or design methods and/or documents for gathering data that will allow them to focus specifically on their performance in their assessed assignments during the Delta course, and briefly explain the reasons for choice(s). Candidates may also refer to any other lessons they are teaching during the Delta course.

Stage 3 (maximum 750 words)

Candidates complete the first two of their Language Systems/Skills Assignments after which, with reference to their action plan from Stage 2, they:

- identify and comment on any key development(s) they have made in their teaching practices since the diagnostic observation
- reflect on the effectiveness of the approaches, methods, techniques and materials they selected in Stage 2 in terms of how these have helped their development as teachers
- identify and comment on the most significant current weaknesses in their teaching practices
- select approaches, procedures, techniques or materials that will allow them to develop their teaching skills and enhance their learners' learning experiences
- select and/or design methods and/or documents for gathering data that will allow them to focus specifically on their performance in their remaining assignments and briefly explain the reasons for choice(s).

Stage 4 (maximum 750 words)

When all internal assignments have been completed, candidates:

- identify and comment on how their beliefs about teaching and learning and their classroom practice have changed as a result of this assignment
- identify and critically evaluate the most effective procedures and/or methods and/or documents for reflection and observation they have used for their own professional development in this assignment
- outline how they will continue to use these as part of their own continuing professional development.

Specifications for Part B: Experimental Practice

The focus of Experimental Practice is an investigation of a specific lesson approach/teaching procedure/teaching technique with which the candidate is unfamiliar.

It includes:

- reading and research related to the chosen area
- a lesson in which the candidate experiments with the new practice
- identification, selection and/or development of methods, procedures and/or documents to evaluate the effectiveness of the experiment
- an evaluation of its success.

Part B: Experimental Practice: Outline

Length: 1,500–2,000 words to cover a Commentary on the lesson and a post-lesson Reflection and Evaluation.

Additionally, as an appendix not included in the word limit, a lesson outline.

Candidates:

- explain their professional interest in the chosen experimental area with reference to:
  - their own professional development
  - underlying theory
  - teaching context
  - characteristics of the learners
- plan and teach the experimental lesson using the selected approaches/procedures/techniques/materials
- evaluate the lesson in terms of identified learning and teaching objectives including a summary, where appropriate, of the outcomes of evaluation procedures
- identify ways in which this area may be developed/adapted for inclusion in future work or consider why this area is not worth further extension or adaptation.

Professional Development Assignment assessment criteria

Part A — Reflection and Action (RA) and Part B — Experimental Practice (EP)

Successful candidates can present an assignment which:

- is written in language which is clear, accurate, easy to follow and does not impose a strain on the reader (1a)
- is cohesive and clearly ordered and in which component parts of the assignment are relevant to the topic (1b)
- uses appropriate terminology accurately (1c)
- refers to and references key sources (1d)
- contains a bibliography of key sources consulted (1e)
- follows widely accepted referencing conventions (1f)
- respects the word limits of individual stages of the assignment and the overall word limit and states the number of words used (1g).

Part A — Reflection and Action (RA)

Successful candidates can focus on their professional development by:

- selecting some key strengths and weaknesses in their teaching practices and providing a rationale for their selection (2a)
- selecting approaches/procedures/techniques/materials to use to address the issues identified in 2a above (2b)
- critically evaluating the effectiveness of the selected approaches/procedures/techniques/materials (2c)
- critically evaluating the effectiveness of methods and/or documents they have selected to gather data to allow them to focus on their teaching practices (2d)
- providing an appropriate action plan to promote their professional development (2e)
- critically reflecting on their teaching practices and beliefs during the course of this assignment (2f).

Part B — Experimental Practice (EP)

Successful candidates can focus on the topic of the assignment by:
- demonstrating understanding of selected approaches/procedures/techniques/materials with reference to any underlying theory (3a)
- justifying the selected approaches/procedures/techniques/ materials (3a) with reference to the teaching context, the specific group of learners and their own professional development (3b)
- evaluating the success or otherwise of the experiment with reference to the planned aims and outcomes for both the learners and the teacher (3c).

Guidance on completing the Professional Development Assignment (PDA)

The aim of this section is to provide support and guidance to Delta Module Two centres in setting up, administering and supporting the PDA. The following are suggestions and should not necessarily be followed to the letter.

Reflection and Action (RA)

Rationale for this part of the PDA

Reflection is increasingly seen as a crucial element in teacher learning.

Teachers develop beliefs about language teaching and learning, and their classroom practices are influenced by these beliefs. Teachers' beliefs and practices often remain unconscious and unchallenged. By consciously exploring and critically reflecting on their existing beliefs and practices, teachers are better able to question and, if necessary, subsequently change aspects of them.

This assignment provides a framework within which candidates can explore their existing beliefs and classroom practices, engage critically with them, reflect on them in the light of feedback, and consider ways in which aspects of them might be adapted.

Setting up

It is important that candidates understand the rationale for the RA part of the PDA, and that they see it as something which is helping their learning and contributing to other parts of Module Two. This may involve discussing with them the importance of critical, action-based reflection and of exploring existing beliefs and classroom practices. Tutors might like to consider using a beliefs questionnaire (see Lightbown, P. and Spada, N. (1993) *How Languages are Learned*, OUP, for an example), either as a pre-course task or in one of the initial input sessions.

Staging

An important feature of the RA is that it is an ongoing piece of work. In order to be an effective learning tool, candidates need to go through the four stages in a structured and timely manner. Tutors are advised to draw up a suggested schedule for candidates which suits the nature of the course being provided, to make this schedule explicit to all candidates, and to include it in their course programme. (Table 1 on page 65 (page 428 of the volume) gives a suggested time frame in relation to other assessments in *Module Two*.) Tutors are also advised to consider the extent to which tutorials and/or feedback on drafts of each stage should be incorporated into the schedule.

Support and guidance to candidates

The following specific suggestions might help tutors administer the RA:

Beliefs questionnaire
• Beliefs are often unconscious and candidates may need help in raising

them to a level of consciousness. Questionnaires may be useful for this purpose.

- It may be useful to encourage candidates to explore the extent to which they feel their teaching reflects their beliefs.
- Any questionnaire(s) used to explore beliefs in Stage 1 can be revisited in Stage 4.

Diagnostic observation

- The diagnostic observation should take place shortly after the beginning of the course to ensure candidates have sufficient time to complete Stages 1 and 2 before the first assessed lessons. There should be a post-lesson discussion and written feedback.
- It is useful if candidates produce a lesson plan for the diagnostic observation and include some rationale for their lesson. This gives an indication of their beliefs and can form the basis for constructive discussion with the tutor after the lesson.

Strengths and weaknesses

- Candidates can refer to the following in their comments: previous feedback on their teaching (e.g. from their institution, learners, colleagues); their own awareness of previous strengths and weaknesses; previous teacher training courses and in-service teacher training (INSET); observations made by their tutor; their own observations; the learners' performance and responses during and/or after the diagnostic lesson.
- Candidates should prioritise weaknesses that most affect their students' ability to learn and their own practices as a teacher.
- Candidates can refer to the following:
  - their preferred teaching styles, techniques and procedures
  - their beliefs about learning and teaching
  - a pervading view of teaching present in their context that may or may not be best suited to all learners within that context
  - the needs and teaching preferences of institutions they have worked for
  - over-application of 'favourite' techniques and procedures
  - coursebook methodologies (not) suited to specific contexts
  - (in)ability to adapt their methods/techniques/procedures to specific contexts

- lack of knowledge in particular linguistic or methodological areas
- lack of confidence in carrying out particular methods, techniques and procedures
- any initial teacher training and developmental training they have experienced in their teaching career.

Action plan

- The purpose of the action plan in Stage 2 is to provide structure to candidates' development and to allow them to carefully consider steps they need to take to improve the weaknesses they have identified in their teaching.
- Therefore, they need to prioritise a number of key areas to work on (typically this would be three to five areas), outline what they intend to do and how, giving some idea of the time frame within which they intend to work on these areas.
- Centres may consider producing a proforma for candidates' action plans.
- Possible approaches/procedures/techniques might include some of the following: reading specific books, observing experienced colleagues and/or tutors, experimenting with aspects of their teaching related to the weakness identified, being observed, videoing their own lessons, getting feedback from students, etc.
- Although Stages 3 and 4 do not require detailed action plans as such, some indication is required in both cases as to how candidates intend to continue improving aspects of their teaching.

Table 1 Suggested schedule for Reflection and Action (RA)

RA Stage	Activity	Documentation for portfolio
At the beginning of the course	• Candidate completes beliefs questionnaire selected by tutor • Tutorial to discuss beliefs either before or after diagnostic observation	Questionnaire results (appendix) Candidate's own notes
Stage 1	• Diagnostic observation • Post-lesson discussion with tutor • Candidate makes notes for Stage 2	Lesson plan (appendix) Tutor feedback (appendix)
Stage 2	• Candidate writes Reflection and Action plan* 800–1,000 words (*Existing beliefs and practices/Strengths and weaknesses as a teacher/Action plan*)	Completed RA Stage 2

(To be continued)

(*Continued*)

RA Stage	Activity	Documentation for portfolio
Between Stage 2 and Stage 3	• Observations of other teachers • **LSA1** (Language Systems or Skills) • Feedback on **LSA1** (including reference to Stage 2 action plan)** • Candidate prepares Stage 3 • Observations of other teachers • **LSA2** (Language Systems or Skills) • Feedback on **LSA2** (including reference to Stage 2 action plan)** • Candidate prepares Stage 3	Written tutor feedback on **LSA1** and RA Stage 2 Completed observation tasks Written tutor feedback on **LSA2** and RA Stage 2 Completed observation tasks
Stage 3	• Reflection and Action 600–750 words* (*Developments in practices/Reflect on Stage 2 action plan/Current weaknesses and future actions*)	Completed RA Stage 3
Between Stage 3 and Stage 4	• Observations of other teachers • **LSA3** (Language Systems or Skills) • Feedback on **LSA3** (including reference to RA Stage 3)** • Candidate prepares Stage 4	Written tutor feedback on **LSA3** and RA Stage 3 Completed observation tasks
Stage 4	• Reflection and Action 600–750 words (*Developments in beliefs and practices/ Reflect on future actions*) • Tutor marks assignment **LSA4** (Externally assessed)	Completed RA Stage 4

* *Tutors may wish to comment on drafts before submission.*
** *Discussion and feedback on the RA could take place at this point either in a separate tutorial or as part of the feedback discussion following an assessed lesson.*

Documents for gathering data

- It would be useful for centres and tutors to consider how to encourage candidates to consciously focus on their prioritised weaknesses in their assessed LSAs, and to make use of tutor feedback on these lessons for the RA.
- Where possible, the peer observations required for Module Two should be used to gather data for the action plan. Candidates may use data from their own observations of colleagues as well as their colleagues' observations of them.
- Videos of candidates' lessons may be used.
- Feedback in the form of student questionnaires may be used.
- Any documents used should be put in the appendix, but referred to in the text.

Word limit for each stage

- Overall, the RA is expected to be 2,000–2,500 words, therefore it is recommended that the three written sections are as follows:

- Stage 2: 800–1,000 words (reflection/beliefs/strengths/weaknesses 500, action plan 500)
- Stage 3: 600–750 words (reflection on developments/evaluation 300, current weaknesses 150, future action 300)
- Stage 4: 600–750 words (reflection on developments 300, evaluation 200, future action 250).

• It is recommended that centres and tutors consider having separate submission deadlines for each of the three written parts of the RA.

Drafting and feedback

• Centres and tutors may wish to collect in and give feedback on Stage 2 before candidates continue writing the remaining parts of the assignment. It is likely to be of more use to candidates to receive feedback at this stage than at the end of the process. Each centre will need to decide and make explicit to candidates their own approach to drafting and feedback for the various stages of the RA.

Tutorials

• Candidates may not have done systematic reflection in this manner before and are likely to benefit from ongoing individual support and guidance if they are to get the most out of this assignment as a learning experience. It is suggested that centres and tutors conduct face-to-face or online tutorials during the course with the specific purpose of discussing this assignment. These may be incorporated into feedback sessions following assessed teaching observations. (See Table 1.)
• Centres may also consider setting up an interactive online facility (such as Moodle) in order to encourage regular and systematic reflection and interaction among candidates and tutors.
• Candidates may be encouraged to keep a regular journal (with possible entries online) to guide their reflections.

Experimental Practice (EP)

Rationale for this part of the PDA

Teachers develop routines during their early years of teaching which enable them to deal with the complexities of their teaching situation and to plan lessons and respond to classroom events as they occur. Developing new routines is a challenging and complex process; numerous contextual and personal factors make it hard for teachers to change their existing routines and to experiment with alternative practices. This assignment provides a framework within which candidates can experiment with, what is for them, a new aspect of teaching, and helps them to reflect on its effectiveness for them and their learners' learning.

Setting up

It is important that candidates understand the rationale for the EP part of the PDA, and that they see it as something which is helping their learning and contributing to other parts of Module Two. This may involve discussing with them the importance of experimental practice and showing how this relates to the exploration of beliefs and classroom practices they carried out in the RA part of the PDA.

Staging

An important feature of the EP is that candidates explore an approach/procedure/technique with which they are not familiar. Centres may support the learning process through tutorial support and/or by commenting on the outline plan and commentary.

Support and guidance to candidates

The following specific suggestions might help centres and tutors in administering the EP:

Link to Reflection and Action (RA)

- Where possible, candidates should be advised to relate the topic of the EP to their action plan for the RA assignment.

Word limit for each stage

- Overall the EP is expected to be 1,500–2,000 words, not including the lesson outline (but including the post-lesson evaluation, c.500 words):
  - Commentary 1,000–1,600 depending on length of evaluation.
  - Post-lesson evaluation: 400–500 words.
- The lesson outline and accompanying materials go in the appendix and do not count towards the word limit.

Lesson outline

- Candidates should provide a lesson outline and accompanying materials for a lesson of 40–60 minutes.

The lesson outline forms an appendix to the EP. It should not be a full lesson plan but must include:

- aims and objectives from the learners' and teacher's points of view
- procedures
- any material used
- ways of finding out whether and to what extent these aims and objectives have been met, including copies of any completed evaluation documents (collated data, sample observation sheets, questionnaires etc.). A *summary* of the results should form part of the Reflection and Evaluation.

Peer observations

- Where possible, centres and tutors may endeavour to arrange for candidates to peer observe each other teaching their experimental practice lesson. Candidates may then refer to their colleague's feedback in their post-lesson evaluation.

Post-lesson evaluation

- The word limit is 500 words for the post-lesson evaluation, which candidates are advised to plan approximately as follows:
  - Evaluation of lesson: 250–300 words.
  - Future action: 150–200 words.

Language Systems and Skills Assignments specifications

The focus of the Language Systems/Skills Assignments is an investigation into different areas of language systems and language skills and issues related to teaching the chosen areas.

Each assignment includes:

- a background essay (2,000–2,500 words) involving reading and research, analysis of a chosen area of language systems or skills, and discussion and critical evaluation of specific approaches, methods,

techniques and materials that might enable the teaching/learning of the chosen area
- planning and delivering a lesson (40–60 minutes) designed to teach the chosen area to a specified group of English language learners
- reflection on and evaluation of the candidate's own teaching practices with reference to the chosen area of language systems/skills and the lesson taught (300–500 words).

Background essay

Length: 2,000–2,500 words

Candidates should make reference in their essay to their reading, research and experience gained through their own teaching.

Topic of essay

Candidates should:

- identify for analysis a specific area of a language system (grammar, lexis, phonology or discourse) or a specific skills area (listening, speaking, reading or writing)
- define the scope by stating what aspect of the identified area the assignment will focus on, with reference to, e.g. learner needs, level of learners, specific learning context, language area, text type, and, where relevant, teaching approach or method
- outline the reasons for choosing the particular aspect by making reference to classroom experience, observation, research and reading.

Analysis of area and discussion of learning problems and teaching issues

Candidates should:

- analyse the specific area of the selected language system or skill — this could be in terms of form, meaning/use and phonology in the case of language systems, and in terms of linguistic, discoursal and communicative features and/or subskills in the case of skills
- in relation to the scope identified above, identify and discuss common learning problems and key teaching issues in a range of learning contexts, e.g. different learner characteristics and/or goals.

Suggestions for teaching

Candidates should:

- describe, show familiarity with and critically evaluate a selected range of procedures, techniques, resources and/or materials which are designed to develop learners' competence in the selected area.

Background essay assessment criteria

Quality of writing — Assessment category 1

Successful candidates demonstrate that they can effectively present an essay which:

- is written in language which is clear, accurate, easy to follow and is cohesive and clearly ordered (1a)
- uses appropriate terminology accurately (1b)
- refers to and references key sources (1c)
- follows the conventions of a standard referencing system for in-text referencing and the bibliography (1d)
- respects the word limit (2,000–2,500 words) and states the number of words used (1e).

Clarity of topic — Assessment category 2

Successful candidates demonstrate that they can effectively make clear the topic of the essay by:

- identifying for analysis a specific area of the grammar, lexis, phonology or discourse system of English, or a skills area (listening, speaking, reading or writing) (2a)
- defining the scope of the area they will analyse with reference to, e.g. learners, teaching approach, method, learning context, learner needs or text type (2b)
- explaining with reference to classroom experience, reading and research why they have chosen this area (2c)
- making all parts of the essay relevant to the topic and coherent (2d)
- following through in later parts of the essay on key issues identified in earlier parts (2e).

Analysis and issues — Assessment category 3

Successful candidates can effectively demonstrate an understanding of the specific area by:

- analysing the specific area with accuracy, identifying key points (3a)
- showing awareness of a range of learning and teaching problems occurring in a range of learning contexts (3b).

Suggestions for teaching — Assessment category 4

Successful candidates demonstrate that they can:

- outline and show familiarity with relevant key procedures, techniques, resources and/or materials (4a)
- evaluate how the selected procedures, techniques, resources and/or materials might be used effectively in classroom practice (4b)
- demonstrate how the procedures, techniques, resources and/or materials address points raised under 'Analysis and issues' (4c).

The lesson (planning, teaching and evaluation)

Lesson requirements

Each Systems/Skills Assignment includes planning, teaching and evaluation of a lesson which is linked to the topic of the background essay, though the lesson will be narrower in scope than the background essay.

Each lesson must be a minimum of 40 minutes and a maximum of 60 minutes.

The class size will vary according to context. There is no maximum class size but the absolute minimum is five learners.

The age range of classes selected for assessment purposes is not specified. Any age group may be taught provided that the research and teaching undertaken allow the teacher to achieve the assessment criteria. (See below.)

For each lesson the candidate must submit a lesson plan, supporting documentation and a post-lesson evaluation (approx. 300–500 words).

Assessment criteria

Planning and evaluation — Assessment category 5

Successful candidates design and present a lesson plan and supporting documentation which:

- includes:

(i) a brief general overview of the group of learners and the course (5ai)

(ii) information about individual learners relevant to the lesson (5aii)

- sets out clear and appropriate overall aims and learning outcomes for the lesson in relation to language systems and/or language skills and learner needs (5b)
- provides relevant analysis of target language in terms of form, meaning/ use and phonology in the case of language systems, and in terms of linguistic, discoursal and communicative features and/or subskills in the case of skills (5c)
- outlines any relevant link(s) between this lesson and relevant aspects of preceding and subsequent lessons, and if relevant, the course as a whole (5d)
- states assumptions made about the learners' knowledge, abilities and interests relevant to the aims and learning outcomes of the lesson (5e)
- anticipates and explains potential problems in relation to the lesson's aims and learning outcomes, the learners and the learning context, and the equipment, materials and resources to be used (5f)
- suggests appropriate solutions to the problems outlined (5g)
- describes suitably sequenced procedures and activities appropriate to achieving the stated overall aims and stage aims (5h)
- states materials and/or resources to be used, which are appropriate to the teaching and learning context, the learners, the lesson aims and learning outcomes, and the time available, and includes a copy/copies of suitably presented materials, sourced where necessary (5i)
- assigns realistic and appropriate timing for each stage and/or group of stages in the procedure (5j)
- includes a commentary, of between 500 and 750 words, which provides a clear rationale for the lesson plan with reference to learner characteristics and needs and the candidate's reading and research in the background essay (5k).

Assessment criteria — Teaching

Creating and maintaining an atmosphere conducive to learning — Assessment category 6

Successful candidates demonstrate that they can effectively:

- teach the class as a group and individuals within the group, with sensitivity to the learners' needs and backgrounds, level and context, providing equal opportunities for participation (6a)
- purposefully engage and involve learners (6b)
- vary their role in relation to the emerging learning and affective needs of learners during the lesson (6c)
- listen and respond appropriately to learner contributions (6d).

Understanding, knowledge and explanation of language and language skills — Assessment category 7

Successful candidates demonstrate that they can effectively:

- use language which is accurate and appropriate for the teaching and learning context (7a)
- adapt their own use of language to the level of the group and individuals in the group (7b)
- give accurate and appropriate models of language form, meaning/use and pronunciation (7c)
- give accurate and appropriate information about language form, meaning/use and pronunciation and/or language skills/subskills (7d)
- notice and judiciously exploit learners' language output to further language and skills/subskills development (7e).

Classroom, procedures and techniques — Assessment category 8

Successful candidates demonstrate that they can effectively:

- use procedures, techniques and activities to support and consolidate learning and to achieve language and/or skill aims (8a)
- exploit materials and resources to support learning and achieve aims (8b)
- deliver a coherent and suitably varied lesson (8c)
- monitor and check students' learning and respond as appropriate (8d).

Classroom management — Assessment category 9

Successful candidates demonstrate that they can effectively:

- implement the lesson plan and where necessary adapt it to emerging learner needs (9a)

- manage the classroom space, furniture, equipment, materials and resources (9b)
- set up whole class and/or group and/or individual activities, as appropriate (9c)
- ensure the learners remain focused on the lesson aims and the learning outcomes (9d).

Assessment criteria

Reflection and evaluation 300–500 words — Assessment category 10

Successful candidates demonstrate that they can effectively:

- reflect on and evaluate their own planning, teaching and the learners' progress as evidenced in this lesson
- identify key strengths and weaknesses in planning and execution
- explain how they will (would) consolidate/follow on from the learning achieved in the lesson.

Appendix C

TKT: Practical band descriptors

Appendix C is taken from pages 66–68 of the *TKT: Practical Handbook* (Cambridge ESOL 2012).

	BAND 1	BAND 2	BAND 3	BAND 4
Aims	Basic aims are stated but may be inappropriate for the learner group, poorly worded and/ or there may be a mismatch between aims and activities.	Aims are stated but may be very general, inappropriate for the learner group and/or unclear.	Appropriate aims are stated and are generally clearly expressed. Minor improvements may be needed.	Aims are appropriate and clearly and fully expressed.
Lesson components	Some components of the lesson plan may be satisfactory while others may show a lack of awareness. There may be some significant gaps. Suggested timings may be unrealistic.	Most components of the lesson plan have been completed satisfactorily. Some need more detail. Some timings may be under or overestimated.	All lesson plan components have been completed and adequately completed. Most are be occasional lack of clarity and/ or need for more detail. Timings are mostly realistic.	The lesson plan components have been completed and are appropriately clear and detailed. Timings are realistic.
Stages, activities, tasks	Individual stages and activities are included but may not be consistently logical or may not always reflect the stated aims.	Stages are generally logical but may not be fully described or thought through. Suitable activities are included but may lack variety.	Stages are generally logical and link well to aims. Activities are generally appropriate and clear and variety is provided.	There is a good balance and variety of logically staged activities which link clearly to the stated aims. The planned lesson is very clear to the reader.

(To be continued)

(*Continued*)

	BAND 1	BAND 2	BAND 3	BAND 4
Language analysis / skills description	Language analysis may lack depth and may contain inaccuracies.	Language analysis is generally accurate but there are some omissions.	Language analysis is mostly accurate but could be more detailed.	Language analysis is thorough.
	The candidate has selected materials for skills development but tasks may not be present or appropriate; terminology may not be used accurately.	The candidate selects some appropriate tasks for skills development but may not use terminology accurately.	The candidate's selection of tasks demonstrates a good understanding of skills development. There may be occasional mismatch between description and task.	The candidate's selection and description of tasks demonstrate good understanding of skills development.
Use of materials	Materials have been selected and are included with the plan but may be inappropriate or poorly exploited; planned use may be unclear.	Appropriate materials have been selected and are included with the plan and there is some evidence of the ability to exploit materials. Planned use may not be fully clear.	Appropriate materials have been selected and included with the plan and there is evidence of the ability to exploit materials well. Planned use is generally clear.	Materials are appropriate and well selected and are exploited to engage and actively involve learners. Some creativity will be evident.
Learning atmosphere	The teacher has some awareness of the role of the teacher in the context, but may not be assertive enough or may be too dominant. There teacher has limited awareness of learners' needs and level and there is minimal learner engagement. Interaction between the teacher and the learners is minimal.	The teacher has reasonable classroom presence for the context but at times may not be assertive enough or may be too dominant. The teacher has some awareness of the learners' needs and level. Learners are not engaged for parts of the lesson. The teacher generally responds appropriately to learners, but attention to learners may be unequal and may not be consistently supportive.	The teacher has a positive and effective classroom presence for the context. The teacher, for the most part, has good awareness of the learners' needs and level. Learners are engaged for most of the lesson. The teacher responds to learners appropriately, but could give more attention to individuals.	The teacher has a positive and effective classroom presence for the context and has good awareness of the learners' needs and level. Learners are engaged throughout the lesson. The teacher responds to learners appropriately and gives good attention to individual learners.

(*To be continued*)

(Continued)

	BAND 1	BAND 2	BAND 3	BAND 4
Focus on language and/or skills	Some language and skills work takes place, but the range of techniques and strategies for dealing with language and skills is insufficient or inappropriate and is not effective in achieving the lesson aims. Information about language may be frequently unclear or inaccurate.	Some language and skills work takes place. The teacher uses a limited range of techniques and strategies for dealing with language and skills but these could be used more extensively to achieve the lesson aims. Information about language may be occasionally unclear or inaccurate.	Language and skills work takes place. The teacher uses a good range of techniques and strategies for dealing with language and skills, but some could be used more effectively to achieve the lesson aims. Information about language is mostly clear and accurate.	Language and skills work takes place. The teacher uses a good range of techniques and strategies for dealing with language and skills, and which are effective in achieving the lesson aims. Information about language is clear and accurate.
Classroom management	Overall the lesson is too teacher-centred. There is minimal student interaction in whole-class, pair and group work activities. Activities could be set up and managed more effectively. The timing and/or pace of stages of the lesson may be inappropriate. Limited use is made of materials and they may not be used effectively to achieve aims.	There is insufficient balance between teacher input and learner activity. Whole-class, individual, pair and group work are included but some activities could be set up more effectively. There are some stages of the lesson where the timing and/or pace could be improved. Some materials are used effectively, but materials may be under or over exploited and could be better exploited to achieve lesson aims.	There is a reasonable balance between teacher input and learner activity, but some stages of the lesson may be too teacher-centred or may need more teacher guidance. Whole-class, individual, pair and group work are generally well set up. The timing and/or pace of stages of the lesson are mostly appropriate. Materials are generally used effectively to achieve lesson aims.	Teacher input and learner activity are appropriately balanced. Whole-class, individual, pair and group work are effectively set up and well managed. The timing of stages and activities is appropriate and the teacher maintains an appropriate pace throughout the lesson. Good use is made of materials to achieve lesson aims.
Use of English	The teacher uses English to manage the lesson, but there may be too much teacher language and the teacher may frequently use language which is unclear or too complex for the learners. L1 may be used too frequently. Language modelled for learners may be frequently unclear or inaccurate.	The teacher generally uses English effectively to manage the lesson. Teacher language may on occasion be unclear or too complex for the learners. Opportunities may be missed, e.g. to elicit, praise or question learners. Language modelled for learners may be occasionally unclear or inaccurate.	The teacher uses English appropriately and effectively to manage the lesson and to encourage and praise learners. The teacher's language is well graded and there is some effective use of eliciting and questioning techniques. Language modelled for learners is mostly clear and accurate.	The teacher uses English appropriately and effectively throughout the lesson to manage the lesson and to encourage and praise learners. The teacher's language is well graded and there is effective use of eliciting and questioning techniques. Language modelled for learners is clear and accurate.

(To be continued)

441

(*Continued*)

	BAND 1	BAND 2	BAND 3	BAND 4
Monitoring, feedback and correction	Some monitoring is present but is not frequent or inclusive enough. Opportunities for correction may not occur, or the teacher may give insufficient attention to correction and/or feedback.	The teacher monitors and checks learning but this could be more helpful. There may be limited opportunities for correction. The teacher makes some use of a limited range of feedback and correction techniques.	The teacher monitors and provides some effective feedback/correction during the lesson although more attention could be given to individuals. Some opportunities to engage with learner output are missed.	The teacher monitors learners effectively and demonstrates a range of strategies to provide effective feedback/correction throughout the lesson. The teacher engages with learner output.
Overall	Overall the teacher displays awareness of some appropriate procedures and techniques but is unable to plan for and implement them consistently, and there is little evidence of learner engagement and participation in the learning process to achieve learning outcomes. The planned lesson does not lead to useful practice or learning.	Overall the teacher is aware of and can plan and implement a range of appropriate teaching procedures and techniques, but needs to do so more consistently and effectively to maximise learner engagement and participation in the learning process. The planned lesson includes some useful activities, but parts of the lesson do not provide useful practice and/or learning.	Overall the teacher has good control of a range of procedures and techniques, and is able to plan and manage a useful lesson. More variety and challenge would increase effectiveness and provide for more learner engagement and participation in the learning process. The planned lesson is appropriate for the learners and provides useful practice and/or learning.	Overall the teacher demonstrates a good range of procedures and techniques and is able to plan and deliver a very effective lesson. The lesson provides for learner interaction, and challenges and engages the learners. The planned lesson is highly appropriate for the learners and promotes effective learning.